The Dictionary of
AMERICANISMS

The Dictionary of
AMERICANISMS

JOHN RUSSELL BARTLETT

CRESCENT BOOKS
NEW YORK

Originally published by
Bartlett & Welford,
New York, 1849

This edition published 1989 by Crescent Books
Distributed by Crown Publishers, Inc.,
225, Park Avenue South,
New York, New York 10003

Copyright © Bracken Books 1989

Printed and bound in Finland

ISBN 0-517-69686-X

h g f e d c b a

INTRODUCTION.

In venturing to lay before the public a Vocabulary of the colloquial language of the United States, some explanation may be necessary for the broad ground I have been led to occupy.

I began to make a list of such words as appeared to be, or at least such as had generally been called Americanisms, or peculiar to the United States, and, at the same time, made reference to the several authors in whose writings they appeared; not knowing whether, in reality, they were of native growth, or whether they had been introduced from England. When this list had expanded so as to embrace a large number of the words used in familiar conversation, both among the educated as well as among the uneducated and rustic classes, the next object was to examine the dialects and provincialisms of those parts of England from which the early settlers of New England and our other colonies emigrated.

The provincialisms of New England are more familiar to our ears than those of any other section of the United States, as they are not confined within the limits of those States, but have extended to New York, Ohio, Indiana, Illinois and Michigan; which States have been, to a great extent, settled by emigrants from New England.

On comparing these familiar words with the provincial and colloquial language of the northern counties of England, a most striking resemblance appeared, not only in the words commonly regarded as peculiar to New England, but in the dialectical pronunciation of certain words, and in the general tone and accent. In fact, it may be said, without exaggeration, that nine tenths of the colloquial peculiarities of New England are derived directly from Great Britain; and that they are now provincial in those parts from which the early colonists emigrated, or are to be found in the writings of well accredited authors of the period when that emigration took place. Consequently, it is obvious, that we have the best authority for the use of the words referred to.

It may be insisted, therefore, that the idiom of New England is as pure English, taken as a whole, as was spoken in England at the period when these colonies were settled. In making this assertion, I do not take as a standard the nasal twang, the drawling enunciation, or those perversions of language which the ignorant and uneducated adopt. Nor would I acknowledge the abuse of many of our most useful words. For these perversions I make no other defence or apology, but that they occur in all countries, and in every language.

Having found the case to be as stated, I had next to decide between a vocabulary of words of purely American origin, or one in which should be embraced all those words usually called provincial or vulgar—all the words, whatever be their origin, which are used in familiar conversation, and but seldom employed in composition—all the perversions of language, and abuses of words into which people, in certain sections of the country, have fallen, and some of those remarkable and ludicrous forms of speech which have been adopted in the Western States. The latter plan seemed the most satisfactory, and this I determined to adopt.

With so broad a ground, many words must necessarily be embraced, which are to be found in the dictionaries of Drs. Johnson and Webster, with the remark that they are low, or vulgar, or only to be heard in familiar conversation. Another class, not in the dictionaries referred to, is contained in the provincial glossaries of England. A third class, entirely distinct from the preceding, consists of slang words which are not noticed by lexicographers, yet are so much employed as to deserve a place in a glossary.

Such is the plan which I have thought most advisable to

adopt, and which I hope will give satisfaction. In carrying out this plan, I have endeavored to give the most accurate definitions, citing the authorities in all cases where I have been enabled to find any. Except as regards words of purely American origin, (e. g. those derived from the Indian languages and from the Dutch,) I have generally kept aloof from etymologies and etymological discussions. These the reader will find in abundance—such as they are—in the works of Johnson, Todd, Webster, and others.

Words of a provincial character, and such as have become obsolete in composition, are often of doubtful signification. Illustrations, from well known authors, wherein such words are employed, are of service in arriving at their true meaning. These have been employed in the present glossary, and serve the double purpose of illustration, and of rendering the book more readable than if confined to a dry collection of definitions. This mode of showing the sense in which words have been employed by authors, was first practised on a comprehensive scale by Dr. Johnson, whose labors are thereby greatly enhanced in value to the philologist; and has since been carried out more completely in Mr. Richardson's dictionary.

The class of words which are purely American in their origin and use, I have also attempted to illustrate, by extracts from American authors, whose writings relate to that class of people among which these words are chiefly found. These books contain descriptions of country life, scenes in the backwoods, popular tales, &c., in which the colloquial or familiar language of particular States predominates. The humorous writings of Judge Haliburton of Nova Scotia, give a tolerably correct though exaggerated specimen of the provincialisms of New England. The letters of Major Downing are of the same character, and portray the dialect of New England with less exaggeration. There are no books in which the Western words and phrases are so fully exhibited; though all the works which aim to illustrate Western life, contain more or less of the idioms peculiar to the people. Judge Hall, Mrs. Kirkland (Mary Clavers), the author of the New Purchase, Charles F. Hoffman, and various tourists, have displayed in their several works the peculiarities of the people of the West, and occasionally their language. Mr. Crockett, however, himself a native of that region, associating from infancy with its woodsmen, hunters, and farmers, whose language is full of quaint words and figures of speech, has unintentionally made us better acquainted with the colloquial language of the West than any other author.

I am also indebted to a series of books published by Messrs. Cary and Hart, called the " Library of Humorous American Works," which consist of a series of tales and adventures in the South-west and West by Wm. T. Porter, editor of the New York Spirit of the Times; John S. Robb and J. M. Field, Esquires, of St. Louis, Missouri; the editor of the New Orleans Picayune, and some anonymous writers. In these several works, the drolleries and quaint sayings of the West are admirably incorporated into tales of the settlers, their manners and customs, vivid descriptions of Western scenery, political and dramatic scenes, etc. We have no books which present so graphic an account of Western life, related in the exaggerated and metaphorical language peculiar to the people of that region.

In Southern provincialisms I find myself most deficient, having seen no books except Major Jones's " Courtship" and "Sketches," "Georgia Scenes," and " Sherwood's Gazetteer of Georgia," in which however a considerable number of local words are to be found.

The newspapers have afforded me many illustrations of the use of words, which I have not failed to make use of. These illustrations, it will be seen, are chiefly from the New York papers, viz. the Commercial Advertiser, the Tribune, and the Herald, for the simple reason that I have been in the practice of reading them daily. When I met with a word or phrase peculiarly American, or one which was employed in a sense differing from the use of the same in England, it was at once noticed and secured. All our newspapers contain more or less colloquial words; in fact, there seems no other way of expressing certain ideas connected with passing events of every day life, with the requisite force and piquancy. In the English newspapers the same thing is observable, and certain of them contain more of the class denominated *slang* words than our own. The Whig papers throughout the United States employ certain political terms in advocating the principles of their party, and in denouncing those of their opponents. The Democratic papers pursue a similar course. The advocates and opponents of Abolition, Fourierism, etc., invent and employ many words peculiar to themselves. So with the religious sects; each new-fangled notion brings into existence some addition to our language, though that addition is not always an improvement.

The value of this glossary would have been greatly enhanced, if, as is usual in the compilation of similar works, I had been able to avail myself of the assistance of persons residing in various parts of our country. No collection of words, professing to contain the colloquial language of the entire country, can approach any degree of completeness or correctness, without the aid of many hands and heads. None but a native of New England, educated on her soil, and who has mingled with all classes of society, has the requisite familiarity with the words and phrases peculiar to her people. So with the Western and Southern provincialisms. One born and brought up where they are spoken, who has heard and used them when a boy, and grown up in their midst, can portray them in their true sense. The aid of such persons it was impossible to procure, and the words here brought together have been, with very few exceptions, collected by myself. The deficiencies and imperfections are such, therefore, as could not be avoided under the circumstances.

The words of Dutch origin, most if not all of which are used or understood in the city of New York and those portions of its vicinity colonized by natives of Holland, were furnished by Mr. Alexander J. Cotheal, a gentlemen born and educated in New York, whose learning in other branches of philological science is well known to many. A few other words have been given me from time to time by other friends, who knew that I was making this collection. To all of these I am happy to express my acknowledgments.

When the work had advanced far towards completion, and one half had been put in type, the occurrence of some terms, common in political language, the exact meaning of which was not clear, led me to apply to my friend John Inman, Esq., editor of the New York Commercial Advertiser, for aid. He readily complied with my request, and kindly furnished the definitions of several terms of daily occurrence in the political language of the day. I regret that I did not have his valuable aid in defining and illustrating the use of words and phrases which occur in the early part of this glossary. The contributions of Mr. Inman are acknowledged where they appear.

To my friend Mr. Wm. W. Turner, I am under great obligations for aid rendered me in preparing this work for the press. Mr. Turner's extensive acquaintance with the European and Oriental languages, together with an unusual sagacity in philological criticism, have peculiarly fitted him to give aid in the preparation of a work like this. I have, therefore, submitted the whole to his supervision, and adopted his views in all my conclusions. At his suggestion, I have struck out many etymologies taken from standard dictionaries, which it was evident were wholly erroneous.

In noticing the words embraced in this glossary, the reader will probably think that many have been admitted which ought not to have a place in a Dictionary of American Provincialisms. From what has already been said, it will be seen that it is very difficult to draw the line between what should be admitted and what excluded; and I have thought it better to err on the side of copiousness, than by too rigid a system of selection to run into the opposite extreme.

A careful perusal of nearly all the English glossaries, has enabled me to select what appeared most desirable to embrace, and what to avoid, in an American book of a similar kind. Cant words, except such as are in general use, the terms used at gaming houses, purely technical words, and those only known to certain trades, obscene and blasphemous words, have been discarded.

For a better understanding of the subject, as well as to show the importance of collecting and preserving the colloquial dialects of our country, I have prefixed to the Vocabulary some remarks on language, in which the reader will find that the study of dialects and provincialisms is considered as worthy the attention of philologists, as the investigation of the language of literature.

DIALECTS OF ENGLAND.

THE most recent investigations in which the science of philology has been brought to bear on the English language, have shown that it is of purely Gothic origin, descended through languages of which sufficient remains to make grammatical as well as etymological comparisons practicable. It is true that some have regarded it as a perfect mongrel, without any natural parent, compounded of various languages and dialects, Greek, Latin, Saxon, French, Welsh, etc., etc. But although the language is very much mixed, it is a question whether it is not as pure, and as closely allied to the Anglo-Saxon and Mœso-Gothic, as the languages in the south of Europe are to the Latin. Or, in other words, it is probable that the English is not more impregnated with words of the Latin stock, than the Italian, French, Spanish, and Portuguese are with words of the Teutonic stock.

The natural tendency of language is to improve; 'and when a people cannot express in a comprehensive manner a particular idea or shade of meaning, they either form a word to denote it from a root or roots already in the language, or borrow a word from other languages which expresses it already.

With regard to the English language this last mentioned process has been adopted to an extent which, while it has enriched our vocabulary with a vast number of terms, has, it must be confessed, greatly impaired its reproductive power. The original substratum of Anglo-Saxon speech has been overlaid with multitudes of common and conversational words from the French, literary and ecclesiastical terms from the Latin, and technicalities from the Greek ; and the process is constantly going on.   Yet in spite of these immense accessions to its vocabulary, the structure of the English has remained in all essential respects the same from the period when it first became a language. Moreover, the number of foreign importations contained in our dictionaries gives by no means a correct idea of the number of such words which we actually make use of.   The greater part of our household, colloquial, and poetical expressions are Saxon, and so are all those important words called particles, on which the whole structure of speech hinges ; whereas an immense number of the words derived from other sources belong exclusively to the language of books, and many even to particular sciences.

There is another fact to be observed, which is that these different classes of words are not used in the same proportion by all members of society.   Persons without education, and who are consequently not familiar with the language of literature, employ almost exclusively in their conversation the simple and expressive Saxon terms ; while persons belonging to the more favored classes of society, supply the place of many of these terms by others derived from the language of books.   The old words thus discarded, which are often far more expressive and more consonant to the genius of the language than the apparently more elegant novelties by which they are supplanted, are from that time considered as the exclusive property of the common people, and receive the name of *provincial, colloquial,* or *vulgar.*

But notwithstanding all this, the common speech often enters largely into composition, and in some instances constitutes the chief excellence of a writer.   In dramatic composition the colloquial language predominates.   In Shakspeare we find every variety of idiom of which the English language is susceptible, from the loftiest flights of the statesman and philosopher to the familiar language of the lowest of the people. In Ben Jonson, Beaumont and Fletcher, Shirley, and other dramatic authors, we find the familiar idiom to be the most prevalent.

If we examine the literature of other countries, we shall find that the colloquial tongue has been employed in written compositions of a similar kind and with equal success. In addition to Aristophanes and Plautus among the ancients, Don Quixote may be mentioned as an example in Spain, and the writings of Rabelais and Molière in France. The colloquial dialect is generally more ancient than the literary language; as the latter is constantly changing, while the former remains nearly stationary.

If any person will take the trouble to examine the early dictionaries of the English language, or the dictionaries of which English forms a part, he will be surprised at the large number of words which have become so completely obsolete as to be undeserving a place in modern compilations. Even the English dictionary of Bailey, which, at the time Dr. Johnson published his, was the standard, abounds in words which are now never used in composition. This class of words was employed by authors from Chaucer's time, or about the year 1400, to the beginning of the seventeenth century. By the middle of that century they had ceased to be used in books, but were preserved in dictionaries for a century longer. The great mass of them, however, are found in one or more of the numerous provincial dialects of England to the present day.

The dialects of the English language now spoken in England have existed from a very early period. It is not pretended by writers on the subject that any are of recent origin. " In early times," says Dr. Bosworth, " there was clearly a considerable dialectic variety in the writings of men residing in different provinces. The differences observable in the language of the most cultivated classes would be still more marked and apparent in the mass of population, or in the less educated community. These, from their agricultural pursuits, had little communication with the inhabitants of other provinces; and having few opportunities and little inducement to leave their own neighborhood, they intermarried among each other, and, from their limited acquaintance and circumscribed views, they would naturally be much attached to their old manners, customs, and language. The same cause operating from age to age would keep united the greater part of the population, or the families of the middle stations of life ; it may, therefore, be well expected that much of the peculiarity of dialect prevalent in Anglo-Saxon times, is preserved even to the present day in the provincial dialects of the same districts. In these local dialects, then, remnants of the Anglo-Saxon tongue may be found in the least altered, most uncorrupt, and therefore its purest state."*

In an ethnological point of view the English dialects afford important materials for elucidating that portion of English history which relates to the early colonization of Great Britain ; for, if history were silent on the subject, a philological test applied to the dialects of the country would show what nations contributed to its colonization.

The Edinburgh Review for April, 1844, in an article on the Provincialisms of the European Languages, gives the following results of an inquiry into the number of provincial words which had then been arrested by local glossaries :

Shropshire, ...	1,993	Sussex, ...	371
Devonshire and Cornwall,	878	Essex, ...	589
Devonshire (North), . .	1,146	Wiltshire, ...	592
Exmoor, ...	370	Hallamshire, ...	1,568
Herefordshire, ...	822	Craven, ...	6.169
Lancashire, ...	1,922	North Country, . . .	3,750
Suffolk, ...	2,400	Cheshire, ...	903
Norfolk, ...	2,500	Grose and Pegge,† . .	3,500
Somersetshire, ...	1,204		
			30,687

" Admitting that several of the foregoing are synonymous, superfluous, or common to each county, there are nevertheless many of them which, although alike orthographically, are vastly dissimilar in signification. Making these allowances, they amount to a little more than 20,000 ; or, according to the number of English counties hitherto illustrated, to the average ratio of 1478 to a county. Calculating the twenty-six unpublished in the same ratio (for there are supposed to be as many words collected by persons who have never published them) they will furnish 36,428 additional provincialisms, forming in the aggregate 59,000 words in the colloquial tongue of the lower classes, which can, for the chief part, produce proofs of legitimate origin."

* Preface to Anglo-Saxon Dictionary, p. xxvi.
† Set down as Metropolitan.

Since the above was written, a most important contribution to this department of literature has been made in the publication of "A Dictionary of Archaic and Provincial Words, Obsolete Phrases, Proverbs, and Ancient Customs, from the fourteenth Century. By J. O. Halliwell. 2 vols. 8vo., London, 1847." This admirable work actually contains 50,000 words, a great portion of which are illustrated by extracts from manuscripts. It will be found by most persons to amply supply the place of the numerous separate glossaries for studying the dialects of England, while it affords indispensable assistance for the correct understanding of the early writers.

As it does not fall within the scope of these inquiries to discuss the languages with which the English bears a relationship, we shall pass over these, and come at once to the Anglo-Saxon. This forms the basis of the English language, and is to be considered as the *mother-tongue*, upon which many words and phrases from other languages, at successive periods, during a space of fourteen centuries, have been engrafted.

The Saxons brought their language into Britain in the year 449, when the invasion under Hengist took place. What the language was at this period it is impossible to show, as no writings of the time have come down to us. It probably approached nearer to its immediate progenitor, the Low German and Mœso-Gothic, than the form it assumed several centuries later, when we first find written documents.*

The large number of invaders who followed Hengist compelled the ancient inhabitants to retire ; and in about a century the whole country was formed into a Saxon kingdom, wherein their language took the place of the Celtic. This language, thus introduced and so firmly established, has been called *pure Saxon* by the learned Dr. Hickes in his "Thesaurus Veterum Linguarum Septentrionalium."

The languages of the Angles and Saxons were closely allied to each other. In fact, from a comparison of the earliest speci-

* It is true that the celebrated Anglo-Saxon poem of Beowulf is said by some writers to be contemporary with Hengist. But Mr. Bosworth states that "the poem contained in the Cottonian MS., British Museum, is not so old. There occur in it Christian allusions which fix this text at least at a period subsequent to A. D. 597."

mens that have come down to us, it is evident that they were merely dialects of the same tongue, spoken by peoples living contiguous to each other. The other Gothic invaders or colonists of Britain, who have left traces of their language, are the Jutes of Jutland and the Friesians of Friesland.

The Danes made their first descent on the English coast in 787, and were soon repelled. Successive invasions followed, and while Charlemagne compelled them to retreat before his victorious armies, they sought a refuge in Britain, laying waste the country and plundering wherever they came. The Saxons always got rid of them as soon as possible, either by force of arms or contributions of money. Yet, in many instances, they established colonies, and after 230 years of warfare they succeeded in raising a Danish king to the throne of England in the year 1017. His reign, however, was short; for in 24 years the Danish dynasty was extinct, and a Saxon king again succeeded.

This is the period where Dr. Hickes places the second stage of the Anglo-Saxon language, being that in which it was affected by the Danish invasions, receiving new words or dialectical changes. Mr. Forby, in his remarks on the dialect of East Anglia, says that no part of England was more completely overrun or longer occupied than this; but he denies that a number of words sufficiently large was imported to give a new color and character to the Saxon tongue.*

" The French element appeared in our language with the battle of Hastings (A. D. 1066), perhaps in a slight degree during the reign of Edward the Confessor."† It is the dialect spoken in the northern parts of France and denominated Norman French, which has had the greatest influence upon the English language.

* Forby's Introd. to the Vocab. of East Anglia, p. 31.
† Latham on the English.Language, p. 45. 1st edit.

AMERICAN DIALECTS.

DIALECTS originate in various ways. First, by the proximity of nations speaking different languages, in which case many words and phrases are borrowed from one into the other; witness the Scotch and Irish dialects of the English. Secondly, by migrations. This is the most fruitful and permanent source of dialects. We see its effects in the English language; for the immigration of various nations into Great Britain from the Saxons down to the period of the Norman conquest are yet distinctly marked in the dialects of that country.

In the United States it is easy to point out causes, which, in the course of a few generations, will materially affect the English language in the particular districts of country where those influences are at work. Dialects will spring up as marked as those of Great Britain. A free intercourse may in some cases check the permanency of these dialects; but in those parts of the country aside from the great thoroughfares, where a dialect has once become firmly established, a thousand years will not suffice to eradicate it.

The State of New York was originally settled by the Dutch. The number of their colonists was never large, nor did they extend their settlements beyond the valley of the Mohawk and lands adjacent; yet we find even in this thickly settled State, after a lapse of two hundred years, that they have left evident traces on our spoken language. In the cities of New York and Albany many Dutch words have become incorporated into the common speech. In some of the inland villages of Dutch origin, the inhabitants still use the language of their fathers; and there are even individuals who never spoke any other.

The words so adopted by us embrace geographical names,—a class of words which the first colonists of a country or the primitive inhabitants themselves generally leave to their posterity or to the subsequent occupants. Many of the other words which the Dutch have left us are terms belonging to the kitchen. These have been preserved and handed down by cooks and domestic servants, until from constant use they are become familiar to all.   Among these terms are *cooky, crullers, olykoke, spack and applejees, rullichies, kohlslaa, pit.*

The terms for various playthings, holidays, &c., preserve among children their original Dutch names ; as *scup, hoople, peewee, pile, pinkster, paas.*   Other words confined to children are *pinky, terawchy.*

Articles of wearing apparel in some instances retain their Dutch names; as *clockmutch.*

Besides these there are terms the use of which is not confined to the districts originally colonized from Holland, but has been extended to New England and several of the Northern States ; such as *stoop,* a porch, *boss,* a master-workman.

If a few Dutch colonists mingled with the English have been able to engraft so many words on our language, what may we expect from the hundreds of thousands of Germans in the State of Pennsylvania ?   There the German language will doubtless exist for centuries ; for, although they are situated in the midst of an English-speaking population far more numerous than themselves, and although the government and laws are conducted through the English language, still the tendency of a people of common origin to cling together,—the publication of newspapers, almanacs, and books in German,—and the cultivation to some extent of German literature, will tend to preserve the idiom and nationality of the people.   It is true the language is already much corrupted, and in the course of time it must give way to the English; but it will leave behind it an almost imperishable dialect as a memento of its existence.   In the State of Ohio, where there are large settlements of Germans, a similar result must follow.

In the State of Illinois is a colony of Norwegians.   These people before coming to America sent out an agent, who selected and purchased for them a large tract of land in one section of that State.   They were accompanied by their clergyman and schoolmaster.   They are thus kept together, and will for a long time preserve their language and nationality.   But it must also eventually give way, after engrafting on the English language in that vicinity a Norwegian dialect.

There are large settlements of Welsh emigrants in the States of Pennsylvania and New York. In the latter, in Oneida county, one may travel for miles and hear nothing but the Welsh language. They have their newspapers and magazines in their native tongue, and support many churches wherein their language alone is preached. The Welsh, however, are not in sufficient numbers, nor are they sufficiently isolated to retain for any length of time their native tongue; neither can they produce any sensible dialectical change in our language, owing to the great difference between it and their own. They will, however, add some words to it.

In the State of Louisiana, which was colonized by the French, and Florida, which was colonized by the Spaniards, there are many words of foreign origin, scarcely known in the Northern States. The geographical divisions, the names of rivers, mountains, bays; the peculiarities of soil and climate; all that relates to the cultivation of the earth, the names of fishes, birds, fruits, vegetables, coins, &c., &c., retain to a great extent the names given them by the first possessors of the country. The same class of words is preserved in Lower Canada, where they were originally given by the French. They are now adopted by the English, and will for ever remain in use. Among the words of French origin are *cache, calaboose, bodette, bayou, sault, levee, crevasse, habitan, charivari.*

The Spanish colonists in Florida, and our intercourse with Mexico and the Spanish main, have been the means of introducing a few Spanish words. Among these are *canyon, cavortin, chaparral, pistareen, rancho, vamos.*

The Indian terms in our language, as might be supposed, are numerous. First, as to geographical names. These abound in every State in the Union, though more in some States than in others. In New England, particularly on the coast, Indian names are very common. Nearly all the rivers, bays, and prominent landmarks bear them, as *Housatonic, Connecticut, Quinnebaug, Pawcatuck, Merrimack, Kennebec, Penobscot, Narraganset, Passamaquoddy,* &c. In other parts of the country too the rivers retain their aboriginal names, as the *Mississippi, Ohio,*

Susquehanna, Roanoake, Altamaha, Chattahoochie, Alabama, &c., &c. And the same may be said of the great lakes, nearly all the bays, mountains, and numerous geographical divisions and localities. Many of the aboriginal names, however, have been discarded for others less appropriate. In New England the towns and villages were chiefly named after the towns in England from which the early colonists emigrated. In the State of New York there is a strange anomaly in the names of places. Before the Revolution the people seemed to prefer the aboriginal names; not only the rivers, lakes, hills, &c., but many of the towns received them. After the war, the names of distinguished statesmen and soldiers were applied to the new counties and towns.

The greatest perversions of the English language arise from two opposite causes. One of them is the introduction of vulgarisms by uneducated people, who not having the command of proper words to express their ideas, invent others for the purpose. These words continue among this class, are transmitted by them to their children, and thus become permanent and provincial. They are next seized upon by stump-speakers at political meetings, because they have an influence and are popular with the masses. Next we hear them on the floor of Congress and in our halls of legislation. Quoted by the newspapers, they become familiar to all, and take their place in the colloquial language of the whole people. Lexicographers now secure them and give them a place in their dictionaries ; and thus they become firmly engrafted on our language. The study of lexicography will show that this process has long been going on in England, and doubtless other languages are subject to similar influences.

But the greatest injury to our language arises from the perversion of legitimate words and the invention of hybrid and other inadmissible expressions by educated men, and particularly by the clergy. This class is the one, above all others, which ought to be the conservators rather than the pervertors of language. It is nevertheless a fact which cannot be denied, that many strange and barbarous words to which our ears are gradually becoming familiar, owe to them their origin and introduction; among them may be mentioned such verbs as to *fellowship*, to *difficult*, to *eventuate*, to *doxologize*, to *happify*, to *donate*, &c., &c.

Political writers have made and are constantly making large additions to our stock of words and phrases. Alex. Hamilton's writings abound in newly coined expressions; many of which have been adopted by Dr. Webster, and have a place in his dictionary. But few, however, have come into general use, as his writings have not been widely diffused, and there is nothing to recommend them for adoption by scholars. Judge Story has contributed his share of new words; but as they are confined to legal treatises and works on the Constitution, they can never seriously affect the language.

Writers of political articles in the newspapers, stump-orators, and the members of legislative bodies, have added much to the English vocabulary. This class of words, though not remarkable for their elegance, are often expressive and become more widely known than other classes. In many instances, however, their existence is but short. They often spring up with a party; and as the parties become extinct, or give place to new ones, the terms which express their peculiar ideas or doctrines likewise fall out of use. In this class may be included such terms as *Old Hunker, Bucktail, Federalist, Barnburner, Loco-foco. Young Democracy, Democratic Republican, Native American, Nullifier, Nullification, Coon, Coonery,* &c.

There are words, however, in this class, whose origin has grown out of our peculiar institutions, and which consequently are of a permanent nature. The origin of some of these is involved in obscurity, while that of others is well known. Sometimes a little incident trivial in itself has brought into existence words which are extremely expressive, and which will remain as long as our institutions exist. In this class we find *Caucus. Buncombe* or *Bunkum, Congress,* to *Lobby, Mileage, Gubernatorial, General Court, General Assembly,* President's and Governor's *Messages, Senatorial,* &c., &c.

The peculiar physical features of the country—its animals. productions, aborigines, forest life, &c.—have been a most fruitful source, from which has sprung perhaps the largest number of new words, as necessary and useful to ourselves as any derived from our Saxon ancestors. These terms are not used in England, for the simple reason that there they are not wanted. Although I cannot agree with Dr. Webster, that " we rarely find a new word introduced into a language which is entirely useless,"—for there are unquestionably thousands of words encumbering our dictionaries which might well be dispensed with,—yet there is no doubt that, in most instances, " the use of new terms is dictated by necessity or utility ; sometimes to express shades of difference in signification, for which the language did not supply a suitable term ; sometimes to express a combination of ideas by a single word, which otherwise would require a circumlocution. These benefits, which are often perceived, as it were, instinctively by a nation, recommend such words to common use, till the cavils of critics are silenced by the weight of authority."—*Letter to J. Pickering*, p. 7.

Were we to classify the periods when names were applied to places in the State of New York, for example, we would call that in which the Indian names were applied, the *Aboriginal* period. This is as far back as it would be safe for ordinary mortals to go, leaving the " ante-diluvian " period to the second sight of such seers as Mr. Rafinesque.*

The Indian names seem to have prevailed till the revolution. Then came a burst of patriotism among the settlers, many of whom doubtless had served in the war, and every new place was christened with the names of the warriors and statesmen of the day. Thus arose Washington county, Washington village, and Washington *hollow;* Jefferson county, village, lake, &c. The State of New York has thus perpetuated, in her towns and villages, the names of Adams, Jay, La Fayette, Hamilton, Madison, Pinckney, Putnam, Pulaski, Schuyler, De Kalb, Steuben, Sullivan, Gates, Wayne, &c. This may well be styled the *Patriotic* period. But New York appreciated also the military and naval geniuses of other countries, for we find a Nelson, a Moreau, a Waterloo, &c. within her borders. The names of statesmen and generals did not suffice for the patriotism of our early pioneers, for we find interspersed among

* See Introduction to History of Kentucky.

them the names of Freedom, Freetown, Freeport, Independence, Liberty, Victory, Hopewell, Harmony, Concord, &c.

Next comes the *Classical* period; for by what other term could we designate a period when towns were christened by the names of such men as Homer, Virgil, Solon, Ovid, Cato, Brutus, Pompey, Tully, Cicero, Aurelius, Scipio, Ulysses, Seneca, Hannibal, Hector, Romulus, Lysander, Manlius, Camillus, and Marcellus; or of such places as Athens, Sparta, Troy, Corinth, Pharsalia, Palmyra, Utica, Smyrna, Rome, and Carthage.

Testimony to the piety (to say nothing of the good taste) of our forefathers is also afforded by the occurrence of such names as Eden, Babylon, Sodom, Jerusalem, Jericho, Hebron, Goshen, Bethany, Bethpage, Bethlehem, Sharon, &c. There are towns named after nearly every country in Europe, as Norway, Sweden, Denmark (with a Copenhagen adjoining), Russia, Greece, Italy, Sardinia, Holland, Wales, as well as after their principal cities. There is a town of Mexico, Canton, Peru, Delhi, Cairo, China, Cuba. Distinguished men in English history, as Milton, Addison, Dryden, Scott, Byron, Chesterfield, Marlborough, Junius, have towns christened with their names. But little fondness is exhibited for dramatic authors, as the name of the greatest of them all has been forgotten. Not even a pond, a hollow, or a swamp has been honored with the name of Shakspeare. If we were to classify all the names of places in the State of New York, we should be puzzled for a place to put the names of Painted Post, Oxbow, Halfmoon, Owl Pond, Oyster Bay, Mud Creek, Cow Neck, Mosquito Cove, and the like. The name of *Pennyan* is said to have been manufactured by the first settlers, part of whom were from Pennsylvania and the rest from New England, by taking the first syllable from " Pennsylvania," and the last from " Yankee."

Now the Mexican war is over, we shall doubtless have a large fund of names to use in our newly acquired territories, and the new States at the West. The old generals of the revolution will be passed by, and the span-new heroes of this war will be handed down to the admiration of posterity in the metamorphosed shape of cities, towns, and villages, yet to come into existence. As the simplicity of the revolutionary period no longer remains, the plain surname will not answer now-a-days; but the love of glory and the love of magniloquence may both be gratified in such euphonious compounds as Quitmanville, Pillowtown, and *Polkopolis!*

The class of words which owe their origin to circumstances or productions peculiar to the United States, such as *backwoods, backwoodsmen, breadstuffs, barrens, bottoms, buffalo-robe, cane-brake, cypress-brake, clapboard, corn broom, corn-shucking, clearing, deadening, diggings, dug-out, flat boat, husking, pine barrens, prairie, prairie dog, prairie hen, shingle, sawyer, salt lick, savannah, snag, sleigh,* &c., are necessary additions to the language.

The metaphorical and other odd expressions used first at the West, and afterwards in other parts of the country, often originate in some curious anecdote or event, which is transmitted from mouth to mouth, and soon made the property of all. Political writers and stump speakers perform a prominent part in the invention and diffusion of these phrases. Among these may be mentioned, *to cave in, to acknowledge the corn, to flash in the pan, to bark up the wrong tree, to pull up stakes, to be a caution, to fizzle out, to flat out, to fix his flint, to be among the missing, to give him Jessy, to see the elephant, to fly around, to tucker out, to use up, to walk into, to mizzle, to absquatulate, to cotton, to hifer,* &c., &c.

Our people, particularly those who belong to the West and South, are fond of using intensive and extravagant epithets, both as adjectives and adverbs, as *awful, powerful, monstrous, dreadful, mighty, almighty, all-fired,* &c.

The words *bankable, boatable, mailable, mileage,* are well formed and useful terms which have been generally adopted by those who have occasion to make use of them. But the words *dubersome, disremember, decedent, docity,* cannot be called useful or necessary additions to our language.

The Indian element in our language, or rather the Indian words which have become adopted in it, consist, 1st. Of geographical names. 2d. Of the names of various animals, birds, and fishes. 3d. Of fruits and cereals; particularly the several preparations of the latter for eating. Thus from Indian corn, we have *samp*, *hominy*, and *supawn ;* from the manioc plant, *mandioca* and *tapioca*. 4th. Such articles known to and used by the Indians, which the Europeans did not possess, as *canoe*, *hammock*, *tobacco*, *moccasin*, *pemmican ;* also, *barbecue*, *hurricane*, *pow-wow*.

The Indian names of animals, fishes, and reptiles, are generally local. Thus a fish may be known by different names in Boston, New York, and Delaware Bay, as *scup*, *paugie*, and *scuppaug*.

There is a diversity in the pronunciation of certain words in different parts of the United States, which is so perceptible that a native of these particular districts may be at once recognised by a person who is observant in these matters. Residents of the city of New York are, perhaps, less marked in their pronunciation and use of words, than the residents of any other city or State, the reason of which is obvious. The population is so fluctuating, so many people from every part of the country, as well as from England, Scotland, and Ireland, are congregated here, who are in daily contact with each other, that there is less chance for any idiom or peculiarity of speech to grow up. The large number of educated men in New England, her admirable schools and higher institutions of education, have had a powerful influence in moulding the language of her people. Yet, notwithstanding this fact, in Boston and other towns in Massachusetts, there exist some glaring errors in the vulgar speech. There are peculiarities also to be observed in the literary language of the Bostonians. The great extent to which the scholars of New England have carried the study of the German language and literature for some years back, added to a very general neglect of the old master-pieces of English composition, have had the effect of giving to the writings of many of them an artificial, unidiomatic character, which has an inexpressibly unpleasant effect to those who are not habituated to it.

The agricultural population who live in the interior of New England, have a strongly marked provincial dialect, by which they may be distinguished from the people of every other part of the Union. The chief peculiarity is a drawling pronunciation, sometimes accompanied by a speaking through the nose, as *eend* for *end*, *dawg* for *dog*, *Gawd* for *God*, &c. Before the sounds *ow* and *oo*, they often insert a short *i*, which we will represent by the letter *y ;* as *kyow* for *cow*, *vyow* for *vow*, *tyoo* for *too*, *dyoo* for *do*, &c. &c. The numerous words employed in New England, which are not heard in other parts of the country, are mostly genuine old words still provincial in the North of England ; very few are of indigenous origin.

The chief peculiarity in the pronunciation of the Southern and Western people is the giving of a broader sound than is proper to certain vowels; as *whar* for *where*, *thar* for *there*, *bar* for *bear*.

In the following table of words, incorrectly pronounced, such as belong to New England are designated by the letters N. E. ; those exclusively Western, by the letter W. ; the Southern words, by S. ; the rest are common to various parts of the Union. In this attempt at classification there are doubtless errors and imperfections ; for an emigrant from Vermont to Illinois would introduce the provincialisms of his native district into his new residence.

arter	for after,	delightsome	for delightful.
ary	" either,	drownded	" drown'd,
attackted	" attack'd,	druv	" drove, W.
anywheres	" anywhere,	dubous	" dubious.
bachelder	" bachelor,	eend	" end.
bagnet	" bayonet,	everywheres	" everywhere,
bar	" bear, W.	gal	" girl,
becase	" because,	gin	" give,
bile	" boil,	git	" get,
cheer	" chair,	gineral	" general,
chimbly	" chimney,	guv	" gave,
cupalo	" cupola,	gownd	" gown,
cotch'd	" caught,	har	" hair, W.
critter	" creature,	hath	" hearth, S.
curous	" curious,	hender	" hinder,
dar	" dare, W.	hïst	" hoist,
darter	" daughter,	hum	" home, N. E.
deu	" do. N. E.	humbly	" homely, N. E.

hull	for whole, W.	sen	for since,
ile	" oil,	shay	" chaise, N. E.
innemy	" enemy,	shet	" shut, S.
janders	" jaundice,	sistern	" sisters, W.
jest	" just,	sich	" such,
Jeems	" James,	sot	" sat, N. E.
jine	" join,	sorter	" sort of,
jīst	" joist,	stan	" stand, N. E.
kittle	" kettle,	star,	" stair, W.
kiver	" cover,	stun	" stone, N. E.
larn	" learn,	stiddy	" steady, N. E.
larnin	" learning,	spettacle	" spectacle,
lives	" lief,	spile	" spoil, N. E.
leetle	" little,	squinch	" quench,
nary	" neither,	streech	" stretch, W.
ourn	" ours,	suthin	" something,
perlite	" polite,	tech	" touch,
racket	" rocket,	tend	" attend,
rale	" real,	tell'd	" told, N. E.
rench	" rince,	thar	" there, W.
rheumatiz	" rheumatism,	timersome	" timorous,
ruff	" roof, N. E.	tossel	" tassel,
sarcer	" saucer,	umberell	" umbrella,
sarce	" sauce,	varmint	" vermin, W.
sarve	" serve,	wall	" well, N. E.
sass	" sauce, N. E.	whar	" where, W.
sassy	" saucy,	yaller	" yellow,
scace	" scarce, N. E.	yourn	" yours.
scass	" scarce, W.		

Before closing these observations on American provincialisms, I should do injustice to previous writers on the same subject, not to speak of their works. The earliest of these, as far as my knowledge extends, is that of Dr. Witherspoon. In a series of essays, entitled " The Druid," which appeared originally in a periodical publication in 1761, he devotes numbers 5, 6, and 7 of these essays, about 20 pages in all, to Americanisms, perversions of language in the United States, cant phrases, &c. They were afterwards published in his collected works, in 4 vols. 8vo., Philadelphia, 1801, and may be found in the fourth volume.

The most important work of the kind is that of the late Hon. John Pickering. He began with an article in the " Memoirs of the American Academy of Arts and Sciences," Boston. This was soon after enlarged and published in a separate volume entitled " *A Vocabulary, or Collection of Words and Phrases which have been supposed to be peculiar to the United States of America.* To which is prefixed an Essay on the present state of the *English Language* in the United States." Boston: 1816. Pp. 206. (Containing about 520 words.) This valuable and interesting work received much attention, and in the following year appeared a pamphlet, entitled " *A Letter to the Hon. John Pickering, on the Subject of his Vocabulary, or Collection of Words and Phrases, supposed to be peculiar to the United States.*" By Noah Webster. 8vo. Boston: 1817. Pp. 69.

In the transactions of the Albany Institute, 1830, vol. I., is an article entitled " *Notes on Mr. Pickering's Vocabulary, &c., with Preliminary Observations.*" By T. Romeyn Beck. In Mr. Sherwood's " *Gazetteer of Georgia,*" is a glossary of words provincial in the Southern States. The latest work on provincialisms, but chiefly of errors in grammar, is " *A Grammatical Corrector, or Vocabulary of the Common Errors of Speech ; Alphabetically Arranged, Corrected, and Explained for the Use of Schools and Private Individuals.*" By Seth T. Hurd. 12mo. Philadelphia: 1847.*

As the charge has been frequently made against us by English critics of perverting our vernacular tongue, and of adding useless words to it, it will not be out of place to state here, that in the belief of the author, the English language is in no part of

---

* In preparing this work, I have examined all the English provincial glossaries, and the principal English dictionaries ; which it was necessary to do in order to know what words and phrases were still provincial in England. Many of the facts in the introductory essay on dialects, have been drawn from similar essays appended to the several glossaries. But I am chiefly indebted to the enlarged preface in Dr. Bosworth's Anglo-Saxon Dictionary, which presents the best historical analysis extant of the English language ; and to the admirable and later work of Professor Latham, "The English Language," London 1841, which is unquestionably the most valuable work on English Philology and Grammar, which has yet appeared.

the world spoken in greater purity by the great mass of the people than in the United States. In making this assertion he does not depend wholly on his own observation ; it has repeatedly been made by intelligent Englishmen who have travelled in the United States, and had an opportunity of judging. On this subject, the author of an English work, entitled the " Backwoods of Canada," has the following judicious remarks :

" With the exception of some few remarkable expressions, and an attempt at introducing fine words, the lower order of Yankees have a decided advantage over our English peasantry in the use of grammatical language ; they speak better English than you will hear from persons of the same class in any part of England, Ireland, or Scotland ; a fact that we should be unwilling to allow at home."—P. 83.

The Rev. Dr. Witherspoon, President of Princeton College, born and educated in Scotland, made a similar remark in 1784. In an essay on language, he says :

" The vulgar in America speak much better than the vulgar in Great Britain, for a very obvious reason, viz. that being much more unsettled, and moving frequently from place to place, they are not so liable to local peculiarities either in accent or phraseology."—*Works*, Vol. IV. p. 281.

We cannot say as much, however, in favor of our literary dialect. The ripest scholars among us acknowledge the fact, that in the best authors and public speakers of Great Britain, there is a variety in the choice of expressions, a correctness in the use of the particles, and an idiomatic vigor and freshness of style to which few or none of our writers can attain. The unfortunate tendency to favor the Latin at the expense of the Teutonic element of our language, which social and educational causes have long tended to foster, has in this country received an additional impulse from the great admixture of foreigners in our population. It is not likely that the pure old idiomatic English style can ever be restored in this country ; but there is no good reason to doubt, that the fusion of the present rather heterogeneous elements of which our society is composed, will result in the production of a style and a literature which will also have their beauties and merits, although fashioned after a somewhat different model.

DICTIONARY

OF

AMERICAN WORDS AND PHRASES.

ABISSELFA. A, by itself, A. It will be recollected by many, that in the olden time, the first letter of the alphabet was denominated " abisselfa" when it formed a syllable by itself, as in the word *able*. The scholar, in spelling the word, was taught to say, " *a*, by itself, *a*, (rapidly, *abisselfa*,) *b, l, e, able.*" We derive this word and the use of it from England, where it is used in Suffolk County.—*Moor's Glossary.*

ABOVE-BOARD. In open sight; without artifice, or trick. "A figurative expression," says Johnson, " borrowed from gamesters, who, when they put their hands under the table, are exchanging their cards."

> It is the part of an honest man to deal *above-board*, and without tricks.— *L'Estrange.*

ABOVE ONE'S BEND. Out of one's power; beyond reach. A common expression in the Western States.

> I shall not attempt to describe the curiosities at Peale's Museum; it is *above my bend.*—*Crockett, Tour down East,* p. 64.

ABSQUATULATE. To run away, to abscond. Used only in familiar language.

> W—— was surrendered by his bail, who was security for his appearance at court, fearing he was about to *absquatulate.*—*N. Y. Herald,* 1847.

ACKNOWLEDGE THE CORN. An expression of recent origin, which has now become very common. It means to confess, or acknowledge a charge or imputation. The following story is told as the origin of the phrase:

> Some years ago, a raw customer, from the upper country, determined

to try his fortune at New Orleans. Accordingly he provided himself with two flat-boats—one laden with corn and the other with potatoes—and down the river he went. The night after his arrival he went up town, to a gambling house. Of course he commenced betting, and his luck proving unfortunate, he lost. When his money was gone, he bet his "truck;" and the corn and potatoes followed the money. At last, when completely cleaned out, he returned to his boats at the wharf; when the evidences of a new misfortune presented themselves. Through some accident or other, the flat-boat containing the corn was sunk, and a total loss. Consoling himself as well as he could, he went to sleep, dreaming of gamblers, potatoes, and corn.

It was scarcely sunrise, however, when he was disturbed by the "child of chance," who had arrived, to take possession of the two boats as his winnings. Slowly awakening from his sleep, our hero, rubbing his eyes, and looking the man in the face, replied: "Stranger, *I acknowledge the corn*—take 'em; but the potatoes you *can't* have, by thunder."—*Pittsburgh Com. Advertiser.*

The Evening Mirror very naively comes out and *acknowledges the corn*, admits that a demand was made, &c.—*New York Herald*, June 27, 1846.

Mr. Tyler, in reply (to certain charges), boldly *acknowledges the corn*, and says that the cards of invitation were signed by him, &c.—*New York Tribune*, Jan. 26, 1845.

Enough, said the Captain. I'm hoaxed, I'm gloriously hoaxed. *I acknowledge the corn.*—*Pickings from the Picayune*, p. 80.

ACCOUNTABILITY. The state of being liable to answer for one's conduct; liable to give account, and to receive reward or punishment for actions.—*Webster.* This word, so much used by our divines, is not to be found in any English Dictionary except the recent one of Mr. Knowles. Mr. Todd, in his additions to Johnson's Dictionary, has *accountableness*, the state of being accountable.

Reason and liberty imply *accountableness.*—*Duncan's Logic.*

We would use *accountability* instead, as in the following example:

The awful idea of *accountability.*—*Robert Hall.*

ADAM'S ALE. Water. A colloquial expression, used both in England and America.

To slake his thirst, he took a drink
Of *Adam's Ale* from river's brink.—*Reynard the Fox.*

TO ADMIRE. 1. To like very much. This verb is much and very absurdly used in New England in expressions like the following: "I should *admire* to see the President."

TO ADMIRE. 2. To wonder at; to be affected with slight surprise.—*Ray.* In New England, particularly in Maine, this word is used in this sense. Some of the old English writers so employed it.

> I perceive these lords
> At this rencontre do so much *admire*
> That they devour their reason.—*Shakspeare.*

ADOBIES. (Sp. *adobes.*) Sun-baked brick used for building houses, fortifications, and making inclosures on the Western frontier of the United States.

TO ADVOCATE. (Lat. *advoco.* Fr. *avocasser.*) To plead, to support, to defend.—*Todd.* To plead in favor of; to defend by argument before a tribunal; to support or vindicate. —*Webster.*

This word has been particularly noticed by recent Lexicographers; as it is one of that class which has fallen into disuse in England, and, by English and American critics not familiar with its history, has been set down as an Americanism. It is a useful word, and has long been employed by our best writers.

In speaking of this word, Mr. Boucher observes in his Glossary, " that it has been said that it is an improvement of the English language, which has been discovered by the people of the United States of North America, since their separation from Great Britain;" but that it can be shown to be a very common Scottish word. Mr. Todd, the learned editor of Johnson's Dictionary, is also unwilling to allow this concession to us, and says, " It is an old English word, employed by one of our finest and most manly writers; and if the Americans affect to plume themselves on this *pretended improvement of our language,* let them, as well as their abettors, withdraw the unfounded claim to discovery, in turning to the prose writings of Milton. In the Dictionaries of the sixteenth and seventeenth centuries, however, as in the Latin of Thomas, the Spanish of Minshew, the Italian of Florio, and the French of Cotgrave, *advoco, advogar, avocare,* and *avocasser,* are rendered, not *to advocate,* but " *to play the advocate.*"

> This is the only thing distinct and sensible that has been *advocated.*— *Burke, Speech on the Reform of Representatives.*

"Though this verb is found in *Milton,*" says Mr. Pickering, " yet it does not appear to have been in common use in England, either at the time he wrote, or since that period.   It has very recenly been adopted by a few other writers, and seems now to be getting into use in England."   Dr. Webster makes no remarks as to the legitimacy of the word, but gives several examples of its use.   From the vocabulary of Mr. Pickering, the Glossary of Mr. Boucher, and the Dictionary of Dr. Webster, the following illustrations have been selected.

The members of the College of Justice have this privilege, that they cannot be pursued before any inferior judge ; and if they be, the lords will *advocate* the cause to themselves.—*Sir Geo. Mackenzie, Institutes of Law.*

How little claim, persons who *advocate* this sentiment, really possess to be considered Calvinists, will appear from the following quotation.—*Mackenzie's Life of Calvin.*

The most eminent orators were engaged to *advocate* his cause.— *Mitford.*

But from his want of sobermindedness, we cannot always prove his earnestness in the cause he *advocated.*—*D'Israeli, Quarrels of Authors.*

From American writers are the following examples :

Some are taking unwearied pains to disparage the motive of those Federalists who *advocate* the equal support of, &c.—*Alex. Hamilton.*

I shall on a future occasion examine impartially, and endeavor to ascertain precisely the true value of this opinion, which is so warmly *advocated* by all the great orators of antiquity.—*J. Q. Adams, Rhetoric.*

The idea of a legislature consisting of a single branch, though *advocated* by some, was generally reprobated.—*Ramsey, Hist. of S. Carolina.*

This seems to be a foreign and local dialect, and cannot be *advocated* by any person who understands correct English.—*Webster, Diss. on the English Langua౸e,* p. 111.

AFEARD. (Ang. Saxon *afered.*)   Afraid ; frightened ; terrified.—*Todd's Johnson.*

This is a good old English word, though now considered a vulgarism ; and as common in ancient times, as *afraid* is at present.   It is provincial in various parts of England, and among uneducated persons in the United States.

A gret ok he coolde breide a doun, as it a smal gerde were,
And here forth in his honde, that fole forte *afere.*—*Robt. of Gloucester.*
With scalled browes blake, and pilled hend ;
Of his visage children were sore *aferd ?*—*Chaucer, Cant. Tales.*

Hal! art thou not horribly *afeard?*—*Shakspeare, Henry IV.*

Chin as woolly as the peach,
And his lips should kissing teach,
Till he cherished too much beard,
And made love or me *afear'd.*—*Ben Jonson, Her Man described.*

It has been supposed, that in Chaucer's time, there was a difference between the significations of *afeard* and *afraid,* as in one instance he employs both in the same verse.

His wife was neither *afeard* nor *afraid.*—*Canterbury Tales.*

The following are examples of the use of the word by American writers:

I an't *afeared* of the old Harry himself, but I vum! I never dare speak to Rhody.—*Margaret,* p. 87.

I promised when I caught him, to give him a licking, and I was *afear'd* I'd have to break the peace.—*J. C. Neal, Sketches.*

AFORE. (Sax. *ætforan.*) Before; sooner in time; in front; rather than.—*Todd's Johnson.*

This old word is gone entirely out of use in elegant language. It is now provincial in England, and in the United States is used only by the illiterate.

If your diligence be not speedy, I shall be there *afore* you.—*Shakspeare K. Lear.*

Approaching nigh, he reared high *afore*
His body monstrous, horrible, and vast.—*Spenser, F. Queen.*

KEEP. *Afore* I'll
Endure the tyranny of such a tongue
And such a pride——
POL. What will you do?
KEEP. Tell truth.—*Ben Jonson.*

AFOREHAND. (Old English.) Beforehand. Aforehand in business, i. e. successful.

Once good English, now a provincialism.

For it will be said, that in the former times, whereof we have spoken, Spain was not so mighty as now it is; and England, on the other side, was more *aforehand* in all matters of power.—*Bacon, War with Spain.*

AFTERCLAPS. Unexpected events happening after an affair is supposed to be at an end.—*Todd's Johnson.*

Although this is a genuine old English word, it is now seldom heard except in familiar conversation.

For the next morrow's meed they closely went,
For fear of *afterclaps* to prevent.—*Spenser, Hub. Tale.*

Let that man, who can be so far taken and transported with the present
pleasing offers of a temptation, as to overlook those dreadful *afterclaps*
which usually bring up the rear of it.—*South, Sermons,* VI.

She wyll thee graunt it liberally perhappes ;
But for all that, beware of *afterclaps.*—*Sir Thomas More.*

AFTER NIGHT. After nightfall ; in the evening ; as, " A
meeting will be held in the court-house *after night.*" This
expression is said to be peculiar to Pennsylvania.—*Hurd's
Grammatical Corrector.*

AGY, for ague ; *fever-nagy,* for ' fever and ague ;' common
among the uneducated, wherever this distressing disease is
known.

AHEAD. Originally a sea-term. Farther onward than another.
—*Johnson.*

This word has now become very common, and signifies
forward, in advance.

Our banks, being anxious to make money for their stockholders, are
probably right to drive *ahead,* regardless of consequences, &c.—*N. Y. Com.
Adv. Nov.* 29, 1845.

ALBANY BEEF. Sturgeon ; a fish which abounds in the
Hudson river ; so called by the people in the State of New York.

ALEWIFE, *plur.* alewives. (Indian, *aloof. Alosa vernalis,*
Storer, Massachusetts Rep't.) A fish of the herring kind,
abounding in the waters of New England.

The name appears to be an Indian one, though it is somewhat changed, as appears by the earliest account we have of
it. In former times, the Indians made use of these fish to
manure their lands, as the *menhaden* are now used. Mr. Win-
throp says, " Where the ground is bad or worn out, they put
two or three of the fishes called *aloofes* under or adjacent to
each corn-hill ; whereby they had many times a double crop
to what the ground would otherwise have produced. The
English have learned the like husbandry, where these *aloofes*
come up in great plenty."—*Philosophical Trans.* 1678.

ALIENAGE. The state of being an alien.—*Webster.*

Neither this nor the following word is to be found in the

English dictionaries, except the recent one of Mr. Knowles. They are common, however, in professional books.

> Where he sues an executor, &c., the plaintiff's *alienage* is no plea.—*Laires' Pleading on Assumpsit*, p. 687.

> To restore estates, forfeitable on account of *alienage.*—*Judge Story.*

ALIENISM. The state of being an alien.—*Webster, Knowles.*

> The prisoner was convicted of murder; on his arraignment he suggested his *alienism*, which was admitted.—2 *Johnson's Reports*, 381.

> The law was very gentle in the construction of the disability of *alienism.*—*Chancellor Kent.*

ALLEY. (Lat. *albus*, white.) An ornamented marble, used by boys for shooting in the ring, &c.; also called in England, a *taw.* It is often made of white marble or of painted clay.

ALL-FIRED. Very, in a great degree. A low American word.

> The first thing I know'd, my trowsers were plastered all over with hot molasses, which burnt *all-fired* bad.—*Maj. Jones's Courtship*, p. 87.

> Old Haines sweating like a pitcher with ice-water in it, and looking *all-fired* tired.—*Porter's Tales of the Southwest*, p. 50.

> I was woked up by a noise in the street; so I jumps up in an *all-fired* hurry, ups with the window, and outs with my head.—*Sam Slick.*

> You see the fact is, Squire (said the Hooshier), they had a mighty deal to say up in our parts about Orleans, and how *all-fired* easy it is to make money in it; but it's no ham and all hominy, I reckon.—*Pickings from the Picayune*, p. 67.

> I'm dying—I know I am! My mouth tastes like a rusty cent. The doctor will charge an *all-fired* price to cure me.—*Knickerbocker Mag.* 1845.

ALL OVER. Bearing a resemblance to some particular object. The word is common in familiar language.

The Southern Standard, in noticing Dombey and Son, says: "We have read this work so far with great interest; it is Dickens *all over.*" Meaning that it partakes fully of the character of Dickens's writings.

By the following example it appears that English writers use the word in the same sense. Sir George Simpson, in speaking of the indolence of the Californians, and of the deficiencies in all the comforts of life, says:

> The only articles on the bare floor, were some gaudy chairs from the Sandwich Islands. This was California *all over;* the richest and most influential individual in a professedly civilized country, obliged to borrow the means of sitting from savages.—*Journey round the World*, Vol. I. p. 173.

ALL-OVERISH.   Neither sick nor well.   A low word, used both in England and America.

TO ALLOT UPON.   To intend, to form a purpose ; as, I *allot upon* going to Boston.   Used by uneducated people in the interior of New England.

TO ALLOW.   To acknowledge, to think.   Used in a very loose manner like the word *guess.*

> The lady of the cabin seemed kind, and *allowed* we had better stop where we were.—*Carlton, The New Purchase.*

ALL SORTS OF.   A Southern expression, synonymous with expert, acute, excellent, capital.   It answers to the English slang term *bang-up.* It is a prevalent idiom of low life, and often heard in the colloquial language of the better informed.   A man who in New England would be called a *curious* or a *smart* fellow, would in the South be called *all sorts of* a fellow.   Sometimes one hears the expression " all sorts of a horse," or, " all sorts of a road."

> She was *all sorts* of a gal—there warn't a sprinklin' too much of her— she had an eye that would make a fellow's heart try to get out of his bosom ;—her step was light as a panther's, and her breath sweet **as a** prairie flower.—*Robb, Squatter Life.*

ALL-STANDING.   Without preparation, suddenly.

This, like many other common expressions, seems to be borrowed from the sea.   Thus, a ship in full career, whose course is suddenly checked by striking against a rock, or by a squall of wind, is said to be brought-to *all-standing*, i. e. with all her sails set and unprepared for stopping.   And hence we say, for instance, of a horseman or an orator whose course is suddenly checked, that he is brought up *all-standing.*

> It was no stumble, no pitching head first over a steep precipice ; but on the contrary, I walked directly off the giddy height—to use a common expression, went ove · *all-standing.*—*Kendall's Santa Fé Expedition.*

ALL-TO-SMASH.   Smashed to pieces.   This expression is often heard in low and familiar language.   It is an English provincialism.   Mr. Halliwell says, that a Lancashire man, telling his master the mill-dam had burst, exclaimed, " Maister, maister, dam's brossen, and *aw's-to-smash.*—*Archaic and Prov. Dictionary.*

ALL-WINSOME. Winsome is a word used in the north of England, (Ang. Sax. *winsum*, pleasant,) sweet, pleasant. I have never heard the word, although an American writer thus uses it:

> What absence of that anagogical, all-prevalent, *all-winsome* Brahminism in Christ!—*Margaret*, p. 258.

ALONE. Sole. The German *allein* is used in like manner; thus, *alleinbesitz*, sole, exclusive possession; *alleinhandel*, sole trade, monopoly. Mr. Todd says, the English word was formerly written *all-one*, and was used in this sense by old writers. Mr. Pickering says, "It is often heard from our pulpits in expressions like the following : The *alone* God ; the *alone* motive," &c. It is now rarely used, although I heard it in a prayer during the present year (1848). The following examples from English writers cited by Johnson and Pickering show its use:

> God, by whose *alone* power and conversation we all live, and move, and have our being.—*Bentley*.

> The Legislature never pretended to omnipotence ; that is the *alone* attribute of the people.—*British Critic*, Vol. IX. p. 234.

TO AMALGAMATE. This word, which properly denotes the compounding or mixing of metals, is universally applied in the United States to the mixing of the black and white races.

AMALGAMATION. The mixing or union of the black and white races.

AMAZING. Wonderfully ; very, in a great degree. A vulgarism.

> Everything in New York on a May-day looks *amazin'* different, and smells *amazin'* different, I can tell you.—*Maj. Downing*, p. 43.

AMAZINGLY. Exceedingly, very much. Used only in colloquial language and applied to trifling things.

> Major, I like this 'ere churn *amazingly*.—*Ibid.* p. 58.

AMBITION. In North Carolina this word is used instead of the word *grudge*, as, "I had an *ambition* against that man." I am credibly informed that it is even used in this manner by educated men.

TO AMBITION. (Fr. *ambitionner*.) Ambitiously to seek after. —*Webster*.

> This is what I *ambition* for my own country.—*Jefferson's Writings*.

This word is not common. It is not in the English Dictionaries; yet examples may be found of its use by late English writers.

> On dress occasions, the ladies of the upper ranks despise the mantilla, *ambitioning* nothing so much as a fashionable French bonnet.—*London Spectator, June* 7, 1845.

AMENABILITY. State of being amenable or answerable.—*Judge Story. Webster.*

Not in the English Dictionaries.

AMERICANISM. A way of speaking peculiar to this country. —*Witherspoon.*

"By Americanism," says Dr. Witherspoon, "I understand a use of phrases or terms, or a construction of sentences, even among persons of rank and education, different from the use of the same terms or phrases, or the construction of similar sentences, in Great Britain. In this sense it is exactly similar in its formation and signification to the word Scotticism."—*Works*, Vol. IV. p. 82.

TO AMERICANIZE. To render American; to naturalize in America.—*Webster.*

AMOST. Almost. A vulgarism alike common in England and the United States. *E'en amost* is often heard in New England.

AMONG, for *between*. This word is often used when reference is made only to two persons. Ex. " The money was divided among us two."

AMPERSAND. The character &, representing the conjunction *and*. It is a corruption of " *and, per se, and*" (and, by itself, and). This expression was formerly very common in this country, but seems now to have gone out of use. It may, however, be retained in the interior, where the modern system of education has not reached. Mr. Halliwell, who notices this word in his *Archaic and Prov. Dict'y*, says, that it is or was common in England. In Hampshire it is pronounced *amperzed*, and very often *amperze-and*. Strutt, in his *Sports and Pastimes*, mentions an ancient alphabet of the fourteenth century, now in the Harleian Library, at the end of which is " X Y wyth ESED AND per se—Amen."

ANGELOLOGY. A discourse on angels; or the doctrine of angelic beings.—*Webster*.

> These questions may easily be answered, by a proper survey of the *angelology* of the Scripture.—*Stuart on the Apocalypse*, Vol. II. p. 397.

ANNULMENT. (Fr. *annullement*.) The act of annulling. —*Pickering's Vocab.*

This word was not in any English Dictionary before Todd's edition of Johnson.

> The *annulment* of the belligerent edicts.—*Cor. of Sec'y of State to Mr. Pinckney*, 1810.

AN'T, or AINT. A common abbreviation in colloquial language for *am not* and *are not*. It is often improperly used for *is not*. It is equally common in England.

ANTAGONIZING. Conflicting, opposing.—*Pickering's Vocabulary*.

This word, says Mr. Pickering, has been censured by an American critic, in the following passage :

> Nor can I forbear to remark the tendency of *antagonizing* appeals.— *John Q. Adams's Letter to H. G. Otis.*

The verb is given by Johnson, but not the participle, nor is it noticed by Webster. Prof. Goodrich has inserted it in his new edition (1848) of Webster's Dictionary.

ANTI-FEDERALIST. "This word was formed about the year 1788, to denote a person of the political party that opposed the adoption of the Constitution of the United States, which was then always spoken of by the name of the *Federal* Constitution. The word is not now much used ; having been superseded by various other names, which have been successively given to the same party."—*Pickering's Vocabulary*.

ANTI-SLAVERY. Hostile to slavery.

ANTI-MASON. One hostile to masonry or free-masonry.— *Worcester*.

ANTI-MASONIC. Hostile to masonry.

ANY HOW. At any rate, on any account, in any way.

> We have no confidence in cobble-stone pavement for Broadway *any how*. —*New York Tribune*, October 25, 1845.

This expression is not peculiar to this country.

> All Nelson wanted was to go to Copenhagen ; and he said, "Let it be by the Sound, or by the Belt, or *any how*."—*Nelson's Despatches*, Vol. IV.

ANY HOW YOU CAN FIX IT.   At any rate whatever.

ANY MANNER OF MEANS.   An expression much used instead of *any means.*

TO APE ONE'S BETTERS.   To imitate one's superiors.

> The negroes are good singers; they are an imitative race, and it is not to be wondered at that in this, as in other things, they *ape their betters.—Newspaper.*

APPELLATE.   Relating to appeals.

> In all cases affecting ambassadors, &c. the supreme court shall have *original* jurisdiction: In all other cases before mentioned, the supreme court shall have *appellate* jurisdiction.—*Constitut. of the U. States, Art.* **3.**

> The king of France is not the fountain of justice; the judges neither the original nor the *appellate* are of his nomination.—*Burke, Revolution.*

For a fuller account of this word, about which there has been much discussion by lexicographers, see Mr. Pickering's Vocabulary, where many authorities are cited. It was first given by Mason in his supplement to Johnson's Dictionary, and was afterwards adopted by Todd.

APPLE BUTTER.   A sauce made of apples stewed down in cider. This is generally made in quantity, and kept for use during the winter.

APPLE BRANDY, ⎫ A liquor distilled from cider; also called
APPLE JACK.   ⎬ cider brandy.

APPLE-PIE ORDER.   An expression used in familiar conversation, denoting perfect order. It is used alike in England and America.—*Halliwell's Dict'y.*

> As the period for the assembling of Congress approaches, an air of bustling activity is noticeable in everything, from the preparation of the "Message" down to the scrubbing of door-plates. The landladies are putting their lodgings in *apple-pie order* for the members, &c.—*Newspaper.*

> The ferry-boats are kept running in *apple-pie order* under the vigilant superintendence of Capt. Woolsey.—*New York Tribune.*

APPLICANT.   A diligent student.—*Pickering's Vocab.* One who applies himself closely to his studies. A sense of the word common in New England. The English appear to use the word only in the sense of "one who applies for anything," in which sense it is most commonly employed by us.

APPOINTABLE.   That may be appointed or constituted; as officers are appointed by the Executive.—*Federalist, Webster.*

TO APPRECIATE. *v. a.* To raise the value of.—*Webster.*

This sense of the word is not in any English dictionary except Knowles's, which is quite a recent work.

Lest a sudden peace should *appreciate* the money.--*Ramsay.*

The common use of this verb, however, is, as in England, to set a just value on. Also, *v. n.* to rise in value; as, "the currency of the country appreciates."—*Webster.*

APPRECIATION. A rising in value; increase of worth or value.—*Webster.*

This noun, like the verb from which it is derived, is commonly used by us in its appropriate meaning of a just valuation; and this will hereafter be understood of all similar words where a peculiar meaning is assigned to them, unless an express statement is made to the contrary.

TO APPROBATE. (Lat. *approbo*, to approve.) To express approbation of; to manifest a liking, or degree of satisfaction; to express approbation officially, as of one's fitness for a public trust.—*Webster.*

Dr. Webster observes that this is a modern word, but in common use in America. Mr. Todd introduces it in his edition of Johnson, from Cockeram's old vocabulary, the definition of which is, to allow, to like. Mr. Todd says it is obsolete.

All things contained in Scripture is *approbate* by the whole consent of all the clergie of Christendom.—*Sir T. Elyot's Governor,* fol. 226.

"This word," says Mr. Pickering, "was formerly much used at our colleges, instead of the old English word *approve.* The students used to speak of having their performances *approbated* by their instructors. It is now in common use with our clergy as a sort of technical term, to denote a person who is *licensed to preach :* they would say, such a one is *approbated,* that is, *licensed to preach.* It is also common in New England to say of a person, who is licensed by the County Courts to sell spirituous liquors, or to keep a public house, that he is *approbated ;* and the term is adopted in the law of Massachusetts on this subject."—*Pickering's Vocabulary.*

TO ARGUFY. To import, to have weight as an argument; to argue.

This vile word has a place in several of the English glossaries. In this country it is only heard among the most illiterate.

ARK.   The common abbreviation for " Arkansas."

ARK.   A large boat, used on some of the Western rivers, to
transport merchandise. Before the use of steamboats, they
were employed on the Ohio and Mississippi rivers.   Dr.
Harris thus describes them : " They are made with plank,
fastened upon ribs or knees, by wooden bolts. They are
from twelve to fifteen feet wide, and from forty to sixty long ;
carrying, commonly, sixty or eighty tons burden. They float
down the stream with the current, and are not worked with
oars, except to direct and propel them to the shore. These
boats go down the river to New Orleans ; and after discharging their cargoes, they are taken apart, and sold for lumber
with very little loss."—*Tour in Ohio in* 1803.

ARY, either.   A vulgarism used by the illiterate.

AS GOOD AS GO.
AS GOOD'S GO. In the phrase, I'd as *good's go* to New York,
instead of " I might as well go to New York."   " I'd *as
good's* do this," for, I may as well do this.   Only heard among
the illiterate.

ASH-HOPPER.   A lie cask, or an inverted pyramidal box to
contain ashes, resembling a hopper in a mill. They are
common in the country, where people make their own soap.

ASSOCIATION.   In ecclesiastical affairs, a society of the
clergy, consisting of a number of pastors of neighboring
churches, united for promoting the interests of religion and
the harmony of the churches.—*Webster.*

ASSOCIATION.   In civil affairs, this word is much used at the
present day, to denote the principle of uniting the producing
classes in societies, for the purpose of obtaining for themselves
a larger share of the fruits of their labor.

   The citizens of Illinois are well prepared for *Association.* They are, to
a great extent, freed from the prejudices and bigotry which pervade every
nook and corner of the older States.   There is here a feeling of liberality
—a spirit of inquiry, before which spurious Civilization cannot long make
headway.   We say to all friends of *Association,* come West.   But we

say, at the same time, don't come, until you are convinced it is for your interest and the interest of the cause of *Association* that you should come.— *New York Tribune.*

We do not claim that our Rules are perfect, but we wish to make them so; being firmly convinced that the Science taught by Fourier will ultimately lead us into true *Association*, if we follow it as a science, and that we must have some correct rules of progress to govern us during the transition period from Civilization to *Association.*—*Ibid.*

ASSOCIATIONAL. Pertaining to an association of clergymen. —*Webster.*

In order to obtain a license, and afterwards to be admitted to ordination, they (the students in divinity) must, in each case, pass through the *Associational* or Presbyterian examination.—*Quarterly Rev.*, 1815.

ASSOCIATIONIST. One who advocates the Fourier doctrine of association.

AT, for by. Used in this expression, "Sales *at* auction."

The English say—" Sales *by* auction," and this is in analogy with the expressions—Sales *by* inch of candle ; sales *by* private contract.—*Pickering's Vocab.*

Sometimes English writers use the word as we do.

Those execrable wretches, who could become purchasers *at* the auction of their fellow-creatures.—*Burke's Reflections.*

ATHENÆUM. A building or an apartment, where a library, periodicals, and newspapers are kept for public use, or for a reading room.—*Webster.*

ATOP. On or at the top, upon. Atop of a horse. A vulgarism common in England and America.

ATTACKTED, for attacked. This corruption is only heard among the most illiterate.

It is common also in the dialect of the lower classes in London.—*Pegge's Anecdotes.*

ATTITUDINIZE. To assume affected attitudes.—*Worcester.*

AUSPICATE. (Lat. *auspicio.*) To foreshow or foretell the event.—*Richardson.* This old word, though unnoticed by Johnson, may be found in Holland's translations, Ben Jonson and other early writers. It is but rarely used at the present day.

King Edward therefore presented himself before the strong towne of Berwick, with a mighty haste, there to *auspicate* his entrance to a conquest of England.—*Speed, History of Great Britain.*

Would to God I could *auspicate* good influences.—*Webster's Speech.*

AUTHORESS. A female writer who has printed her compositions.—*Jodrell's Philology.*

The use of this word has been questioned in England. It is not in Johnson's Dictionary, and as he says, it is not much used. This was sixty years ago. The British Critic, in the year 1793, says of it, " We do not acknowledge the word." Since that time Mr. Todd has inserted it in his edition of Johnson's Dictionary, from Cotgrave, (French, *authrice,* or autrix, *authoress,* or actress,) and defines it, " a female efficient." This sense of the word is different from that in which we use it.

> O Amarillis, *auth'ress* of my flame !—*Fanshawe, Past. Fido.*

> Albeit, his (Adam's) loss, without God's mercy, was absolutely irrecoverable ; yet we never find he twitted her as *authoress* of his fall.—*Feltham.*

> Mrs. Montagu, the justly celebrated authoress of the Essay on the Genius and Writings of our Author.—*Steeven's Notes, Hamlet.*

AUTHORITY. In Connecticut the justices of the peace are denominated *the civil authority.*—*Webster.*

Mr. Pickering says, " This word is also used in some of the States in speaking collectively of the professors, &c. of our colleges, to whom the government of those institutions is intrusted."

> " The *authority* required him to give bonds for his good behavior."—*Miss H. Adams's Hist. of New England,* p. 64.

AVAILED. Dr. Witherspoon notices this word as used in the following example :—" The members of a popular government should be continually *availed* of the situation and condition of every part."—*Works,* Vol. IV. p. 296.

The newspapers sometimes say " an offer" (for instance) " was made but not *availed of.*"

AVAILS. Profits, or proceeds. It is used in New England for the proceeds of goods sold, or for rents, issues, or profits.—*Webster.*

> Expecting to subsist on the bounty of government, rather than on the *avails* of their own industry.—*Stoddard's Louisiana.*

It is used in other parts of the country in like manner.

AVERSE. On the use of this word, Mr. Pickering has the following remarks : " American writers, till within some years past, generally employed the preposition *to* instead of *from* with this adjective. Dr. Witherspoon thinks, that " as *averse* properly signifies turned away, it seems an evident improvement to say *averse from ;*" and the Scottish writers generally seem to have preferred this. Dr. Campbell, however, observes, that " the words *averse* and *aversion* are more properly construed with *to*, than with *from*. The examples in favor of the latter preposition, are, beyond comparison, outnumbered by those in favor of the former. The argument from etymology is here of no value, being taken from the use of another language. If, by the same rule, we were to regulate all nouns and verbs of Latin original, our present syntax would be overturned."—*Campbell's Rhetoric*. Dr. Webster remarks to the same effect. Mr. Todd says many examples may be brought to show the prevalent use of the word *from* in connection with *averse*, before Clarendon ; but now the usage of *to* prevails.

AWFUL, *adj.* 1. Disagreeable, detestable, ugly.

A word much used among the common people in New England, and not unfrequently among those who are educated. The expression, " an *awful*-looking woman," is as often heard as " an ugly woman."

The country people of the New England States make use of many quaint expressions in their conversation. Everything that creates surprise is *awful* with them : " what an *awful* wind ! *awful* hole ! *awful* hill ! *awful* mouth ! *awful* nose !" &c.—*Lambert's Travels in Canada and the U. S.*

The practice of moving on the first day of May, with one-half the New-Yorkers, is an *awful* custom.—*Maj. Downing, May-day in N. Y.*

AWFUL. Very great, excessive. This sense of the word is peculiar to the West.

Pot-pie is the favorite dish, and woodsmen, sharp set, are *awful* eaters.—*Carlton, The New Purchase*, vol. I. p. 182.

It is even used in this sense adverbially, and with still greater impropriety, like many other adjectives. Thus we not unfrequently hear such expressions as " an *awful* cold day."

AWFULLY. Exceedingly, excessively.

The chimneys were *awfully* given to smoking.—*Carlton, New Purchase*

We give an example of the same use of this word by a popular English writer.

> The Ottoman horseman, raised by his saddle to a great height above the humble level of the back which he bestrides, and using an *awfully* sharp bit, is able to lift the crest of his nag, &c.—*Eöthen*, p. 13.

TO AXE. (*Ang. Sax. acsian, axian.*) To ask.

This word is now considered a vulgarism; though, like many others under the same censure, it is as old as the English language. Among the early writers it was used the same as *ask* is now. In England it still exists in the colloquial dialect of Norfolk and other counties. A true born Londoner, says Pegge, in his *Anecdotes of the English Language*, always *axes* questions, *axes* pardon, and at quadrilles, *axes* leave. In the United States it is somewhat used by the vulgar.—*Forby's Vocabulary. Richardson's Dic.*

> And Pilate *axide* him, art thou Kyng of Jewis?   And Jhesus answeride and seide to him, thou seist.—*Wiclif, Trans. of the Bible.*

> A poor lazar, upon a tide,
> Came to the gate, and *axed* meate.—*Gower, Con. Anc.*

Margaret, Countess of Richmond and Derby, in a letter to her son, Henry VII., concludes with—

> As herty blessings as ye can *axe* of God.—*Lord Howard.*

In the next reign, Dr. John Clarke writes to Cardinal Wolsey, and tells him that—

> The King *axed* after your Grace's welfare.—*Pegge's Anecdote.*

> Day before yesterday, I went down to the Post Office, and *ax'd* the Postmaster if there was anything for me.—*Maj. Jones's Courtship*, p. 172.

> I have often *axed* myself what sort of a gall that splendiferous Lady of the Lake of Scot's was.—*Sam Slick in Eng.*, ch. 30.

B.

TO KNOW *b* FROM A *bull's foot*. It is a common phrase to say, "He does not know B from a bull's foot," meaning that a person is very illiterate, or very ignorant. The term *bull's foot* is chosen merely for the sake of the alliteration; as in the similar phrases, "He does not know B from a *broomstick*," or "B from a *battledoor*." It is a very old saying; Mr. Halliwell finds it in one of the Digby MSS.

I know not an A from the wynd mylne,
Ne a *B from a bole-foot*, I trowe, ni thiself nother.
Archaic and Provincial Glossary.

BAA-LAMB. A pet term for a lamb in England and America.

BACHELOR'S BUTTON. (*Lychnis sylvestris.*) The common name of a flower, supposed by country people to have some magical effect upon the fortunes of love. It seems to have grown into a phrase for being unmarried, " to wear *bachelor's buttons*," in which, probably, a quibble was intended.—*Nare's Glossary.*

> He wears *Bachelor's Buttons*, does he not ?—*Heywood, Fair Maid.*

BACK, is often used for *ago ;* as in the phrase, " a little while back," i. e. " a short time ago."

BACK AND FORTH. Backwards and forwards, applied to a person in walking, as, " He was walking *back and forth.*" A common expression in the familiar language of New England.

BACKWOODS. The partially cleared forest region on the western frontier of the United States, called also the *back settlements.* This part of the country is regarded as the back part or rear of Anglo-American civilization, which fronts on the Atlantic. It is rather curious that the English word *back* has thus acquired the meaning of *western*, which it has in several Oriental languages, and also in Irish.

BACKWOODSMAN. In the United States, an inhabitant of the forest on the Western frontier.—*Webster.*

> The project of transmuting the classes of American citizens and converting sailors into *backwoodsmen*, is not too monstrous for speculators to conceive and desire.—*Fisher Ames's Works*, p. 144.

> I presume, ladies and gentlemen, it is your curiosity to hear the plain, uneducated *backwoodsman* in his home style.—*Crockett's Tour*, p. 126.

TO BACK OUT. To retreat from a difficulty, to refuse to fulfil a promise or engagement. A metaphor borrowed from the stables.

Mr. Bedinger, in his remarks in the House of Representatives on the Mexican war, Jan. 25, 1848, said :

> He regretted the bloodshed in Mexico, and wished it would stop. But, he asked, would gentlemen be willing *to back out*, and forsake our rights ? No, no. No turning back. This great country must go ahead.

The Whigs undertook to cut down the price of printing to a fair rate. but at last *backed out*, and voted to pay the old prices.—*N. Y. Tribune.*

To all appearance, we are on the eve of a bloody contest, if not a revolution. What will be the consequence? One or the other party must *back out*, or no one can tell what will be the result.—*Nat. Intelligencer.*

BACK. *Behind the Back.* When a person is slandered in his absence, it is said to be done *behind his back*, that is, in secret, or when his back is turned. It is the same as *backbiting.*

> Where *behind a man's back*
> For though he praised, he fint some lacke.—*Gower's Conf. A.* 62.

BAD, *for Ill*, as, I feel very *bad* to-day; also, for *much.*

BAD BOX. *To be in a bad box*, is to be in a bad predicament.

> I began to be afraid now I'd got into rather a *bad box.*—*Maj. Downing.*

BACON. *To save one's bacon.* A vulgar expression, meaning to save one's *flesh* from injury, to preserve one's *flesh* from harm or from punishment. We say also, *to escape with a whole skin.* A very old phrase.

> What frightens you thus, my good son? says the priest;
> You murder'd, are sorry, and have been confest.
> Oh, father! my sorrow will scarce *save my bacon;*
> For 'twas not that I murder'd, but that I was taken.—*Prior's Poems.*

BAGGAGE. Literally, what is contained in a bag or bags. The clothing or conveniences which a traveller carries with him on a journey. This word is applied by us to the trunks, clothing, &c. of a traveller. The English now use the less appropriate term *luggage.* *Baggage* was formerly used by them.

> Having dispatched my *baggage* by water to Altdorf.—*Coxe.*

This is sometimes called more fully *bag and baggage.*

> Seventeen members of Congress arrived to-day with their *bag and baggage.*—*Washington Paper.*

BAGGING. A coarse linen cloth, chiefly manufactured in Kentucky, for packing cotton in.

BAIL. (Fr. *baille*.) The handle of a pail, bucket, or kettle.—*Forby's Glossary.* A common word throughout New England.

TO BAIL, OR BALE. Literally, to lade out with a bail or bucket. A sailor's term, applied to lading water from a boat.

BALANCE. A mercantile word originally introduced into the ordinary language of life by the southern people, but now common throughout the United States, signifying the *remainder* of anything. The *balance* of money, or the *balance* of an account, are terms well authorized and proper ; but we also frequently hear such expressions as the "*balance* of a speech ;" " the *balance* of the day was idly spent ;" " a great many people assembled at the church : a part got in, the *balance* remained without."

> The yawl returned to the wreck, took ten or eleven persons and landed them, and then went and got the *balance* from the floating cabin.—*Albany Journal, Jan.* 7, 1846.

> Most of the respectable inhabitants held commissions in the army or government offices ; the *balance* of the people kept little shops, cultivated the ground, &c.—*Williams's Florida*, p. 115.

BALDERDASH. Empty babble, nonsensical talk. The etymology of this word is doubtful, for in no word do writers more widely differ. It seems to be connected with the Icelandic *bullder*, "the prating of fools" (Jamieson) ; and the Welsh *ball dardd* or *ball dordd*, "to babble, prate, or talk idly" (Boucher). It is chiefly used in conversation.

> They would no more live under the yoke of the sea, or have their heads washed with his bubbly spurm or barber's *balderdash*.—*Nashe*.

> Mine is such a drench of *balderdash*.—*Beaumont and Fletcher*.

> Enough (the king) all *balderdash!*
> I'll none of it ! so cease the trash !—*Reynard the Fox*, p. 24

BALLYHACK—Go to Ballyhack ; a common expression in New England. I know not its origin. It savors in sound, however, of the Emerald Isle.

> You and Obed are here too.
> Let Obed *go to Ballyhack*. Come along out.—*Margaret*, p. 55

TO BAMBOOZLE. To deceive ; to impose upon ; to confound.—*Todd's Johnson*. To make a fool of any one ; to humbug or impose upon him.—*Grose, Prov. Dic.*

Mr. Todd calls it a cant word from *bam*, a cheat. It is provincial in England, and is seldom heard here except at political meetings or in familiar conversation.

> After Nick had *bamboozled* about the money, John called for counters.—*Arbuthnot*.

All the people upon earth, excepting those two or three worthy gentle-men, are imposed upon, cheated, babbled, abused, *bamboozled!—Addison.*

The New Yorkers have appointed Van Buren men as delegates to the Baltimore convention. If the Calhoun men can abide such dictation with-out a wry face, they deserve to be thus babbled and *bamboozled.—Boston Atlas.*

The fact is—we reiterate it with increased corroboration from accumu-mulating evidences—the fact is, the South are to be *bamboozled* upon this subject of the tariff. Yes, sir, in the language of Col. Benton, which in the Senate, on Clay's bank bill, he proved to be legitimate English from Richardson's quarto Dictionary, "they are to be *bamboozled,* sir--they are to be *bamboozled!"—Congressional Debates.*

BANG. To beat, i. e. excel, to surpass. "This bangs all things."—*Ohio.*

BANKER. A vessel employed in fishing on the banks of New-foundland. "There were employed in the fisheries 1232 vessels, viz. 584 to the Banks, 648 to the Bay and Labra-dor; the *Bankers* may be put down at 36,540 tons."

The vessels that fish at the Labrador and Bay are not so valuable as the *bankers,* more particularly those from Maine, Connecticut and Rhode Island.—*J. Q. Adams on the Fisheries,* p. 219.

BANKABLE. Receivable at a bank, as bills; or discountable as notes.—*Webster.*

Among the great variety of bank notes which constitute our circulating medium, many are below par, and conse-quently are not received at the Banks. Those only, which are redeemed with specie or its equivalent, are received at the Banks, and are of the class called *bankable.*

In New York, at auction sales, the auctioneer, in stating the conditions of the sale, if for cash, invariably states, that the money must be *bankable ;* otherwise the purchaser would be likely to pay him in bank notes below par.

BANK-BILL. A bank-note.

Neither Johnson nor the other lexicographers have the term bank-*note,* though they all have bank-*bill,* which Johnson defines, "a note for money laid up in a bank, at the sight of which the money is paid."

In the United States these are invariably called *bank-bills ;* while in England this term is obsolete, and *bank-notes* uni-versally used.

BANNOCK. (Gaelic, *bonnach*. Irish, *boinneag*.) In Scotland, a cake of oatmeal baked on an iron plate.

> Behind the door a bag of meal;
> And in the kist was plenty
> Of good hard cakes his mither bakes;
> And *bannocks* were nae scanty.—*Scotch Songs*, II. 71.

In New England, cakes of Indian meal, fried in lard, are called *bannocks*.

BAR, for bear. The common pronunciation in certain parts of the Southern and Western States.

BANQUETTE. The name for the side-walk in some of our Southern cities.

BARBECUE. A term used in the Southern States and in the West Indies, for dressing a hog whole; which being split to the back-bone, is laid flat upon a large gridiron, and roasted over a charcoal fire.—*Johnson. Webster.*

Formerly it was customary to make a fire in a large hole in the ground, lined with stones, and then to put the hog in whole and cover it up until cooked.

> Oldfield, with more than harpy throat endu'd,
> Cries, " Lend me, gods, a whole hog *barbecued*.—*Pope*.

TO BARK ONE'S SHINS. To knock the skin off the shins by stumbling or striking against something.

Mr. Hartshorne calls this a very old metaphor, and says it is found in the ancient popular poetry of Scotland.—*Shropshire Glossary*.

> Berding her selffe to hym apace
> She cryed him mercy then,
> And pylled the barke even of hys face
> With her commaundments ten.

> Neist Sanderson fratch'd wid a hay-stack,
> And Deavison fught wi' the whins;
> Smith Leytle fell out wi' the cobbles,
> And *peel'd aw the bark off his shins.*—*Cumberland Ballads*.

TO BARK OFF SQUIRRELS. A common way of killing squirrels among those who are expert with the rifle, in the Western States, is to strike with the ball the bark of the tree immediately beneath the squirrel; the concussion produced

by which, kills the animal instantly without mutilating it.—
Audubon, Ornithology, Vol. I. p. 294.

TO BARK UP THE WRONG TREE. A common expression
at the West, denoting that a person has mistaken his object,
or is pursuing the wrong course to obtain it. A metaphor
of Western origin. In hunting, a dog drives a squirrel or
other game into a tree, where, by a constant barking, he at-
tracts its attention, until the hunter arrives. Sometimes the
game escapes, or the dog is deceived and *barks up the wrong
tree.*

> When people try to hunt (office) for themselves, ... and seem to be
> *barking up the wrong sapling*, I want to put them on the right trail.—
> *Crockett's Tour*, p. 205.

BARRACLADE. (Dutch *barre kledeeren*, cloths undressed or
without a nap.) A home-made woolen blanket without
nap. This word is peculiar to New York city, and those
parts of the State settled by the Dutch.

BARN-DOOR FOWL. The common fowl; also so called in
Scotland.—*Jamieson.*

> Never had there been such slaughtering of capons, and fat geese, and
> *barn-door fowls.*—*Bride of Lammermoor.*

BARRENS. Elevated lands, or plains upon which grow small
trees, but never timber. Pine *barrens* are common throughout the United States.

BASE. A game of hand-ball.

TO BASE. To lay the foundation of an argument. This
word is not in the English Dictionaries in this sense. We
say, for example, " He *bases* his arguments on these facts."
It is used in good language both in England and America.

The Washington correspondent of the N. Y. Journal of
Commerce, in speaking of a rumor that Mr. Pakenham had
made overtures to our Government, says :

> The rumor is *based* upon a very general belief that Mr. P. has instruc-
> tions of a discretionary kind to resume the negotiation.

> We learn, that the revolution (in Mexico) is *based* upon the disavowal
> by the late Mexican Congress of the treaties made with the Yucatecos by
> Santa Anna.—*New Orleans Picayune.*

BAYOU. (French, *boyau*, a gulf.) In Louisiana, the outlet of
a lake; a channel for water.

BARNBURNERS. The nickname of one of the present divisions of the great Democratic party, otherwise called the Young Democracy; the other is called the Old Hunker.

The following editorial of the Ohio Union, a Democratic paper in Cincinnati, will define the political sentiments of these parties:

> There is one class of the Democratic party which seeks the retention of power in the hands of a few—the direction of the disposition of offices—would if possible restrain the impulses of the Democracy—would check its progressive tendency—is unfavorable to, or fearful of, the extension of the "area of freedom," and in fine, in the language of Alexander Hamilton, would restrain " the amazing violence of the popular or democratic spirit." Who would likewise prescribe a fixed rule for present and future, by which the Democracy of every man should be judged, leaving no margin for honest differences on minor points, and would proscribe all who do not fit the dimensions of their intellect, feelings, and opinions, to the Procrustes bed which they have made for them. This is the class which we denominate " *Old Hunkers.*"
>
> There is another class, who would *divide power* among the many; would leave it entirely where it belongs, with the *masses* of the *people*—who would have offices filled by men, taken from among the people, and not confined to those who live by office and make politics a trade—who have sympathies with the people, understand their interests and feelings, and will seek to have both satisfied, while they honestly and faithfully discharge the duties of their offices—who care less about the disposition of offices than they do about the principles of Democracy and the measures and policy of the Government—who desire always and continually the "extension of the area of freedom"—who believe that the Democratic impulses are right and should be obeyed, and not thwarted—who would admit to the ranks of Democracy ALL who agree with us, upon the great cardinal principles of Democracy and upon the great national policy, now acted upon by the General Government—who believe in and favor *progress,* and would not prescribe a *fixed rule* in *all minor* matters for *all time*, but would adapt action to the circumstances and exigencies which arise in the *progression* of events, and to the rights and interests which accompany or result from that progression and its changes. And finally, who have in their hearts "sworn eternal hostility against every form of tyranny over the mind of man." These we denominate "the young Democracy." This is progressive " *Young Democracy.*"
>
> " OLD HUNKERS." We have been requested to give a definition of this term. Party nicknames are not often logically justified; and we can only say that that section of the late dominant party in this State (the democratic) which claims to be the more radical, progressive, reformatory, &c.

bestowed the appellation " Old Hunker" on the other section to indicate that it was distinguished by opposite qualities from those claimed for itself. We believe the title was also intended to indicate that those on whom it was conferred had an appetite for a large *hunk* of " the spoils"—though we never could discover that they were peculiar in *that*. On the other hand, the opposite school was termed *Barnburners*, in allusion to the story of an old Dutchman who relieved himself of rats by burning his barns which they infested—just like exterminating all Banks and Corporations to root out the abuses connected therewith.   The fitness or unfitness of these family terms of endearment is none of our business.—*N. Y. Tribune.*

They have gone into such depths of *Barnburning* Radicalism, that a large portion of the rank and file are determined not to follow.—*Ibid.*

BE (Ang. Sax. *beo*, 1st person sing. and 1st, 2d, and 3d plur. See *Rask's Gram.* p. 84), instead of *am* and *are*. Ex. *Be* you cold ?   Where *be* you going ?   This use of this word is confined to uneducated people.   It is common in several of the provincial dialects of England.   In the Bible it often occurs instead of *are*.

Let them shew the former things what they *be*, that we may consider them.—*Isaiah* xli. 22.

BEAD.   The bubbles which rise on a glass of wine or spirits, by which the strength and quality of the article is known.

Deacon Penrose.   Will the Parson taste a little of our New England rum ?   We call it a prime article, and think it the very best we ever made.

Abel Wilcox.   It has as handsome a *bead* as I ever saw ; and we think it possesses a flavor like the West Indies.

Parson Welles.   Truly in the words of Scripture, we must say, " Give strong drink to him that is ready to perish."   We need something to make our faces shine these dark times.—*Margaret*, p. 310.

Mr. Bagley broke three slim glasses in the attempt to raise a *bead*.—*Drama at Pokerville.*

BEAKER.   (Germ. *becher*, Dutch *beker*.) A tumbler.   " This word," says Mr. Pickering, " not many years ago was in common use in New England, as well as in some other parts of the United States ; but it is now seldom heard except among old people."   We derive it from our ancestors from Norfolk and Suffolk counties, where it is still provincial.   It is also used in the north of England and in Scotland.—*Jamieson. Forby.*

And into pikes and musketeers,
Stamp'd *beakers*, cups, and porringers.—*Butler's Hudibras.*

TO BE AMONG THE MISSING. To be absent, to leave,
to run away.

> There comes old David for my militia fine ; I don't want to see him, and
> think I will *be among the missing.*

BEAR, for *bar.* Connecticut and Virginia.

BEAR. A word to denote a certain description of stock-jobbers.—*Johnson.*

The same term is used among the brokers and stock-jobbers
of Wall street, New York. Their plans of operation are as
accurately described in the annexed extract from Warton, as
they can be at the present moment :

He who sells that of which he is not possessed, is proverbi-
ally said to sell the skin before he has caught the *bear.* It
was the practice of stock-jobbers, in the year 1720, to enter
into a contract for transferring South Sea stock at a future
time for a certain price ; but he who contracted to sell, had
frequently no stock to transfer, nor did he who bought intend
to receive any in consequence of his bargain ; the seller was
therefore called a *bear,* in allusion to the proverb, and the
buyer a *bull,* perhaps only as a similar distinction. The contract was merely a wager, to be determined by the rise or fall
of stock ; if it rose, the seller paid the difference to the buyer,
proportioned to the sum determined by the same computa-
tion to the seller.—*Dr. Warton on Pope.*

The stock speculators of Wall street are denominated *Bull-
backers* or *Bear-traps,* according to the nature of their operations.   The first signifies that they have bought stock largely
and hold it; and the second, that they have sold stock which
they have not got, and trust to circumstances to be able to
supply it.   The brokers themselves in these cases are called
Bulls and *Bears.*—*A Walk in Wall Street,* p. 80.

> There has been a very important revolution made in the tactics of a cer-
> tain extensive operator in Wall street.   The largest *bull* in the street has
> become a *bear,* and the rank and file have been thrown into the greatest
> confusion and left without a leader.—*N. Y. Herald.*

> Some of the operators (in Wall street, owing to the rise in stocks), who
> were the strongest *bears* last week, are now roaring *bulls.*—*Ibid.*

> An attack has recently been made upon the Reading Road in one of the
> city papers, evidently suggested by the *bears.*—*N. Y. Tribune,* 1848.

TO BEAR A HAND. A seaman's phrase. To be ready; to go to work; to assist.

BEAST. A common name for a horse in the Southern States.

TO BEAT. To excel, surpass in a contest. Thus we say, one racer or steamer *beats* another.

Also, to overcome with astonishment, to surprise. We sometimes hear, especially from the mouths of old people, such expressions as " I felt *beat*," " I was quite *beat*," i. e. utterly astonished.

TO BEAT ALL HOLLOW. To surpass or overcome completely; thus, " Eclipse *beat* Sir Henry *all hollow.*" Also, to take wholly by surprise.

> The number of ships in New York *beat me all hollow*, and looked for all the world like a big clearing in the West, with the dead trees all standing. —*Crockett, Tour down East,* p. 27.

This phrase seems to be common in England. There, however, they do not use the word *all*, which invariably forms a part of it here.

> The author of " The Diary of a Physician" *beats* Walter Scott *hollow*, in the attempt which he describes his martyr-philosopher as making to correct La Place.—*London Athenæum, Dec.* 6, 1845.

A late English traveller under the assumed name of Rubio, says:

> I used to think the English might defy all creation for bad coffee; but the Americans *beat us hollow.*—*Travels in the United States.*

BECASE, for because. A common vulgarism.

BED-SPREAD. In the interior parts of the country, the common name for a *bed*-quilt, or coverlet.

BEE. An assemblage of people, generally neighbors, to unite their labors for the benefit of one individual or family. The *quilting-bees* in the interior of New England and New York, are attended by young women, who assemble around the frame of a bed-quilt, and in one afternoon accomplish more than one person could in weeks. Refreshments and beaux help to render the meeting agreeable. *Husking-bees*, for husking corn, are held in barns, which are made the occasion of much frolicking. In new countries, when a settler arrives, the neighboring farmers unite with their teams, cut the timber and build him a log-house in a single day; these are termed *raising-bees.* *Apple-bees* are occasions when the neighbors assemble to gather apples, or to cut them up for drying.

BEE-LINE. To take a bee-line, is to take the most direct or straight way from one point to another. Bees in returning to their hives after having loaded themselves with honey always fly back to the hive in a direct line. For a further explanation see the phrase *lining bees.*

> This road is one of nature's laying. It goes determinedly straight up and straight down the hills, and in a " *bee line*" as we say.—*Mrs. Clavers*

> I acknowledge the corn, boys, that when I started my track warn't anything like a *bee-line;*—the sweeten'd whiskey had made me powerful thick-legged.—*Robb, Squatter Life.*

BEECH-LE-MAR. (Fr. *biche de mer.*) A kind of slug taken on the coast of some of the South sea islands, where it is cured for the China trade.—*See Morell's Voyage.*

BEING. (Also pronounced *bein, been.*) Pres. part. of the verb *to be,* equivalent to *because.*

This word is noticed by Boucher, as much in use in the Middle States of America, and as an idiom of the Western counties of England. It is also heard among the illiterate in New England.

> " I sent you no more peasen, *been* the rest would not have suited you."—*Boucher's Glossary.*

> The mug cost 15d. when 'twas new, but *bein* it had an old crack in it, I told her she needn't pay but a shilling for it.—*Maj. Downing.*

> Bein' ye'll help Obed, I'll give ye the honey.—*Margaret*, p. 20.

BELITTLE. To make smaller; to lower in character.—*Webster.*

This word is but little used, either in conversation or in composition. President Jefferson is the only writer of authority who has used it.—*Notes on Virginia.*

> I won't stand that, said Mr. Slick, I won't stay here and see you *belittle* Uncle Sam for nothin'. He ain't worse than John Bull, arter all.—*Sam Slick in England,* ch. 19.

BELLWORT. The popular name of plants of the genus *Uvularia.*

BENDER. In New York, a spree; a frolic. To go on a bender, is, to go on a spree.

> Thus did Harry Whitmore address C. M——, when the met, the morning after the trio had determined to go on a *bender.*—*Mysteries of N. York.*

BENT GRASS. (*Genus, agrostis.*) The popular name in the Northern States for a common grass, sometimes called *red-top.*

BERATE. To revile; to abuse in vile language.—*Worcester.*

This is a common word in New England, and is not in the English glossaries. Mr. Worcester quotes Holland for his authority.

BESTOWMENT. 1. The act of giving gratuitously; a conferring.—*Webster.*

This word, which is much used by our theological writers, is not in the English dictionaries.

> God the Father had committed the *bestowment* of the blessings purchased, to his Son.—*Edwards on Redemption.*

> If we consider the *bestowment* of gifts in this view.—*Chauncey, U. Lab.*

2. That which is conferred or given.—*Webster.*

> They strengthened his hands by their liberal *bestowments* on him and his family.—*Christian Magazine*, iii. 665.

> The free and munificent *bestowment* of the Sovereign Judge.—*Thodey.*

Mr. Todd has *bestowal* in his edition of Johnson, but cites no authority for its use. Dr. Webster thinks *bestowment* preferable on account of the concurrence of the two vowels in *bestowal.*

BETTER, for *more ;* as, " It is *better* than a year since we met."

BETTERMENTS. (Generally used in the plural number.) The improvements made on new lands, by cultivation and the erection of buildings.—*Pickering's Vocabulary.*

" This word," adds Mr. Pickering, " was first used in the State of *Vermont,* but it has for a long time been common in the State of *New Hampshire ;* and it has been getting into use in some parts of *Massachusetts,* since the passing of the late law, similar to the *Betterment Acts* (as they are called) of the States above mentioned. It is not to be found in Mr. *Webster's,* nor in any of the *English* dictionaries that I have seen except Ash's ; and there it is called ' a bad word.' It is thus noticed by an English traveller in this country, in speaking of those people who enter upon new lands without any right and proceed to cultivate them :

> These men demand either to be left owners of the soil or paid for their *betterments*, that is, for what they have done towards clearing the ground.— *Kendall, Travels in the United States*, Vol. III. p. 160.

BETTERMOST.   The best.   Used in New England.

> The *bettermost* cow, an expression we do not find in Shakspeare or Milton.—*Mrs. Kirkland.*

BETTY.   (Ital. *boccetta*.)   A pear-shaped bottle wound around with straw in which olive oil is brought from Italy.   Called by chemists a Florence flask.

B'HOYS. i. e. Boys, a name applied to a class of noisy young men of the lower ranks of society in the city of New York.

> The New York Commercial Advertiser, April 12, 1847, in speaking of the approaching election, uses the following language :
>
> All the *b'hoys* will vote, aye, more than all.   Let every Whig do his duty.   Another year with a Democratic Mayor—and such a Mayor as the *b'hoys* would force upon the city !   Who can tell what the taxes will be ?

BIDDY.   A domestic fowl ; a chicken.   A term generally used in calling fowls to eat.

BIBLE CHRISTIANS.   The Philadelphia Mercury thus gives a summary of the creed of this new sect : " This denomination abstain from all animal food and spirituous liquors, and live on vegetables and fruits.   They maintain the unity of God, the divinity of Jesus, and the salvation of man, attainable only by a life of obedience to the light manifested to his mind and a grateful acknowledgment of his indebtedness to the great Giver of all.   The congregation numbers about seventy members."

BIG-BUGS.   People of consequence.

> Then we'll go to the Lords' house—I don't mean to the meetin' house, but where the nobles meet, pick out the *big-bugs*, and see what sort o' stuff they're made of.— *Sam Slick in England*, ch. 24.
>
> These preachers dress like *big-bugs*, and go ridin' about on hundred-dollar horses, a-spungin' poor priest-ridden folks, and a-eaten chicken-fixens so powerful fast that chickens has got scarce in these diggins.—*Carlton's New Purchase*, Vol. II. p. 140.

BIG-WIGS.   People of consequence.   The same as the last.

> Demagogues and place-hunters make the people stare by telling them how big they talked and what great things they did to the *big-wigs* to home.—*Sam Slick.*

BIG FIGURE. To do things on the big figure, means to do them on a large scale. This vulgar phrase is used at the West and South.

Well, I glory in her spunk, but it's monstrous expensive and unpleasant to do things *on the big figure* that she's on now.—*Maj. Jones's Courtship.*

BILBERRY, (*genus vaccinium.*) The popular name of a shrub of several species, and bearing fruit resembling the whortle-berry.

BIME-BY. By-and-by, soon, in a short time.

BINDWEED. The popular name in Massachusetts for the *convolvulus.*—*Bigelow's Flora.*

BINDERY. A place where books are bound.—*Webster.*
The Penny Cyclopedia thinks this a new, but not a bad word.

BISHOP. An appendage to a lady's wardrobe, otherwise called a *bustle.*

BIT, *past part.* of the verb *bite.* Cheated, taken in. In York-shire, England, a cheat is called a *bite.* Dr. Johnson notices this vulgarism.

Asleep and naked as an Indian lay,
An honest factor stole a gem away ;
He pledg'd it to the Knight ; the Knight had wit,
So kept the diamond, and the rogue was *bit.*—*Pope.*

A BIT. A little ; a little while. As " wait a bit ;" " after a bit."

BIT. (Span. *pieza.*) The name in the Southern States of a silver coin of the value of one-eighth of a dollar. The Spanish real (*de plata*).

BITTER COLD. Very cold. This common colloquial ex-pression is used alike in England and America.

Those who say it is a very easy thing to get up of a cold morning, ... ought to stand around one's bed of a *bitter cold* morning, and lie before their faces.—*Leigh Hunt. The Indicator*, p. 134.

BITTERS. A liquid or spirituous liquor, containing an infu-sion of bitter herbs and roots.—*Worcester.*

Bitters, before the temperance reform, were much in fash-ion, taken before breakfast to give an appetite. The custom is now confined to the back parts of the country, or to professed tipplers.

> What was that I saw you taking for your *bitters*, a little while ago ?—
> *Cooper, Satanstoe*, p. 68.

BITTERSWEET. (*Solanum dulcamara*.) The popular name of a medicinal plant, which has a place in most dispensatories. It is also called the Woody Nightshade.—*Big. Flora.*

BLACK. *To look black at one*, to look at one with anger or deep resentment depicted on the countenance.

BLACK AND BLUE. The color of a bruise; a familiar expression for a bruise, here and in England.

> Mistress Ford, good heart, is beaten *black and blue*, that you cannot see a white spot about her.—*Shakspeare, Merry Wives of Windsor.*
>
> And, wing'd with speed and fury, flew
> To rescue Knight from *black and blue*.—*Hudibras.*

BLACK AND WHITE. To put a thing into *black and white*, is, to commit it to writing. In use in Scotland.—*Jamieson.*

> I was last Tuesday to wait on Sir Robert Walpole, who desired that I would put it in *black and white*, that he might show it to his Majesty.—*Culloden Papers*, p. 108.

BLACK-BOOK. A book was kept in the English monasteries, during the reign of Henry VIII., in which details of the scandalous enormities practised in religious houses were entered for the inspection of visitors, in order to blacken them and hasten their dissolution. Hence the vulgar phrase, " I'll set you down in my *black-book*."

BLACK-LEG. The common term here and in England for a gambler.

BLACK-MAIL. Formerly, money paid to men allied with robbers to be protected by them from being robbed.—*Cowell.* In the United States it means money extorted from persons under the threat of exposure in print, for an alleged offence, or defect.

BLACKSTRAP. Gin and molasses. The English sailors call the common wines of the Mediterranean *blackstrap*.—*Falconer's Marine Dictionary.*

> Come, Molly, dear, no *black-strap* to-night, switchel or ginger pop.—
> *Margaret*, p. 300.

BLACK WOOD. Hemlock, pine, spruce, and fir.—*Maine.*

BLADDER-TREE (*genus straphylea*). A handsome shrub, from six to ten feet high, remarkable for its large inflated capsules.—*Bigelow's Flora Bostoniensis.*

BLADDER-WORT. (*Utricularia vulgaris*). The popular name of an aquatic plant, appearing above water only with its stalk and flowers.—*Ibid.*

BLAME. A euphemistic evasion of the horrible word *damn.* Ex. " Blame me," or, " I'll be blamed, if;" also, " You be blamed!"

It is used both in England and in the United States, chiefly in New England.

> I wasn't goin' to let Dean know ; because he'd have thought himself so *blam'd* cunning.—*Mrs. Clavers's Western Clearings*, p. 70.

BLARNEY. Marvellous stories, flattery. Ex. He deals in the wonderful, he is full of *blarney.* Grose derives this word from the *Blarney* stone, a triangular stone on the very top of an ancient castle of that name in the county of Cork, in Ireland, extremely difficult of access ; so that to have ascended it, was a proof of perseverance, courage, and agility, whereof many are supposed to claim the honor who never achieved the adventure. Hence, in England, they say, " He has licked the Blarney stone," i. e. he deals in the wonderful.—*Dictionary of the Vulgar Tongue.*

Dr. Jamieson doubts the Irish origin of this word, and adopts the French etymon *baliverne*, a lie, a fib, gull ; also, a babbling, idle discourse.—*Cotgrave, Dictionary.*

BLATHER. Impudence. " None of your blather."—*Western.*

BLATHERSKITE. A blustering, noisy, talkative fellow.— *Western.*

BLAUSER. The name given by the Dutch settlers to the hog-nosed snake, from its habit of distending or blowing up the skin of its neck and head. The other popular names in New York are Deaf-adder and Buckwheat-nosed.—*Nat. Hist. of New York.*

BLAZE. In traversing the dense forests of the West, a person would soon lose his way and find it difficult to retrace his steps without some land-mark. This is effected by cutting a piece out of the side of trees at a sufficient distance from each other to enable the traveller readily to discover them and thus follow the direct path or road. Such a mark is called a *blaze,* and trees thus marked are said to be *blazed.*

Three *blazes* in a perpendicular line on the same tree indicating a legislative road, the single *blaze,* a settlement or neighborhood road.—*Carlton. The New Purchase.*

After traversing a broad marsh, however, where my horse seemed loth to venture, I struck a burr-oak opening, and soon found my way by the *blazed* trees back to the mail trail.—*Hoffman, Winter in the West.*

TO BLAZE AWAY. To keep up a discharge of fire-arms. A good English phrase.

The hunter (of the west) attacks the oldest and largest bull he can find, and continues to *blaze away* at him with his pistols, until he brings him down.—*Kendall's Sante Fé,* Vol. I. p. 79.

BLAZES. *Like blazes,* that is, furiously.—*Moor's Suffolk Words.*

> As they cut away, the company
> Stil kep upon the glare ;
> An' when comin' in, the hosses ded
> Along *like blazes* tear.—*Poem in Essex Dialect,* p. 21.

This expression is common in low language with us. At the South it seems to be used as a euphemism for *devil,* etc.

I've been serving my country like a patriot, goin' to town-meetings, hurraing my daylights out, and getting as blue as *blazes.*—*J. C. Neal.*

All the hair was off his head, and his face was as black as the very old *blazes.*—*Chron. of Pineville,* p. 49.

BLAZING STAR. (*Aletris farinosa.*) A plant, the root of which is greatly esteemed by the Indians and people of the West for its medicinal virtues. It is also called *star- oo* and *devil's hit.*—*Flint's Mississippi Valley.*

TO BLINK. To shut the eyes, to wink. Hence, to shun, to avoid, shy at, as some animals avoid an alarming object, at the same time shutting their eyes so as not to see it. The leathern flaps on a horse's bridle, over the eyes, are called *blinkers.* We use the verb in a metaphorical sense of avoiding or flinching from delicate topics. Thus we say, " He *blinks* the question," that is, he shuns the true point of the argument.

> It's no use to *blink* matters. The skunk has been abroad, and he must have a blunt nose that can't wind him.—*Crockett's Tour*, p. 107.

BLIZZARD. A poser. This word is not known in the Eastern States.

> A gentleman at dinner asked me for a toast, and supposing he meant to have some fun at my expense, I concluded to go ahead, and give him and his likes a *blizzard.*—*Crockett's Tour*, p. 16.

BLOCK. A term applied in America to a square mass of houses included between four streets. It is a very useful one.

BLOCK-HOUSE. A small fort built of logs which project some six or eight feet over a wooden or stone foundation, fifteen or twenty feet high.

BLOUSE. (Fr. *blouse.*) A loose garment made of brown linen, fastened round the waist with a belt ; worn by men and boys in France, and lately introduced partially into this country.

TO BLOW. To taunt ; to ridicule.

TO BLOW. To turn informer on an accomplice.

BLOW. A gale of wind. Ex. A heavy blow ! originally a seaman's word, but now come into general use.

BLOW OUT. A feast ; also called a *tuck out.* Both expressions are English as well as American.

TO BLOW OVER Said properly of a storm ; and hence generally, to pass away without effect. This metaphor is very common. We say, there is a great excitement about a certain matter; but it will *blow over*, i. e. pass away.

> Storms, though they *blow over* at divers times, may yet fall at last.—*Bacon's Essays.*

> A storm is brewing in the political horizon, which may defeat our candidate ; but it will soon *blow over.*—*Newspapers of the day.*

BLOW-UP. A quarrel ; a dispute. A common expression, used in familiar conversation.

> There was a regular *blow-up* at Tammany hall, between the friends of Mr. Van Buren and Mr. Calhoun, which ended in a row, and broke up the meeting.—*Newspapers of the day.*

TO BLOW UP. To scold, to abuse, either in speaking or

writing. A vulgar expression borrowed from sailor's language.

> Oh ho! I see, it's a piece about the major's book. I suppose somebody's been *blowin' him up*, and he ain't used to it.—*Maj. Jones's Courtship.*

> I thought I could stand a *blowing up* pretty well—I have had some experience in that way, as the old woman's tongue can testify.—*Pickings from the Picayune*, p. 121.

> He was ravin' about the disputed territory, a *blowin' up* the governor of New Brunswick sky-high.—*Sam Slick*, 3d ser. chap. vii.

BLUE. Gloomy, severe; extreme, ultra.

In the former sense it is applied especially to the Presbyterians, to denote their severe and mortified appearance. Thus, beneath an old portrait of the seventeenth century, in the Woodburn Gallery, is the following inscription:

> A true *blue Priest*, a Lincey Woolsey Brother,
> One legg a pulpit, holds a tub the other;
> An Orthodox grave, moderate Presbyterian,
> Half surplice cloake, half Priest, half Puritan.
> Made up of all these halfes, hee cannot pass
> For anything entirely but an ass.

In the latter sense it is used particularly in politics.

> The *bluest* description of old Van Rensselaer Federalists have followed Col. Prentiss (in Otsego county).—*N. Y. Tribune.*

BLUE. A synonym in the tippler's vocabulary for *drunk*.

BLUE-BERRY. (*Vacinium tenellum.*) A fruit resembling the whortleberry in appearance and taste.

TO LOOK BLUE AT ONE, is to look at one with a countenance expressive of displeasure or dissatisfaction.

> The Bishop would not cease to rate,
> Were I to give the church's blessing
> To any fold of her transgressing:
> Besides, the provost would *look blue.*—*Reynard the Fox*, p. 124.

BLUE-BOOK. A printed book containing the names of all the persons holding office under the Government of the United States, with the amount of their pay. It answers to the Red-Book of England.

BLUE DEVILS. To have the *blue devils* is to be dispirited.

BLUE LAWS. " Where, and how, the story of the New Haven *Blue Laws* originated, is a matter of some curiosity. Accord-

ing to Dr. Peters, the epithet *blue* was applied to the laws of
New Haven, by the neighboring colonies, because these laws
were thought peculiarly sanguinary : and he says, that *blue*
is equivalent to *bloody*.   It is a sufficient refutation of this account of the matter, to say, that if there was any distinction
between the colony of New Haven, and the other united
Colonies of New England, in the severity of their punish-
ments, New Haven was the last of the number to gain this
bad pre-eminence.   Others have said, that certain laws of
New Haven, of a more private and domestic kind, were
bound in a blue cover; and hence the name.   This explanation has as little probability as the preceding, for its support.
It is well known, that on the restoration of Charles II. the
Puritans became the subject of every kind of reproach and
contumely.   Not only what was deserving of censure in their
deportment, but their morality was especially held up to
scorn.   The epithet *blue* was applied to any one, who looked
with disapprobation on the licentiousness of the times.   The
Presbyterians, under which name all dissenters were often
included, as they still dared to be the advocates of decency,
were more particularly designated by this term ; their religion
and their moralit being marked by it as mean and contemptible.   Thus Butler :

> For his religion, it was fit
> To match his learning and his wit;
> 'Twas Presbyterian true *blue.—Hudib.* Canto I.

" That this epithet of derision should find its way to the
colonies was a matter of course.   It was here applied not only
to persons, but to customs, institutions, and laws of the Puritans, by those who wished to render the prevailing system
ridiculous.   Hence probably a belief with some, that a distinct system of laws, known as the ' blue laws,' must have
somewhere a local habitation."—*Prof. Kingsley's Hist. Disc.*

BLUE-NOSE.   The slang name for a native of Nova Scotia.

"Pray, sir," said one of my fellow passengers, " can you tell me why
the Nova Scotians are called ' Blue Noses ?' "

"It is the name of a potatoe," said I, " which they produce in great perfection, and boast to be the best in the world.   The Americans have, in
consequence, given them the nick-name of *Blue-noses.*"—*Sam Slick.*

After a run (in the steamer) of fourteen days, we entered the harbor of Halifax, amid the hearty cheers of a large number of *Blue-noses.*—*Sir George Simpson's Overland Journey*, Vol. I. p. 19.

THE BLUES. A euphemism for *blue devils.* To have a fit of the *blues*, is to have a fit of the *blue devils*, to be low-spirited.

BLUE-SKINS. A nickname applied to the Presbyterians, from their alleged grave deportment.

BLUE STOCKING. The American avoset (*recurvirostra Americana*). A common bird in the Northern States.—*Nat. Hist. New York.*

BLUE STOCKING. A ridiculous epithet applied here as well as in England to literary ladies, and borrowed from that *gallant* nation the French. Called also simply a *blue.*

BLUFF. A high bank, almost perpendicular, projecting into the sea.—*Falconer's Marine Dic.*

In America it is applied to a high bank, presenting a steep front, in the interior of the country.

Here you have the advantage of mountain, *bluff*, interval, to set off the view.—*Margaret*, p. 282.

BLUFF. Steep, bold ; as a hill.

Its banks, if not really steep, had a *bluff* and precipitous aspect from the tall forest that girded it about.—*Margaret*, p. 7.

TO BLUFF OFF. To put off a troublesome questioner, or dun, &c.

BLUMACHIES. (Dutch.) This Dutch word for flowers is still preserved in the New York markets.

TO BLURT OUT. To speak inadvertently, and without reflection.

They blush if they *blurt out*, are well aware
A swan is white, or Queensbury is fair.—*Young.*

Mr. Pickens, in explaining that his report was a peaceable one, *blurted out* the whole character and conduct of his countrymen.—*Lord Sydenham's Memoirs*, p. 307.

(This matter) is only fit to be talked on over a cigar alone. It don't answer a good purpose to *blurt* everything *out.*—*Sam Slick in England.*

BLUSTERATION. The noise of a braggart.—*Brockett's North County Words.* Used among us only in low colloquial language.

BOATABLE. Navigable for boats, or small river-craft.—
Webster.

This useful word has only recently been adopted in the
English dictionaries.

> The Seneca Indians say, they can walk four times a day from the *boat-able* waters of the Allegany, to those of the Tioga.—*Morse's Geography.*

This word, says Dr. Webster, though of modern origin, is
well formed according to the English analogies, like *fordable,
creditable,* &c. The advantage of using it is obvious, as it
expresses an important distinction in the capacity of water
to bear vessels. *Navigable* is a generic term of which boatable is the species; and as the use of it saves a circumlocution, instead of being proscribed, it should be received as a
real improvement.—*Letter to J. Pickering on his Vocabulary,*
p. 6.

The objection to this word is, that it is a hybrid, composed
of a Saxon noun and a Latin ending. It is like *fordable,*
but not like *creditable,* which is all Latin. We would hardly
use the word *trustable.*

BOATING. Transporting in boats.—*Webster.*

BOB. A knot of worms on a string used in fishing for eels.—
Webster.

TO BOB. To fish for eels with a bob. This word is common
in New England, and is used in the same sense in England.

> These are the baits they *bob* with.—*Beaumont and Fletcher.*

BOBBERY. A squabble, a row; common both in England and
America.—*Moor, Forby.*

> That woke up the confounded rooks from their first nap, and kick'd up such a *bobbery.*—*Sam Slick in England,* ch. 2.

> I've been writing to Aunt Keziah, about the *bobbery* you New Yorkers always get into about the first of May.—*Maj. Downing.*

BOBOLINK. The popular name of the rice-bunting (*icterus*),
a bird which frequents the wild rice and marshes; on Long
Island it is called the rice bird. In other places it is called
the skunk-blackbird.

> It sticks to me like a *bobolink* on a saplin, in a wood.—*Margaret,* p. 87.

BOB-SLED. A sled prepared for the transportation of large
timber from the forest to a river or public road.—*Maine.*

BOBTAIL. (From *bob*, in the sense of *cut*). Cut tail, short tail.—*Johnson.*

> Avaunt, you curs !
> Be thy mouth or black or white,
> Or *bobtail* tike, or trundle tail,
> Tom will make him weep or wail.—*Shakspeare, King Lear.*

BOCKEY.—A bowl or vessel made from a gourd. A term probably derived from the Dutch, as it is peculiar to the city of New York and its vicinity.

BOCKING. A kind of baize, or woollen cloth, either plain or stamped with colored figures, used to cover floors or to protect carpets. It is also called *floorcloth.*

BODETTE. (Fr. *beaudette.*) In Canada the common name for a cot-bedstead.

BODY.—A person. A colloquial expression used both in England and America.

> Good may come out of evil, and a *body's* life may be saved, without having any obligations to his preserver.—*L'Estrange.*

> This hot weather makes a *body* feel odd. How long would a *body* be going to Washington ? How the mosquitoes bite a *body.*—*Davis, Travels in America in* 1798, p. 223.

BOG-TROTTER. One that lives in a boggy country. A derisive epithet applied to Irishmen.

BOGUS. A liquor made of rum and molasses.

BOGUS MONEY. Counterfeit silver coin. A few years since, a large quantity of this coin was in circulation at the West, where it received this name.

TO BOLT. To swallow food without chewing.—*Forby.*

> Often my dame and I at home
> Eat rav'nously of honey comb;
> For lack of more substantial food,
> We *bolt* this down, and call it good.—*Reynard the Fox*, p. 26.

TO BOLT. To start off suddenly in any direction. It is said in the first place of a horse starting from his course; and is then transferred to persons. Thus :

> In she come, *bolting* into our room.—*Maj. Downing*, p. 54.

It is also applied especially to politicians who suddenly desert their party.

Mr. Poindexter has *bolted* from the Whigs, and united with the Democratic party for the war and the whole of Mexico.—*Newspaper.*

BOLT-UPRIGHT. Perfectly upright.—*Johnson.* Used alike in England and the United States.

As I stood *bolt-upright* upon one end, one of the two ladies burst out.—*Addison.*

In the mean time, Shadrach stood *bolt-upright*, with his hands crossed before him, his nose elevated to the ceiling, and his eyes shut.—*Paulding's Koningsmarke*, ch. v.

BOOM ALONG. To move rapidly. A sea term. A ship is said to *boom along* when under full sail.

You're right in the way; and if you don't *boom along*, we'll have to play clearance with you.—*J. C. Neal's Sketches.*

TO MAKE NO BONES OF. To do a thing without hesitation. A metaphor borrowed from eating with dispatch as if it contained no bones.

Knowing (according to the old rule of Thales) that he who had not stuck at one villanie, will easily swallow another; perjury will easily down with him that hath *made no bones* of murther.—*Bp. Hall.*

BONESET. (*Eupatorium perfoliatum*). The popular name of a medicinal plant. Its properties are sudorific and tonic.

BONNY-CLAPPER.
BONNY-CLABBER. (Irish, *baine*, milk, and *clabar*, mire.) An Irish term for sour buttermilk.—*Nares' Glossary.*

We scorn for want of talk, to jabber
Of parties o'er our *bonny-clabber*;
Nor are we studious to inquire,
Who votes for manors, who for hire.—*Swift.*

BOO! BOH! An exclamation of terror among children. To one who is timid, it is common to say, " You dare not say *boo* to a goose."

I dare not, for the honor of our house,
Say *boh* to any Grecian goose.—*Homer Travestied.*

(The old squatter Jones) was awful. He could jest lick anything that said *boo* in them diggins, out swar Satan, and was as cross as a she bar with cubs.—*Robb, Squatter Life.*

TO BOO-HOO. To cry loudly.

The little woman *boo-hoo'd* right out, threw herself incontinently full on his breast, hung around his neck, and went on in a surprising way for such a mere artificial as an actress.—*Field, Drama in Pokerville.*

TO BOOSE.   To tipple.

BOOSY.   Fuddled ; a little intoxicated. A low word, only used colloquially, and alike common to England and America.

> With a long legend of romantic things
> Which in his cups, the *bouzy* poet sings.—*Dryden.*

BOOSILY.   Lazily, in a state of intoxication.

> In the sun before the house, lay Mr. Tapley, *boosily* sleeping with his bare head pillowed on a scythe-snathe.—*Margaret,* p. 214.

TO BOOST.   To lift or raise by pushing.—*Webster.*

Chiefly used by boys, who apply it to the act of pushing one another up a tree or over a fence. " *Boost* me up this tree, and I'll hook you some apples."

> He clambered back into the box (in the theatre), the manager assisting to *boost* him with the most friendly solicitude.—*Field, Drama in Pokerville.*

TO BOOT.   (Ang. Sax. *to-bote.*) In addition ; over and above ; that which is given to make the exchange equal.—*Johnson.*

> Man is God's image ; but a poor man is Christ's stamp *to boot :* both images regard.—*Herbert.*

> He might have his mind and manners formed, and be instructed *to boot* in several sciences.—*Locke.*

BOOTEE, dimin. of *boot.*   A boot without a top, or a shoe made like a boot without a leg.

BO-PEEP—*To play at bo-peep.*   To peep out suddenly from a hiding place, and cry *bo !* a children's game.

> They then for sudden joy did weep,
>   And I for sorrow sung,
> That such a king should play *bo-peep,*
>   And go the fools among.—*Shakspeare.*

> There the devil plays at *bo-peep,* puts out his horns to do mischief, then shrinks them back for safety.—*Dryden.*

TO BORE.   Used as a metaphor. To tease by ceaseless repetition ; like the unvaried continued action of a *borer.*—*Richardson.*

> *Buc.* I read in 's looks
> Matter against me, and his eyes revil'd
> Me as his abject object ; at this instant
> He *bores* me with some tricks.—*Shakspeare.*

BORE.   A tiresome person or unwelcome visitor, who makes himself obnoxious by his disagreeable manners, or by a repetition of visits.

BORN DAYS. One's life-time ever since one was born; a vulgar expression used in various parts of the country. It is also used in the same sense in England.—*Craven Glossary.*

> In a' my *born days*, I never saw sic a rascal.—*Carr's Craven.*

An expression nearly similar is used by Froissart:

> I know not in all my *lyfe days* how to deserve it.

> Odswinge! this is brave! canny Cumberland, oh!
> In aw my *born days* sec a sight I ne'er saw.—*Westm. and Cum. Poems.*

> I never seed such a sight in all my *born days.* Heaven and earth! thinks I, where could they come from?—*Maj. Jones's Courtship*, p. 39.

> Where have you been all your *born days*, not to know better than that? *Sam. Slick in England*, ch. ii.

> Bime-by the General begun to let off steam, and such a whizzin' you never heard in your *born days.*—*Maj. Downing's Letters*, p. 200.

> The more (the schoolmaster) read the advertisement, the more he was astonished at the rashest act of temerity he had ever witnessed in his *born days.*—*Knickerbocker Mag.* vol. xvii. p. 33.

NOT BORN IN THE WOODS TO BE SCARED BY AN OWL. Too much used to danger, or threats, to be easily frightened.

> I just puts my finger to my nose, and winks, as much as to say, "I aint such a cursed fool as you take me to be!" Guess he found that was no go; for I warn't *born in the woods to be scared by an owl.*—*Sam Slick.*

BORN WITH A SILVER SPOON IN HIS MOUTH. To inherit a fortune by birth.

Mr. Hood, in his History of Miss Kilmansegg, says:

> She was one of those, by Fortune's boon, who
> Are *bor-*, as they say, with a *silver spoon*
> *In her mouth*, not a wooden ladle;

BOSS. (Dutch, *baas.* Danish, *bas*, a master.) A master, an employer of mechanics or laborers. It probably originated in New York, and is now used in many parts of the United States. The blacks often employ it in addressing white men in the Northern States, as they do *massa* (master) in the Southern States.

BOSS. (Lat. *bos.*) Among the hunters of the prairies, a name for the buffalo.

BOSSY. A familiar name applied to a calf.

BOTHER. Trouble, confusion.

BOTTOM. Low land with a rich soil formed by alluvial deposits, and formerly the bottom or bed of a stream or lake. This is an old use of the word. Dr. Johnson defines it, a dale; a valley; a low ground.

> He stood among the myrtle-trees that were in the *bottom.—Zech.* i. 8.
>
> In the purleius stands a sheep-cote, west of this place, down in the neighboring *bottom.—Shakspeare.*
>
> On both shores of that fruitful *bottom*, are still to be seen the marks of ancient edifices.—*Addison on Italy.*
>
> Both the *bottoms* and the high grounds are alternately divided into wood lands and prairies.—*Stoddard's Louisiana*, p. 213.

BOTTOM-LANDS. In the Western States, this name is given to the rich flat land on the banks of rivers, which in New England is generally called interval land, or simply interval. —*Pickering's Vocab. Webster.*

> Our sleigh, after winding for some time among this broken ground, and passing over one or two small but beautiful pieces of *bottom land* among the ravines, reached at last the top of the bluff.—*Hoffman.*

BOUGHTEN. Which is bought. This is a common word in the interior of New England and New York. It is applied to articles purchased from the shops, to distinguish them from similar articles of home manufacture. Many farmers make their own sugar from the maple-tree, and their coffee from barley or rye. West India sugar or coffee are then called *boughten sugar*, etc. This is a home-made carpet; that a *boughten* one, or one of foreign manufacture, bought at a shop.

BOUNCING. Large, heavy. Often applied, in familiar language, as in the phrase, "a bouncing girl."

TO BOUGE. (Old Fr. *bouge*, swelling.—*Cotgrave*). To swell out, to bulge. This old word is noticed by Dr. Johnson. It is nearly obsolete in England, but is preserved in the interior of New England.

> When the sun gets in one inch, it is ten o'clock; when it reaches the stone that *bouges* out there, it is dinner time.— *Margaret*, p. 6.

BOWIE-KNIFE. (Pron. *boo-ee*). A knife from ten to fifteen inches long and about two inches broad, so named after its inventor, Colonel Bowie. They are worn as weapons by persons in the South-western States only, and concealed in the back part of the coat.   No gentleman at the North thinks it necessary to wear such a weapon.

BOW-DARK TREE. (Fr. *bois d'arc.*)   A western tree, the wood of which is used to make bows with.

BRACK. (Goth. *braka.* Ang. Sax. *bracan,* to break.)   A breach, a broken part.—*Johnson.*

Mr. Pickering says, " This old English word is still used in some parts of New England, where it is applied to a break or flaw in a piece of cloth." It is to be found in old authors and is still provincial in England.

> Let not a *brack* i' th' stuff, or here and there
> The fading gloss, a general loss appear.—*Beaumont and Fletcher.*

BRAKE. The common name for *fern.* In Sweden the female fern is called *bracken.* In the north of England it is called *brackens.*—*Brockett's North County Words.*

It is a common saying in the Northern States, on the opening of spring, If you break the first *brake,* and kill the first snake, you will go through all you undertake.

BRAKE. A lever used for stopping cars on railways.

BRAKEMAN. The man whose business it is to stop cars on railways, by pressing a lever against the wheels.

BRAND-NEW.
BRAN-NEW. } (Teut. *brand new.*)   Quite new.

This word is provincial in the North of England, and is used in colloquial language in other parts, as well as in the United States. Mr. Todd suggests whether the expression may not have been originally *brent-new,* or *bren-new,* from the Saxon *brennan,* to burn, equivalent in meaning to *fire-new,* i. e., anything new from the forge; hence the secondary sense, just finished, quite new. The Dutch expression is explained by Kilian by *vier-new.*—*Forby—Brockett.*

Dr. Jamieson calls this a Scottish word.

> —— Waes me, I hae forgot,
> With hast of coming off, to fetch my coat.
> What shall I do ? It was almaist *brand new ;*
> 'Tis bat a hellier since't came off the clew.—*Ross's Helenore,* p. 53.

BRASH. Brittle. In New England this word is used in speaking of wood or timber that is brittle. In New York it is often heard in the markets, applied to vegetables. Ex. " These radishes are *brash*," i. e. brittle. In many parts of England, twigs are called *brash*.

Although this word is not used in the same sense in England, it seems to be properly derived from the Dutch *braash*, brittle. *Brashy*, in the north of England, means, delicate in constitution.—*Brockett's Glossary*.

BRAVELY. Excellently. The adjective *brave* was formerly used in the sense of *excellent ;* as it still is, for instance, in German and French. It has now lost this meaning ; but we continue to use the adverb in such phrases as " Templeton sang *bravely*," " The sick man is now doing *bravely*."

BREACHY. A term applied to unruly oxen in New England, particularly to such as break down fences or through inclosures. It is provincial in the south of England in the same sense.—*Halliwell's Arch. and Prov. Dic.*

BREAD-STUFF. Bread-corn, meal, or flour; bread.—*Webster. Pickering.*

This very useful word is American. Mr. Pickering says, " It was first used in some of the official papers of our government, soon after the adoption of the present Constitution. . . . . . It has probably been more readily allowed among us, because we do not, like the English, use the word *corn* as a general name for all sorts of grain, but apply it almost exclusively to *Indian corn* or maize." He cites the following authorities :

> The articles of exports . . . . . . are *bread-stuffs*, that is to say, bread-grains, meals, and bread. *Report of the Secretary of State (Mr. Jefferson) on Commercial Restrictions*, Dec. 16, 1793.

> One great objection to the conduct of Britain, was her prohibitory duty on the importation of *bread-stuff*, &c.—*Marshall, Life of Washington*, Vol. V. p. 519.

In Jamaica, the term *bread-kind* is applied to esculent roots, &c. substituted for bread.

BREAD-ROOT. (*Psoralea esculenta.*) A plant resembling the beet in form, which is found near the Rocky mountains, sometimes growing from twenty to thirty inches in circumfer-

ence.   It contains a white pulpy substance, sweet and palat-
able.—*Scenes in the Rocky Mountains,* p. 50.

TO BREAK UP LAND.   To plough up land that has lain long
as a meadow, is the sense as understood in the United States.
In England, according to Grose, land that has long lain fal-
low or in sheep-walks, is so called during the first year after
the alteration.

> Where peasen ye had, and a fallow thereon,
> Sow wheat ye may well, without dung thereupon :
> New *broken up land,* or with water opprest,
> Or overmuch dunged, for wheat is not best.—*Tasser, Husbandry.*

BRICKLEY, for brittle.   Used in Georgia.—*Sherwood's Gazetteer.*

TO BRIDGE.   To build a bridge, or bridges; as, ' to bridge a
river.'—*Webster.*

Mr. Todd, in his edition of Johnson's Dictionary, says this
unusual word was thought to be peculiar to Milton, who some
supposed coined it; but that he has found it in Sherwood's
Dictionary of 1632, with the explanation, " that hath a
bridge over it."

> Xerxes, the liberty of Greece to yoke,
> From Susa, like Memnonian palace high,
> Came to the sea ; and, over Hellespont
> *Bridging* his way, Europe with Asia joined.—*Milton, Par. Lost.*

> Here a road is formed by causeys of logs ; or, in the language of the
> country, it is *bridged* —*Kendall's Travels in the United States.*

BRIEF.   Rife; common; prevalent.   This word is much used
by the uneducated in the interior of New England, when
speaking of epidemic diseases.   Mr. Halliwell, in his Provincial Dictionary, says, it is used in the same sense in England, and denotes the quickness with which the contagion
spreads.   *Brief* is also used when speaking of diseases in Virginia.   It is not in any English dictionary except Bailey's, in
which it is defined as ' common, rife.'

BRIGHT.   Ingenious; possessing an active mind.—*Webster.*

This is a common use of the word in the United States.
Neither Johnson nor Todd gives this definition of it.   Two of
their definitions are, " illuminated with science ; sparkling

with wit." We say, a *bright* child, but would not say that Newton or Bacon was *bright,* for the term does not express enough to be applied to those great minds. In poetry, however, it does well enough, even when applied to one of these great philosophers.

> If parts allure thee, think how Bacon shin'd,
> The wisest, *brightest,* meanest of mankind.—*Pope.*

TO BRISK UP. To come up with life and speed; to take an erect or bold attitude.—*Webster.* An Americanism.

BROADBILL. (*Anas marila.*) The common name of a wild duck, which appears on our coast in large numbers in October. On the Chesapeake it is called *Black-head ;* and in Virginia, *Raft-duck.*—*Nat. History of New York.*

BROGANS. ⎱
BROGUES. ⎰ The first word is used in the United States, to distinguish a heavy, coarse shoe, between a boot and a shoe. In England coarse or wooden shoes are called *brogues.* When filled with nails they are called clouted *brogues.*—*Nares's Glossary.*

> I thought he slept,
> And put my clouted *brogues* from off my feet, whose rudeness
> Answer'd my steps too loud.—*Cymbeline,* IV. 2.

BROOM-CORN. (*Sorghum saccharatum.*) A species of corn which grows from six to eight feet high, from the tufts of which brooms are made.

BROTHER-CHIP. A fellow-carpenter; in a more general sense, a person of the same trade.

BROTHER JONATHAN.—The origin of this term, as applied to the United States, is given in a recent number of the Norwich Courier. The Editor says it was communicated by a gentleman now upwards of eighty years of age, who was an active participator in the scenes of the Revolution. The story is as follows:

When General Washington, after being appointed commander of the army of the Revolutionary war, came to Massachusetts to organize it and make preparations for the defence of the country, he found a great want of ammunition and other means necessary to meet the powerful foe he had to contend with, and great difficulty to obtain them. If attacked in such condition, the cause at once might be hopeless. On one occasion at that anxious period, a consultation of the officers and others was had, when it seemed no way could be devised to make such preparation as was necessary. His Excellency, Jonathan Trumbull, the elder, was then Governor of the State of Connecticut, on whose judgment and aid the General placed the greatest reliance, and remarked, " We must consult ' Brother Jonathan' on the subject."   The General did so, and the Governor was successful in supplying many of the wants of the army.   When difficulties afterwards arose, and the army was spread over the country, it became a by-word, " We must consult Brother Jonathan." The term Yankee is still applied to a portion, but " Brother Jonathan " has now become a designation of the whole country, as John Bull has for England.

BROWN STUDY.   Deep thought ; absence of mind.   " He is in a brown study," i. e. in deep thought, or intent upon his book.

The adjective is here used in a metaphorical sense ; brown being considered a dull, sober color.   Comp. art. Blue.

Why, how now, sister, in a motley mouse ?
*   *   *   *   *   *   *   *
Faith, this brown study suits not with your black,
Your habit and your thoughts are of two colors.—Ben Jonson.

They live retired, and they doze away their time in drowsiness and brown studies ; or, if brisk and active, they lay themselves out wholly in making common-places.—Norris.

BROWN THRASHER. (Ferruginous thrush. Audubon Ornith.) The popular name of the brown thrush.   It is also called the ground mocking-bird.—Nat. History of New York.

1 love the city as dearly as a brown thrasher loves the green tree that sheltered its young.—C. Mathews, Works, p. 125.

BRUSH.   A skirm ish, or fight.—Johnson.   Grose.

It could not be possible, that, upon so little a brush as Waller had sustained, he could not be able to follow and disturb the king.—Clarendon.

TO BRUSH UP.   To prepare oneself ; to take courage.

When Miss Mary came, I brushed up, and was determined to have a rite serious talk with her, not knowin but she mought be captivated by some of them Macon fellers.—Major Jones's Courtship.

BUBBLER.   A fish found in all the waters of the Ohio.   Its name is derived from the singular grunting noise which it makes, a noise which is familiar to every one who has been much on the Ohio.—Flint's Mississippi Valley.

BUCK-EYE. In the Western States, the people of each are known by certain nicknames. The natives of Ohio are called *Buck-eyes*.

TO BUCKLE-TO. To set about any task with energy and a determination to effect the object. It probably comes from harnessing or *buckling to* a carriage, the horses, before starting. In Scotland, *buckle to* means to join in marriage.— *Jamieson*.

> I have no objections, said the schoolmaster, to sing you a psalm tune, since you're anxious to hear it ; but after that you must *buckle-to*, and stick to the elements.—*Knickerbocker Mag*. Vol. XVII. p. 87.

BUCKRA. A white man. A term universally applied to white men by the blacks of the African coast, the West Indies and the Southern States. In the language of the Calabar coast, *buckra* means devil ; not, however, in the sense we apply to it, but that of a demon, a powerful and superior being. The term *swanga buckra*, often used by the blacks, means, an elegantly dressed white man, or dandy. I am indebted to the Rev. J. L. Wilson, who is familiar with the African language alluded to, for the etymology of this word.

> Which country you like best ? *Buckra* country very good, plenty for yam (food), plenty for bamboo (clothing). *Buckra* man book larn. *Buckra* man rise early—he like a cold morning ; nigger no like cold.— *Carmichael's West Indies*, Vol. 1. p. 311.

BUCKTAIL. The name of a political party in the State of New York, which sprung up about the year 1815. Its origin is thus described by Mr. Hammond : "There was an order of the Tammany Society who wore in their hats as an insignia, on certain occasions, a portion of the tail of the deer. They were a leading order, and from this circumstance the friends of De Witt Clinton gave those who adopted the views of the members of the Tammany Society, in relation to him, the name of *Bucktails ;* which name was eventually applied to their friends and supporters in the country. Hence the party opposed to the administration of Mr. Clinton, were for a long time called the "BUCKTAIL PARTY."—*Polit. Hist. of New York*, Vol. I. p. 450.

BUCKWHEAT. A species of grain (genus *polygonor*), the flour of which is much used in the United States.

An etymology of this word has been suggested to me by a friend, which, as it is new, deserves mention. The Saxon for *beech* is *boc*, Dutch, *bock*. The mast or nut of the beech is of the same form and color as the grain of the *buckwheat*; hence we have the Dutch *bock weyt*, beech-wheat, and English *buckwheat*, or wheat resembling the *buck* or *beech* nut.

BUFFALO. A sort of fresh-water fish, resembling the sheep's head, found in the Mississippi.

BUFFALO CHIPS. The dry dung of the buffalo, used for fuel on the prairies.

> Wood is now very scarce, but "*buffalo chips*" are excellent—they kindle quick and retain heat surprisingly. We have this evening buffalo steaks broiled upon them that had the same flavor they would have had on hickory coals.—*Letter from a California Emigrant.*

BUFFALO GRASS. A species of short grass from two to four inches high, covering the boundless prairies on which the buffaloes feed. A remarkable characteristic of some varieties of this grass, is that " the blade, killed by the frost of winter, is resuscitated in the spring, and gradually becomes green from the root up, without casting its stubble or emitting new shoots."—*Scenes in the Rocky Mountains*, p. 287.

BUFFALO-ROBE. The skin of the buffalo, dressed for use.

BUG. In the United States *coleopterous* insects are invariably called *bugs*; thus May bug, June bug, golden bug, &c. In England they are called *beetles*, and the word *bug* is restricted to the species found in bedding.

BUGGY. A light waggon for one horse.

> Lend me a hundred and buy yourself a *buggy*,—why don't you get a *buggy*, to begin with ?—*J. C. Neal's Sketches.*

BUGLE-WEED. (*Lycopus Virginicus.*) A plant which has much reputation for its medicinal properties. It is also known as the *Virginian Water-horehound*.

BULGER. Large.—*A Western term.*

> We soon came in sight of New York ; and a *bulger* of a place it is.—*Crockett*, p. 37.

BUILD UP. To erect; and metaphorically to establish, to found.

> In this manner it was thought we should sooner '*build up a settlement*,' as the phrase goes. In America, the reader should know, everything is *built*. The priest *builds up* a flock; the speculator, a fortune; the lawyer, a reputation; and the landlord, a settlement.—*Cooper, Satanstoe.*

> Mr. R. has never done anything to the Courier and Enquirer to make them hunt him down or cast ridicule on him, while endeavoring to *build up* for himself, an unsullied character among his fellow-men.—*N. Y. Tribune,* 1848.

BULL. A stock exchange term for one who buys stock on speculation for time, i. e. agrees with the seller, called a *bear*, to take a certain sum of stock at a future day, at a stated price; if at that day stock fetches more than the price agreed on, he receives the difference; if it falls or is cheaper, he either pays it, or becomes a " lame duck." This description of a *bull* from Grose's Slang Dictionary, corresponds precisely with the *bulls* of Wall street, who speculate in stocks in the same manner. See *Lame Duck* and *Bear*, the names of other classes who figure in the stock exchange.

> There was a *sauve qui peut* movement to-day in the Stock Market, and the clique of *bulls* finding it impossible to stem the rush, gave up the attempt to sustain the market and let things go down with a run. . . . Such a state of the market as is now exhibited, is nearly as bad for the bears as the *bulls.*—*N. Y. Tribune,* Dec. 10, 1845.

> There is something of a panic in Wall street, and the *bulls* fare hard.—*N. Y. Journal of Commerce,* Dec. 10, 1845.

It is usual for the brokers to collect in Wall street, sometimes in such numbers as to obstruct the way. This led to a petition to the board of aldermen complaining of

> " An encumbrance upon the sidewalks, for that every week-day morning, between 9 and 11, certain *bulls* and bears do congregate upon the sidewalk, on the northerly side of Wall street nearly opposite Hanover street, in such numbers as entirely to obstruct the way of foot passengers, so that they are compelled to take the middle of the street, or cross over to the walk on the opposite side." The prayer is, " that the nuisance may be abated." Ald. Dod moved to lay the memorial on the table. Ald. McElrath said that the petition was very respectably signed, and trusted it would receive a respectful consideration : the petitioners were serious, asked the removal of an obstruction, and used the terms well known.—*N. Y. Tribune,* 1847.

BULL'S EYES, *n.* A coarse sweetmeat mixed with flour, and

streaked various colors, greedily devoured by children.—
Hartshorne's Shropshire Glossary.

The same word is used here.

BUMBLE-BEE. The wild bee ; also called the humble bee.
In Yorkshire, England, *to bumble* means to make a humming
noise.—*Dr. Willan, in Archæologia*, Vol. XVII.

Chaucer uses the verb *bumble* to describe the noise made by
the bittern.

BUNCOME,
BUNKUM. } Judge Halliburton of Nova Scotia, thus
explains this very useful and expressive word, which is
now as well understood as any word in our language :

"———All over America, every place likes to hear of
its members of Congress, and see their speeches ; and if they
don't, they send a piece to the paper, enquirin' if their member died a natural death, or was skivered with a bowie knife,
for they hante seen his speeches lately, and his friends are
anxious to know his fate.   Our free and enlightened citizens
don't approbate silent members ; it don't seem to them as if
Squashville, or Punkinsville, or Lumbertown was right
represented, unless Squashville, or Punkinsville, or Lumbertown makes itself heard and known, ay, and feared too.   So
every feller in bounden duty, talks, and talks big too, and the
smaller the State, the louder, bigger, and fiercer its members
talk.

" Well, when a critter talks for talk sake, jist to have a
speech in the paper *to* send to home, and not for any other
airthly puppus but electioneering, our folks call it *Bunkum.*
Now the State of Maine is a great place for *Bunkum*—its
members for years threatened to run foul of England, with
all steam on, and sink her about the boundary line ; voted a
million of dollers, payable in pine logs and spruce boards, up
to Bangor mills ; and called out a hundred thousand militia
(only they never come), to captur a saw mill to New Bruns-
wick. That's *Bunkum*—all that flourish about Right o' Search
was *Bunkum*—all that brag about hangin' your Canada
sheriff was *Bunkum*—all the speeches about the Caroline,
and Creole, and Right of Sarch, was *Bunkum*.   In short,

almost all that's said *in Congress*, in *the Colonies*, (for we set the fashions to them, as Paris gals do to our milliners,) and all over America, is *Bunkum*.

" Well, they talk *Bunkum* here, too, as well as there. Slavery speeches are all *Bunkum ;* so are reform speeches, too," etc.

The origin of the phrase, as I have read it, is somehow so : A tedious speaker in Congress being interrupted and told it was no use to go on, for the members were all leaving the house, replied, " Never mind ; *I'm talking to Buncombe.*" Buncombe, in North Carolina, was the place he represented.

> Washington is the theatre of the worst passions in our nature: chicanery lurks within the cabinet, distrust and envy without, while fawning sycophancy environs it round about. To sum it up, it is a little of government—a great deal of *bunkum*, sprinkled with a high seasoning of political juggling, with but one end and aim—the spoils of Uncle Sam.—*Robb, Squatter Life,* p. 17.

BUNK. (Ang. Sax. *benc.* Germ. *bank.* Danish, *baenk*, a bench, a form.) A wooden case used in country taverns and in offices which serves alike for a seat during the day and for a bed at night. They are common throughout the Northern States.

Dr. Jamieson has the word *bunker*, a bench, or sort of low chests that serve for seats—also, a seat in a window, which serves for a chest, opening with a hinged lid.—*Etym. Dict. Scottish Language.*

> Ithers frae off the *bunkers* sank,
> We e'en like the collops scor'd.—*Ramsay's Poems,* Vol. I. p. 280.

In some parts of Scotland a *bunker* or *bunkart*, which Dr. Jamieson thinks to be the same word, means an earthen seat in the fields. In the North of England, a seat in front of a house, made of stones or sods, is called a *bink*.

BUNK. A piece of wood placed on a lumberman's sled to enable it to sustain the end of heavy pieces of timber.— *Maine.*

BUNGTOWN-COPPER. The old English half-penny, or copper. So called in various parts of New England.

> These flowers wouldn't fetch a *bungtown copper.*—*Margaret,* p. 19.

TO BUNDLE. Mr. Grose thus describes this custom :

"A man and woman lying on the same bed with their clothes on ; an expedient practised in America on a scarcity of beds, where, on such occasions, husbands and parents frequently permitted travellers to *bundle* with their wives and daughters."—*Dictionary of the Vulgar Tongue.*

Bundling is said to be practised in Wales.   Whatever may have been the custom in former times, I do not think *bundling* is now practised in the United States.

Mr. Masson describes a similar custom in Central Asia :

"Many of the Afghan tribes have a custom in wooing, similar to what in Wales is known as *bundling-up*, and which they term *namzat bazé*.   The lover presents himself at the house of his betrothed with a suitable gift, and in return is allowed to pass the night with her, on the understanding that innocent endearments are not to be exceeded.—*Journeys in Balochistan, Afghanistan, &c.* Vol. III. p. 287.

TO BUNT.   To push with horns ; to butt.   This word is given by Webster, but is not in the English dictionaries.   Mr. Hartshorne notices this word in his *Shropshire Glossary.*

BURGALOO.   A kind of pear.

BURGOO.   A seafaring dish made with oat meal and water, seasoned with salt, butter, and sugar.—*Falconer's Marine Dict.*

BURNT HIS FINGERS.   When a person has suffered loss by a speculation, he is said to have *burnt his fingers*.   It is used in the same sense in England.

> We were sick of speculating in cotton.   We had *burnt our fingers* once with the article, and would not try it again.—*Perils of Pearl Street*, p. 165.

BURR-STONE.   A species of silex or quartz occurring in morphous masses, partly compact, but containing many irregular cavities.   It is used for mill-stones.—*Cleveland's Mineralogy.*

BUSHWHACKER.   A raw countryman, a green-horn.

> Do you think all our eastern dignitaries combined could have compelled young *bushwhackers* to wear coats and shoes in recitation rooms.—*Carlton's New Purchase*, Vol. II. p. 87.

BUSS.   A kiss.   This word, once of sufficient dignity to be

used by our dramatic authors, has now become so obsolete as
to be heard only from the vulgar.

> Come, grin on me ; and I will think thou smil'st,
> And *buss* thee as my wife.—*Shakspeare, K. John*, iii. 4.

> Kissing and bussing differ both in this,
> We *buss* our wantons, but our wives we kiss.—*Herrick's Works,* p. 219.

TO BUST. To burst ; to fail in business.

> Simple persons who have been smarter or earlier in the field of fortune'
> will *burst up* some fine morning, and leave the road open to others.—*Black-*
> *wood's Mag.* April, 1847, p. 498.

> I was soon fotch'd up in the victualling line—and I *busted* for the benefit
> of my creditors.—*J. C. Neal, Dolly Jones.*

BUSTER. Anything large in size ; a man of great strength.
A common vulgarism, which appears to be of foreign origin.

Dr. Jamieson, in his Scottish Dictionary, has the word
bustuous, busteous, huge, large in size ; also, strong, powerful ; which is the same meaning usually understood by our
vulgar word *buster*.

> —— The same time sendis sche
> Down to the folkis at the cost of the se,
> Twenty fed oxin, large, grete, and fyne,
> And one hundreth *busteous* boukes of swyne.—*Douglas, Virgil*, 33, 8.

We sometimes hear this word applied to a gale of wind, as,
" This is a *buster*," i. e. a powerful or heavy wind. In the
old Scottish poems there are examples of a similar use of the
word.

> That terrible trumpet, I hear tel,
> Beis hard in heavin, in eirth and hel ;
> Those that were drownit in the sey,
> That *busteous* blast they sal obey.—*Lindsay's Works*, 1592, p. 167.

The Icelandic *bostra*, great noise, seems to be analagous
to the word.

BUSTER, or bust. A frolic, a spree. " They were on a *buster*,
and were taken up by the police."

BUSTLE. A pad stuffed with cotton, feathers, bran, &c., worn
by ladies for the double purpose of giving a greater rotundity
or prominence to the hips, and setting off the smallness of the
waist.

> Some of the ladies had *bustles* on that would have literally throwed the

whiskers, and the thing that wore them, entirely in the shade. I never knowed what a *bustle* was before. Would you believe it, Mr. Thompson, that I saw *bustles* up to Athens, that, if they'd been made out of real flesh and blood, would broke the back of any gall in Georgia to carry 'em ? It's a fact. Why, some of them looked jist as much out of proportion as a bundle of fodder does tied to the handle of a pitchfork. If anything would make me sue for a divorce, it would be to see my wife toting about sich a monstrous pack on her back as some of them I saw up to Athens.—*Maj. Jones's Courtship*, p. 168.

BUTTE. (French.) This word is of frequent occurrence in books that relate to the Rocky Mountain and Oregon regions, " where," says Col. Frémont, " it is naturalized, and if desirable to render into English, there is no word which would be its precise equivalent. It is applied to the detached hills and ridges which rise abruptly, and reach too high to be called hills or ridges, and not high enough to be called mountains. *Knob*, as applied in the Western States, is their most descriptive term in English ; but no translation or paraphrasis would preserve the identity of these picturesque land-marks."— *Exped. to the Rocky Mountains*, p. 145.

Sir Geo. Simpson in his " *Overland Journey round the World*," when traversing the Red River country, west of Hudson's Bay, speaks of a conspicuous land-mark in the sea of plains, known as the *Butte* aux Chiens, ... towering with a height of about four hundred feet over a boundless prairie as level and smooth as a pond.—Vol. I. p. 54.

BUTTER-CUP. The flower of the *ranunculus ficarius*. It seems to have obtained its name from a vulgar error, that butter is improved in flavor and color by cows eating this plant ; though it is well known that they avoid it, on account of its *acrid taste.*—*Craven Glossary*.

BUTTERNUT. (Lat. *Juglans cinerea*.) Also called the oil-nut. The tree resembles the black walnut.

BUTTONING UP. A Wall street phrase. When a broker has bought stock on speculation and it falls suddenly on his hands, whereby he is a loser, he keeps the matter to himself and is reluctant to confess the ownership of a share. This is called *buttoning up.*—*A Walk in Wall Street*, p. 47.

BUTTON BUSH. (*Cephalanthus occidentalis*.) A shrub which

grows along the water side, its insulated thickets furnishing a safe retreat for the nests of the black-bird. Its flowers appear at a distance like the balls of the sycamore tree; hence its name.—*Bigelow's Flora Bostoniensis.*

BUTTON WOOD. (*Platanus occidentalis.*) The popular name in New England of the sycamore tree; so called from the balls it bears, the receptacle of the seeds, which remain on the trees during the winter.—*Michaux's Sylva.*

BY THE BYE. To Mr. Richardson we are indebted for a fuller examination of this phrase, than other lexicographers have given it. In this expression the latter *bye* seems to be the same *bye* as in *by-law*, &c., and of course to admit a similar explanation. In Lord Bacon; "there is *upon* the by to be noted," that is, upon the way, in passing, indirectly, this being a collateral and not the main object of pursuit. In Ben Jonson; "those who have saluted poetry on the by;" on their way, in passing; poetry being the collateral and not the direct or main object of their pursuit. *By the bye* then is *by the way*, in passing, such being a collateral and not a main object.—*Richardson, Dictionary.*

BY THE SKIN OF ONE'S TEETH. When a man has made a narrow escape from any dilemma, it is a common remark to say, that he has saved himself ' by the skin of his teeth.'

BY-BIDDER. A person employed at public auctions to bid on articles put up for sale, in order to obtain higher prices. In New York city also called *Peter Funks*, which see.

BY GOSH! An inoffensive oath, used mostly in New England. Negroes often say, *By Golly !*

BY GUM! The same as the preceding. It is also noticed by *Moor* in his *Suffolk Glossary.*

BY GOOD RIGHTS. By right, by strict justice; as, "*By good rights* Mr. Clay ought to be President of the United States," meaning that he is entitled to it by right, or by justice, and for the services he has rendered his country.

C.

CAB. A small one horse carriage, lately introduced into our principal cities from England.

CABBAGE. A cant word for shreds and patches made by tailors in cutting out clothes.—*Todd*. From this comes *to cabbage*, to steal in a small way.

CABOOSE. The common pronunciation for *camboose* (Dutch *kombuis*), a ship's cooking-range or kitchen.

CACHE. (French.) A hole in the ground for hiding and preserving provisions which it is inconvenient to carry ; used by settlers in the West.—*Webster*.

CADDY. A small box generally made of laquered ware, and lined with sheet lead, for keeping tea in.

CAHOOT. Probably from *cohort*, Spanish and French, defined in the old French and English Dictionary of Holly-band, 1593, as " a company, a band." It is used at the South and West to denote a company or union of men for a predatory excursion, and sometimes for a partnership in business.

> If I could only get the township and range, I'd make a *cahoot* business with the old man.—*Simon Suggs*, p. 37.

> Pete Hopkins aint no better than he should be, and I wouldn't swar he wasn't in *cahoot* with the devil.—*Chronicles of Pineville*, p. 74.

> I'd have no objection to go in *cahoot* with a decent fellow for a character, but have no funds to purchase on my own account.—*New Orleans Picayune*, p. 136.

> The hoosier took him aside, told him there was a smart chance of a pile on one of the (card) tables, and that if he liked, he would go in with him— in *cahoot !*—*Field, Western Tales*, p. 198.

CALASH. (Fr. *calèche*.) A two-wheeled carriage, resembling a chaise, used in Canada.

CALASH. A covering for the head, usually worn by ladies to protect their head-dresses when going to evening parties, the theatre, etc.

TO CALCULATE. This word, which properly means to compute, to estimate, has been erroneously transferred from the language of the counting-house to that of common life, where it is used for the words, to esteem ; to suppose ; to believe; to think; to expect; intend, &c. It is employed in a similar way to the word *guess*, though not to so great an extent. Its use is confined to the illiterate of New England.

Mr. Cram requested those persons who *calculated* to join the singin' school to come forward.—*Knickerbocker Mag.* Vol. xvii.

CALABOOSE. (Fr. *calabouse*. Span. *calabozo*.) In New Orleans, the common jail or prison.

CALIBOGUS. Rum and spruce-beer. An American beverage.—*Grose.*

CALICO. Supposed to be derived from *Calicut* in India. The word was originally applied to white cottons from India. In England, white cotton goods are still called calicoes. In the United States the term is applied exclusively to printed cotton cloth. Dr. Webster says, to printed cotton cloth having but *two* colors. This is a mistake. Calicoes may have two or ten colors in them. The number of colors does not change the name.

TO CALK. In some parts of America, to set upon a horse or ox shoes armed with sharp points of iron, to prevent their slipping on ice.—*Webster.*

CALLITHUMPIANS. It is a common practice in New York, as well as other parts of the country, on New-Year's eve, for persons to assemble with tin horns, bells, rattles, and similar euphonious instruments, and parade the streets making all the noise and discord possible. This party is called the *Callithumpians*, or the *Callithumpian Band*. On wedding nights the happy couple are sometimes saluted with this discord by those who choose to consider the marriage an improper one, instead of a serenade. See *chiravari.*

CALUMET. (Old Fr.) Among the aboriginals of America, a pipe, used for smoking tobacco, whose bowl is usually of soft red marble, and the tube a long reed, ornamented with feathers. The calumet is used as a symbol or instrument of peace and war. To accept the calumet, is to agree to the terms of peace; and to refuse it, is to reject them. The calumet of peace is used to seal or ratify contracts and alliances, to receive strangers kindly, and to travel with safety. The calumet of war, differently made, is used to proclaim war.—*Webster, Dic.*

CAMP OUT. To encamp out of doors for the night.

> The surveying party did not always return to the hut at night, but it *camped out*, as they called it, whenever the work led them to a distance.— *Cooper, Satanstoe*, Vol. II. p. 88.

CANADA RICE. (*Zizania aquatica.*) A plant which grows in deep water along the edges of ponds and sluggish streams, in the Northern States and Canada. It is called in some places wild rice and water oats.

CANDLE. Hold a candle. To hold a candle to one, is to wait on him. Hence, ' you are not fit to hold a candle to him,' is equivalent to, you are not fit to be even his servant ; or not to be compared to him.

> I have heard in my time a good many men speak French, but I never see the man yet who could *hold a candle* to the Prince de Joinville. It was like lightnin', jist one long-endurin' streak. It was beautiful, but I couldn't understand it, it was so everlastin' fast.—*Sam Slick in England*, ch. 22.

> Talking about the popularity and glory of his administration—" Why," says the General, "nothing can *hold a candle to it*."—*Maj. Downing's Letters*, p. 233.

CANE-BRAKE. A thicket of canes. They abound in the low lands of Louisiana and Mississippi.

CANOE. (*Canóa*, West Indies.) An Indian boat made of bark or skins.

TO CANT. To turn about ; to turn over ; a common use of the word, not mentioned by Johnson or Todd. It is, however, in Ash's Dictionary, who defines it, a sudden kind of turn in moving a piece of timber.

> The cart reeled and rattled. It jolted over stones, *canted* on knolls, sidled into gutters.—*Margaret*, p. 17.

CANT-HOOK. A wooden lever, with an iron hook at one end, with which heavy articles of merchandise or timber are canted over.

CAN'T COME IT, is a vulgar expression for cannot do it. " You *can't come it* over me so," i. e. you cannot effect your purpose. Mr. Hamilton notices this expression among the provincialisms of Yorkshire.—*Nugæ Literariæ*, p. 353.

CANTELOPE. A species of muskmelon.

CANTICOY, or Cantica. An Indian word, denoting a dancing assembly, still used by aged people in New York and on Long Island. Also, a noisy conversation.

> At their *canticas* or dancing matches, where all persons that come are freely entertained, it being a festival time.—*Denton's Description of New York*, 1670.

CANYON. (Span. *cañon*.) A narrow, tunnel-like passage between high and precipitous banks, formed by mountains or table-lands, with a river running beneath. These occur in the great western prairies.

> The Platte forces its way through a barrier of table lands, forming one of those striking peculiarities incident to mountain streams, called a *cañon*. —*Scenes in the Rocky Mountains*, p. 111.

TO CAP. To excel; to surpass. Ex. *To cap all.* Used in familiar language in New England. Mr. Hartshorne, in his *Shropshire Glossary*, has the expression, *to cob all*, meaning the same.

TO CAP THE CLIMAX, is to surpass everything. A letter from Mexico, in speaking of the excesses of the American soldiers, says:

> Several robberies were committed by them at Jalapa, but at Cautepec they robbed almost every house, and, *to cap the climax*, robbed the church. —*Alexandria Gazette*.

> The western hunter, when he wishes to *cap the climax* of braggadocio with respect to his own prowess, says, " he can whip his weight in wild-cats."—*Thorpe's Backwoods*.

TO SET HER CAP FOR HIM. To direct her attentions to him; to endeavor to win his affections. Dr. Johnson notices the phrase, which he says belongs to modern times. It is common in the United States, and may be heard in the best society, in familiar conversation.

CAPSHEAF. A small sheaf of straw forming the top of a stack.—*Dorset Glossary*. Figuratively used in the United States to denote the highest degree, the summit.

> Of all the days that I ever did see in this 'ere world, moving-day in New York is the *capsheaf*.—*Maj. Downing, May-day in N. Y.*, p. 43.

TO CAPSIZE. To upset or overturn.—*Webster*. Originally a seaman's word; but now often heard among landsmen.

TO CAPTIVATE, *v. a.* (Lat. *captivo*, from *capto*, to take; Fr. *captiver*.) To take prisoner; to bring into bondage.— *Johnson*. To seize by force; as an enemy in war.—*Webster*.

> How ill-becoming is it in thy sex,
> To triumph like an Amazonian trull
> Upon their woes whom fortune *captivates.—Shakspeare.*

They stand firm, keep out the enemy, truth, that would *captivate* or disturb them.—*Locke.*

The unnatural brethren who sold their brother into captivity, are now about to be *captivated* themselves, and the *binder* himself to be bound in his turn.—*Dr. Adam Clarke, Reflec.* 4th Genesis.

The Edinburgh Review, in its notice of the American Mineralogical Journal, published in New York in 1810, after speaking of other words, says, " Other examples, proving the alteration to which our language has been exposed, chiefly by the introduction of *gallicisms,* may be noticed in the rest of this Journal, resembling expressions found in American newspapers, where for a " *ship taken,*" we read of " *a ship captivated !*"

In his remarks on this word, Mr. Pickering says it was new to him, and that he had never seen it in the newspapers. Subsequently, however, he discovered it in two or three of our authors. It cannot be said to be in use among writers at the present day. It is well known that Congress, in adopting the Declaration of Independence prepared by Mr. Jefferson, omitted certain passages contained in the original draft. Among these was the omission of the paragraph relating to the slave trade :

> He has waged cruel war against human nature itself, violating its most sacred rights of life and liberty in the persons of a distant people, who never offended him, *captivating* and carrying them into slavery in another hemisphere, or to more miserable death in transportation thither.

In noticing the above passage, Lord Brougham says, The word " *captivating* " will be reckoned an Americanism (as the Greeks used to say of their colonists a Solæcism). But it has undoubted English authority—Locke among others.— *Statesmen of George III.*

> Twenty-three people were killed in this surprisal, and twenty-nine were *captivated.—Belknap, Hist. New Hampshire,* Vol. I. ch. 10.

> The singularly interesting event of *captivating* a second Royal army (Lord Cornwallis's) produced strong emotions.—*Ramsay, History American Revolution,* Vol. II. p. 274.

CARDINAL. The name of a woman's cloak; from the red or scarlet habit worn by cardinals.—*Todd's Johnson.* The cardinal worn by ladies at the present day is a short cloak usually made of velvet, satin, or other rich material.

> But we've no time, my dear, to waste,
> Come, where's your *cardinal*, make haste.—*Lloyd, Chit-chat.*

CAROLINA POTATO. The sweet potato (*convolvulus batata*), so called in the Eastern States.

CARPET WEED. A small spreading plant, common in cultivated ground (*mollugo*).—*Bigelow's Plants of Boston.*

CARROTY. *Carroty-hair*, red hair. A term common alike to England and America.

> While "Tall-and-thin," with his hair all *carroty*,
> Looks thrice as red, with fright, as his head,
> And his face bounds plump, at a single jump,
> Into horror, and out of hilarity!—*New Tale of a Tub.*

Seth's short, bow-legged figure was thatched with the most obstinate bunch of *carroty* hair that ever bid defiance to bear's oil.—*Robb, Squatter Life.*

CARRYALL. A four-wheeled pleasure carriage, capable of holding several persons, or a family; hence the term, *carryall.* The name is common in the Northern States. In Canada it is applied to a sleigh.

TO CARRY A HORSE TO WATER, instead of *lead* or *ride him to water.* A Southern expression.—*Sherwood, Georgia.*

TO CARRY ON. To riot; to frolic.

> We notice some young scapegraces, who get up their wild freaks at night and continue them till morning. Sometimes they *carry on* even longer than this.—*N. Y. Tribune.*

CARRYINGS-ON. Riotings, frolickings.

> Everybody tuck Christmas, especially the niggers, and sich *carryins-on*—sich dancin' and singin'—and shootin' poppers and sky-rackets—you never did see.—*Maj. Jones's Courtship.*

> She had better not come about me with any of her cantankerous *carryings-on* this mornin'.—*Chron. of Pineville.*

> When he reflected that wherever there were singin' schools, there would be *carryings-on*, he thought the cheapest plan would be to let them have their fun out.—*Peter Cram in Knickerbocker Mag.*

TO CASCADE. To vomit—from the resemblance to a waterfall. It is a common word in England.

CASSAVA, or CASSADA. (*Cassabi*, W. Ind.) The native name of a shrub of Central and South America, from the root of which the tapioca and mandioca are extracted.

CATAMARAN. In the State of Maine, a raft for crossing rivers.

CATAMOUNT. Although this animal is peculiar to North America, a similar name, that of *catamountain*, for the wild cat, is common in the old authors, from which we probably borrowed it. The catamount of North America is a larger and very different animal from the wild cat of Europe.

> As *cattes of the mountayn*, they are spotted with diverse fykle fantasyes. —*Bale on the Revel.* (1550), p. 2.

> Would any man of discretion venture such a gristle,
> To the rude claws of such a *cat-a-mountain*?—*Beaumont and Fletcher.*

CATAWAMPTIOUSLY CHAWED UP. Completely demolished, utterly defeated. One of the ludicrous monstrosities in which the vulgar language of the Southern and Western States abounds.

> In this debate Mr. B. was ' catawamptiously chawed up ;' his arguments were not only met, but his sarcasm returned upon himself with great effect.—*Charleston Mercury.*

TO CATCH A TARTAR. To attack one of superior strength or abilities. This saying originated from the story of an Irish soldier in the Imperial service, who, in a battle against the Turks, called out to his comrade that he had caught a Tartar. "Bring him along then," said he. "He won't come," answered Paddy. "Then come along yourself," replied his comrade. "Arrah," cried he, "but he won't let me."— *Grose.*

> In this defeat they lost about 5000 men, besides those that were taken prisoners ; so that, instead of *catching the Tartar*, they were catched themselves.—*Life of the Duke of Tyrconnel,* 1689.

TO CATCH A WEASEL ASLEEP. It is a common belief that this little animal is never caught napping, for the obvious reason that he sleeps in his hole beyond the reach of man. The expression is applied to persons who are watchful and always on the alert, or who cannot be surprised ; as, "You cannot deceive me, any sooner than *you can catch a weasel* *asleep,''* or, '' You can't catch a weasel asleep.'' The expressions are common.

CATERWAUL. The wailing of cats in the night-time; and hence, any ludicrous, disagreeable noise that resembles it.

> What a *caterwauling* you do keep here! If my lady has not called up her stewart Malvolio, and bid him turn you out of doors, never trust me.— *Shakspeare, Twelfth Night.*

> It indeed appeared a little odd to me, to see so many persons of quality of both sexes, assembled together at a kind of *caterwauling;* for I cannot look upon the performance to have been anything better, whatever the musicians themselves might think of it.—*Spectator*, No. 361.

> Yes, gentlemen, as the eagle is the proud representative of this great nation, so is Mr. Van Buren the proud representative of the Democracy. (Cheers, groans, and *caterwaulings.*)—*Report of Speech, N. Y. Herald.*

CATFISH. (*Genus Prinelodus.* Cuvier.) This fish in several varieties is common throughout the Atlantic States under different popular names. It is also called by the name of Horned-pout, Bull-head, Mud-pout, and Minister. There is a very large species called the *channel cat-fish*, which is noticed by Dr. Kirtland in his Report on the Geology of Ohio.

CATMINT, or CATNIP. (*Nepeta cataria.*) A well known medicinal herb.

CATS-PAW. *To be made a cats-paw of.* To be made a tool or instrument to accomplish the purpose of another; an allusion to the story of a monkey, who made use of a cat's paw to scratch a roasted chestnut out of the fire.—*Grose.*

CATSTICK. A bat or cudgel used by boys in a game at ball. It is known by the same name in England, though used for a different play. I have never heard the word here except in Rhode Island.

> When the cat is laid upon the ground, the player with his cudgel or *catstick* strikes it smartly, it matters not at which end, and it will rise high enough for him to beat it away as it falls in the same manner as he would a ball.—*Strutt, Sports and Pastimes.*

> Your petitioner most earnestly implores your immediate protection from the insolence of the rabble, the batteries of *catsticks*, and a painful lingering death.—*Tattler*, No. 134.

CAT-TAILS. Hares-tail rush (*eriophorum vaginatum*). So called from its resemblance to a cat's tail. This name is common alike to England and America. It is used as a material for stuffing bed-ticks.

> The *cat-tails* whiten through the verdant bog ;
> All vivifying Nature does her work.—*Davidson's Poems*, p. 10.

CAT-TAIL GRASS.   Herds grass, or timothy.

CATTLE-RANGE.   In Kentucky, a park.

CATTY-CORNERED.   Diagonally.   In his *Craven Glossary*, Mr. Carr gives the word *cater corner'd*.

CAUCUS.   A private meeting of the leading politicians of a party to agree upon the plans to be pursued in an approaching election.

Gordon's History of the American Revolution, 1788, contains the earliest account of this word.

" The word *caucus*, and its derivative *caucusing*, are often used in Boston.   All my repeated applications to different gentlemen have not furnished me with a satisfactory account of its origin. . . . . . More than fifty years ago, Mr. Samuel Adams's father, and twenty others, one or two from the north end of the town, where all ship-business is carried on, used to meet, make a *caucus*, and lay their plan for introducing certain persons into places of trust and power.   When they had settled it, they separated, and used each their particular influence within his own circle," &c.   Vol. I. p. 240.

" From the above remarks of Dr. Gordon on this word," says Mr. Pickering, " it would seem that these meetings were in some measure under the direction of men concerned in the '*ship business ;*' and I had therefore thought it not improbable that *caucus* might be a corruption of *caulkers'*, the word meetings being understood.   I was afterwards informed that several gentlemen in Salem and Boston believed this to be the origin of the word."

> I'll be a voter, and this is a big character, able to shoulder a steamboat, and carry any candidate that the *caucus* at Baltimore may set up against the people.   What's the people to a *caucus?*   Nothing but a dead ague to an earthquake.—*Crockett's Tour*, p. 206.

On the whole, this may be called a very useful word, the sense being so well understood in every part of the Union.

CAUSEY.   A causeway, or way raised above the natural level

of the ground, by logs, stones, earth, etc., serving as a dry passage over wet ground. This word is seldom used now.

Mr. Church said he would go and fetch his horse back, which was going off the *causey* toward the enemy; but before he got over the *causey*, he saw the enemy run.—*Church's Indian Wars*, 1716.

TO BE A CAUTION. To be a warning. A common expression used in familiar language.

The way the Repealers were used up, *was a caution* to the trinity of O'Connell, Repeal, and Anti-Slavery, when they attempt to interfere with true American citizens.—*New York Herald*.

There's a plaguy sight of folks in America, Major, and the way they swallow down the cheap books *is a caution* to old rags and paper-makers. —*Maj. Downing, May-day in New York*, p. 3.

A large portion of Capt. Marryatt's " Travels of Mons. Violet," is stolen from the New Orleans Picayune; and it will not be surprising if Kendall [the author] lets his sting into this trans-Atlantic robber. He can do it in a way that will *be a caution.*—*Providence Journal*.

The way Mr. Van Buren is a democrat, *is a caution,* all over. He is dyed in the wool, through and through.—*Crockett's Tour*, p. 207.

He was a sneezer that; and when he flourished his long whip-stick, that looked like a fishin'-rod, and yelled like all-possessed, he *was a caution,* that's a fact.—*Sam Slick in England*.

Our route was along the shore of the lake in a northerly direction, and the way the icy blast would come down the bleak shore *was a caution.*—*Hoffman, Winter in the West*, p. 234.

Moses wound up his description of the piano, by saying that the way the dear creeturs could pull music out of it, *was a caution* to hoarse owls.—*Thorpe's Mysteries of the Backwoods*, p. 24.

CAVALLARD. (Sp. *caballardo*.) A term used by the caravans which cross the prairies, to denote a band of horses or mules.

The chef d'œuvre of this Indian's rascality was exhibited in his stealing our whole *cavallard*, consisting of ten head of horses and mules, which he drove to the mountains.—*Scenes in the Rocky Mountains*, p. 80.

TO CAVE IN. Said of the earth which falls down when digging into a bank. Figuratively, to break down; to give up.

At the late dinner, Mr. W—— arose to make a speech, but soon *caved in.*—*Washington Paper*.

The South-western and Western Locos, it is thought, will *cave in*, and finally go for the Treaty [of peace with Mexico], though they talk loud against it now.—*New York Tribune*, March 4, 1848.

The Northern Democrats are *caving in* on the " three million bill ;" they have determined to sacrifice the proviso against slavery ; their temporary firmness, though mostly affected, has already failed.—*N. Y. Tribune.*

CAVESON. (French *caveçon.*) A muzzle for a horse.—*New England.*

> There, Chilion, it is just as I told you. The rake-shame put a *caveson* on him.—*Margaret,* p. 304.

CAVORTIN. (Span. *cavar,* to paw, applied to horses.) A word chiefly used in the Southern States. The following illustrations will show the sense in which it is used :

> There's some monstrous fractious characters down in our beat, and they musn't come a *cavortin* about me when I give orders.—*Major Jones's Courtship,* p. 20.
>
> A whole gang of fellers, and a heap more of young ladies, came ridin' up and reinin' in, and prancin' and *cavortin'.*—*Ibid.* p. 41.
>
> He tossed himself into every attitude which man could assume on horseback. In short, he *cavorted* most magnanimously.—*Georgia Scenes.*
>
> Old Alic had a daughter, that war a most enticin' creatur ; and I seed Tom Settlers *cavortin'* round her like a young buffalo.—*Robb, Squatter Life.*

CENSUS. In the United States, an enumeration of the inhabitants of all the States, taken by order of Congress, to furnish the rule of apportioning the representation among the States, and the number of representatives to which each State is entitled in the Congress ; also, the enumeration of the inhabitants of a State, taken by order of the Legislature.—*Webster.*

CENT. A copper coin of the United States, whose value is the hundredth part of a dollar.—*Webster.*

CHAIR. In the Southern States, this name is given to that kind of one-horse pleasure carriage, which, in the Northern States, is generally called by the old English name, *chaise.*—*Pickering.* The same word, in England, is applied to a vehicle drawn by one horse.

> E'en kings might quit their state, to share
> Contentment and a one-horse *chair.*—*T. Warton.*

TO CHALK OUT. To mark or trace out as with chalk.—*Johnson.* To *chalk out* a plan or proceeding, is to devise or lay out a plan.

His own mind *chalked out* to him the just proportions and measures of behaviour to his fellow creatures.—*South.*

The time falls within the compass here *chalked out* by nature very punctually.—*Woodward, Nat. Hist.*

The Liverpool Times, when speaking of Sir Robert Peel's Tariff, says:

The United States cannot long be insensible to the enlightened views in commercial matters, which English philosophers have *chalked out*, and which English statesmen have carried.—*June* 19, 1846.

CHALK. *Not by a long chalk.* When a person attempts to effect a particular object, in which he fails, we say, " He can't do it *by a long chalk.*"

CHAP. A boy, lad; a fellow.

> For you are to consider these critical *chaps*
> Do not like to be snubb'd; you may venture, perhaps,
> An amendment, where they can see somewhat amiss;
> But may raise their ill blood, if you circulate this.—*Byron, Critical Remarks.*

CHAPARRAL. In Spain, a *chaparral* is a bush of a species of oak. The termination *al* signifies *a place abounding in ;* as, *chaparral,* a place of oak-bushes; *almendral,* an almond orchard; *parral,* a vineyard; *cafetal,* a coffee-plantation, &c. &c.

This word having recently become quite common in our newspapers in consequence of the lamentable war with Mexico, the following description of a *chaparral* was given last year by a correspondent of the New Orleans Picayune, then at Matamoras: It is a series of thickets of various sizes, from one hundred yards to a mile through, with bushes and briars, all covered with thorns, and so closely entwined together as to prevent the passage of anything through larger than a wolf or hare. When they are in the course of a traveller, he must travel around them, sometimes four or five miles before he can make half a mile on his route. In the middle of most of them you will find a small prairie, with numerous beds of prickly pears, the fruit of which is often ventured for by those who are accustomed to its use, and " know the ropes."

CHATTER-BOX. One whose tongue runs incessantly.— *Todd.*

TO CHAW. (Saxon, *ceowan ;* German, *kawen.*) To champ between the teeth ; to masticate ; to chew.—*Johnson. Webster.* This, according to all lexicographers, is the legitimate word, and should be so written and pronounced. Custom and fashion, however, have changed it to *chew,* which is now invariably used among educated people.

> I home returning, fraught with foul despite,
> And *chawing* vengeance all the way I went.—*Spenser, F. Queen.*

> The man who laught but once, to see an ass
> Mumbling to make the cross-grained thistles pass,
> Might laugh again, to see a jury *chaw*
> The prickles of unpalatable law.—*Dryden.*

TO CHAW UP. To use up ; demolish.

> I heerd Tom Jones swar he'd *chaw me up,* if an inch big of me was found in them diggins in the mornin'.—*Robb, Squatter Life,* p. 63.

> Miss Patience smiled, and looked at Joe Cash. Cash's knees trembled. All eyes were upon him. He sweat all over. Miss Patience said she was gratified to hear Mr. Cash was a musician ; she admired people who had a musical taste. Whereupon Cash fell into a chair, as he afterwards observed, *chawed-up.*—*Thorpe's Backwoods,* p. 28.

CHAY. A chaise. Common in New England, where these vehicles are chiefly used.

CHEBACCO BOAT. Probably the same as the *xebec* of the Mediterranean. A description of fishing vessel employed in the Newfoundland fisheries. They are also called Pinksterns. The word may be a corruption of *chedabucto,* the name of a bay in Nova Scotia, from which vessels are fitted out for fishing.—*Adams on the Fisheries,* p. 220.

CHECKERS, or chequers. The common name for the game which is called *draughts* in England. Mr. Todd, in his edition of Johnson's Dictionary, has the word *checker,* a *chessboard,* or *draught-board.*

> The *checkers,* at this time a common sign of a public house, was originally intended, I should suppose, for a kind of draught-board, called tables, and showed that there the game might be played.—*Brand, Popular Antiquities.*

CHEQUER BERRY. (*Mitchella.*) A handsome little creeping plant, the only species of its genus.—*Bigelow's Flora Bostoniensis.*

CHEWINK. The ground robin; so called from its peculiar note. On Long Island it is called the *towhee goldfinch ;* and in Louisiana, from its plumpness, *grasset.—Natural History of New York.*

CHICKABIDDY. A young chicken. Used also as a term of endearment to children, and not peculiar to America.

> I'm a *chickabiddy* see,
> Take me now, now, now.—*Nursery Rhymes.*

CHICKADEE. The black-cap titmouse, a very common little bird, so called from its peculiar note.—*Audubon, Ornith.*

CHICKAREE. (Lat. *sciurus Hudsonii.*) The popular name of the red squirrel.

CHICKEN-FIXINGS. In the Western States, a chicken fricassee.

> We trotted on very fast, in the assurance of rapidly approaching a snug breakfast of *chicken-fixins*, eggs, ham-doins, and corn slap-jacks.—*Carlton's New Purchase*, Vol. II. p. 69.
>
> The remainder of the breakfast table [in New York], was filled up with some warmed-up old hen, called *chicken-fixings*.—*Rubio, Travels in the U. S.*
>
> I guess I'll order supper. What shall it be, corn-bread and common-doins, or wheat bread and *chicken-fixins?—Sam Slick*, 3d Ser. p. 118.

CHICKWEED. (*Stellaria media.*) A very common plant, growing in every situation, even between the bricks in the side-walks.—*Bigelow's Flora.*

CHIGRES (commonly called *jiggers*). Sand-fleas, which penetrate under the skin of the feet, but particularly the toes. As soon as they accomplish this, an itching sensation is felt; when the *chigre* ought to be removed by means of a needle breaking the skin. No uneasiness follows; but should this precaution be neglected, the insect breeds in the toe, and produces sometimes dreadful sores. These insects are found in the West Indies, and the adjacent shores of the Gulf of Mexico.—*Carmichael's West Indies*, Vol. I. p. 188.

TO CHINK. To rattle, jingle; to cause to rattle or jingle. Used especially of the noise of coin shaken in a purse or bag.

> At length the busy time begins,
> " Come, neighbours, we must wag."—
> The money *chinks*, down drop the chins,
> Each lugging out his bag.—*Cowper, Yearly Distress.*

He *chinks* his purse, and takes his seat of state ;
With ready quills the dedicators wait.—*Pope, Dunciad.*

CHINK. A term for money ; used in various parts of **England,** as well as in the United States.—*Grose. Forby.*

Though never so much a good huswife doth care
That such as do labour have husbandly fare ;
Yet feed them and cram them, till purse do lack *chink*,
'No spoon-meat, no bellyfull,' laborers think.
Kill crow, pie, and cadow, rook, buzzard, and raven,
Or else go desire them to seek a new haven.—*Tusser, Husbandry.*

When joyful tidings reach the ear,
And dad retires by Heaven's commands,
To leave his *chink* to better hands.—*Somerville, Fables,* 2.

CHINKING AND DAUBING. The process of filling with clay the interstices between the logs of houses in the new countries. In the north of England it is called *daubing and filling.*—*Moor.*

Our log-house quarters, however, were closely *chinked and daubed,* and we passed a comfortable night.—*Kendall's Santa Fé Exp.* Vol. I. p. 28.

The interstices of the log wall were " *chinked* "—the *chinking* being large chips and small slabs, dipping like strata of rocks in geology ; and the *daubing,* yellow clay ferociously splashed in soft by the hand of the architect.—*Carlton, The New Purchase,* Vol. I. p. 61.

CHINQUIPIN. (*Castanea pumila.*) A species of chestnut. The water *chinquipin* of the United States, is the ' sacred bean ' of the Egyptians (*nelumbo nucifera*).

CHIP. " A chip of the old block," a child who either in person or sentiments resembles his father.—*Grose.* A common expression in the United States.

I was introduced to about one hundred young gentlemen, true *chips of the old block,* ready to be rocked in the old cradle of liberty [Faneuil Hall].
—*Crockett, Tour,* p. 66.

Hosses and galls, Sam, are all you think of (says father). You're a *chip of the old block,* my boy. There ain't nothin' like 'em, is there ?—
Sam Slick in England, ch. 19.

CHIPMUK, or **CHIPMONK.** The popular name for the striped squirrel (*sciurus striatus*). Probably an Indian word.

The children were never tired of watching the vagaries of the little *chipmonk* as he glanced from branch to branch.—*Mrs. Clavers's Forest Life.*

CHARIVARI. (Commonly pronounced *shevaree.*) A custom

which prevails in those parts of the United States which were originally colonized by the French, as Louisiana, some parts of Florida, Missouri and Michigan. It is also common in Canada. When an unequal match takes place, when an old bachelor marries, or a widow or widower soon after the death of his or her partner, their friends assemble on the night of the marriage, with tin horns, bells, pans, kettles, and everything that will make a discordant noise. This "serenade" is continued night after night until the party is invited in and handsomely entertained.—See *Callithumpian.*

TO CHIRK. To make a peculiar noise by placing the tongue against the roof of the mouth, to urge horses on.

He painted a horse-rider cheering and *chirking* his horse, yet reining him hard as he champed upon his bit.—*Holland, Pliny,* B. 35, ch. 10.

CHIRK. Lively; cheerful; in good spirits; in a comfortable state; as when one enquires about a sick person, it is said, he is *chirk.* The word is wholly lost except in New England.—*Webster.* It is doubtless derived from the old verb *to chirk* (Ang. Sax. *cercian*), i. e. to chirp, which is found in old English writers.

Afore I had mixed a second glass of switchel, up they came, and the General looked as *chirk* and lively as a skipper.—*Maj. Downing's Letters.*

TO CHIRRUP. To cheer up; to quicken or animate a horse by a peculiar sound or chuck, or by chirping. It is not noticed by Johnson, though it is common in England.

The mustang needs but a *chirrup* to arouse him, and set him off at a gate which an eastern horse can hardly attain.—*Prairie Scenes.*

TO CHISEL. To cheat; the same as *to gouge.* A Western word.

CHITLINS. Fragments; small pieces.

While I was in this way rolling in clover, they were tearing my character all to *chitlins* up at home.—*Robb, Squatter Life.*

TO CHOCK. To put a wedge under a thing to prevent its moving; as, to 'chock a barrel,' i. e. to put a piece of wood or something under it to keep it steady.

CHOCK UP. Close, tight; said of a thing which fits closely to another.

When the bells ring, the wood-work thereof shaketh and gapeth, and exactly *chocketh* into the joynts again.—*Fuller's Worthies.*

CHOCK-FULL. Entirely full; see also *Chuck-full.*

I'm *chock-full* of genius and running over, *said Pigwiggin.—Neal.*

By this time we got into a shabby looking street, *chock-full* of hogs and boys.—*Maj. Downing, May-day in N. York.*

CHOKE-CHERRY. The popular name of the *prunus Virginiana,* so called from its astringent properties.

TO CHOKE OFF. A figurative expression, borrowed from the act of choking a dog to make him loosen his hold. To arrest or stop a public speaker when addressing an audience, is called *choking him off.* This is done by shuffling the feet, applauding where applause is uncalled for, by putting questions of order, or in any way impeding or arresting the speaker. It is sometimes resorted to when a tedious man occupies the floor, and when vacant seats do not satisfy him that no one will listen to him.

I spent a couple of hours in the House, amused by watching the dignified proceedings of our Representatives. The operation of "*choking off*" a speaker was very funny, and reminded me of the lawless conduct of fighting school-boys.—*New York Express,* Feb. 21, 1848.

TO CHOMP. To champ; to chew loudly and greedily. *Champ* is an old word, but not often used now, except in connection with a horse.—*Forby's Vocab. Chomp* is quite common in New England, and is applied to persons who eat fast or greedily.

A tobacco-pipe happened to break in my mouth; and the pieces left such a delicious roughness on my tongue, that I *champed* up the remaining part.—*Spectator.*

CHOO! *interj.* (Old Fr. *chou.*) Used to drive away pigs and set dogs upon them. Cotgrave says, " *Chou* is a voice wherewith we drive away pullein." And why not pigs?—*Forby's Vocab.*

CHOP. A Chinese word signifying quality; first introduced by mariners in the China trade, but which has now become common in all our sea-ports. Originally the word was only applied to silks, teas, or other goods from China; now it is applied to everything, for we hear of first *chop* teas, first *chop* tobacco, and first *chop* potatoes.

A smart little hoss, says I, you are a cleaning of; he looks like a *first chop* article.—*Sam Slick in England,* ch. 2.

I went to board at a famous establishment in Broadway, where sundry young merchants of the *first chop* were wont to board.—*Perils of Pearl St.*

TO CHOP. " To chop and change," is an old expression which we still make use of, meaning to change often, to shift about. It is also applied particularly to the wind, so that a ' chopping wind or sea' is one that is constantly changing its direction.

For we are not as many are, which *choppe* and chaunge with the worde of God; but even oute of purenesse, and by the power of God, and in the syghte of God, so spake we of Chryste.—*Bible,* 1551. 2 Cor. ch. 2.

> Long time you fought, redoubl'd battery bore,
> But after all, against yourself you swore—
> Your former self, for ev'ry hour you form,
> Is *chopp'd* and chang'd, like winds before a storm.—*Dryden.*

The wind was at south-east, south-south-east, and south; which brought in a short *chopping* sea.—*Cook's Voyages.*

CHORE, or CHAR. The word *chore,* which has been thought peculiar to America, is without doubt the same as the word *char,* which, both as a verb and a noun, may be found in the English dictionaries. " In America," says Mr. Webster, " this word denotes small work of a domestic kind, as distinguished from the principal work of the day. It is generally used in the plural, *chores,* which includes the daily or occasional business of feeding cattle and other animals, preparing fuel, sweeping the house, cleaning furniture," &c.

According to the English dictionaries, *char* means work done by the day, a single job or task ; from which has arisen the words *char-man* and *char-woman.* In Jenning's Glossary of Somersetshire, is the word *choor,* a job, or any dirty household work ; *choor-woman,* a woman who goes out to do any kind of odd or dirty work. In Wiltshire, it is pronounced *cheare.* This as well as the Somerset word is very near the American word in pronunciation.

That *char* is *charr'd,* as the good woman said when she had hang'd her husband (i. e. The business is done).—*Ray's Proverbs.*

His hands to woll, and arras worke, and woman's *chares* he laide.— *Warner's Albion's England,* ii. 11.

> A woman, and commanded
> By such poor passion as the maid that milkes
> And does the meanest *chares.*—*Shakspeare, Ant. & Cleop.*

> *Bob.* I approve
> Your counsel, and will practise it; bazi los manos;
> Here's two *cheares chear'd.*—*Beaum. and Fletch. Love's Cure.*

> The harvest done, to *char*-work did aspire;
> Meat, drink, and two pence, were her daily hire.—*Dryden, Theoc.*

Get three or four *char-women* to attend you constantly in the kitchen, whom you pay only with broken meat, a few coals, and all the cinders.—*Swift.*

Hunting cattle is a dreadful *chore!* remarked one of our neighbors, after threading the country for three weeks in search of his best ox.—*Mrs. Clavers's Forest Life*, Vol. I. p. 142.

I'm looking for a place where I can board and do *chores* myself.—*Mrs. Clavers, A New Home,* p. 87.

Radney comes down, and milks the cow, and does some of my other little *chores.*—*Margaret,* p. 388.

Girl hunting is certainly among our most formidable *chores.*—*Mrs Kirkland, Western Clearings.*

The editor of the Boston Daily Star, in relinquishing his editorial charge, gives the following notice :

> Any one wishing corn hoed, gardens weeded, wood sawed, coal pitched in, paragraphs written, or small ' *chores*' done with dispatch and on reasonable terms, will please make immediate application to the retiring editor.

TO CHOUSE. The origin of this word has been referred by Etymologists to the Swed. *kiusa,* the old French *joucher,* and the Dutch *kosen,* to cozen. Skinner, and Gifford in his notes to Ben Jonson, think the word is of Turkish origin, from *chiaous,* a messenger of the Turkish emperor. A messenger, or *chiaous,* from he Grand Senior, in 1609, committed a gross fraud upon the Turkish and Persian merchants resident in England, by cheating them out of £4,000. Hence from the notoriety of the circumstance, to *chiaous, chause,* or *chouse,* was to do as this man did, i. e. to cheat, or defraud. This origin of the word seems quite probable; for the name of a notorious defaulter in New York has recently been used in a similar manner.

> *Dap.* And I will tell, then ? By this hand of flesh,
> Would it might never write good court-hand more,
> If I discover. What do you think of me,
> That I am a *chiause?*

Fac. What's that? The Turk was here,
As one would say, do you think that I'm a Turk?—*Ben Jonson.*

Freedom and zeal have *chous'd* you o'er and o'er;
Pray give us leave to bubble you once more.—*Dryden.*

For which reason, however they may pretend *to chouse* one another, they make but very awkward rogues; and their dislike to each other is seldom so well dissembled but it is suspected.—*Tattler,* No. 213.

CHOWDER. A favorite dish in New England, made of fish, pork, onions, and biscuit, stewed together. Picnic parties to the sea-shore generally have a dish of *chowder,* prepared by themselves in some grove near the beach, from fish caught at the same time. Grose describes the same as a sea dish.

CHRISTIANIZATION. This substantive is to be found occasionally in our religious publications. The verb *to christianize,* which is in the dictionaries, is in use among the English writers; but the substantive is never employed by them.—*Pickering, Vocab.*

CHUCK-FULL. Entirely full. Common in familiar language as well as *chock-full,* which see for other examples.

[At dinner] the sole labor of the attendants was to keep the plates *chuck-full* of something.—*Carlton, The New Purchase,* Vol. I. p. 181.

I'll throw that in, to make *chuck-full* the "measure of the country's glory."—*Crockett, Tour,* p. 86.

CHUCK-WILL'S-WIDOW. The common name of a bird of the whippoorwill family (*caprimulgus Caroniensis*). Mr. Audubon says, "About the middle of March, the forests of Louisiana are heard to echo with the well-known notes of this interesting bird. No sooner has the sun disappeared, and the nocturnal insects emerge from their burrows, than the sound '*Chuck-Will's-widow,*' repeated with great clearness and power, six or seven times in as many seconds, strike the ear."—*Ornithology,* Vol. I. p. 273.

TO CHUCK. To throw, by a quick and dexterous motion, a short distance.—*Dorsetshire Glossary. Todd.* This word is noticed by Dr. Webster as a vulgarism.

To *chuck* under the chin, is a common expression here as in England.

Who loves no hurries, routs, or din;
But gently *chucks* her husband's chin.—*Fawkes, The Vicar's Reply.*

CHUCKLEHEAD. A fool. Not peculiar to America.

CHUFFY. Blunt; surly; clownish.—*Todd's Johnson.*

In New England, says Mr. Webster, this word expresses that displeasure which causes a swelling or surly look and grumbling, rather than heat and violent expressions of anger.

The etymology of this word is uncertain. Shakspeare applied the term *fat chuffs* to rich and avaricious people, as a term of contempt. In old French, *joffu* has a similar meaning to our *chuffy.*

> The goddess drank; a *chuffy* lad was by,
> Who saw the liquor with a grudging eye,
> And grinning, cries, She's greedy more than dry.—*Ovid. Met.* b. v.

CHUK. A noise made in calling swine. Always repeated at least three times.

CHUM. A chamber-mate; a term used in colleges.—*Junius Etymologicon.* We sometimes use it in the more extended meaning of companion, fellow.

> A young student laid a wager with his *chum*, that the Dean was at that instant smoking his pipe.—*Philips's Life and Poems*, p. 13.

> I am again your petitioner in behalf of that great *chum* of literature, Samuel Johnson.—*Smollett, in Boswell.*

CHUNK. A short, thick piece of wood.—*Webster.* This word is provincial in the South of England.—*Ray. Grose.*

It is sometimes called a *junk* in this country, as well as in England. The English dictionaries have the word *chump,* which is used in the same sense as *chunk.* This word is also applied to other things beside wood. I have often heard the butchers in market say, a '*chunk* of beef.'

CHUNKY. Short and thick. This word, formed from *chunk,* is only used when speaking of the stature of a person, as 'a *chunky* little fellow.'

CHURCH. Mr. Pickering has the following remarks on this word: " A church, as *a body of persons,* is distinguished in New England, from a *congregation,* by the privileges which the former in general reserve to themselves of receiving exclusively in that church the sacrament and baptism, in consequence of their having publicly declared their assent to the creed which that church maintains. Marriage, burial, and public worship, are open to the members of the congregation at large, according to the forms and methods employed in each church; as are also catechizing for children and visits to the sick."—*Vocabulary*.

CIRCUMBENDIBUS. A circuitous, roundabout way, either of getting to a spot, or of telling a story.—*Holloway's Dic. of Prov.*

CISCO. The popular name of a fish of the herring kind which abounds in Lake Ontario, particularly in Chaumont Bay at the east end, where thousands of barrels are annually caught and salted. I do not find this name mentioned by Dr. DeKay, in his work on the fishes of New York, in the Natural History of the State.

TO CITIZENIZE. To make a citizen; to admit to the rank and privileges of a citizen.—*Webster*. Rarely used.

> Talleyrand was *citizenized* in Pennsylvania, when there in the form of an emigrant.—*T. Pickering*.

CITESS. This word, Mr. Pickering says, as well as *citizeness,* was used during the first years of the French Revolution, as a translation of the revolutionary title, *citoyenne ;* but it has for several years been wholly disused.—*Pickering's Vocabulary*.

> It is unnecessary to recite the discussions on this word by the British critics, the Quarterly Review, &c. as it was never adopted into our language. Dr. Webster and the English lexicographers have the word *citess* in their dictionaries, but only in the sense of " a city woman."

CIVISM. Love of country; patriotism.—*Webster*. This, like the preceding word, is one of the productions of the French Revolution; and, though frequently used several years ago, is now obsolete here as well as in France.—*Pickering's Vocabulary*.

CIVILIZEE. A civilized man; one advanced in civilization.

> The barbarian likes his seraglio ; the *civilizee* admires the institution of marriage. The barbarian likes a roving, wandering life ; the *civilizee* likes his home and fireside.—*New York Observer*.

CLAM. The popular name of a very common shell-fish. " As happy as a clam at high water," is a very common expression in those parts of the coast of New England where clams are found.

> Many sorts of fishes are caught on the coast; lobsters, crabs, *clams*, limpits, and periwinkles.—*Fordyce, Statistics of Scotland.*

> Tak thee a fiddle or a flute to jest,—
> Thy clouted cloak, thy scrip and *clam-schells*,—
> Cleik on thy cross, and fair on into France.—*Kennedy, Evergreen*, p. 74.

CLAM-BAKE.   The baking of clams on those parts of the sea-coast where they abound, particularly in Massachusetts and Rhode Island, furnishes one of the most popular dishes as well as most favorite amusements of which the people partake. The method of baking is as follows : A cavity is dug in the earth, about eighteen inches deep, which is lined with round stones. On this a fire is made ; and when the stones are sufficiently heated, a bushel or more of clams (according to the number of the persons who are to partake of the feast) is thrown upon them.   On this is put a layer of rock-weed gathered from the beach, and over this a second layer of sea-weed.   This prevents the escape of the steam, and preserves the sweetness of the clams.   Clams baked in this manner, are preferred to those cooked in the usual way in the kitchen.

Parties of ten or twenty persons, of both sexes, are the most common.   Often they extend to a hundred, when other amusements are added ; and on one occasion, that of a grand political mass-meeting in favor of Gen. Harrison on the 4th of July, 1840, nearly 10,000 persons assembled in Rhode Island, for whom a *clambake* and *chowder* were prepared. This was probably the greatest feast of the kind that ever took place in New England.

CLAM-SHELL.   The lips, or mouth.   There is a common though vulgar expression in New England, of " Shut your *clam-shell*," that is, Shut your mouth, hold. your tongue.

TO CLAP, or CLAP DOWN.   To set down ; charge to one's account.

> If a man be highly commended, we think him sufficiently lessened, if we *clap* one sin, or folly, or infirmity, into his account.—*Jeremy Taylor, Holy Living.*

CLAPBOARD.   A thin narrow board, used to cover the sides of houses, and placed so as to overlap the one below it.   In

England, according to Bailey's Dictionary, a *clapboard* is a thin board formed ready for the cooper's use, in order to make casks or vessels.

CLAPE. The common name of the golden-winged woodpecker in the State of New York. Dr. DeKay thinks it "a provincial word, introduced by the early English colonists." It is elsewhere called High-hole, Yucker, Flicker, Wake-up, and Pigeon woodpecker; in Louisiana, *Pique bois jaune.*—*Nat. Hist. of New York.*

CLAP-TRAP. An artifice for attracting applause. Used chiefly in theatrical or political language.

> The managers have resorted to all sorts of mummery and *clap-trap*, for the purpose, forsooth, of promoting American manufactures.—*Newspaper.*

> There are those in both parties in Congress, who will vote down the *clap-traps* of such men as A—— in the Senate.—*N. Y. Tribune.*

CLEAN, *adv.* (Ang. Sax. *clæne.*) Quite; perfectly; fully; completely. This sense is now little used.—*Johnson.* In the United States it is common among the illiterate, but rarely seen in composition.

> Spenser labored to restore such good and natural English words as have been a long time out of use, and almost *cleane* disherited.—*Obs. on Spenser's Fairy Queen, by E. K.*

> The people passed *clean* over Jordan.—*Joshua*, iii. 17.

> Is his mercy *clean* gone for ever?—*Psalm* lxxvii. 8.

> Let's hew his limbs till they be *clean* consum'd.—*Shakspeare, Titus And.*

> Since the prelates were made lords and nobles, there is no work done. They hawk, they hunt, they dice, they pastime with gallant gentlemen. And by their lording and loitering, preaching and ploughing is *clean* gone. —*Bp. Latimer's Sermon of the Plough.*

> He gave him a kick that sent him *clean* over the fence, into the Deacon's potato-patch.—*Maj. Downing's Letters*, p. 23.

THE CLEAN THING. A low expression denoting propriety, or what is honorable.

> It is admitted, that sending out ships to plunder your neighbor or adversary, is as much as mere words in making war. I don't like it. It isn't the *clean thing.*—*Crockett, Tour*, p. 193.

CLEARING. A place or tract of land cleared of wood for cultivation; a common use of the word in America.—*Webster.*

> After we reached the boundaries of the *clearing* and plunged into the

timbered land, this heat was exchanged for a grotto-like coolness.—*Mrs. Clavers's Forest Life*, Vol. I. p. 64.

TO CLEAR OUT.   To take oneself off; to depart, decamp. A vulgar expression.

> This thing of man-worship I am a stranger to; I don't like it ; it taints every action of life ; it is like a skunk getting into a house—long after he has *cleared out*, you smell him in every room and closet, from the cellar to the garret.—*Crockett's Speech, Tour*, p. 74.

> I turned round and was going *to clear out*. But says he, Stop Mister !— *Maj. Downing's May-day in N. Y.*

CLEAVAGE.   The state of being cleft.

> The color of the stone is darker than appears to be natural in a fresh *cleavage.*—*Schoolcraft in Amer. Ethnolog. Trans.* Vol. I.

CLEVER.   Good-natured, obliging. In *Great Britain*, a *clever* man is a dextrous man, one who performs an act with skill or address.   Mr. Pickering says, that " in speaking of any- thing but *man*, we use the word much as the English do. We say a *clever* horse, &c. ; and it is common to see in the London newspapers advertisements in this form—" To be sold, a *clever* gray gelding," &c.

> A choice of ministers and diplomatic agents constitutes one of the most important duties of a wise and *clever* monarch.—*Millengen, Mind and Mat- ter*, 1847.

> The landlord of the hotel was a very *clever* man, and made me feel quite at home in his house.—*Crockett's Tour down East*, p. 22.

CLEVERLY.   " This is much used in some parts of New England instead of *well* or *very well*.   In answer to the com- mon salutation, *How do you do ?* we often hear, I am *cleverly*. It is also applied to other things, as well as to health, and means either adroitly or exactly ; according to the case."— *Pickering*.   It is also used in the sense of fairly, completely. Dr. Johnson's definition is dextrously, fitly, handsomely.

> The landlord comes to me, as soon as I was *cleverly* up this morning, looking full of importance.—*Sam Slick in England*, ch. 8.

CLEVERNESS.   Mildness or agreeableness of disposition ; obligingness ; good nature. Used in New England.—*Webster*.

CLEVIS, or CLEVY.   An iron bent to the form of an ox-bow, with the two ends perforated to receive a pin, used on the end of a cart-neap, to hold the chain of the forward horse or oxen; or, a draft-iron on a plow. Provincial in New England.—*Webster*.

CLINCHER. A smart reply.—*Bailey's Dictionary*. This word is used in a figurative sense. To *clinch* a nail, renders it immovable and impossible to draw out. So a *clincher* in conversation is an argument or opinion which cannot be controverted.

> That was supposed to be a *clincher*, even in New England [that Gen. Jackson was in favor of a judicious tariff], until after power lifted him above the opposition of the supporters of a tariff.—*Crockett's Speech*.

CLING.
CLING-STONE. } A variety of the peach in which the flesh adheres, or clings, firmly to the stone. When the stone readily separates from the peach, they are called *free-stones*. The word *peach* frequently designates the free-stone, while the others are called *clings*.

CLINKER. A vitrified substance found in grates and stoves where anthracite coal has been burnt.

CLIP. A blow or stroke with the hand; as, He hit him a *clip*.—*Webster*. Provincial in New England and the Northern States.

TO CLIP. To cut, to run. Probably from the motion of a bird's wings, which strike or beat the air as it flies or runs.

> Some falcon stoops at what her eye designed,
> And, with her eagerness the quarry missed,
> Straight flies at check, and *clips it* down the wind.—*Dryden*.

> I hadn't much time left, ... so I ran all the way, right down as hard as I could *clip*.—*Sam Slick in England*, ch. 8.

CLIPPER. A cutter; a small schooner with raking masts, built and rigged with a view to fast sailing. Larger vessels are sometimes built after their model, when they are called *clipper-built*.

CLITCHY. Clammy, sticky, glutinous.—*Pickering's Vocab*. Mr. Pickering says, he has " heard this word used in a few instances by old people in New England; but it is rarely heard." In Devonshire, in England, the word *clatchy*, meaning the same, is provincial. In Holloway's Dictionary of Provincialisms is *clit*, clayey, stiff, applied to the soil.

CLOCKMUTCH. (Dutch, *klapmuts*, a night-cap.) A woman's cap composed of three pieces,—a straight centre one, from the forehead to the neck, with two side pieces. A New York term.

CLODHOPPER. A rustic ; a clown.

> Jack, are ye turned *clodhopper* at last ?—*St. Ronan's Well.*
>
> She was not much concerned to do justice to one whom she had known as a *clodhopper.*—*Mrs. Clavers's Forest Life.*

CLOSE-FISTED. Stingy, mean. Common in various dialects of England.—*Halliwell.*

> Ibycus is a carking, griping, *close-fisted* fellow.—*Bp. Berkeley's Maxims.*

CLOSURE. A shutting up ; a closing.—*Pickering.*

> Very soon after the *closure* of imports, I did submit to the consideration of the Senate a proposition.—*J. Q. Adams,* 1808.

Mr. Pickering observes that he has never seen this word, except in the extract quoted, in any American publication. Dr. Johnson gives the word in the same sense from the French *closure,* and cites several authorities for its use.

> And must so break with men on such occasions, as to leave room and to prepare the way for a *closure.*—*Atterbury, Sermons,* IV. 330.

CLOTHES-HORSE. A frame-work for hanging clothes on to dry after they have been washed and ironed, in the form of an opening screen.

CLOTHIER. A man whose occupation is to full and dress cloth.—*Webster.* In England, a *clothier* is one who makes clothes, which seems to have been the meaning of the word in the time of Shakspeare. Mr. Pickering observes, that " although we use *clothier* for *fuller,* yet the place where the cloth is cleansed and dressed, is called a *fulling-mill.*"

CLOUT. A blow or stroke, most properly with the fist. This word is found in several old English authors, and in the Shropshire and Dorset glossaries of the present day. With us it is a vulgar expression frequently heard.

> The kynges sone, kene and proud,
> Gaf king Richard swylke a ner *clout*
> That the fyr of his heyen sprong.—*Richard Cœur de Lyon,* v. 768.
>
> The late queene of Spaine took off one of her chapines, and *clouted* Olivarez about the noddle with it.—*Howell, Familiar Letters.*

CLOUT-NAILS. Short nails with large heads for the soles of strong shoes.—*Hartshorne's Shropshire.*

CLUB-TAIL. (Genus *alosa.*) The common shad, the fatter portion of which have the tail swollen, and on the coast of Carolina where they are taken, are called *club-tails.*—*Nat. Hist. N. Y.*

COAL-HOD. A kettle for carrying coals to the fire. More frequently called, as in England, a *coal-scuttle.* Mr. Halliwell in his Dic. of Prov. has *coal-hood,* which is used in the eastern part of England.

CONCERN. In mercantile usage, an establishment or firm for the transaction of business. It is provincial in England, and denotes a small estate ; from whence our use of the word is derived.

TO CONDUCT, instead of ' to conduct *oneself ;*' leaving out the reflexive pronoun. This offensive barbarism is happily confined to New England, where it is common both in speech and writing. Like many other expressions in the same predicament, it has received the tacit sanction of Dr. Webster, himself a New England man.

CONGRESS. This term is applied by us especially to three differently constituted bodies of representatives of the people that have succeeded each other in the government of the country. The first is the *Continental Congress,* assembled in 1774, and which conducted the national affairs until near the close of the Revolution. The second is the *Federal Congress,* which met under the Articles of Confederation, adopted March, 1781, and ruled the country till 1789. The third is the *Congress of the United States,* which first met under the Constitution, on the 4th of March, 1789.

Mr. Pickering remarks, that English writers, in speaking of American affairs, generally say, " *the* Congress," using the article. Such was formerly our own practice ; but in the course of time it has acquired with us the force of a proper name, so that we now speak of *Congress,* as the English do of *Parliament.* When the present Constitution was adopted, the usage was still fluctuating, as the following examples will show :

The Congress shall assemble at least once in every year ; and such meeting shall be on the first Monday in December, unless they shall by law appoint a different day.—*Art.* I. *Sec.* 4.

Neither House, during the session of *Congress*, shall, without the consent of the other, adjourn for more than three days, nor to any other place than that in which the two Houses shall be sitting.—*Art.* I. *Sec.* 5.

CONGRESSIONAL. Pertaining to a congress, or to the Congress of the United States ; as, Congressional debates.— *Webster.*

The *congressional* institution of Amphictyons, in Greece.—*Barton.*

The conflict between *Congressional* and State authority, originated with the creation of those authorities.—*Marshall, Life of Washington.*

CONSCIENCE. Reason, reasonableness. A common use of the word in familiar language, even in the best society ; as, " What *in conscience* are you doing that for ?" " That's enough, *in all conscience.*"

Half a dozen fools are, *in all conscience,* as many as you should require. —*Swift.*

CONSIDERABLE, used adverbially for *very,* is a common vulgarism.

A body has to stir about *considerable* smart in this country, to make a livin', I tell you.—*Sam Slick in England,* ch. 6.

CONSIDERABLE. This word is frequently used in the following manner in the Northern States, " He is *considerable* of a surveyor ;" " *Considerable* of it may be found in the country." —*Pickering.*

CONSOCIATION. Fellowship or union of churches by their pastors and delegates ; a meeting of the pastors and de gates of a number of congregational churches, for aiding a supporting each other, and forming an advisory council in ecclesiastical affairs.—*Webster. Consociation* of churches, is their mutual and solemn agreement to exercise communio in such acts as aforesaid, amongst themselves, with specia reference to those churches, &c.—*Result of the Synod,* 1662.

TO CONSOCIATE. To unite in an assembly or convention, as pastors and messengers or delegates of churches.—*Webster.*

CONSTABLE. Mr. Webster notices the following distinction between the application of this word in England and in the

United States: "In England there are high constables, petty constables and constables of London. In the United States constables are town or city officers of the peace, with powers similar to those possessed by the constables in Great Britain." Mr. Pickering says that "in many of the cities, boroughs, and other local jurisdictions in England, they have peace officers called *constables*, whose powers are not materially, if at all, different from those of our constables."

CONSTANTS. Quantities or data that are constant, not subject to variation or change.

> The perceptions of a public are as subtle-sighted, as its passions are blind. . . . . . These involuntary opinions of people at large explain themselves and are vindicated by events, and form at last the *constants* of human understanding.—*Washington and the Generals of the Amer. Rev.*

CONSTITUTED AUTHORITIES. The officers of government collectively, in a kingdom, city, town, &c. This expression has been adopted by some of our writers from the vocabulary of the French Revolution.—*Pickering.*

> Neither could he perceive danger to liberty except from the *constituted authorities*, and especially from the executive.—*Marshall's Washington.*

CONSTITUTIONALITY. Used chiefly in political language, to signify the state of being agreeable to the constitution of a State or of the United States.

> The argument upon this question has naturally divided itself into two parts, the one of *expediency*, the other of *constitutionality.*—*Debates in Congress in* 1802.

> The judges of the supreme court of the United States have the power of determining the *constitutionality* of laws.—*Webster.*

CONTEMPLATION. The phrase, "I have it in *contemplation* to do so and so," instead of "I intend," &c., has been transferred by us, like many other Latinisms of a like kind, from the language of books to that of common conversation.

TO CONVENE. This is used in some parts of New England in a very strange sense; that is, *to be convenient*, fit, or suitable. Ex. This road will *convene* the public; i. e. will be convenient for the public. The word, however, is used only by the illiterate.—*Pickering.* I have never heard the phrase.

COODIES. The name of a political sect in the State of New

York, which originated in the year 1814. At that time a series of well written articles appeared in a New York paper signed *Abimeleck Coody.* He professed to be a mechanic. " He was a federalist, and addressed himself principally to the party to which he belonged. He endeavored to show the impropriety of opposing the war, and urged them to come forward in defence of their country. He also attacked De Witt Clinton with great severity." The writer was ascertained to be Mr. Gulian C. Verplanck, then as now distinguished for his talents. He was replied to by a writer under the signature of " A Traveller," said to be De Witt Clinton, who thus speaks of this party : " The political sect called the *Coodies,* of hybrid nature, is composed of the combined spawn of federalism and Jacobinism, and generated in the venomous passions of disappointment and revenge, without any definite character ; neither fish, nor flesh, nor bird, nor beast, but a non-descript made up of ' all monstrous, all prodigious things.' "—*Hammond's Political Hist. of N. Y.*

COOKEY. A cake. A Dutch word used in New York.

> Mrs. Child thinks it best to let the little dears have their own way in everything, and not to give them more *cookies* than they, the dear children, deem requisite.—*Sunday Mercury, N. Y.*

COLD AS PRESBYTERIAN CHARITY. I know not the origin of this saying, and am not aware that there is less charity in this sect than in any other.

> They are as *cold as Presbyterian charity,* and mean enough to put the sun in eclipse, are the English.—*Sam Slick in England,* ch. 7.

> Why, Colonel, the river is pretty considerable for a run ; but the water is *cool as Presbyterian charity.*—*Crockett's Tour,* p. 145.

COOL-WORT. (*Tiarella cordifolia.*) The popular name of an herb, the properties of which are diuretic and tonic. It is prepared by the Shakers.

COOL. Used in familiar language, in England and in the United States, in the sense of impudent. Punch gives a dialogue between the years 1845 and 1846, which is a good illustration of this word.

> 1846. " Come, answer me, answer me, old Forty-Five,
> As an old man a young should answer ;

I've much to learn ; so, while you're alive,
Just resolve me this point if you can, sir :
What's the *coolest* thing that you've seen, Forty-Five ?"

1845. " Why, PEEL, when he said to Commons and Peers
That the Income Tax should end in three years—
That was, p'raps, the *coolest* thing."

1846. " What else have you seen that was *cool,* Forty-Five ?"

1845. " Why, Jonathan threatening that he'd annex us,
If we grumbled about his annexing Texas—
That struck me as rather *cool.*"

COON. A popular contraction of the word *raccoon.* A nick-name applied to those who belong to the Whig party.

COONERY. Whiggery. See preceding article.

Democrats of the old Bay State, one charge more and the work is thoroughly done. " Once more to the breach," and you will hear the shouts of Democratic victory, and the lamentations of the vanquished. We must achieve a victory—the people must be free—'*coonery* must fall with all its corruptions and abominations, never more to rise. Democrats —freemen !—keep your council-fires burning brightly. Let no one remain listless, or doubt, or hesitate; " push on your columns," rout the '*coons,* beat them, overwhelm them, and let the welkin ring with the soul-stirring tidings that Massachusetts is safe—is free from the curse of whiggery.— *Boston Post.*

COPPER. A copper coin, especially a British halfpenny or American cent.

My friends filled my pockets with *coppers.*—*Franklin.*

COOT. The name of a small water-fowl. It is often applied by us to a stupid person, as, " He is a poor *coot.*" Mr. Halliwell notices the old proverbial saying, " As stupid as a *coot.*"

Little *coot !* don't you know the Bible is the best book in the world ?— *Margaret,* p. 134.

CORDUROY ROAD. A road or causeway constructed with logs laid together over swamps or marshy places. When properly finished, earth is thrown between them, by which the road is made smooth ; but in newly settled parts of the United States, they are left uncovered, and thereby are extremely rough and bad to pass over with a carriage. Sometimes they extend many miles. They derive their name from their resemblance to a species of ribbed velvet, called *corduroy.*

CORK. The steel points fixed under the shoes of horses, in the winter, to prevent them from falling on the ice. It is the same thing that in Johnson's and other Dictionaries is called *frost-nails.—Pickering*. In Ash's Dictionary, the word *corking* is defined, " turning up the heels of a horse's shoes."

CORN. Maize, throughout the United States, is called *Indian corn*, or simply *corn*. What is called corn in England, is here called grain ; or rather *corn* is considered in England a general term, and is applied to grain used for bread.

CORN-BLADE. The leaf of the maize. Corn-blades are collected and used as fodder in some of the Southern States.—*Webster*.

CORN-BROOM. Brooms made from the tops of a species of corn, called *broom-corn*.

CORN COCKLE. The popular name of a purple-flowering plant (genus *agrostemma*).—*Bigelow's Flora Bostoniensis*.

CORN-CRACKER. The nickname for a native of Kentucky.

CORN-DODGER. A kind of cake made of Indian corn, and baked very hard.

> The Sucker State, the country of vast projected rail-roads, good *corn-dodgers*, splendid banking-houses, and poor currency.—*Robb, Squatter Life*, p. 28.

CORNED. Drunk. Used in the same sense in England.

CORN-JUICE. Whisky. A western term.

> I informed the old fellow that Tom wanted a fight; and as he was too full of *corn-juice* to cut carefully, I didn't want to take advantage of him.—*Robb, Squatter Life*.

CORN-STALK. A stalk of corn, particularly the stalk of the maize.—*Webster*. Mr. Pickering says, " the farmers of New England use this term, and more frequently the simple term *stalks*, to denote the upper part of the stalks of Indian corn (above the ear), which is cut off while green, and then dried to make fodder for their cattle."—*Vocabulary*.

CORN-SHUCKING. An occasion on which a farmer invites the young people of the neighborhood to his house or barn, to aid him in stripping the shucks from his corn.—See *Husking*.

The young people were all gibberin', and talkin', and laughin', as if they'd been to a *corn-shuckin'*, more'n to a meetin' house.—*Major Jones.*

TO CORNER. To corner a person, is to get the advantage of him in an argument, as though he were physically placed in a corner from which he could not escape.

TO CORNER. A Wall street word, which means to take advantage of a person in a peculiar manner.

"There is a large class of brokers in Wall street, who sometimes control a good deal of money, and who make speculation their business. These generally unite in squads, for the purpose of *cornering*—which means, that they first get the control of some particular stock, and then, by making a great many contracts on time, compel the parties to pay whatever difference they choose, or rather what they can get; for they sometimes overrate the purse of those they contract with."—*A Week in Wall Street*, p. 81.

The remarkable fluctuations in the Stock market, are chiefly the result of a successful *cornering* operation.—*N. Y. Journal of Com.*

The Erie Rail-road *cornering* has been a very unfortunate affair for many members of the board.—*N. Y. Herald.*

COSEY. Snug, comfortable. Dr. Jamieson calls it a Scottish word.

Then cannie in some *cozie* place
They close the day.—*Burns.*

To keep you *cosie* in a hoord,
This hunger I with ease endur'd.—*Allan Ramsay.*

All observers of primitive life, know that animals, quadruped and biped too, have from time immemorial indulged in the *cozey* habits of burrowing in the earth, huddling close together, &c.—*London Athenæum.*

Mid comforts abounding, well clothed and well fed,
The bright fire surrounding, or *cosy* in bed.—*N. Y. Tribune*, 1845.

COSSET. A lamb brought up without the aid of the dam.—*Bailey.* This word is used in New England in this sense, and also to signify a favorite or darling.

And if thou wilt bewayle my woful teene,
I shall give thee yond *cosset* for thy payne.—*Spenser.*

TO COTTON TO. 'To cotton to one,' is to take a liking to him; to fancy him; literally *to stick to him*, as cotton would. The term is very common at the South and West.

> There were divers queer characters on board the steamer, with whom Tom was a great favorite; but none of them *cotton'd* to him more kindly than an elderly hoosier, from the innermost depths of Indiana.—*Field.*

COTTONOCRACY. A term applied to the Boston manufacturers, especially by the 'Boston Whig' newspaper.

COUNTERACTION. Mr. Pickering has noticed this word in his Vocabulary, and observes that it is sometimes, though rarely, used by American writers in the following manner : "He prevailed over his enemies by the *counteraction* (counteracting) of their designs."

No English lexicographer had then noticed the word. The dictionaries of Mr. Todd and Dr. Webster now contain it. The definition of the latter is, " Action in opposition ; hindrance."

> The beauties of writing are . . . . . . wholly subject to the imagination, and do not force their effects upon a mind pre-occupied by unfavorable sentiments, nor overcome the *counteraction* of a false principle or of stubborn partiality.—*Johnson, Rambler*, No. 93.

> All the eloquence and fire of Demosthenes could not rouse the Athenian people to a timely dread or steady *counteraction* of the formidable plans of Philip.—*British Critic*, Vol. I. p. 51.

COUNTRIFIED. Rustic, rude. A word of recent formation in our language, and in no dictionary, but now much used.— *Todd.* It is in the last edition of Webster.

> The inhabitants of Herefordshire, though near the metropolis, are as likely to be *countrified* as persons living at a greater distance from town. —*Grose's Local Proverbs.*

> This man pretty soon espied a *countrified* looking fellow whom he approached.—*Perils of Pearl Street.*

> Mr. Seymour Bullitt brought the message to Caroline ; and such a splendid fellow—but then, old recollections, and such a *countrified* name.—*Mrs. Clavers's Forest Life.*

COUNTY. " In speaking of *counties*," says Mr. Pickering, " the names of which are composed of the word *shire*, we say the *county* of *Hampshire*, the *county* of *Berkshire*, &c. In England they would say, either *Hampshire* or *Berkshire* simply, without the word *county* ; or, the county of *Hants*, the county of *Berks*, &c. The word *shire* of itself, as everybody knows, means *county* ; and in one instance (in Massachusetts), this latter word is used instead of *shire*, as a part of the *name*—'The county of *Duke's County*.'"—*Pickering's Vocabulary*.

COUPON. A financial term, which, together with the practice, is borrowed from France. In the United States, the certificates of State stocks drawing interest are accompanied by coupons, which are small tickets attached to the certificates. At each term when the interest falls due, one of these *coupons* is cut off (whence the name); and this being presented to the State treasurer, or to a bank designated by him, entitles the holder to receive the interest. The *coupons* attached to the bonds of some of the Western States have not been cut off for several years.

COURT. In New England this word is applied to a legislative body composed of a House of Representatives and a Senate; as, the *General Court* of Massachusetts.

COVERCLIP. (Genus *achirus*. Lacipede.) The popular name of the sole, a fish common in the waters of New York. *Calico* is another name for it.—*Nat. Hist. of New York*.

COVERLID. A bed-quilt, counterpane.

> Her bed consisted of a mattress of beech-leaves spread on the floor, with tow and wool *coverlids*.—*Margaret*, p. 12.

TO COW. To depress with fear.—*Webster*.

> By reason of their frequent revolts, they have drawn upon them the pressure of war so often, that it seems to have somewhat *cowed* their spirits.—*Howell, Vocal Forest*.

> For when men by their wives are *cow'd*,
> Their horns of course are understood.—*Hudibras*.

> The Spaniards ought to defend the Despena Perros; but they go to the plains to be beaten, and thus *cow* the troops, who would otherwise defend themselves in the mountains.—*Wellington's Despatches*, No. 346.

> They were in a terrible sweat all the time, for fear I'd get *cowed*, and wouldn't succeed in my oration.—*Maj. Jones's Courtship*, p. 154.

COWBERRY. (*Vaccinium vitis idæa*.) A plant resembling the common cranberry, but larger. It is found on certain mountains in Massachusetts.—*Bigelow's Flora Bostoniensis*.

COWHIDE. A particular kind of whip made of raw hide; it is also called a *raw-hide*.

TO COWHIDE. To flog with a cowhide.

To be out of office and in for a *cowhiding*, is not a pleasant change from eight dollars a day and all sorts of nice pickings. [Alluding to an ex-member of Congress.]—*N. Y. Tribune.*

COW-LICK. A twist, or wreathing in the hair, which, in a calf, might be supposed to have been licked by the cow out of its natural position.—*Forby's Vocabulary.* In some parts of England it is called a *calf-lick.*

COW PARSNIP. (*Heracleum latanum.*) The popular name of a plant classed among the herbs prepared by the ' Shakers,' as containing properties carminative and diuretic.

CRACK. This word is used by us as in England to signify most famous, best. Thus we speak of " a *crack* ship," " a *crack* officer," &c.

CRACKED. Crazy.

To such an extent may these discrepancies be carried, that a man of genius is considered *cracked*;—an expression which led Dr. Parr to say, " that such men were decidedly *cracked*, but that the crack let in the light."—*Millengen, Mind and Matter,* 1847.

CRACKER, or FIRE-CRACKER. A little paper cylinder filled with powder or combustible matter, imported from China. It receives its name from the noise it produces in exploding. In England it is called a *squib.*

CRACKER. A small hard biscuit; probably so called from the noise it emits when broken. The word seems to be peculiar to the United States.

The following anecdote was related to me by the Hon. Albert Gallatin. When travelling in England with his family in 1818, he stopped at an inn and ordered a servant to bring them some " crackers and cheese " for their lunch. But what was his surprise to see the servant return with a plate of cheese and half a dozen *nut-crackers !*

CRACKER. A nick-name applied to the backwoodsmen of Georgia.

CRACKLINGS. Cinders, the remains of a wood fire. A word used in the Southern States.

When it lightened so, she said t'other eend of the world was afire, and we'd all be burnt to *cracklin's* before morning.—*Maj. Jones's Courtship.*

TO CRACK UP. *To crack,* i. e. to brag or boast, is a verb common in old authors, from Chaucer downwards, and still provincial in the north of England. We use it only in the phrase *to crack up.* Thus we say, " A Yankee is sure to *crack up* his own country ;" " That is not what it is *cracked up* to be."

CRADLE-SCYTHE. Called also simply *cradle.* It consists of a common scythe with a light frame-work attached, corresponding in form with the scythe. It is used for cutting grain instead of the sickle ; and by the regular manner in which it lays the grain, it enables the farmer to perform treble the work that could be accomplished with the latter implement.

TO CRADLE. ' To *cradle* grain,' is to cut it in the same manner that grass is cut or mowed, with the implement above described.

> The operation of *cradling* is worth a journey to see. The sickle may be more classical ; but it cannot compare in beauty with the swaying, regular motion of the cradle.—*Mrs. Clavers's Western Clearings.*

CRAMBO. A diversion in which one gives a word, to which another finds a rhyme. If the same word is repeated, a forfeit is demanded. It was also a term in drinking, as appears from Dekker.—*Halliwell's Arch. and Prov. Dictionary.*

This amusement is practised in New York, where it is also called, " What is my thought like ?"

CRAMP-BARK. (*Viburnum oxycoccus.*) The popular name of a medicinal plant ; its properties anti-spasmodic. It bears a fruit intensely acid. In New England it is called the tree cranberry.

CRANES-BILL. (*Geranium maculatum.*) The popular name of a native geranium, which grows about fences and the edges of woods.—*Bigelow.*

CRASH. A coarse kind of linen cloth used for towels.

> Margaret was up early in the morning. She washed at the cistern, and wiped herself on a coarse *crash* towel.—*Margaret.* p. 17.

CRAWFISH. (*Astacus Bartonii.*) The popular name of the fresh-water lobster.

CREATURE. In the plural number this word is in very com-

mon use among farmers as a general term for horses, oxen,
&c. Ex. The *creatures* will be put into the pasture to-day.—
Pickering.

> The owners or claimers of any such *creatures* [i. e. " swine, neat cattle,
> horses, or sheep"], impounded as aforesaid, shall pay the fees, &c.—*Pro-*
> *vincial Laws of Mass.—Statute* 10, *Wm. III.*

CREEK. A small river or brook. In New York, the Western
States, and in Canada, a small stream is called a *creek ;* in
New England it is called a brook. The term is incorrectly
applied ; as its original signification, according to the dictionaries, is a small port, a bay or cove ; from which it has gradually been extended to small rivers. In New England, the
old English sense of the word is retained.

CREEPMOUSE. A familiar word in the nursery. Mr. Hal-
liwell calls it a term of endearment still in use in England.
He refers to *Palsgrave's Acolastus,* 1540.—*Archaic and Prov.*
Dic.

CREOLE. In the West Indies and Spanish America, a native
of those countries descended from European ancestors.—
Webster. But this is not its only acceptation.

"The word Creole," says Mrs. Carmichael, "means a
native of a West India colony, whether he be black, white,
or of the colored population."—*West Indies,* p. 17.

In the United States, we generally understand a Creole to
have a portion of black blood in him ; which may be explained by the following extract :

"Children born in the West Indies from Spaniards," says
an anonymous author, "are called *creollos,* which signifies,
one born in that country ; which word was made by the
negroes, for so they call their own children, born in those
parts, and thereby distinguish them from those born in Guinea."
—*History of Peru,* p. 397.

CREVASSE. (French, a disruption.) The breaking away of
the embankments or levees on the lower Mississippi, by a
pressure of the water. See *Levee.*

CRIMANY. Interj. of sudden surprise.—*Forby's Vocabulary.*
Used in low language in the United States.

CRISS-CROSS. A mark in the shape of a cross; especially that of those who cannot sign their own names. Mr. Hartshorne, in his interesting work on British Antiquities, has the following account of this custom: "From the earliest period since the introduction of Christianity, it has been customary for those who were unable to sign their names, to affix the mark of a cross instead. Witred, king of Kent, decreed, anno 694, that no deed was valid unless it bore this stamp. It is constantly observable in the charters of the Anglo-Saxon and Spanish kings, and in all those documents which recite property bequeathed for ecclesiastical purposes. Numerous proofs still remain, which testify that royal and noble personages were not ashamed to confess their ignorance of letters. Witred acknowledges, in a charter printed in Spelman's Concilia, p. 193, that on account of his ignorance of letters, he had confirmed what he had dictated by the signature of a cross.—*Salopia Antiqua*, p. 379.

CRISS-CROSS. A game played on slates by children, at school.

CROCK. (Ang. Sax. *crocca*.) An earthen vessel, a pot or pitcher, a cup.—*Webster*.
This old English word is still used in some parts of New England.

> Therefore the vulgar did about him flocke,
> Like foolish flies into an honey *crocke*.—*Spenser, F. Queen*, V. 2. 33.

CROCK. The black of a pot; smut, the dust of soot or coal. This word is provincial in various parts of England, and is there used precisely as in the United States.

> At one of our frolics, there was one long-haired fellow, looked as though he'd been among the pots and kettles, and got a great gob of *crock* on his upper lip.—*Lafayette Chron.*

TO CROCK. To black with soot or other matter collected from combustion, or to black with the coloring matter of cloth.—*Webster*.
Provincial in Norfolk and Suffolk, England.

CROCKY. Smutty. Used alike in England and America.

CROOKED AS A VIRGINIA FENCE. A phrase applied to anything very crooked; and figuratively to persons of a stubborn temper, who are difficult to manage, that is, to make straight or correct. The fences of Virginia are mostly made of rails, laid up in a zig-zag manner, and of course very crooked.

CROSS-EYE. That sort of squint, by which both the eyes turn towards the nose, so that the rays, in passing to the eye, cross each other.—*Forby's Vocabulary.* Since the newly discovered means of restoring and curing *squint* or *cross eyes* by a surgical operation, the scientific name of *strabismus* has been substituted.

CROSS-FOX. A fox whose color is between the common reddish-yellow and the silver-gray, having on its back a black cross. These animals are rare, and their skins command a high price.

CROSS-GRAINED. Perverse; troublesome; vexatious.— *Johnson.*

> Or what the plague did Juno mean,
> That *cross-grain'd,* peevish, scolding queen,
> That scratching, caterwauling puss,
> To use an honest fellow thus ?—*Cotton, Virgil Travestie,* B. 1.

CROSS-PATCH. An ill-tempered person. A vulgar word, used alike in England and America. *Patch* is a very old word of contempt in Shakspeare and other writers. At the present day it is used only in connection with *cross.*

CROTCHETY. Whimsical; fanciful.

CROTCHICAL. Cross, perverse, peevish. A common colloquial word in New England.

> You never see such a *crotchical* old critter as he is. He flies right off the handle for nothin'.—*Sam Slick in England.*

CROW-BAR. A bar of iron sharpened at one end, used as a lever. In England it is called a *crow ;* though *crow-bar* is " a name often *provincially* applied to an iron *crow* or lever." —*Rees's Cyclopedia.*

CROWSFEET. The wrinkles under the eyes, or from the outward corners of the eyes, which are the effect of age, and which are thought to resemble the impression of the feet of crows.—*Todd.*

> So long mote ye liven, and all proud,
> Till *crowes feet* growin under your eie,
> And send you then a mirrour in to prie.—*Chaucer, Troil. and Cres.*

And by myne eye the *crow* his *claw* doth wright.—*Spenser, Shepherd's Cal. Dec.*

CRULLER. (Dutch *kruller*, a curler.) A cake made of a strip of sweetened dough, boiled in lard, the two ends of which are twisted or *curled* together. The New Yorkers have inherited the name and the thing from the Dutch.

TO CRUNCH, or CRAUNCH. To crush with the teeth; to chew with violence and noise.—*Webster.* Mr. Hartshorne notices this word among the provincialisms of England, and gives early examples of its use. It is sometimes pronounced *cranch.—Shropshire Glossary.*

> To *cranchen* ous and al our kynde.—*Piers Ploughman.*
>
> She can *cranch*
> A sack of small coale! eat you lime and hair.—*Ben Jonson.*
>
> The flames seized and *crunched* the gnarled top of an old oak.—*Margaret,* p. 350.

CRUSTY. Sturdy; morose; snappish. A low word.—*Johnson.* Provincial in various parts of England. A word, says Dr. Webster, used in families, but not deemed elegant.

> Maister Reef, are ye so *crusty?—Preston's King Cambyses,* O. P. (1562.)

TO CRY. To publish the bans of marriage in church, formerly so called in the interior of New England.

> I should not be surprised if they were *cried* next Sabbath.—*Margaret.*

CUBBY-HOLE, or CUBBY-HOUSE. A snug place for a child. Common to various English dialects.—*Barnes's Dorset Glossary.* Seldom heard with us except among children.

TO CUDDLE, or CUDDLE UP. To hug or fondle. So used in some parts of England.

CULTIVABLE. Capable of being tilled or cultivated.—*Webster.* This word, Mr. Todd says, has lately been adopted by English writers on agriculture.

CUNNUCK. A name applied to Canadians by the people in the Northern States.

CURB-STONE. A border to a pavement, consisting of stone slabs set on edge, which form the separation between it and the carriage-way.

> I will sit here as unmoved as a *curb-stone.—Margaret,* p. 82.

Here the watchman struck his club against the *curb-stone.—Pickings from the Picayune*, p. 31.

CURIOUS. "This word is often heard in New England among the common farmers, in the sense of *excellent*, or *peculiarly excellent ;* as in these expressions : 'These are *curious* apples ;' 'this is *curious* cider,' &c. This use of the word is hardly known in our seaport towns."—*Pickering.*

CUPALO, for *cupola*, is a common error of pronunciation. It is also a very old one, as appears from the following passage :

> Whose roof of copper shineth so,
> It excells Saint Peter's *cupello.—Political Ballads*, 1660.

CURMUDGEON. An avaricious, churlish fellow ; a miser. In explaining this word, Dr. Ash made a ludicrous mistake, from his ignorance of the French language. He took the word from Johnson, who derives it from *cœur-méchant*, and who gives as his authority an "unknown correspondent." As these words immediately followed the French, Dr. Ash supposed them to be the English of *cœur-méchant*, and accordingly says, "*Curmudgeon*, from the French *cœur*, unknown, and *méchant*, correspondent."

> A man's way of living is commended, because he will give any rate for it ; and a man will give any rate, rather than pass for a poor wretch, or a penurious *curmudgeon.—Locke.*

TO CURRY FAVOR. To seek or gain favor by flattery, caresses, kindness, or officious civilities.—*Webster.*

> He judged them still over-abjectly to fawn upon the heathens, and to *curry favor* with infidels.—*Hooker.*
>
> This humor succeeded so well with the puppy, that an ass would go the same way to work to *curry favor* for himself.—*L'Estrange.*

CUSTOMABLE. Subject to the payment of duties called *customs.* (*Law of Massachusetts.*)—*Webster.*

The word *dutiable* is much used among merchants in New York, but I never heard the word *customable*.

CUSTOMER. A cant term, meaning one that one has to deal with, that one comes across. In use, it answers nearly to the word "fellow," and is often heard in such phrases as "He's a *queer customer*," "You'll find him an *ugly customer*."

What is any home game, or the wild boar of which British Lloyds write so pleasantly, when compared with such a *customer* as the buffalo bull?—*London Athenæum*, No. 195.

CUT. A quantity of yarn, twelve of which make what is called a *hank* or *skein.* Common in England and America.

TO CUT. This word is in general use in conversation in the United States, and is employed precisely in the same way as defined by Grose in the following passage:

"To renounce acquaintance with any one, is to *cut* him. There are several species of the cut; such as the cut direct, the cut indirect, the cut sublime, the cut infernal, &c. The *cut direct* is to start across the street, at the approach of the obnoxious person, in order to avoid him. The *cut indirect* is to look another way, and pass without appearing to observe him. The *cut sublime* is to admire the top of King's College Chapel, or the beauty of the passing clouds, till he is out of sight. The *cut infernal* is to analyze the arrangement of your shoe-strings, for the same purpose."—*Class. Dict. Vulgar Tongue.*

> The Bankrupt,
> With his debts' schedule large, and no assets,
> By all his decent friends entirely *cut.*—*London Bench.*

> "I'll *cut your acquaintance*," said Harry to John,
> In a furious passion, "if thus you go on!"
> "To *cut my acquaintance*," said John, "you are free,—
> *Cut* them all, if you please, so you do not *cut* me!"—*Mrs. Osgood.*

CUT. An infliction; a rebuke.

A thief, arrested at Baltimore and brought to this city in the steamboat Ohio this morning, escaped from the officer, who was lying fast asleep, just as the boat reached the wharf. The unkindest *cut* of all was, that he walked off with the officer's baggage.—*N. Y. Tribune.*

TO CUT. To run; to be off.

The whole was borne along upon the shoulders of men who contrived to *cut* along with their burdens at a great pace.—*Eöthen*, p. 158.

The wedding over, about twelve o'clock the company began to *cut* hom, all of 'em just as sober as when they came.—*Major Jones's Courtship.*

Down *cut* the mesmeric professor, through the bar-room; out I *cut* after him; over went the stove in the rush after us.—*Field, Western Tales.*

TO CUT AND RUN. To be off; to be gone.—*Holloway's Prov. Dictionary.*

Originally a nautical term. To cut the cable of a ship and make sail without waiting to weigh anchor.—*Falconer's Dictionary.*

> They caught the leaders [in the Canadian revolt] and hanged them ; tho' most of the first chop men *cut and run,* as usual in such cases.—*Sam Slick.*

TO CUT DIRT. To run ; to go fast. A vulgar expression, probably derived from the quick motion of a horse or carriage over a country road, which makes the dirt fly.

> Well, the way the cow *cut dirt* was cautionary ; she cleared stumps, ditches, windfalls, and everything.—*Sam Slick in England,* ch. 18.

> Now *cut dirt!* screamed I ; and, Jehu Gineral Jackson ! if he didn't make a straight shirt-tail for the door, may I never make another pass.— *Field, Western Tales,* p. 132.

TO CUT DIDOES. Synonymous with *to cut capers,* i. e. to be frolicksome.

> Who ever heerd them Italian singers recitin' their jabber, showin' their teeth, and *cuttin' didoes* at a private concert.—*S. Slick in England,* ch. 15.

> Watchman ! take that 'ere feller to the watchhouse ; he comes here a *cutting up his didoes* every night.—*Pickings from the Picayune,* p. 86.

TO CUT A DASH. In modern colloquial speech, to make a great show ; to make a figure.—*Johnson.* A fashionable or gaily dressed lady in walking the streets is often said *to cut a dash.* In Scotland, according to Dr. Jamieson, the phrase to *cast a dash,* to make a great figure or a splendid appearance, is used.

> Bowden wi' pride o' simmer gloss,
> To *cast a dash* at Reikie's cross ?—*Fergusson's Poems,* 2. 32.

> I saw the curl of his waving lash
>   And the glance of his knowing eye,
> And I knew that he thought he was *cutting a dash,*
>   As his steed went thundering by.—*O. W. Holmes's Poems,* p. 105.

TO CUT A CAPER. (Italian, *tagliar le capriole.*) The act of dancing in a frolicksome manner.—*Todd.* We use it also in a more general sense. Thus, of a person who conducts himself in a strange or ridiculous manner, we would say, " He *cuts* strange *capers.*"

> Flimnap, the treasurer, is allowed to *cut a caper* on the straight rope, at least an inch higher than any other lord in the whole empire.—*Gulliver's Travels.*

A man may appear learned, without talking sentences; as in his ordinary gesture he discovers he can dance, though he does not *cut capers*.—*Spectator*, No. 4.

TO CUT A FIGURE. To make an appearance, either good or bad.

We are not as much surprised at the poor *figure cut* by the Whigs in the committees of the House, as by the position of some of the Loco Focos.—*N. Y. Tribune*, Dec. 10, 1845.

TO CUT OUT. To supersede one in the affections of another. A familiar expression in common use: " Miss A was engaged to be married to Mr. B; but Mr. C *cut him out*." It also means to supplant or excel in any way.

TO CUT OUT OF. To cheat, deprive of.

Having been *cut out of* my speech in Congress, by the " previous question."—*Crockett, Tour*, p. 24.

THE CUT OF HIS JIB. The form of his profile, the cast of his countenance; as, " I knew him by the *cut of his jib*." A nautical vulgarism.

CUT AND COME AGAIN. An expression in vulgar language, implying that having *cut* as much as you pleased, you may *come again;* in other words, plenty; no lack; always a supply.—*Todd*.

TO CUT UP. To criticise with severity; as, he was severely *cut up* in the newspapers.

Some correspondent asked you, just for a change, to give " a spicy and personal *cut up* of an author."—*N. Y. Literary World*, Vol. iii. p. 125.

TO CUT UP. To wound one's feelings, to mortify. Ex. " He was very much *cut up* by the neglect of his friend."

CUT AND DRIED. Ready made.

I am for John C. Calhoun for the presidency; and will not go for Mr. Van Buren, the man attempted to be forced upon us by this *cut-and-dried* party machinery.—*Mr. Walsh's Speech. Com. Adv.* Sept. 1847.

TO CUT UP SHINES. To cut capers, play tricks.

A wild bull of the prairies was *cutting up shines* at no great distance, tearing up the sod with hoofs and horns.—*Knickerbocker Mag.*

What have these men been doing? asked the Recorder.

Oh, they were *cutting up* all kinds of *shines;* knocking over the ashes barrels, shying stones at lamps, kicking at doors, and disturbing the peace of the whole city.—*Pickings from the Picayune*, p. 61.

TO CUT A SWATHE. The same as *to cut a dash*.

The expression is generally applied to a person walking who is gaily dressed, and has a pompous air or swagger in his or her gait. In allusion to the sweeping motion of a scythe, when *cutting a swathe*.

TO CUT SHORT. To hinder from proceeding by sudden interruption.—*Johnson*.

> The judge *cut* off the counsel very *short*.—*Bacon*.

> Achilles *cut* him *short*; and thus replied,
> My worth, allow'd in words, is in effect denied.—*Dryden*.

TO CUT STICK, or TO CUT ONE'S STICK. To be off; to leave immediately and go with all speed. A vulgar expression, and often heard. It is also provincial in England.

> Dinner is over. It's time for the ladies to *cut stick*.—*Sam Slick in England*, ch. 15.

> If ever you see her and she begins that way, up hat and *cut stick*, double quick.—*Ibid*. ch. 29.

TO CUT UNDER. To undersell in price.—*New York*.

CUT-OFF. Passages cut by the great Western rivers, particularly the Mississippi, affording new channels, and thus forming islands. These *cut-offs* are constantly made.

> When the Mississippi, in making its *cut-offs*, is ploughing its way through the virgin soil, there float upon the top of this destroying tide, thousands of trees that covered the land and lined its curving banks.—*Thorpe's Backwoods*, p. 172.

TO DRAW CUTS. A common way of deciding by lot, is to place several slips of paper or straws, of different length, in a person's hand, which are drawn out by others. This is called *drawing cuts*. The practice and the term are very old, as will be seen by the following examples:

> And ther they were at a long stryf which of them shulde go; and so at last they acorded and sware, and made promyse before all the company, that they shulde *drawe cuttes*, and he that shulde have the *longest strawe* shulde go forthe, and the other abyde.—*Lord Berners, Froissart Cronycle*, Vol. I. p. 288.

> My lady Zelmane, and my daughter Mopsa may *draw cuts*, and the shortest cut speak first.—*Sidney*.

CUT-GRASS. (*Leersia oryzoides*.) The common name of a

species of grass, with leaves exceedingly rough backward, so as to cut the hands if drawn across them.—*Bigelow's Flora Bostoniensis.*

CUTE. (An abbreviation of *acute.*) Sharp; cunning; acute. It is provincial in various parts of England. In New England it is a common colloquialism, though never used by educated people.

> Now, says I, I'm goin' to show you about as *cute* a thing as you've seen in many a day.—*Maj. Downing's Letters,* p. 214.

> Mr. Marcy was a right *cute,* cunning sort of a man; but in that correspondence Gen. Taylor showed himself able to defend himself against the fire in the rear.—*Mr. Gentry's Remarks at the Taylor Meeting in N. Y.*

> He had a pair of bright twinkling eyes, that gave an air of extreme *cuteness* to his physiognomy.—*Knickerbocker Mag.* Aug. 1845.

CUTTER. A one horse sleigh.

> And then—we'll go sleighing, in warm raiment clad,
> With fine horses neighing as if they were glad.
> The shining bells jingle, the swift *cutter* flies,
> And if our ears tingle, no matter; who cries?—*N. Y. Tribune.*

CUTTOES. (French *couteau,* a knife.) A large knife used in olden times in New England.

> There were no knives and forks, and the family helped themselves on wooden plates, with *cuttoes.*—*Margaret,* p. 10.

CYPRESS-BRAKE. A basin-shaped depression of land near the margin of shallow, sluggish bayous, into which the superabundant waters find their way. In these places are vast accumulations of fallen cypress-trees, which have been accumulating for ages. These are called *cypress-brakes.*—*Dickeson on the Cypress Timber of Louisiana.*

D.

DAB, or DABSTER. One who is expert in anything; a proficient. A vulgar colloquialism in England and America.

> One writer excels at a plan, or title-page; another works away at the body of the book; and the third is a *dab* at an index.—*Goldsmith.*

> He's sich a *dabster* at a plough,
> Few match'd him nigh or far.—*Essex Dialect Poems.*

DADDOCKS. The heart or body of a tree thoroughly rotten. —*Ash*.

This old word is not noticed by Johnson, Todd, or Webster. It is introduced by Mr. Worcester in his new dictionary.

> The great red *daddocks* lay in the green pastures, where they had lain year after year, crumbling away, and sending forth innumerable forms of vegetable life.—*Margaret*, p. 215.

DAD, or DADDY. Old and very common words for *father*.

> I was never so bethumpt with words
> Since first I call'd my brother's father *dad.*—*Shakspeare*.

DAMAGE. The pay or return for service rendered; the cost of any thing. "What's the *damage?*" i. e. What's the cost?

> Many thanks, but I must pay the *damage*, and will thank you to tell me the amount of the engraving.—*Lord Byron to Murray*, Let. 114.

DANDER. Scurf; dandruff.

DANDER. *To get one's dander up*, is to get into a passion.

This word is noticed in Barnes's Dorset Glossary. Halliwell says it is common in various English dialects.

> The Department of State did not keep back the letters of Mr. Rives, in which he boasts that he had outwitted the French. Well, this sort of *put up the dander* of the French.—*Crockett, Tour*, p. 198.

> As we looked at the immense strength of the Northumberland's mast, we could not help thinking that Neptune must have his *dander* considerably *raised* before he could carry it away.—*N. Y. Com. Adv.*

> I felt my *dander risin'* when the impertinent cuss went and tuck a seat along side of Miss Mary, and she begun to smile and talk with him as pleasin' as could be.—*Maj. Jones's Courtship*, p. 77.

> The fire and fury that blazed in her eye gave ocular evidence of her *dander being up.*—*Pickings from the New Orleans Picayune,* p. 163.

DARKY. A common term for a negro.

DARNED. A substitute for the profane word *damned*, and generally called a Yankeeism. It is used, however, in England.

> If e'er their jars they've made yu feel,
>   This gude adwise you'll call;
> For sich warmin's gripe—or I'll be *darned*
>   'Twood soon make ye sing small.—*Essex Dialect, Noakes and Styles.*

> " Buttermilk, by Jingo," exclaimed the disappointed pedagogue. Saint Jingo was the only saint, and a " *darnation*," or " *darn you*," were the only

oaths, his puritan education ever allowed him to use.—*Cooper, Satanstoe,* Vol. I. p. 68.

TO DAWDLE. To loiter, to lounge, especially over one's work. A word much used by women.

> Come, some evening, and *dawdle* over a dish of tea with me.—*Johnson's Letters.*

> Looking out of the window, I can see a dozen of these industrious burghers, *dawdling* about a bar-room opposite.—*Hoffman, Winter in the West,* Let. 35.

A DAWDLE. In women's language, one who loiters over his or her work.

TO DEACON A CALF, is to knock it in the head as soon as it is born.—*Connecticut.*

DEADENING. In newly settled parts of the West, where it is designed to make a " clearing," some of the trees are cut down ; the others are girdled, or *deadened*, as they say. If the majority of trees are thus girdled, the field is called *a deadening,*—otherwise it is a clearing.—*Carlton, The New Purchase,* Vol I. p. 240.

DEAD. This word is vulgarly used in the sense of utter, complete. Ex. " A *dead* beat," i. e. a complete beating ; " a *dead* shave, or a *dead* suck," i. e. an utter swindle ; " *dead* ripe," fully ripe.

DEAD-ALIVE. Dull, inactive, moping.—*Barnes's Dorset Glossary.* We often hear the expression, " He is a *dead-alive* sort of a man."

DEAD AS A DOOR NAIL. Utterly, completely dead. The figure is that of a nail driven into wood, and, therefore, perfectly immovable ; the word *door* is used for the sake of the alliteration. It is sometimes changed with us into the less appropriate phrase, " As dead as a *hammer.*"

> For James, the gentil, suggeth in his bokes,
> That faith without fact ys febelere than nouht,
> And *dead as a door nayle.*—*Piers Ploughman,* p. 22.

> If I do not leave you all as *dead as a door nail,* I pray God I may never eat grass more.—*Shakspeare, Henry VI.* p. 2.

DEAR ME, or **DEARY ME.** An exclamation of surprise, used in the same sense as " Oh dear !"

DEATH. To *be death for*, or *go one's death for* a thing, is to be in favor of it or pursue it to the last extremity.

> I'm *death* for the 'Mug,' Mr. Bloater.—*Mathews, Puffer Hopkins.*

DECEDENT. A deceased person.—*Laws of Pennsylvania.*

DECENT. Tolerable; middling; fair.

DECENTLY. Tolerably; fairly.

> The greater part of the pieces it contains may be said to be very *decently* written.—*Edinburgh Review*, Vol. I. p. 426.

DECLENSION. " We sometimes see this word used in the newspapers, in speaking of a person's declining to be a candidate for office. Ex. In consequence of a *declension* of our candidate, we shall be obliged to vote for a new one.—*Pickering.*

TO DEED. To convey or transfer by deed. A popular use of the word in America; as, he *deeded* all his estate to his eldest son.—*Webster.*

TO A DEGREE. To a great extent. An expression common in all parts of the country.

> We learn that the situation of the inhabitants was distressing *to a degree.*—*Charleston, S. C. Gaz.* Aug. 10, 1813.

DEL. The common abbreviation for Delaware.

DEMIJOHN. A glass vessel or bottle, with a large body and small neck, protected and strengthened by a covering of wicker-work. Mr. Webster derives it from the French *dame-jeanne*, but gives no further explanation. I met the word in *Niebuhr's Travels in Arabia* :

> But we imprudently put our wine into great flasks, called in the East *damasjanes*, and large enough each of them to contain twenty ordinary bottles.—Vol. I. p. 169.

This induced the belief that the word was *Arabic ;* but, on referring to the Arabic dictionary, no such word could be found. I made inquiry of several philologists, none of whom could give its origin. One day I asked a Frenchman who dealt in wines, why the French called them *dame-jeannes ?* He replied at once, that they were invented in France at a time when large hoop-dresses were worn at court, and from the resemblance of those large bottles to the small waists and

full dresses of the ladies, they were called *dame-jeannes*, i. e.
Lady Janes.

DEMORALIZATION. The act of subverting or corrupting
morals; destruction of moral principles.—*Webster.* A word
of modern origin, but of very extensive use, which, says Mr.
D'Israeli, "was the invention of horrid Capuchin Chabot."

> *Demoralization* is a long, hard word, which has lately been a good deal
> intruded upon us, as expressive of the change that has taken place lately,
> not only in the actual morals or manners of the lower orders of people, but
> in their *feelings.*—*Arch. Nares, Heraldic Anomalies*, p. 218.

> The cause [of the crimes of the Creoles] is to be found in the existence
> of Slavery; and the inevitable *demoralization* which this accursed practice
> produces, is not checked by any system of religious instruction.—*London
> Quarterly Rev.* Nov. 1810.

TO DEMORALIZE. To corrupt and undermine the morals
of; to destroy or lessen the effect of moral principles on.—
Webster. Like the preceding, this word has a place in Todd's
Johnson, where it is noticed as a word of late introduction
into our language. Professor Lyell, who visited Dr. Webster,
says, "When the Dr. was asked how many words he had
coined for his dictionary, he replied, only one, 'to demoralize,'
and that not for his dictionary, but in a pamphlet published
in the last century."—*Travels in the U. States*, p. 53. Mr.
Jodrell, in his "Philology of the English Language," gives the
word a place, and cites as an example, a passage from a
speech by Lord Liverpool, in the House of Lords, March 11,
1817:

> They had endeavored to guard and protect the people against the
> attempts which were made to corrupt and *demoralize* them.

> The native vigor of the soul must wholly disappear, under the steady
> influence and the *demoralizing* example of profligate power and prosper-
> ous crime.—*Walsh, Letters on France.*

DEPARTMENTAL. Pertaining to a department, or division.
—*Webster.*

> The game played by the revolutionists in 1789 was now played against
> the *departmental* guards, called together for the protection of revolutionists.
> —*Burke, Pref. to Brissot's Address.*

> Which it required all the exertion of the *departmental* force to suppress.
> —*H. M. Williams, Letters on France.*

TO DEPUTIZE.   To depute ; to appoint a deputy ; to empower to act for another, as a sheriff.—*Webster*.

This word is not in any of the English dictionaries except one of the early editions of Bailey, where it appears in the preface among words in modern authors, collected after the dictionary was printed.   Mr. Pickering remarks, that "the word is sometimes heard in *conversation*, but rarely occurs in *writing*,   .   .   .   and that it has always been considered as a mere vulgarism."   Since the publication of Mr. P.'s Vocabulary, this word has been adopted in general use, and cannot now by any means be considered a vulgarism.

> They seldom think it necessary to *deputize* more than one person to attend to their interests at the seat of government.—*Port Folio,* Jan. 1811.

TO DERANGE.   To turn out of the proper place ; to disorder, to put out of order.—*Todd's Johnson.   Webster.*

" About twenty years ago," says Mr. Todd, " this word was condemend as a Gallicism."   The following are among the earliest instances of its use :

> That Robespierre might fall without *deranging* the general system.—*British Critic,* Vol. 5. p. 77.

> The republic of regicides has actually conquered the finest parts of Europe ; has distressed, disunited, *deranged,* and broke to pieces all the rest. —*Burke on a Regicide Peace.*

DESK.   The pulpit in a church, and figuratively, the clerical profession.   The man appears well at the desk.   He intends one son for the bar, and another for the desk.—*Pickering*. This New England word is not generally used in other parts of the country.

> The pulpit, or as it is here [in Connecticut] called, the *desk,* was filled by three if not four clergymen ; a number which, by its form and dimensions, it was able to accommodate.—*Kendall's Travels,* Vol. I. p. 4.

> They are common to every species of oratory, though of rarer use in the *desk,* &c.—*Adams's Lecture on Rhetoric.*

DESPERATE, commonly pronounced *desput,* and used to denote exceedingly ; as " I'm *desput* glad to see you."   Bad as this use and pronunciation of this word are, they are both to be found in England.   Mr. Hamilton notices this word among the provincialisms of Yorkshire ; as, " Thou's *desperate* hopeful !"—*Nugæ Literariæ, p.* 353.

Waes me ! what's this that lugs sae at my heart,
And fills my breast with such a *despert* smart ?—*Poems in Westmoreland and Cumberland Dialect*, p. 117.

DEUCE. A euphemism for *devil;* as, 'The *deuce* is in it;' '*Deuce* take it.' Common both in England and America.

DEVIL. A kind of expletive, expressing wonder or vexation; a ludicrous negative, in an adverbial sense; a term for mischief.—*Johnson.* In these several senses the word is used in the United States.

The things, we know, are neither rich nor rare;
But wonder how the *devil* they got there ?—*Pope.*

The devil was well, the *devil* a monk was he !—*A Proverb.*

A war of profit mitigates the evil;
But to be tax'd and beaten, is the *devil.—Granville.*

It is also, says Johnson, a ludicrous expletive of elder times, coupled with *all ;* implying, after an enumeration of some things, several understood. Bale was very fond of applying it, in his zeal against popery. It is yet absurdly retained in low language.

Baptysed bells, bedes, organs, songs, wax-lyghts, pycteres, reliques, banners, crosses, altars, holye-water, and the *devyl and all* of soche idolatrouse beggary.—*Bale, Yet a Course at the Romishe Foxe* (1543).

DEVILISH. Atrocious, enormous; excessively, exceedingly. Of the latter or adverbial use of the word Grose says, " It is an epithet, which, in the English vulgar language, is made to agree with every quality or thing; as, devilish bad, devilish good; devilish sick, devilish well; devilish sweet, devilish sour; devilish hot, devilish cold, &c."—*Slang Dictionary.*

A *devilish* knave ! besides, the knave is handsome, young, and blithe ; all those requisites are in him that delight.—*Shakspeare.*

Thy hair and beard are of a different die,
Short of one foot, distorted of one eye ;
With all these tokens of a knave complete,
If thou art honest, thou'rt a *devilish* cheat.—*Addison.*

DEVIL'S DARNING NEEDLE. A common name for the Dragon-fly.

DEVIL-FISH. (Genus, *Sophius.* Cuvier.) The common name of the *American Angler,* so called from its hideous form. It is also known by the names of Sea-devil, Fishing-frog,

Bellows-fish, Goose-fish, Monk-fish, and others.—*Storer's Fishes of Mass.*

DEVILTRY. Mischief; devilry. Provincial in England.

> The office-holding gentry at Washington will meet with their match in an indignant people, when they come to find out their *deviltry.*—*Crockett's Speech, Tour,* p. 106.

> Peter Funk is ready to be employed in all manner of deceit and *deviltry·* He cares not who his employers are.—*Perils of Pearl Street,* p. 51.

DICKENS. A euphemism for *devil;* used in the same manner as *deuce.* ' What *the dickens* are you about ?'

> Whence had you this pretty weather-cock ?
> ——I cannot tell what the *dickens* his name is my husband had him of.
> —*Shakspeare, Merry Wives of Windsor.*

TO DICKER. To barter. Used in the State of New York.

DICK'S HATBAND. This very singular expression I have often heard in Rhode Island. Mr. Hartshorne calls it " one of those phrases which set philologists and antiquarians at defiance." It is in general use throughout Shropshire, where it is applied as a comparison for what is obstinate and perverse. Ex. " As curst as *Dick's hatband,* which will come nineteen times round and wont tie at last ;" " As contrary as *Dick's hatband ;*" " As false as *Dick's hatband ;*" " As cruikit as *Dick's hatband ;*" " As twisted as *Dick's hatband ;*" " All across, like *Dick's hatband ;*" " As queer as *Dick's hatband.*"

DIFFICULTED. Perplexed. This is not a common word. Mr. Sherwood has it among the words peculiar to Georgia, and there are examples of its use to be found in some of our well-known authors. It is in common use at the Bar : ' The gentleman, I think, will be *difficulted* to find a parallel case.'

> There is no break in the chain of vital operation ; and consequently we are not *difficulted* at all on the score of the relation which the new plant bears to the old.—*Bush on the Resurrection,* p. 57.

Dr. Jamieson has the verb *to difficult* in his Scottish Dictionary.

DIGGING. Dear or costly ; as, ' a mighty *digging* price.' A Southern word.—*Sherwood's Georgia.*

DIG. A poke, punch ; and metaphorically, a reproof.

> A sly *dig* like the above in "The Sun" [newspaper] is worth having any day, when it is a *dig* on the right side.—*N. Y. Tribune.*

DIGGINGS. A word first used at the Western lead mines, to denote places where the ore was dug. Instead of saying this or that mine, it is *these diggings*, or *those diggings*. The phrase *these diggings* is now provincial in the Western States, and is occasionally heard in the Eastern, to denote a neighborhood, or particular section of country.

Mr. Charles F. Hoffman visited the Galena lead mines, and while there was shown about to the various estates, where the people were *digging* for ore. The person who accompanied him said :

> Mr. ———, from your State, has lately struck a lead, and a few years will make him independent. We are now, you observe, among his *diggings.*—*Winter in the West*, Let. 25.

> Boys, fellars, and candidates, I am the first white man ever seed in these *diggins*. I killed the first bar [bear] ever a white skinned in the county, and am the first manufacturer of whisky, and a powerful mixture it is too. —*Robb, Squatter Life.*

> He can shoot the closest of any chap, young or old, in these 'are *diggins*. —*Carlton, The New Purchase*, Vol. I. p. 155.

> I ain't a vain man, and never was. I hante a morsel of it in my composition. I don't think any of us Yankees is vain people ; it's a thing don't grow in our *diggins.*—*Sam Slick in England*, ch. 24.

> Guess they don't often see such an apostle in these *diggins.*—*Ibid.*

TO DILL. (Probably the same as *to dull*.) To soothe. The word is used in the north of England.

> I know what is in this medicine. It'll *dill* fevers, dry up sores, stop rheumatis, drive out rattle-snake's bite, kill worms, &c.—*Margaret*, p. 140.

TO DILLY-DALLY. To delay. A colloquial expression common in the United States.

> The note this verra morning shall be writ,
> And gien on Sunday to the parish clerk ;
> There ne'er comes luck of *dilly-dallying* work.—*Glossary and Poems*

DIME. (Fr. *dixme* or *dime*, tenth.) A silver coin of the United States, in value the tenth of a dollar, or ten cents.

This term, peculiar to our decimal currency, is now in common use at the South and West ; but in the Eastern and

Northern States, where the Spanish real and half-real have long formed a large portion of the circulation, and where the *dime* is only now beginning to be common, it is usually called a *ten-cent piece*, and the half-dime a *five-cent piece*.

> Small articles are sold in the New Orleans markets by the picayune or *dime's* worth. If you ask for a pound of figs you will not be understood : but for a *dime's* worth, and they are in your hands in a trice.—*Sketches of New Orleans. N. Y. Tribune.*

TO DING. To beat, to bang. Used metaphorically to denote tedious repetition ; as, ' Why do you keep *dinging* that in my ears ?'

DING. Excessively. A Southern word.

> It was *ding* hot ; so I sot down to rest a bit under the trees.—*Chron. of Pineville.*

DINGED. Very. An expletive, peculiar to the South.

> You know it's a *dinged* long ride from Pineville, and it took me most two days to get there.—*Maj. Jones's Courtship.*

TO DISH. To ruin ; to frustrate.

> She's *dished* us, too, said the officer. How shall we find out where she's gone to ?—*Maj. Downing.*

TO DIP SNUFF. A mode of taking tobacco, practised by women in some parts of the United States, and particularly at the South, may be thus described : A little pine stick or bit of rattan about three inches long, split up like a brush at one end, is first wetted and then dipped into snuff ; with this the teeth are rubbed sometimes by the hour together. Some tie the snuff in a little bag, and chew it. These filthy practices, which originate in the use of snuff for cleansing the teeth, seem to be rapidly going out of use, at least at the North.

DIPPER. A small aquatic bird common throughout the United States ; also called the Water-witch and Hell-diver. (*Horned grebe.* Nuttall, Ornith.)—*Nat. Hist. of New York.*

TO DISREMEMBER. To forget ; also, to choose to forget. Used chiefly in the Southern States.

DOCITY. A low word, used in some parts of the United States to signify *quick comprehension.* It is only used in conversation, and generally with a negative, thus : He has no *docity.*—

Pickering. This word is provincial in England, where it means docility, quick comprehension.—*Ash.*

DOCTOR. The cook on board a ship; so called by seamen.

DOGS. To go to the dogs. To go to destruction; to be ruined, destroyed, or devoured.—*Johnson.*

> Had whole Culpepper's wealth been hops and hogs,
> Could he himself have sent it *to the dogs?*—*Pope.*

TO DOG. To hunt as a dog, insidiously and indefatigably.—*Johnson.*

> I have been pursued, *dogged*, and way-laid through several nations, and even now scarce think myself secure.—*Pope.*

> The landlord gets his rents by looking after 'em; he fairly *dogs* it out of his tenants. He's as keen as a blood-hound, and will follow them day and night till he gets it.—*Maj. Downing, May-day in N. Y.*

DOG'S BANE. (*Apocynum androsæmifolium.*) The common name of a shrub, which grows along the road-side and borders of woods. The root is bitter, and has emetic properties.—*Bigelow's Medical Botany.*

DOG SICK, or SICK AS A DOG. A common expression, meaning very sick at the stomach.

> He that saieth he is *dog sick*, or *sick as a dog*, meaneth doubtless, a sick dog.—*Dyet's Dry Dinner* (1599).

DOG CHEAP. Anything exceedingly cheap; or, as Dr. Johnson says, as cheap as dog's meat.

> Good store of harlots, say you, and *dog cheap?*—*Dryden.*

> I bought fifty green sprigs of the morus multicaulis at a dollar a-piece, which was *dog cheap* to what they had been selling.—*Knickerbocker Mag.*

DOGWOOD. (*Rhus vernix.*) The popular name of the poison sumac. It grows in swamps, and from the beauty of its leaves has the appearance of a tropical plant. It is a violent poison to many when it is handled or even approached. To others it is harmless. The Dogwood-tree (*Cornus Florida*) is a different plant, and is used in medicine.—*Bigelow's Flora.*

DOLLAR MARK ($). The origin of this sign to represent the *dollar* has been the cause of much discussion of late in the newspapers. One writer says it comes from the letters U. S. (United States) which, after the adoption of the Federal Constitution, were prefixed to the Federal currency, and which afterwards, in the hurry of writing, were run into one another; the U being made first and the S over it. Another, that it is derived from the contraction of the Spanish word *pesos*, dollars, or *pesos fuertes*, hard dollars. A third, that it is a contraction of the Spanish *fuertes*, hard, to distinguish silver or hard dollars from paper money. The more probable explanation is, that it is a modification of the figure 8, and denotes a piece of eight reals, or, as a dollar was formerly called, a *piece of eight*. It was then designated by the figures $\frac{8}{8}$.

> As to my boat, it was a very good one; and that he saw, and told me he would buy it of me for the ship's use; and asked me what I would have for it? I told him that I could not offer to make any price of the boat, but left it entirely to him; upon which he told me he would give me a note of hand to pay me eighty *pieces of eight* for it in Brazil. He offered me also sixty *pieces of eight* more for my boy Xury, which I was loath to take; not that I was not willing to let the Captain have him, but I was loath to sell the poor boy's liberty, who had assisted me so faithfully in procuring my own.—*Robinson Crusoe*, sec. 4.

DONATE. To give as a donation; to contribute. This word is not in the dictionaries, but has only reached the newspapers and reviews.

> There have been received from the Foreign Bible Society $7000, not including $1000 recently *donated*.—*Baptist Missionary Herald*. Rep. 1846.

> The display of articles exhibited [at the Fair in Albany] was very tasteful and attractive; and the friends of the cause in Massachusetts, and other places, *donated* liberally.—*N. Y. Tribune*, Nov. 6, 1846.

DONATION PARTY. A party, consisting of the friends and parishioners of a country clergyman, assembled together, each individual bringing some article of food or clothing as a present to him. Where the salary of a clergyman is small, the contributions at a *donation party* are very acceptable. It is also called a *giving party*.

DONE, instead of *did;* as, 'They *done* the business.' A common vulgarism in the State of New York.

DONE BROWN. Thoroughly, effectually cheated, bamboozled. Of recent origin.

DO DON'T, for *do not* or *don't*, is a common expression in Georgia, and not by any means confined to the uneducated classes.

DONE FOR. Cheated ; taken advantage of.

> Wall street, it appears, is infested with mock-auction shops,—a country-man was *done for* at No. 15, to the tune of twenty-four dollars.—*New York Tribune*, Nov. 1, 1845.

DONE DID IT, for has done it, or performed it.—*Sherwood's Georgia.*

DONE COME. Come. A vulgarism peculiar to the South.

DONE GONE. Ruined ; destroyed ; rendered useless ; entirely gone. A Southern vulgarism.

> The horse and cart is *done gone*, and everything in it.—*Chron. of Pineville*, p. 107.

>> Oh ! she waked me in the mornin', and it's broad day ;
>> I look'd for my canoe, and it's *done gone* away.—*Porter's Tales of the Southwest*, p. 133.

DONE UP. Ruined by gaming and extravagance.—*Grose.* We use it colloquially, where a person is ruined in any way, whether by gaming or by trade.

DON'T. The proper colloquial contraction for *do not ;* and which should therefore be used only in the first person singular and the plural. Yet we very often hear it used instead of *doesn't* for *does not ;* as, ' He *don't* tell the truth.'

I DON'T KNOW AS I SHAN'T, for I don't know but I shall. This uncouth expression, Mr. Hurd says, is very common in the eastern towns of Massachusetts, near Cape Cod.—*Grammatical Corrector.*

DOREE. A fish commonly called *John Dory* with us as in England. This last name is a corruption of the French *jaune dorée*, golden yellow, which is the color of this fish.

DO TELL ! A vulgar exclamation common in New England, and synonymous with really ! indeed ! is it possible !

> A bright-eyed little demoiselle from Virginia came running into the dairy of a country house in New Hampshire, at which her mother was spending the summer, with a long story about a most beautiful butterfly she had been chasing ; and the dairy maid, after hearing the story through, exclaimed, " *Do tell !* " The child immediately repeated the story, and the good-natured maid, after hearing it through a second time, exclaimed again, in a tone of still greater wonder, " *Do tell !* " A third time the story was told, and the third time came the exclamation of wonder, " *Do tell !* " The child's spirits were dashed, and she went to her mother with a sad tale

about Ruth's teasing her ; while poor Ruth said that " those *daown* country gals were so strange ; keep telling me the same thing over and over,—I never see anything like !"—*N. Y. Com. Adv.*

DOMESTICS. Used only in the plural. Cotton goods of American manufacture.

TO DOOM. To tax at discretion. A New England term.

When a person neglects to make a return of his taxable property to the assessors of a town, those officers *doom* him ; that is, *judge* upon, and fix his tax according to their discretion.—*Pickering*.

> The estates of all merchants, shop-keepers, and factors, shall be assessed by the rule of common estimation, according to the will and *doom* of the assessors.—*Massachusetts Colony Laws*, p. 14, ed. 1660.

DOOMAGE. A penalty or fine for neglect. *Laws of New Hampshire.*—*Webster.*

DORMAR-WINDOW. A window made in the roof of a house. —*Worcester.* The word seems formerly to have been *dormant*, as in the following :

> Old *dormant* windows must confess
> Her beams; their glimmering spectacles, &c.—*Cleveland.*

Here and there was a house with gambled roof and *dormar* windows.— *Margaret*, p. 33.

DOUCHE. A term lately introduced into the language from the French by the followers of Priessnitz. It technically denotes a jet of water employed as a remedy.

DOUGH-FACES. A contemptuous nickname, applied to the northern favorers and abettors of negro slavery.

> The Wilmot proviso was lost, and the *dough-faces* of New York did the deed.—*N. Y. Expres*, March, 1847.

> There is one very probable result, to wit: that there will be "*dough-faces*" enough among the Northern Democrats to sustain the policy of extending the area of African slavery to the shores of the Pacific.—*N. Y. Com. Adv.* Jan. 8, 1848.

> The truth is, that while the Southerners need and are willing to pay for the services of the *dough-faces*, they dislike their persons and despise their discourse.—*N. Y. Tribune*, April, 1848.

DOUGH-NUT. A small roundish cake, made of flour, eggs, and sugar, moistened with milk, and boiled in lard.—*Webster.* Halliwell has *donnut* in his Provincial Dictionary, which is no doubt the same word.

DOVE. Dived. Very common among seamen.

DOWD. A woman's night-cap, composed of two pieces of cloth, the seam running from the forehead to the neck. It is sometimes called a " squaw-shaped cap." *New York.*

DOWN IN THE MOUTH. Dispirited, dejected, disheartened. —*Brockett's Glossary.*

DOWN UPON. To be down upon, is to seize with avidity, as a bird of prey would pounce *down upon* its victim. Alluding to the state of the poultry market, the New York Tribune says :

> The boarding-house keepers are *down upon* geese.

This phrase is also used to express disapprobation, dislike, or enmity ; as, " I'll be *down upon* you," i. e. I'll come up with you, or pay you off for some injury or insult, &c. A common expression at the West is, " I'll be *down upon* you like a thousand of brick."

TO DOXOLOGIZE. To give glory to God, as in doxology.— *Webster.*

> No instance is to be found in which primitive Christians *doxologized* the spirit of God as a person.—*Christian Disciple*, Vol. II. p. 295.

Mr. Pickering says he " never met with the word in any other American work, nor in any English publication ; but that it may possibly be a part of the professional language of divines." Mr. P. farther observes, that he found it in the early editions of the dictionaries of Ash and Bailey, from which it was afterwards discarded. Mr. Worcester has inserted the word in his new dictionary.

TO DRABBLE. To draggle; to make dirty by drawing in dirt and water ; to wet and befoul ; as, to drabble a gown or cloak. A word common in New England.—*Webster.*

Dr. Jamieson calls *drabble* a Scottish word. The sense here is the same as in Scotland.

DRAGGED OUT. Fatigued; exhausted; worn out with labor.

DRAT. A good-humored sort of half oath, as Moor calls it in his *Suffolk Words.* It is probably an abbreviation of *od rot,* and originally *God rot.* The expression is only heard at the South.

> " A wolf ! a wolf !" they cry, " have at him !
> If he escape us this time, '*drat* him !"—*Reynard the Fox*, p. 69.

> Your bag ! says Pete, *drat* your infernal picter, who told you to hang up a bag, for white folks to get into ?—*Maj. Jones's Courtship*, p. 194.

> '*Drot* it ! what do boys have daddies for, any how ? 'Taint for nothin' but jest to beat 'em and work 'em.—*Simon Suggs.*

DRATTED. A Southern word, derived from the former. It is an expletive, and means very, exceeding, etc.

> I never was so *dratted* mad ; for the fellows were coming in in gangs, and beginnin' to call for me to come out and take the command.—*Maj. Jones's Courtship*, p. 22.

> It was about eleven o'clock before the *dratted* thing came along.—*Ibid.*

> You may thank me that you have got eyes left in yer *dratted* head to look for yer blind horse.—*Chronicles of Pineville*, p. 108.

DREADFUL. Very, exceedingly. This and the words *awful, terrible, monstrous,* &c., are indiscriminately used by uneducated people for the purpose of giving emphasis to an expression.

> There was a swod of fine folks at Saratoga, and *dreadful* nice galls.—*Maj. Downing's Letters*, p. 35.

> It's a fact, Major, the public has a *dreadful* cravin' appetite for books.—*Ibid. May-day in N. Y.*, p. 4.

> The young ladies thought Mr. Harley's new storekeeper a *dreadful* nice young man, if he hadn't such a horrid nose.—*Chronicles of Pineville.*

> She was a *dreadful* good creature to work.—*Mrs. Clavers.*

It is used in the same way in England, in the Westmoreland and Cumberland dialects:

> I send to this an, to tell thee amackily what *dreadful* fine things I saw i' th' road tuv at yon Dublin.—*Poems and Glossary*, p. 125.

TO DRIVE A BARGAIN. To make a bargain. A common colloquial expression, as old as the language.

> This *bargain* is *full drive*, for we ben knit ;
> Ye shal be paied trewely by my troth.—*Chaucer, Franklin's Tale.*

DRIVER. An overseer of slaves.

DRIVER. He or that which drives ; a coachman, a carman. —*Worcester.* The English always call a driver of a carriage a coachman.

TO BE DRIVING AT. ' What are you driving at ?' that is, what are you about ? what object have you in view ? A colloquial expression, in very common use.

> We confess that we are exceedingly puzzled to know exactly what our long-cherished friend is *driving at*, in his repeated discussions of the question above involved.—*N. Y. Com. Advertiser.*

> People ludicrate my situation, and say they don't know what the deuce I'm *driving at.*—*Neal's Charcoal Sketches.*

> I have heard enough now, said the Recorder, to know what you and he would be *driving at.*—*Pickings from the Picayune*, p. 135.

TO DRIVE WELL. A Southern phrase, thus explained by Mr. Davis : This gentleman applied for a situation as teacher in a college in South Carolina, when the following dialogue took place :

> *Planter.* Can you *drive well*, Sir.
> *Tutor.* *Drive*, Sir, did you say ? I really do not comprehend you.
> *Planter.* I mean, Sir, can you keep your scholars in order ?
> The phrase, adds our author, is used by the overseer on a plantation, who, in preserving subordination among the negroes, is said *to drive well.*—*Davis's Travels in the United States.*

DROGER. Lumber droger ; cotton droger, etc. A vessel built solely for burden, and for transporting cotton, lumber, and other heavy articles.

DROUTH, or **DROWTH.** (Ang. Sax. *drugothe.*) Dry weather ; want of rain ; drought. This is the oldest pronunciation of the word, and is still heard in some parts of England and in Scotland, as well as amongst us.

> Great *drouths* in summer, lasting till the end of August ; some gentle showers upon them, and then some dry weather.—*Bacon.*

> As torrents in the *drowth* of summer fail.—*Sandys.*

> He speaks in his drink, what he thought in his *drouth.*—*Scottish Proverb.*

DROWNDED, for drowned. Often used by illiterate people in England and America.—*Craven Glossary.*

> Then rising up he cried amain,
> Helpe, helpe ! or else I am *drownded.*—*Baffled Knight.*

DRUMMING, in mercantile phrase, means the soliciting of customers. It is chiefly used in reference to country merchants, or those supposed to be such. Instead of patiently waiting for these persons to come and purchase, the merchant or his

clerk goes to them and solicits their custom.   In this manner
the sale of goods is often expedited; and though the practice
of *drumming* is held by some to be neither very modest nor
very dignified, still it must be owned to add very largely, in
certain cases, to the amount of goods sold.   Indeed, without
drumming, it is suspected that sundry houses, which make a
remarkable show and noise, would do very little business.

The expenses of *drumming* amount to no small sum.
Besides employing extra clerks and paying the extra price for
their board at the hotels, the merchant has to be very liberal
with his money in paying for wine, oyster-suppers, theatre
tickets, and such other means of conciliating the favor of the
country merchant, as are usually resorted to by *drummers.*

Another part of the system of mercantile *drumming* is to
" become all things to all men."   Drummers are apt to be
exceedingly flexible in matters of religion, and of morals too
—being orthodox with the orthodox, and heterodox with the
heterodox; going to church with those who incline church-
ward, and to the theatre with those who prefer the theatre;
taking cold water with those who are opposed to brandy, and
drinking brandy with those who eschew cold water.—*Perils
of Pearl Street,* ch. 9.

DUBERSOME.   Doubtful.   A vulgarism common in the interior of New England.

> I have been studyin' Tattersall's considerable, to see whether it is a safe
> shop to trade in or no.   But I'm *dubersome;* I don't like the cut of the
> sporting folks here.— *Sam Slick in England,* ch. 28.

A LAME DUCK.   A Wall-street phrase for a Broker or Stock
Jobber, who is unable to pay his losses or differences.   He is
short in his payments; he is a lame duck.   It is among the
rules of the Stock Exchange, that a broker ceases to be a member when he cannot or will not meet his engagements.

The same phrase is employed at Exchange Alley in London,
where the delinquent is said to " *waddle out of the Alley,* not
to appear again till his debts are paid; should he attempt it,
he would be hustled out by the fraternity."—*Grose, Slang
Dictionary.*

DUDS.   (Gaelic, *dud.*)   Rags; old clothes.   A common word, which is used in the same sense in various parts of England and the United States.

> Sae I pack'd up my *duds* when my quarter was out,
> And wi' weage i' my pocket, I saunter'd about.—*Westmoreland and Cumb. Dialect*, p. 226.

> Give a man time to take off his *duds*, and then lick him if you can.—*Crockett's Tour*, p. 193.

DUG-OUT. The name in the Western States for a canoe or boat, hewn or *dug out* of a large log. They are common in all the rivers and creeks of the United States and Canada. In the latter country they are called *log canoes*.

> After a fashion I got to my *dug-out*, with no weapon along but the paddle. Snags were plenty. I felt strong as a hoss, too ; and the *dug-out* hadn't leaped more'n six lengths afore—co-souse I went—the front eend jest lifted itself agin a sawyer and emptied me into the element.—*Robb, Squatter Life.*

DULL MUSIC. A term applied to anything tedious.

DUMB-FOUNDED. Stupefied ; struck dumb with fear and confusion. This word is in the English provincial glossaries and in Webster's Dictionary.

DUMMY. A dumb, i. e. silent person ; a stupid person. We use the word most frequently to denote a silent partner at cards. *To play dummy*, is to play with one person less than the requisite number.

> Auld Gabbi Spec wha was sae cunning,
> To be a *dummie* ten years running.—*Allan Ramsay.*

TO DUMP. To unload wood, coal, &c. from a cart by tilting it up. A word very common in New York, and probably of Dutch origin.

> Why, nothing in all creation can come up to blackberrying, but gettin' *dumped* out of a sleigh into a snow-bank.—*Lafayette Chronicle.*

DUMPS. Sorrow ; melancholy ; sadness.—*Johnson.* We say of a person who is dull or sad, ' He has the dumps,' or ' is in the dumps.'

> Sudden *dumps*, and dreary sad disdain
> Of all worlds' gladness, more my torment feed.—*Spenser.*

> Edwin, thus perplexed with troubled thoughts, in the dead of the night, sate solitary under a tree in *dumps*, musing what was best to be done.—*Speed. Chronicle.*

DUMPISH. Sad; melancholy.—*Johnson.*

> The life which I live at this age is not a dead, *dumpish*, and sour life; but cheerful, lively, and pleasant.—*Herbert.*

> But I fear now I have overcharged the reader's mind with doleful, *dump-ish*, and uncomfortable lines.—*Camden, Remains.*

DUMPY. Short and thick. Provincial in various parts of England, where, as with us, it is generally applied to a person who is both short and fat.

> Whenever he was with me, his short, *dumpy*, gouty, crooked fingers, were continually teazing my spinnet, to his own harmonious croaking.—*Student*, 2, 225.

TO DUN. (Ang. Sax. *dynan*, to clamor.) To urge for payment; to demand a debt in a pressing manner.—*Johnson.*

> But you have something to add, Sancho, to what I owe your good will also on this account, and that is to send me the subscription money, which I find a necessity of *dunning* my best friends for before I leave town.—*Sterne, Works,* Let. 94.

DUNDERHEAD. Blockhead; dolt. The same as the English provincialisms *dunder-knoll* and *dummer-head.*

DUNFISH. (From *dun*, a dark yellow color.) Codfish cured in a particular manner, by which they retain a *dun* color. They command a higher price, and are much superior to those cured in the ordinary way.

DUNNING. A peculiar operation for curing codfish.—*Webster.* Fish for *dunning* are caught early in the spring, and often in February. At the Isles of Shoals, off Portsmouth, in New Hampshire, the cod are taken in deep water, split and slack-salted; then laid 'n a pile for two or three months, in a dark store, covered, for the greatest part of the time, with salt hay or eel-grass, and pressed with some weight. In April or May they are opened and piled as close as possible in the same dark store, till July or August, when they are fit for use.—*J. Haven.*

DUST. 'To kick up a dust,' is to make a row, to cause a great disturbance. A phrase common in England and the United States.

DUTIABLE. Subject to the imposition of duties or customs.—*Webster.* This is a very convenient word, and is in common use, both by the officers of the customs, and by merchants having transactions with them. Instead of saying that certain articles of merchandise are subject to duty, the common terms are *dutiable* and *free*.

DYED IN THE WOOL. Ingrained; thorough.

> The Democrats, on the authority of Mr. Cameron's letter, are beginning to claim General Taylor as a democrat *dyed in the wool*, as a democrat of the Jeffersonian order of 1798.—*N. Y. Com. Adv.* May 24, 1847.

E.

EAGLE. A gold coin of the United States, of the value of ten dollars.

EARS. To be *by the ears*. A familiar and very old phrase, denoting to quarrel or fight. It alludes to the practice of dogs, which, when fighting, seize each other by the ears.

> Poor naked men belabored one another with shagged sticks, or daily fell together *by the ears*, at fisty-cuffs.—*More*.

> She used to carry tales from one to another, till she had set the neighborhood together *by the ears*.—*Arbuthnot*.

EASY. A word in common use among merchants and bankers. 'Our bank is easy,' meaning that its loans are not extended, or that money is plentiful. 'The money market is easy;' i. e. loans of money may easily be procured.

TO EAT, *v. a.* To supply with food. A Western sense of the word. Comp. *Subsist*.

> *Hooshier.* Squire, what pay do you give?
> *Contractor.* Ten bits a day.
> *Hooshier.* Why, Squire, I was told you'd give us two dollars a day and *eat* us.—*Pickings from the Picayune*, p. 47.

TO EDGE. To move sideways; to move gradually.—*Webster*.

> Well, says I, I must be a goin'; I can't think of paying eighty dollars. And I began to *edge* along a little.—*Maj. Downing, May-day*.

> I danced with her at some on the balls, and thar I gin to *edge up* and talk tender at her, but she only laughed at my sweetnin'.—*Robb, Squatter Life*.

EDUCATIONAL. Pertaining to education; derived from education; as, *educational habits*.—*Webster*. The authority cited by Webster for the use of this word is "*Smith*"—a rather indefinite one. Mr. Pickering says the word was new to him until he saw it in the following extract:

> It is believed that there is not an individual of the college who would, if questioned, complain that he has, in any instance, felt himself pressed with opinions which interfered with his *educational* creed.—*Dr. Grant's Report to the College of New Jersey*, 1815.

EEL-GRASS. (*Zostera marina.*) A plant thrown ashore in large quantities by the sea. It is also called Sea-wrack.

EEL-SPEAR. A sort of trident for catching eels.

E'EN A'MOST, for *almost.* A vulgarism.

> The repudiation of debts by several of our States, has lowered us down *e'en a'most* to the bottom of the shaft.—*Sam Slick in England*, ch. 14.

> He knows the Catechism, and has got the whole Bible *eeny most* by heart.—*Margaret*, p. 113.

> The village boys would raise a party of gals, and start off early in the morning for Toad-hill, where the blackberries was *e'en a'most* as plentiful as mosquitoes in these diggings.—*Lafayette Chronicle.*

EEND, for *end.* A vulgar pronunciation of the word. It is also common in various parts of England.

ELBOW-GREASE. Persevering exercise of the arms, exciting perspiration; hard rubbing.—*Glossaries of Brockett and Carr.*

> These were the manners, these the ways,
> In good Queen Bess's golden days;
> Each damsel owed her bloom and glee
> To wholesale *elbow-grease* and me.—*Smart, Fable* 5.

TO ELECT. To prefer, to choose, to determine in favor of.—*Webster.* This sense of the word is not noticed by Johnson or Todd. It is not common with us. President Polk used it thus:

> In pursuance of the joint resolution of Congress, " for annexing Texas to the United States," my predecessor, on the third day of March, 1845, *elected* to submit the first and second sections of that resolution to the Republic of Texas, as an overture, on the part of the United States, for her admission as a State into our Union. This election I approved.—*Message to Congress*, Dec. 1, 1845.

TO ENERGIZE. To give strength or force to; to give active vigor to.—*Webster.* To excite action.—*Todd.* This word is not found in Johnson's Dictionary, and is of modern origin. Mr. Pickering says, the use of it in the British Spy, published in Virginia, was censured in the Monthly Anthology, as unauthorized.

> Instead of aiding and *energizing* the police of the college.—*British Spy.*

Bishop Horsley uses the word *energizing;* also Harris:

> As all energies are attributes, they have reference, of course, to certain *energizing* substances.—*Harris, Hermes,* i. 9.

ENLIGHTENMENT. Act of enlightening; state of being enlightened or instructed.—*Webster.* Used by the Quarterly Review, Oct. 1837.

ESQUIRE. In England this title is given to the younger sons of noblemen, to officers of the king's courts and of the household, to counsellors at law, justices of the peace while in commission, sheriffs, and other gentlemen. In the United States, the title is given to public officers of all degrees, from governors down to justices and attorneys. Indeed, the title, in addressing letters, is bestowed on any person at pleasure, and contains no definite description. It is merely an expression of respect.—*Webster.*

The New York Commercial Advertiser, in an article on the subject of titles, had the following remarks on *esquire :* " In our own dear title-bearing, democratic land, the title of *esquire,* officially and by courtesy, has come to include pretty much everybody. Of course everybody in office is an esquire, and all who have been in office enjoy and glory in the title. And what with a standing army of legislators, an elective and ever-changing magistracy, and almost a whole population of militia officers, present and past, all named as esquires in their commissions, the title is nearly universal."

EULOGIUM. On this word Mr. Pickering has the following remarks : " A writer in the Monthly Anthology (Vol. I. p. 609) observes that 'eulogium is not an English word.' But the writer is certainly mistaken. It is in common use with all the English and Scottish reviewers; and occurs much oftener, I think, than the Anglicized term *eulogy.*"—*Pickering's Vocabulary.*

It is singular that this word is not to be found in either edition of Johnson's Dictionary, nor in the additions of Mr. Todd, or Mason. Walker did not insert it until his fourth

edition in 1806.   Mr. Jodrell has inserted the word in his
Philology on the English Language, and gives examples of
its use; it may also be found in the 9th edition (1840) of
Knowles's English Dictionary.

> The epitaph on Cragg's monument, in Westminster Abbey, is an *eulo-*
> *gium* on that statesman, taken from Pope's Epistle to Addison.—*Sir John*
> *Hawkins, Life of Johnson,* p. 538.

> I cannot make a higher *eulogium* of Mrs. Stanley, than to say that she
> is every way worthy of the husband whose happiness she makes.—*Cœlebs,*
> Vol. I. p. 142.

> To prevent posterity being deceived by the pompous *eulogiums* bestowed
> on this bridge, which has been styled the wonder of the world, &c.—*Lon-*
> *don and Environs,* Vol. IV. p. 143. (1761).

TO EVENTUATE.   To issue; to come to an end; to close; to
terminate.—*Webster.*   This word is not in any of the English dictionaries, except Knowles's 9th edition, London, 1840;
and Mr. Pickering says, " it is rarely, if ever, used by English
authors."

EVERLASTING.   Very; exceedingly.

> New York is an *everlasting* great concern.—*Maj. Downing, May-day in*
> *New York.*

EVERY-DAY.   Common; usual.

> Men of genius forget things of common concern, which make no slight
> impression on *every-day* minds.—*Shenstone.*

EVERY NOW AND THEN.   Repeatedly, at intervals.
This phrase is common with us, and is used also in England.

> [The young woman] looks demurely on the ground, a smile playing on
> her lips, *every now and then* turning on her swain such sparkling glances
> from her bright eyes.—*Kingston, Lusitanian Sketches.*

EVERY ONCE IN A WHILE.   A singular though very common expression, signifying the same as *every now and then.*

EVIDENTIAL.   Affecting evidence; clearly proving.—*Web-*
ster.

> Dr. Webster cites *Scott* as his authority, but gives no ex-
ample.   Mr. Pickering has the following example from an
English work:

> Equivalent to that belief itself, and *evidential* of it.—*Christian Observer,*
> Vol. XIII. p. 765.

TO EVOKE. To call forth.—*Todd. Webster.* Several newspapers criticised the use of this word by the Hon. J. Q. Adams in a letter to the Hon. H. G. Otis :

Every phantom of jealousy and fear is *evoked.*

The following examples will show that it has been used by English writers. Mr. Todd says, it is in Cockeram's old Vocabulary, but that he has not found it in use till near a century later.

I had no sooner *evoked* the name of Shakspeare from the rotten monument of his former editions, &c.—*Bp. Warburton to Hurd* (1749), Let. 6.

The only business and use of this character, is to open the subject in a long prologue, to *evoke* the devil, and summons the court.—*Warton, Hist. of Eng. Poetry.*

He was so subjugated by them, as frequently to pass many hours of the night in churchyards, engaged in *evoking* and attempting to raise apparitions.—*Wraxall, Hist. Memoirs,* Vol. I. p. 178.

EXCHANGEABILITY. The quality or state of being exchangeable.—*Webster.*

Though the law ought not to be contravened by an express article admitting the *exchangeability* of such persons.—*Washington.*

THE EXECUTIVE. The officer, whether king, president, or other chief magistrate, who superintends the execution of the laws ; the person who administers the government ; executive power or authority in government.—*Webster.*

TO EXPECT, instead of *suspect.* To suppose, think, imagine. A very common corruption.

In most parts of the world people *expect* things that are to come. But in Pennsylvania, more particularly in the metropolis, we *expect* things that are past. One man tells another, he *expects* he had a very pleasant ride, &c. . . . . . . I have heard a wise man in Gotham say, he *expected* Alexander, the Macedonian, was the greatest conqueror of antiquity.—*Port Folio,* 1809.

Nor is it confined to ourselves. It is not only provincial in England, but we are even startled at meeting with it in the London Athenæum. In an article on the Penny Cyclopedia, a writer says :

The most sustained departments are those of mathematics, classical literature, astronomy, geography, topography, geology, materia medica, and agriculture. In the articles on these subjects we *expect* that one hand has written or one head has guided the whole series, and thus completeness has been obtained.—*Athen.* No. 858.

F.

FACTORY. (Contracted from *manufactory*.) This word is not
in Johnson's Dictionary or in any other before his time. It is
now common both in England and the United States, and is
applied to a place where anything is made.

FAGGED OUT. Fatigued; worn out.

FAIR SHAKE. A fair trade ; a satisfactory bargain or exchange. A New England vulgarism.

FALL. The fall of the leaf; autumn; the time when the
leaves drop from the trees.—*Todd's Johnson.   Webster.*
   This beautifully picturesque expression, which corresponds
so well to its opposite *spring*, has been said to be peculiar to
the United States. Mr. Pickering notices the following remark in Rees's Cyclopedia : " In North America the season
in which the fall of the leaf takes place, derives its name
from that circumstance, and instead of *autumn* is universally
called the *fall*."—ART. *Deciduous Leaves*. It is used, however, in England in the same sense, though *autumn* is as
generally employed there, as *fall* is in the United States.

> What crowds of patients the town doctor kills,
> Or how last *fall* he raised the weekly bills.—*Dryden's Juvenal.*

> Hash worked the farm, burnt coal in the *fall*, made sugar in the spring,
> drank, smoked, &c.—*Margaret*, p. 13.

TO FALL. To fell, to cut down ; as, ' *to fall* a tree.'—*Webster.*
This use of the word is now common in America, although it
has been condemned as a barbarism. It is found in the English
dictionaries of Ash, Sheridan, Walker, and Knowles; but
many others leave it out. Besides the dictionaries, there are
other authorities for the use of this word, sufficient to elevate
it above the rank of a barbarism. For a fuller account of it,
see Mr. Pickering's Vocabulary.

FANCY STOCKS. A species of stocks which are bought and
sold to a great extent in New York. Unlike articles of
merchandise, which may be seen and examined by the dealer,
and which always have an intrinsic value in every fluctuation

of the market, these stocks are wholly wrapped in mystery; no one knows anything about them, except the officers and directors of the companies, who, from their position, are not the most likely men to tell you the truth. They serve no other purpose, therefore, than as the representative of value in stock gambling. Nearly all the fluctuations in their prices are artificial. A small fluctuation is more easily produced than a large one ; and as the calculations are made on the par value, a fluctuation of one per cent. on stock worth $20 a share, is just five times as much on the amount of money invested, as it would be on a par stock. Consequently, if a " Flunkie " can be drawn in, he may be fleeced five times as quick in these, as in good stocks.—*A Week in Wall St.* p. 83.

FARZINER. A vulgar contraction of *far-as-I-know*, extensively used through New England and New York, including Long Island.

FEAST. (A corruption of the Dutch *vies*, nice, fastidious.) ' I am *feast* of it,' is a literal translation of the Dutch *Ik ben 'er vies van*, i. e. I am disgusted with, I loathe it. A New York phrase, mostly confined to the descendants of the Dutch.

FEAT. Ready, skilful.—*Johnson.* This word is now only known as a provincialism in England and America.

> Never master had a page so kind, so diligent ;
> So *feat*, so nurse-like.— *Shakspeare, Cymbeline.*

The following will illustrate its use in New England :

> She was so *feat* and spry, and knowing, and good-natured, she said she could be of some use to somebody.—*Margaret*, p. 21.

TO FEATHER ONE'S NEST. To collect riches together : alluding to birds which collect feathers, among other materials, for making their nests.—*Johnson.*

> Tradition says he *feathered his nest*
> Through an agricultural interest,
> In the Golden Age of Farming.—*Hood's Miss Killmansegg.*

FEDERAL CURRENCY. The legal currency of the United States. Its coins are the gold *eagle* of ten dollars, half and quarter eagles of proportionate value. The silver *dollar* of one hundred cents, its half, qaarter, tenth, and twentieth parts. The coin of ten cents value is called a *dime*, that of five cents, a *half-dime*. The lowest coin in common use is the copper *cent*. Half-cent coins have been made, but none of late years. In the commercial cities and along the sea-board, Spanish coins of a dollar and the fractional parts of a dollar are very common, and pass currently for their original value, except at the Custom Houses and Post Offices, where, by a recent ordinance, the quarter dollar and its parts are only received at twenty-five per cent. discount.

Previous to the adoption of our Federal currency, pounds, shillings, and pence were used. But this currency became unstable, in consequence of the great depreciation which took place in the paper money issued by the colonies.

In the year 1702, exchange on England was $33\frac{1}{3}$ per cent. above par ; and silver and gold bore the same relative value to paper money. The depreciation in the latter continued to increase until, in the year 1749, £1100 currency was only equal to £100 sterling, or eleven for one. In 1750, a stop was put to the farther depreciation of the money of the province of Massachusetts by a remittance from England of £183,000 sterling, in Spanish dollars, to reimburse the expense the province had been at in the reduction of Cape Breton in the old French war. The depreciated money was then called in, and paid off at the rate of a Spanish dollar for 45 shillings of the paper currency. At the same time a law was made fixing the par of exchange between England and Massachusetts at £133$\frac{1}{3}$ currency for £100 sterling, and 6 shillings to the Spanish dollar.

The difference of exchange, or depreciation of the paper money, regulated in the same manner the currencies of the other colonies. Throughout New England, as has been before stated, it was 6*s*. to the dollar of 4*s*. 6*d*. sterling. In New York, 8*s*., or about 75 per cent. depreciation. Pennsylvania, 7*s*. 6*d*., or about 66 per cent. depreciation. In some of the Southern States it was 4*s*. 6*d*. to the dollar, and accordingly no depreciation. In Halifax currency, including the present British provinces, it was 5*s*. to the dollar, or about 11 per cent., etc. etc. The old system of reckoning by shillings and pence is continued by retail dealers generally ; and will continue, as long as the Spanish coins remain in circulation.

In consequence of the abovenamed diversity in the colonial currencies, in New England the Spanish real of $\frac{1}{8}$ of a dollar or $12\frac{1}{2}$ cents is called *ninepence ;* in New York, *one shilling ;* in Pennsylvania, *elevenpence* or a *levy ;* and in many of the Southern States, a *bit.* The half real of $\frac{1}{16}$ of a dollar is called in New York a *sixpence ;* in New England, *fourpence ha'penny,* or simply *fourpence ;* in Pennsylvania, a *fip ;* and at the South, a *picayune.*

FEDERALIST. An appellation in America given to the friends of the Constitution of the United States, at its formation and adoption; and to the political party which favored the administration of President Washington.—*Webster.*

TO FEDERALIZE. To unite in compact, as different States ; to confederate for political purposes.—*Webster.*

FEEZE. ' To be *in a feeze,*' is to be in a state of excitement.

> When a man's in a *feeze*, there's no more sleep that hitch.—*Sam Slick in England*, ch. 2.

FELLOW-COUNTRYMEN. This word is often used by public speakers. It is improper, as the last word expresses the meaning of both. Mr. Pickering however mentions an example of the use of the word by *Southey* in his *Life of Nelson.*

FELLOWSHIP. Companionship ; consort ; society.—*Johnson.* With us it is often used in religious writings and discourses instead of the word *communion*, to denote " mutual intercourse or union in religious worship, or in doctrine and discipline."

TO FELLOWSHIP. A verb formed from the preceding noun. *To fellowship with,* is to hold communion with ; to unite with in doctrine and discipline. This barbarism now appears with disgusting frequency in the reports of ecclesiastical conventions, &c., and in the religious newspapers generally. Mr. Pickering, in the Supplement to his Vocabulary, says he had just become acquainted with the word. The following is the first example which he gives :

> We considered him heretical, essentially unsound in the faith; and on this ground refused to *fellowship* with him.—*Address to the Christian Public, Greenfield*, 1813.

> If the Christian Alliance could not *fellowship* with the Southern slave-holders for gain, they ought to say so outright.—*Speech at the Christian Alliance Conference*, May 8, 1847.

ON THE FENCE. In politics, *to be on the fence,* is to be neutral, or to be ready to join the strongest party, whenever it can be ascertained which is so. A man sitting on the top of a fence, can jump down on either side with equal facility. So with a politician who is *on the fence;* selfish motives govern him, and he is prepared at any moment to declare for either party.

FETCH. (Ang. Sax. *facen,* fraud, trick, deceit.) A trick, or invention to deceive.—*Grose.* This word is in several of the English glossaries. In the United States it is never heard except colloquially.

> An envious neighbor is easy to find,
> His cumbersome *fetches* are seldom behind ;
> His *fetch* is to flatter, to get what he can ;
> His purpose once gotten, a pin for thee then.—*Tusser, Husb.*

> It is a *fetch* of wit ;
> You laying these slight sullies on my son,
> As 'twere a thing a little soil'd i' th' working.—*Shakspeare.*

FETTICUS. } Vulg. *Fáttikows.* (Bot. *Valerianella ; Fedia*
VETTIKOST. } *olitoria.* Fr. *Doucette, mache.*) Corn-salad, or lamb's-lettuce. A word used in New York.

TO FETCH UP. To stop suddenly. This sense of the word is not noticed in the English dictionaries, nor by Webster. We often hear the phrase ' He *fetched up* all standing,' that is, he made a sudden halt. It is a nautical vulgarism, the figure being that of a ship which is suddenly brought to, while at full speed and with all her sails set.

FEVER BUSH. (*Laurus benzoin.*) An aromatic shrub with a flavor resembling Benzoin.—*Bigelow's Flora Bostoniensis.*

FID OF TOBACCO. A chew, or quid of tobacco. A word only used by those who make use of the weed. It is also used in England, according to *Grose.*

TO HANG UP ONE'S FIDDLE, is to desist from any labor or project ; a metaphor derived from a musician, who, when he ceases playing, is supposed to *hang up his fiddle.*

FIDDLE FADDLE. Trifling discourse ; nonsense.—*Grose. Johnson.* Also used adjectively and as a verb.

She said that her grandfather had a horse shot at Edgehill, and their uncle was at the siege of Buda; with abundance of *fiddle faddle* of the same nature.—*Spectator.*

She was a troublesome *fiddle faddle* old woman, and so ceremonious that there was no bearing of her.—*Arbuthnot.*

—————— Ye may as easily
Outrun a cloud, driven by a northern blast,
As *fiddle faddle* so.—*Ford, The Broken Heart,* Act I. Scene 3.

FIDDLER. A kind of small crab, with one large claw and a very small one. It lives on the salt meadows, where it makes its burrows. Used in New York and New Jersey.

TO PLAY SECOND FIDDLE, is to take an inferior part in any project or undertaking. A metaphor borrowed from a musical performer who *plays the second* or counter to the one who plays the first or the " air."

On the question of removing the seat of government from Kingston to Montreal, the population of which is chiefly French, a paper in the former city observes that—

We had rather become a portion of the United States, much as we detest that government, and rank with the Western States of Michigan and Iowa, than *play second fiddle* to the French.

FIDGET. Restless agitation. ' He has the *fidgets*,' is said of one who cannot sit long in a place.—*Todd. Grose.*

Why, who can the Viscountess mean ?
Cried the square hoods in woeful *fidget ;*
The times are altered quite and clean.—*Gray, Long Story.*

But sedentary weavers of long tales
Give me the *fidgets*, and my patience fails.—*Cowper, Con.*

I was in a *fidget* to know where we could possibly sleep.—*Mrs. Clavers, A New Home,* p. 13.

FIDGETING, or **FIDGETY.** Restless; impatient. A low word.—*Todd.*

Fungus is one of those *fidgeting*, meddling quidnuncs with which this unhappy city is pestered.—*Paulding, Salmagundi,* Vol. I. p. 40.

Peter seemed monstrous *fidgety*, and bimeby he allowed it was time to go.—*Maj. Jones's Courtship,* p. 191.

TO FIDGET. To be restlessly active.—*Richardson.*

It was evident that there was something on his mind, as he *fidgetted* before the glass.—*J. C. Neal, P. Ploody,* p. 21.

FIGURE. Amount of a reckoning. 'What's the figure?' a flash expression for, What is to pay?—*Grose.*

BIG FIGURE. See *Big.*

FILLIPEEN or PHILLIPINA. (Germ. *Vielliebchen.*) There is a custom common in the Northern States at dinner or evening parties when almonds or other nuts are eaten, to reserve such as are double or contain two kernels, which are called *fillipeens.* If found by a lady, she give sone of the kernels to a gentleman, when both eat their respective kernels. When the parties again meet, each strives to be the first to exclaim, *Fillipeen !* for by so doing he or she is entitled to a present from the other. Oftentimes the most ingenious methods are resorted to by both ladies and gentlemen to surprise each other with the sudden exclamation of this mysterious word, which is to bring forth a forfeit.

In a recent book on German life and manners, entitled " A Bout with the Burschens, or, Heidelberg in 1844," is an account of the existence of this custom in Germany, which at the same time furnishes us with the etymology of the word :

> Amongst the queer customs and habits of Germany, there is one which struck me as being particularly original, and which I should recommend to the consideration of turf-men in England ; who might, perhaps, find it nearly as good a way of getting rid of their spare cash as backing horses that have been made safe to lose, and prize fighters who have never intended to fight. It is a species of betting, and is accomplished thus : Each of two persons eats one of the kernels of a nut or almond which is double. The first of the two who, after so doing, takes anything from the hand of the other, without saying *Ich denke,* ' I think,' has to make the other a present, of a value which is sometimes previously determined, and sometimes left to the generosity of the loser. The presents are called *Vielliebchens,* and are usually trifles of a few florins' value ; a pipe, riding-whip, or such like.

FILLS. A common pronunciation for *thills,* the shafts of a waggon or chaise.

FINDINGS. The tools and materials which a journeyman shoemaker is to furnish in his employment.—*Webster.*

TO FIND ONE'S SELF. To provide for one's self. When a laborer engages to provide himself with victuals, he is said to *find himself,* or to receive *day wages.*—*Craven Glossary.*

In the advertisements of our steamboats and ships, it is stated that passengers are taken for so much and *found*, that is, provided with their meals.

> The singing master's proposals were to keep twenty evenings for twenty dollars and *found*, or for thirty and *find himself.*—*Maj. Downing*, p. 109.

FINEFIED. Made fine ; dandified.

> If this new judge is the slicked up, *finefied* sort on a character they pictur' him, I don't want to see him.—*Robb, Squatter Life*, p. 73.

FINICAL. Nice; foppish; pretending to superfluous elegance. —*Johnson.*

> Be not too *finical*, but yet be clean;
> And wear well-fashioned clothes like other men.—*Dryd. Ov. Art of Love.*

> At nineteen he painted his own portrait, in the *finical* manner of Denner, and executed the heads of an old man and woman in the same style afterwards.—*Walpole, Anecdotes of Painting*, Vol. IV.

FIPPENNY BIT, or contracted, **FIP.** Fivepence. In the State of Pennsylvania, the vulgar name for the Spanish half-real. (See *Federal Currency*.) *Fippence*, for fivepence, is also provincial in England.

TO FIRE. To fling with the hand, as a stone or other missile.

TO HAVE ONE'S FAT IN THE FIRE, is to have one's plans frustrated. A vulgar expression borrowed from the vocabulary of the kitchen.

> But take care that you don't, like the Paddy, touch off your machine at the wrong end; for the consequence, being unlooked for, might be bad, perhaps fatal, and then *the fat would all be in the fire*, and you would be where the devil could give more reliable information about you than any other of your near relations.—*N. Y. Herald.*

TO FIRE AWAY. To begin; to go on. An expression borrowed from the language of soldiers and sailors.

A well-known auctioneer in Pearl street, when putting up an article, says: "Come gentlemen, give us a bid, *fire away* ;" that is, go on.

> The Chairman rose and said: "We are not ready yet, we must go on in order." Calls for Mr. H——. Mr. H—— from the midst of the audience said, "Gentlemen, I beg to be excused, I came here to listen, not to speak." (Loud cries of "Go ahead," "Out with it," "*Fire away*.") Whereupon he commenced.—*N. Y. Herald, Sketch of a Political Meeting.*

TO FIRE INTO THE WRONG FLOCK, is a metaphorical

expression used at the West, denoting that one has mistaken his object, as when a sportsman fires at a different flock from what he intended.

> I said, when General J—— cocked his gun and began his war upon the Senate, he would find he had *fired into the wrong flock.*—*Crockett's Speech, Tour,* p. 81.

FIRE-NEW. New from the forge; brand-new.—*Johnson.* This old and nearly obsolete expression is sometimes used by us.

> You should then have accosted her; and with some excellent jests, *fire-new* from the mint, you should have banged the youth into darkness. —*Shakspeare, Twelfth Night,* III. 2.

> The Democracy of Washington, both in and out of Congress, huzzaed, sang, flaunted torches, held mass-meetings, to exult over the liberation of the French; they virtually insisted that this was all *their* thunder, and that Whigs had no business to participate in their rejoicings; but when the liberation of *Americans* from a much severer and more abject bondage came under consideration, they were and are ferocious for the *punishment,* by law or violence, not of the enslavers, but of the liberators! Instantly they are seized with a *fire-new* reverence for the Constitution and laws!— as if the French Revolution had not been effected in defiance of the consti-tuted authorities—as if the serfs of Metternich and Esterhazy were not as rightfully and truly theirs as those of Calhoun, Hope Slatter, and Mrs. M——.—*N. Y. Tribune,* April 25th, 1848.

FIRST RATE. Of the first class or order; superior; superex-cellent. An expression now in very common use, applied, as most superlatives are in the United States, with very little discrimination. It was formerly said of large and important things, as ' a *first rate* ship.' Now we hear of '*first rate* pigs,' '*first rate* liquors,' '*first rate* lawyers.' It is also used adverbially; thus if we ask a person how he is, he replies, ' I am *first rate,*' i. e. in excellent health, very well.

> The *first rate* importance of the subject, and the real merits of the work, are deserving of a portion of our space.—*Westminster Rev.* July, 1847.

> A young woman wants a situation as a chambermaid. She is a *first rate* washer and ironer, and plain sewer.—*Adv. in N. Y. Tribune.*

> Well, there's some men whose natural smartness helps them along *first rate.*—*Major Jones's Courtship,* p. 31.

> Mary liked all the speakers *first rate,* except one feller who gin the galls all sorts of a shakin.—*Ibid.* p. 168.

FIRSTLY. Mr. Pickering remarks that this adverb is frequently used by American writers. It is not noticed by Dr. Webster or any of the English lexicographers. The following is the only instance where Mr. P. found it in an English work :

> They will in some measure be enabled to determine, *firstly*, &c.—*British Critic*, Vol. XLIV. p. 577.

FIRST-SWATHE. First quality ; first chop. A New York word.

> Nothing 'll serve you but a *first-swathe* mug, about twenty-three years old.—*C. Mathews, Puffer Hopkins.*

FISH. ' To have *other fish to fry,*' is a common colloquial expression denoting that a person has other occupations, or other objects which require his attention.

> But as it seems they wete more wary,
> They'd *other fish to fry* than tarry.—*Maro*, p. 62.

FISH FLAKE. A frame covered with faggots for the purpose of drying fish.—*New England.*

FIT. Any short return after intermission ; a turn ; a period or interval.—*Webster.*

> The houses in many parts of Italy are unprepared for winter ; so that when a *fit* of cold weather comes, the dismayed inhabitant presents an awkward image of insufficiency and perplexity.—*Hunt's Indicator*, ch. 3.

BY FITS AND STARTS. At short and sudden intervals ; interruptedly.

> As prayer is a duty of daily occurrence, the injunction implies that it is ready to be imparted to Christians, not by *fits and starts*, or at distant intervals, but in a stated regular course.—*Robert Hall, Works*, Vol. I. p. 445.

FIX. A condition ; predicament ; dilemma.

> Some feller jest come and tuck my bundle and the jug of spirits, and left me in this here *fix.*—*Chron. of Pineville*, p. 47.

> The gentleman must be stronger in the faith than ourselves, if he does not find himself in an awkward *fix.*—*N. Y. Com. Adv.* Oct. 18, 1845.

> Are you drunk too ? Well, I never did see you in that *fix* in all my livelong born days.—*Georgia Scenes*, p. 163.

TO FIX. In popular use, to put in order ; to prepare ; to adjust ; to set or place in the manner desired or most suitable. —*Webster.*

Mr. Lyell, in his late book of Travels in North America, chap. iii. has the following remarks on this word : " At one of the stations where the train stopped, we heard one young woman from Ohio exclaim, ' Well, we are in a pretty *fix !*' and found their dilemma to be characteristic of the financial crisis of these times, for none of their dollar notes of the Ohio banks would pass here.   The substantive '*fix*' is an acknowledged vulgarism ; but the verb is used in New England by well-educated people, in the sense of the French ' arrange,' or the English ' do.'   To *fix* the hair, the table, the fire, means to dress the hair, lay the table, and make up the fire ; and this application is, I presume, of Hibernian origin, as the Irish gentleman, King Corney, in Miss Edgeworth's tale of Ormond, says, ' I'll *fix* him and his wounds.' "

In Upper Canada this word is equally common, where it was probably introduced by the American settlers :

> One of their most remarkable terms is *to fix*.   Whatever work requires to be done must be *fixed*. ' *Fix* the room,' is to set it in order. ' *Fix* the table,' '*Fix* the fire,' says the mistress to her servants ; and the things are *fixed* accordingly.—*Backwoods of Canada*, p. 82.

FIX IT.   A vulgarism of recent origin, but now very common. It is heard in such phrases as, ' I will not do so and so *any how you can fix it*,' or still worse, ' *no how you can fix it*,' i. e. not in any way that you can arrange it ; not by any means.

> A wet day is considerable tiresome, *any way you can fix it*.—*Sam Slick in England*, ch. 2.
>
> If I was an engineer, I'd clap on steam—I'd fire up, I tell you ; you wouldn't get me to stop the engine, *no way you could fix it*.—*Pickings from the Picayune*.
>
> The master called them up, and axed them the hardest questions he could find in the book, but he couldn't stump 'em *no how he could fix it*.— *Maj. Jones's Courtship*, p. 36.
>
> Workin' aint genteel nor independent, *no how you can fix it*.—*Pickings from the Picayune*, p. 74.

TO FIX ONE'S FLINT, is a phrase taken from backwoods life, and means the same as to settle ; to do for ; to dish.

> " Take it easy, Sam," says I, " *your flint is fixed* ; you are wet through ;" and I settled down to a careless walk quite desperate.—*Sam Slick in England*, ch. 2.

The Bluenose hante the tools; and if he had, he couldn't use them. That's the reason any one a'most can "*fix his flint for him.*"—*Ibid.*

FIXED FACT. A positive or well established fact.

The Boston Post, in speaking of the trial of Capt. Stetson for piratically running away with a ship and cargo, says:

That he did dispose of a large quantity of oil, and afterwards desert from the vessel, are *fixed facts.*—*June,* 1847.

FIXINGS. A word used with absurd laxity, especially in the South and West, to signify arrangements, embellishments, trimmings, garnishings of any kind.

A man who goes into the woods, as one of these veteran settlers observed to me, has a heap of little *fixin's* to study out, and a great deal of projecting to do.—*Judge Hall, Letters from the West,* Let. 18.

The theatre was better filled, and the *fixings* looked nicer than in Philadelphia.—*Crockett, Tour down East,* p. 38.

All the fellows fell to getting grapes for the ladies; but they all had their Sunday *fixins* on, and were afraid to go into the brush.—*Maj. Jones's Courtship,* p. 42.

"Ah!" exclaimed the teamster [to a gentleman who had a good deal of luggage], "what anybody on earth can want with such lots of *fixins,* I'm sure's dark to me."—*Mrs. Clavers, Forest Life,* Vol. I. p. 97.

One half of the country is overflowed in the winter, and t'other half, which is a darned sight the biggest, is covered with cane, pimento, and other *fixins.*—*Porter's South-western Tales,* p. 123.

The following advice was given to the editor of a new Western paper:

Advartise our doins in gineral, such as we got to sell, and throw yourself wide on the *literary fixins* and poetry for the galls; and, Mister, if you do this with spirit, the whole town will take your paper.—*Robb, Squatter Life,* p. 31.

For a use of the term as applied to food, see *Chicken Fixings.*

TO FIZZLE OUT. To be quenched, extinguished; to prove a failure. A favorite expression in Ohio.

The *factious* and *revolutionary* action of the fifteen has interrupted the regular business of the Senate, disgraced the actors, and *fizzled out !*—*Cincinnati Gazette.*

Is the new hotel [one called the Burnet House] to be given up, or to go on? To go on. It cannot be possible, after all that has been said and done about a "splendid hotel," that our enterprising business men will let it *fizzle out.*—*Ibid.*

FLAP-JACK. A fried cake; a pan-cake; a fritter. A word used alike in England and the United States, where it is also called *slap-jack*. See *Chicken-fixings*.

> We'll have flesh for holidays, fish for fasting-days, and moreo'er, puddings and *flap-jacks.—Pericles,* II. 7, *Supplement to Shakspeare.*

> Until at last, by the skill of the cook, it is transformed into the form of a *flap-jack,* which, in our translation, is called a pancake.—*Taylor's Jack-a-lent,* I. p. 115.

TO FLARE UP. To blaze out; to get excited suddenly; to get into a passion.

> It is expected that this grand discussion will take place soon; and then, if any member of the Cabinet chooses to *flare up,* he will have a fair chance, and may anticipate by resignation the ostracism of the Senate.—*N. Y. Com. Adv.* Nov. 20, 1847.

TO FLASH IN THE PAN. To fail of success. A metaphor borrowed from a gun, which, after being primed and ready to be discharged, *flashes in the pan.*

FLAT. In cant language, a foolish fellow; a simpleton.—*Worcester.*

> The London Times, of Sept. 5, 1847, in speaking of the letters of Mr. Tyler and Gen. Houston, showing by what means Texas was annexed to the United States, says:

> Oh! Messrs. Tyler, Donelson, and the rest, what *flats* you are all made to appear, by this revelation from the man in the blanket coat!

FLAT. In America this word is applied to low alluvial lands. " The Mohawk flats" is a term universally applied to the valley of the Mohawk river, on either side of which are alluvial lands. See *Bottom Lands.* It is also applied to river shoals, where they are of much extent.

FLAT. A species of flat-bottomed boat, used on the Mississippi and other rivers.

TO FLAT OUT. To collapse; to prove a failure. A Western phrase applied to a political meeting, as, ' The meeting *flatted out.*'

FLAT-FOOTED. Firm-footed, resolute; firmly, resolutely. A term belonging to the Western political slang with which the halls of Congress, as well as the newspapers, are now deluged.

Col. M—— attempted to define his position, but being unable, exclaimed : I'm an independent, *flat-footed* man, and am neither for nor against the mill-dam.—*Tennessee Newspaper.*

Mr. Pickens, of South Carolina, has come out *flat-footed* for the administration—a real red-hot democrat, dyed in the wool—denounces Mr. Calhoun—and is ready now to take any high office. But the mission to England is beyond his reach.—*N. Y. Herald*, June 30, 1846.

A Washington correspondent of the New York Commercial Advertiser, in speaking of the opinions to be advanced by President Polk in his Message, says :

The ground taken is to be *flat-footed* for the Sub-Treasury—*flat-footed* for the repeal of the Tariff of 1842, and the substitution of a 20 per cent. maximum, &c.

FLEA-BANE. (*Erigeron Canadense.*) One of the most hardy and common weeds. It propagates itself rapidly, and since the discovery of America, has been introduced and spread through most countries in Europe.—*Bigelow's Flora Bost.*

This plant is sold by the Shakers for its medicinal properties, which are astringent and diuretic.

FLINDERS. Shreds; splinters; broken pieces.—*Brockett.* Used also in New England.

Smate with sic fard, the airis in *flendris* lap.—*Douglas, Virgil.*

The tough ash spear, so stout and true,
Into a thousand *flinders* flew.—*Lay of the Last Minstrel*, ch. 3, 6.

Sure enough, when the General came to take off his boots, there was his best gold-rim specs, all broke to *flinders.*—*Maj. Downing's Letters*, p. 125.

Old Harley skeered the horse, upset the cart, and like to mashed everything all to *flinders.*—*Chronicle of Pineville*, p. 122.

FLING. A sneer; a contemptuous remark.—*Todd's Johnson.*

No little scribbler is of wit so bare,
But has his *fling* at the poor wedded pair.—*Addison.*

Nay, if that had been the worst, I could have borne it; but he had a *fling* at your ladyship too, and then I could not hold; but, faith, I gave him his own.—*Congreve, The Way of the World*, Act 3.

FLITTER. A corruption of the word *fritter*, a pan-cake.

FLOOR. Used in Congress, in this expression, *to get the floor;* that is, to obtain an opportunity of taking part in a debate. The English say, *to be in possession of the House.*—*Pickering's Vocabulary.*

FLOP. (Another form of the word *flap.*) Souse ; plump ; flat. Ex. ' His foot slipped, and down he came *flop.*'—*Forby's Vocabulary.*

TO FLOP. To flap.

> Fanny, during the examination, had *flopped* her hat over her eyes, which were also bathed in tears.—*Fielding, Joseph Andrews.*

TO FLOUR. To grind and bolt ; to convert into flour.—*Webster.* A word used in those parts of the country where there are mills for grinding wheat. Ex. ' This mill can *flour* two hundred barrels a day,' i. e. it can make so many barrels of flour.

FLOURING-MILL. A grist-mill.

FLUFF. Any light, feathery, downy substance ; flue.

FLUFFY. Covered with fluff or flue.

FLUMMERY. (Welsh, *llymru.*) A kind of food made by coagulation of wheat-flour or oat-meal ; and hence, flattery. —*Johnson.* We use it only in the latter or figurative sense.

> I allow of orange and buttermilk possets, of roasted apples, *flummery*, or any other light and cooling thing they call for.—*Boyle, Works.*

> > In wrath the king : " Cease, hypocrite !
> > Your *flummery* helps you not a whit !"—*Reynard the Fox.*

TO FLUMMUX. To perplex ; embarrass ; put to a stand. A very common vulgarism.

> Prehaps Parson Hyme didn't put it into Pokerville for two mortal hours ; and prehaps Pokerville didn't mizzle, wince, and finally *flummix* right beneath him.—*Field, Drama in Pokerville.*

TO FLUNK OUT. To retire through fear ; to back out.

> Why, little one, you must be cracked, if you *flunk out* before we begin. —*J. C. Neal.*

FLUNKY. A servant in livery. A term now used contemptuously.—*Jamieson.*

> > Our laird gets in his racked rents,
> > His coals, his kain, and a' his stents ;
> > He rises when he likes himsel' ;
> > His *flunkies* answer at the bell.—*Burns*, iii. 3.

FLUNKY. A class of people, who, unacquainted with the manner in which stocks are bought and sold, and deceived by appearances, come into Wall street without any know ledge of the market. The consequence is, they make bad investments, or lose their money. These the brokers call *flunkies.—A Week in Wall Street*, p. 81.

A broker who had met with heavy losses, exclaimed, " I'm in a *bear-trap*—this won't do. The dogs will come over me. I shall be mulct in a loss. But I've got time; I'll turn the scale, I'll help the bulls, operate for a rise, and draw in the *flunkies.*"—*Ibid.* p. 90.

FLUSH. Full of, abounding in; applied especially to money.

Lord Strut was not very *flush* in ready, either to go to law, or clear old debts; neither could he find good bail.—*Arbuthnot.*

FLUSTER. Heat; glow; agitation; confusion; disorder.— *Webster.*

When Caska adds to his natural impudence the *fluster* of a bottle, that which fools called fire when he was sober, all men abhor as outrage when he is drunk.—*Tattler*, No. 152.

The parish need not have been in such a *fluster* with Molly. You might have told them, child, your grandmother wore better things new out of the shop.—*Fielding's History of a Foundling.*

FLUSTERED. Heated with liquor; agitated; confused.— *Webster.*

—— He pretended to grow *flustered*, and gave the Barmecide a good box on the ear.—*Addison, Guardian*, No. 162.

FLUSTERATION. Heat; hurry; confusion.—*Brockett's Glossary.* A vulgar word also heard among ourselves.

TO FLY AROUND. To stir about; to be active. A very common expression.

Come, gals, *fly round*, and let's get Mrs. Clavers some supper.—*A New Home*, p. 13.

TO FOB OFF. To delude by a trick.—*Johnson.*

A low word now seldom used, though we have good authority for it.

You must not think to *fob off* our disgrace with a tale.—*Shakspeare, Othello.*

In speaking of the retirement of Mr. Buchanan from the Cabinet, the New York Tribune observes:

Pennsylvania insists on having a representative in the Cabinet, and will not be *fobbed off* with a six months' taste of honors.

FOGY. A stupid fellow; as, ' He is an old *fogy.*'

FOLKS. This old word is much used in New England instead of people or persons. 1. For the persons in one's family; as in this common phrase, ' How do your *folks* do ?' that is, your family. 2. For people in general ; as in expressions of this kind : ' What do *folks* think of it ?' &c. Dr. Johnson observes that " it is now only used in familiar or burlesque language."—*Pickering*.

> Old good man Dobson of the green
> Remembers he the tree has seen,
> And goes with *folks* to shew the sight.—*Swift*.

FOOL-FISH. (Genus, *monocanthus.* Cuvier.) The popular name of the long-finned file-fish. " Our fishermen apply to it the whimsical name of Fool-fish," says Dr. DeKay, " in allusion to what they consider its absurd mode of swimming with a wriggling motion, its body being sunk, and its mouth just on a level with the water."—*Nat. Hist. of New York*.

FORE-HANDED. To be *fore-handed* is to be in good circumstances ; to be comfortably off. The expression is much used in the interior parts of the country.

> Many of the new houses which have been built, have been built by mechanics, *fore-handed* men, as we say in New England, who have accumulated small sums.—*Providence Journal*.

> Mrs. Ainsworth made so long a visit among her Eastern friends, who are now *fore-handed* folks, that she has come back imbued most satisfactorily with a loving appreciation of the advantages of civilization.—*Mrs. Clavers, Forest Life*, Vol. I. p. 50.

TO FORK OVER. To hand over; to pay over, as money. A common expression in colloquial language.

> He groaned in spirit at the thought of parting with so much money. There was, however, no help for it, so he *forked over* the five dollars.—*Knickerbocker Mag*.

> A would-be prophet down South, lately said in one of his sermons, that " he was sent to redeem the world and all things therein." Whereupon a native pulled out two five dollar bills of a broken bank, and asked him to *fork over* the specie for them.—*Newspaper*.

> We want money in our treasury; and as you are making a small sprinklin' off the place with your panorama, you might as well leave a little on it behind ; so *fork over* the license money.—*Newspaper*.

FORKS. In the plural, the point where a road parts into two; and the point where a river divides, or rather where two rivers meet and unite in one stream. Each branch is called a *fork.—Webster*.

FORNENT. Opposite to. This Scottish word is now much used in Pennsylvania and the Western States.

FORTED IN. Intrenched in a fort.

A few inhabitants *forted in* on the Potomac.—*Marshall's Washington*.

FORTINER. (*For-aught-I-know*.) This remarkable specimen of clipping and condensing a phrase, approaches the Indian method of forming words. The word is very common through New England, Long Island, and the rest of New York. See *Farziner*.

TO FOURFOLD. To assess in a fourfold ratio. Mr. Pickering quotes this word from Webster's Dictionary, and observes that it is peculiar to the State of Connecticut. Dr. Webster afterwards expunged it.

FORWARDING MERCHANT. One whose business it is to receive and forward goods for others. The internal navigation and trade of the United States, with the great extent of our country, requires *forwarding merchants* in all the principal towns.

TO FOX BOOTS. To foot boots, i. e. to repair boots by adding new soles, and surrounding the feet with new leather. —*Worcester*. Of American origin; at least it does not appear in the English glossaries.

FOXED. A common term among booksellers. A book is said to be *foxed* when the paper, owing to some fault in its manufacture, becomes spotted with light brown or yellow spots. Many books printed in England between the years 1802 and 1812 have become spotted in this manner.

FOXY. A term applied in Maine to timber partially rotten.

FREESTONE. Red sandstone, so called from the ease with which it is cut and wrought.

FRENCH LEAVE. 'To take *French leave*,' is to depart without taking leave; to run away.

And Love, who on their bridal eve
Had promised long to stay,
Forgot his promise—took *French leave*—
And bore his lamp away.—*Halleck's Poems, Domestic Happiness*.

FRESHET.   A flood or overflowing of a river, by means of
heavy rains or melted snow ; an inundation.—*Webster*.

This word is used in the Northern and Eastern States.
That it is an old English word is evinced by the following
extract from the Description of New England, written and
published in England, in 1658 :

> " Between Salem and Charlestown is situated the town of Lynn, near
> to a river, whose strong *freshet* at the end of the winter filleth all her
> banks, and with a violent torrent vents itself into the sea."—p. 29.

This word appears to be now confined to America ; but the
word *fresh* is still used in the north of England and in
Scotland in precisely the same sense.

FROE.   An iron wedge.   *New England.*

> The shingle-maker stands with *froe* in one hand and mallet in the other.
> endeavoring to rive a billet of hemlock on a block.—*Margaret*, p. 159.

> " He beat his head all to smash with a *froe*," said one.   " No, it was
> with an axe," said another.—*Ibid.* p. 323.

FROST-FISH.   (Genus, *morrhua*.)   A small fish which abounds
on our coast during the winter months.   It is also called
tom-cod.—*Storer, Fishes of Massachusetts.*

FROSTWORT.   (*Cistus Canadensis*.)   A medical plant prepared by the Shakers and used for its astringent and tonic
properties.

FROUGH. ⎰
FROUGHY. ⎱   *Frough* is provincial in the north of England,
and means anything loose, spongy, or easily broken ; often
applied to wood, as *brittle* is to mineral substances.—*Brockett's
Glossary.*   '*Froughy* butter,' is rancid butter.

The latter of these words is in common use in many parts
of New England.   It is doubtless a corruption of *frough*,
which is sometimes used here.—*Pickering.*

FROWCHEY.   (Dutch, *vrouw*, a woman.)   A furbelowed old
woman.   Local in New York and its vicinity.

FRUMP.   To mock ; to insult.   A very old word, occurring in
the dictionaries of Cotgrave and Minshew.

> I was abas'd and *frump'd*, sir.—*Beaumont and Fletcher.*

This old word, though long out of use in England, still lingers among the descendants of the first settlers in New England.

> The sleighs warped from side to side; the riders screamed, cross-bit, *frumped*, and hooted at each other.—*Margaret*, p. 174.

FUDDLED. Tipsy; drunk. This word is common in England and the United States, but is only heard in familiar language.

> I am too *fuddled* to take care to observe your orders.—*Steele, Epist. Corresp.*

> > The table floating round
> > And pavement faithless to the *fuddled* feet.—*Thomson.*

> Mull'd yell and punch flew round lyke steyfe,
> The fiddlers a' got *fuddled.*—*Westmoreland Dialect*, p. 147.

FUDGE. An expression of contempt, usually bestowed on absurd or talking idlers; common in colloquial language.—*Todd.*

> I should have mentioned the very impolite behavior of Mr. Burchard, who, during this discourse, sat with his face turned to the fire, and, at the conclusion of every sentence, would cry out *fudge !*—*Vicar of Wakefield.*

FUFFY. Light; puffy; soft. Used in Yorkshire, England, and preserved in some parts of New England.

> She mounted the high, white, *fuffy* plain; a dead and unbounded waste lay all about her.—*Margaret*, p. 168.

FULL BUTT. With sudden collision. The figure is taken from the violent encounter of animals, such as rams or goats, which butt with their heads.

> He and the babler, or talker, I told ye of, met *full butt;* and after a little staring one another in the face, upon the encounter, the babler opened.—*L'Estrange, Tr. of Quevedo.*

FULL CHISEL. At full speed. A modern New England vulgarism.

> Oh yes, sir, I'll get you my master's seal in a minute. And off he set *full chisel.*—*Sam Slick in England*, ch. 2.

> The moose looked round at us, shook his head a few times, then turned round and fetched a spring right at us *full chisel.*—*John Smith's Letters.*

> At that the boys took arter them *full chisel*, and the galls run as if a catamount had been arter them.—*Downing, May-day in New York*, p. 46.

FULL DRIVE. At full speed. A very common and very old phrase.

> This bargain is *full-drive*, for we ben knit;
> Ye shul be paied trewely by my troth.—*Chaucer, Franklin's Tale.*

> Joe Dobson ran off tappy-luppy; an' just as he turned the nook of Anderson's byre, he came *full-drive* against owd Babby Bell.—*Westmoreland Dialect*, p. 352.

FULL SPLIT. With the greatest violence and impetuosity.— *Craven Glossary.* In common use in the United States in familiar language.

> I after him *full-split*,—he was clippin it across the orchard, so you might put an egg on his coat-flap, and it wouldn't fall off.—*Maj. Downing, Let.*

FULL SWING. Full sway; complete control.

> If the Loco-Focos have *full swing*, they will involve the country in war for the small strip in dispute in Oregon.—*N. Y. Tribune.*

FUNKIFY. To frighten; to alarm. *New England.*

> Scared! says he, serves him right then; he might have knowed how to feel for other folks, and not *funkify* them so peskily.—*Sam Slick in England*, ch. 8.

TO MAKE THE FUR FLY. To claw; scratch; wound severely. Used figuratively.

> Mr. Hannegan was greatly excited, which proved most conclusively that Mr. B. had *made the fur fly* among the 54 40 men.—*N. Y. Tribune.*

FUSSY. Bustling about as if much was to be done and was doing; consequential; very nice or particular in household or other matters. Used in familiar conversation with us, as ' a *fussy* fellow.' It is provincial in England.—*Hunter's Glossary.*

> You see the *fussy* European adopting the East, and calming his restlessness with the long Turkish pipe of tranquillity.—*Eöthen.*

FUZZY. Rough and shaggy.—*Forby's Vocabulary.*

> I inquire, whether it be the thin membrane, or the inward and something soft and *fuzzy* pulp that it contains, that raises and represents to itself these arbitrarious figments and chimeras.—*Dr. Henry More.*

FYKE. (Dutch, *fuyk*, a weel, bow-net.) The large bow-nets in New York harbor, used for catching shad, are called *shad-fykes.*

G.

GA. The abbreviation for *Georgia*.

GAB. Loquacity; prate; idle talk. This is an old word, and still has a place in the provincial glossaries of England.

GABBLEMENT. Gabble. A Southern word.

"This court's got as good ears as any man," said the magistrate, "but they aint for to hear no old woman's *gabblement*, though it's under oath."—*Chron. of Pineville.*

GADABOUT. One who walks about without business.—*Webster.*

GAFF. An artificial spur put upon game-cocks.

GAL-BOY. In New England, a romping girl; called also a *tom-boy.*

GALLOWSES. Suspenders; braces.

His skilts [pantaloons] were supported by no braces or *gallowses*, and resting on his hips.—*Margaret*, p. 9.

GAMBREL. A hipped roof to a house, so called from its resemblance to the hind leg of a horse, which by farriers is termed the *gambrel.*

Here and there was a house in the then new style, three cornered, with *gambled* roof and dormer windows.—*Margaret*, p. 33.

GAME LEG. A lame leg. A term not peculiar to America.

GAMMON. Humbug; deceit; lies. Any assertion which is not strictly true, or, professions believed to be insincere; as, 'I believe you're *gammoning*,' or, 'That's all *gammon;*' meaning, you are jesting with me, or, that's all a farce.

The gentry say death and distress are all *gammon*,
And shut up their hearts to the lab'rer's appeal.—*Punch*, pl. 54.

GANDER-PULLING. A brutal species of amusement practised in Nova Scotia. We quote Judge Halliburton's account of it from the Sayings and Doings of Sam Slick :

" ' But describe this *gander-pulling.*'

" ' Well, I'll tell you how it is,' sais I. ' First and foremost, a ring-road is formed, like a small race-course; then two great long posts is fixed into the ground, one on each side of the road, and a rope made fast by the eends to each post, leavin' the middle of the rope to hang loose in a curve. Well, then they take a gander and pick his breast as clean as a baby's, and then grease it most beautiful all the way from the breast to the head, till it becomes as slippery as a soaped eel. Then they tie both his legs together with a strong piece of cord, of the size of a halyard, and hang him by the feet to the middle of the swingin' rope, with his head downward. All the youngsters, all round the country, come to see the sport, mounted a horseback.

"'Well, the owner of the goose goes round with his hat, and gets so much a-piece in it from every one that enters for the "Pullin'," and when all have entered, they bring their horses in a line, one arter another, and at the words "Go a-head!" off they set, as hard as they can split; and as they pass under the goose, make a grab at him, and whoever carries off the head wins.

"'Well, the goose dodges his head and flaps his wings, and swings about so, it aint no easy matter to clutch his neck; and when you do, it's so greassy, it slips right through the fingers like nothin'. Sometimes it takes so long, that the horses are fairly beat out, and can't scarcely raise a gallop; and then a man stands by the post, with a heavy loaded whip, to lash 'em on, so that they mayn't stand under the goose, which aint fair. The whoopin,' and hollerin', and screamin', and bettin', and excitement, beats all; there aint hardly no sport equal to it. It is great fun to *all except the poor goosey-gander.*'"

GAP. This pure English word is used properly of any breach of continuity, as of the line of a saw's edge, or of the line of a mountain, as projected on the horizon. Hence it is applied to such openings in a mountain as are made by a river, or even a high road. Thus the *Water-Gap ;* and, in Virginia, *Brown's Gap, Rockfish Gap,* &c.

GAT. (Dutch.) A gate or passage. A term applied to several places in the vicinity of New York, as Barnegat, Barnes's gate; Hellegat, now called Hell Gate.

GAWKY. A tall, ungainly, stupid, or awkward person.— *Worcester.*

> Wert thou a giglet *gawky* like the lave,
>   That little better than our nowt behave.—*Ramsay, Gentle Shepherd.*

A large half-length [portrait] of Henry Darnley represents him tall, awkward, and *gawky.—Pennant's Scotland.*

GARNISHEE. In *law,* one in whose hands the property of an absconding or absent debtor is attached, who is warned or notified of the demand or suit, and who may appear and defend in the suit, in the place of the principal. *State of Connecticut.—Webster.*

GEE. A term used by teamsters to their horses and oxen, when they wish them to go faster. It is also used in directing oxen to the right or off-side. In most parts of England it seems to be applied in the same manner.

TO GEE. To agree ; to go on well together.—*Barnes's Dorset Glossary.* Also noticed in the Craven, Norfolk, and Cheshire glossaries.

GENERAL TREAT. A *general treat* is a treat of a glass of liquor given by a person in a tavern to the whole company present.

> I nearly got myself into a difficulty with my new acquaintances by handing the landlord a share of the reckoning, for having presumed to pay a part of a *general treat* while laboring under the disqualification of being a stranger.—*Hoffman*, p. 211.

GENITON APPLE. An early apple, probably *June eating.* Provincial in Suffolk, England.—*Moor's Glossary.* In the old dictionary of Cocker, 1700, is *Geunettings* or *Junetings*, small apples ripe in June.

> Dorothy gave her the better half of a *geniton* apple.—*Margaret*, p. 314.

GERRYMANDERING. To arrange the political divisions of a State, so that in an election, one party may obtain an advantage over its opponent, even though the latter may possess a majority of the votes in the State. This term came into use in the year 1811 in Massachusetts, where, for several years previous, the Federal and Democratic parties stood nearly equal. In that year the Democratic party, having a majority in the Legislature, determined so to district the State anew, that those sections which gave a large number of Federal votes might be brought into one district. The result was that the Democratic party carried everything before them at the following election, and filled every office in the State, although it appeared by the votes returned that nearly two-thirds of the voters were Federalists. Elbridge Gerry, a distinguished politician of that period, was the instigator of this plan, which was called *gerrymandering* after him.

TO GET THE WRONG PIG BY THE TAIL, is to make a mistake in selecting a person for any object. If a charge is made against a man, who on inquiry proves to be the wrong one, it is said they have *the wrong pig by the tail*. This is also called *getting the wrong sow by the ear*.

At the late election in Massachusetts, a Mr. C. C. Bell was elected by the Whigs, but was afterwards induced by the opposite party to give them his vote. Soon after, for fear of being forgotten, he wrote to a high official, presenting his claims for reward, closing as follows :

"If you can assist me now in your official capacity, you will command my everlasting gratitude. I have lived in obscurity and am not ambitious for office, but if my Democratic friends will not support me now, and help me out of my dilemma, why then I must make the best of it I can.

"I did not seek the office I have now, and was not at the meeting when I was elected, but the Whigs supposed they could by some means make me a traitor to my party. But, sir, as the old saying is, *they got the wrong pig by the tail*."

TO GIRDLE A TREE. In America, to make a circular incision, like a belt, through the bark and alburnum of a tree to kill it.—*Webster*. Settlers in new countries often adop this method to clear their land ; for when the trees are dr they set them on fire, and thus save themselves the troubl of chopping them down with the axe.

The emigrants purchase a lot or two of government land, build a log house, fence a dozen acres or so, plough half of them, *girdle* the trees, and then sell out to a new comer.—*Mrs. Clavers, Forest Life*, Vol. I.

GIST. The main point of a question or action ; that on which it lies or turns.—*Jamieson*. A word introduced from the language of law into very common use.

TO GIVE HIM JESSY, is to give him a flogging. A vulgarism of recent origin.

Well, hoss, you've slashed the hide off 'er that feller, touched his raw, and rumpled his feathers—that's the way to *give him jessy*.—*Robb, Squatter Life*, p. 33.

TO GIVE HIM THE MITTEN. This phrase is used of a girl who discards her sweetheart. She *gave him the mitten* means that she gave her lover his dismissal or discarded him. In England the phrase *to give him the sack* or *give him the bag*, denotes the same thing.

TO GIVE IT TO ONE is to rate, scold, or beat him severely. —*Holloway, Prov. Dict.* Used in the same sense in America.

GIVEN NAME. The Christian name, or name that is *given* to a person, to distinguish it from the *surname*, which is not given but inherited.

TO GLIMPSE. To get a glimpse of; as, 'I barely *glimpsed* him.'

GLUT. A wooden wedge.—*New England.* Mr. Pickering says this word is used in England, and refers to Rees's Cyclopedia.

THE GO. The mode; the fashion. ' This is all *the go.*'

> What ! Ben, my old hero, is this your renown ?
> Is this the new *go ?*—kick a man when he's down !
> When the foe has knocked under—to tread on him then :
> By the fist of my father, I blush for thee, Ben!—*Tom Crib.*

GO AHEAD. To proceed ; to go forward. A seaman's phrase which has got into very common use.

> I was tired out and wanted a day to rest; but my face being turned towards Washington, I thought I had better *go ahead.*—*Crockett, Tour down East,* p. 101.

> We slip on a pair of India rubber boots, genuine and impenetrable, and *go ahead* without fear.—*N. Y. Com. Adv.*

> The specific instructions to conquer and hold California were issued to Commodore Sloat, by Mr. Bancroft, on the 12th of July, 1846. Previous to this, however, he had been officially notified that war existed, and briefly instructed to "*go ahead.*"—*Ibid.* June 13.

TO GO BY. To call; to stop at. Used in the Southern States.—*Sherwood's Georgia.* Mr. Pickering says this singular expression is often used at the South. " Will you *go by* and dine with me?" i. e. in passing my house will you stop and dine? " Its origin," observes Mr. Pickering, " is very natural. When a gentleman is about riding a great distance through that country, where there are few great roads, and the houses or plantations are often two or three miles from them, a friend living near his route asks him to *go by* his plantation, and dine or lodge with him."—*Vocab.*

THE GO BY. To give one *the go by* is to deceive him ; to leave him in the lurch.—*Craven Glossary.*

TO GO FOR. To be in favor of.   Thus, ' I *go for* peace with
Mexico,' means I am in favor of peace with Mexico, or, as
an Englishman would say, I *am for* peace with Mexico.
This vulgar idiom is a recent one, and is greatly affected by
political and other public speakers, who ought to be the guard-
ians of the purity of the language instead of its most indefatiga-
ble corruptors.   In the following extract from a religious paper,
the reader of correct taste and feeling will hardly know
which to admire most, the sentiment or the language :

> Will Mr. Greeley say that he or any other citizen has the right to oppose
> " the Country"—that is, its laws—whenever he or they shall choose to
> pronounce them " wrong ?"   We say, *go for* your country—right, as she
> may be in some things—wrong, as she is, perhaps, in others ; but whether
> right or wrong, or right and wrong, (which is always nearer the truth in
> all her proceedings,) still, *go for* your country.—*Gospel Banner.*

To decide in favor of, is another acceptation in which this
phrase is often used, especially in stating for which man or
measure any particular section of the country has decided,
as, ' Ohio has *gone for* Clay,' ' Louisiana has *gone for* the
annexation of Mexico.'   Or still worse, ' Ohio has *gone*
Whig,' ' Louisiana has *gone* Loco-foco.'   Other variations of
the expression follow.

TO GO IT BLIND.   To accede to any object without due consideration.   Mr. Greeley, in speaking of General Taylor's
claims for the presidency, says :

> The Whig candidate must be fair and square on all the great questions
> before the country.   He would speak not of his own course, but the Whig
> people could not *go it blind*.—*N. Y. Tribune.*

Meaning that the Whigs could not vote or go for General
Taylor without a knowledge of his principles.

TO GO IT STRONG.   To perform an act with vigor or without scruple.

> President Polk in his message *goes it strong* for the Sub-treasury.—*N.
> Y. Tribune.*

> The Evening Post *goes it* good and *strong* for the establishment of free
> public baths.—*Newspaper.*

> The Senate has of late years refused to take any part of the book
> plunder, but they have *gone it strong* on the mileage.—*Letters from Wash-
> ington, N. Y. Com. Advertiser.*

TO GO THE WHOLE FIGURE. To go to the fullest extent in the attainment of any object.

> Go the whole figure for religious liberty; it has no meanin' here, where all are free, but it's a cant word and sounds well.—*Sam Slick.*

> One half of you don't know what you are talking about; and t'other half are *goin' the whole figure* for patriotism.—*Ibid.*

TO GO THE BIG FIGURE. To do things on a large scale.

> Why, our senators *go the big figure* on fried oysters and whisky punch. —*Burton, Waggeries.*

TO GO THE WHOLE HOG. A Western vulgarism, meaning to be out and out in favor of anything. A softened form of the phrase is *to go the entire animal.*

> Of the Congressional and State tickets we can only form a conjecture; but the probability is that the Democrats have carried the whole, for they generally *go the whole hog*—they never scratch or split differences.— *Newspaper.*

The phrase has been caught up by some English writers.

> The Tiger has leapt up heart and soul,
> It's clear that he means *to go the whole*
> *Hog*, in his hungry efforts to seize
> The two defianceful Bengalese.—*New Tale of a Tub.*

TO GO THROUGH THE MILL. A metaphor alluding to grain which has been *through the mill.* A Western editor observed that the mail papers looked as if they had been *through the mill*, so much worn were they by being shaken over the rough roads. It is often said of a person who has experienced anything, and especially difficulties, losses, &c.

GODSEND. An unexpected acquisition.

GOING. The state of the roads; the travelling. Ex. 'The *going* is bad, owing to the deep snow or mud in the roads;' 'The *going* is good since the road was repaired.'

GOINGS ON. Behavior; actions; conduct. Used by us as in England mostly in a bad sense. See *Carryings on.*

> Pretty place it must be where they don't admit women. Nice *goings on*, I dare say, Mr. Caudle.—*London Punch.*

GOLD-THREAD. (*Coptis trifolia.*) A plant well known in medicine, valued for its stomachic and tonic properties.

GOMBO. The Southern name for what is called at the North Okra, the pod of the *hibiscus esculentis*.

GOMBO. In the Southern States, a soup in which this plant enters largely as an ingredient.

GONDOLA. A flat-bottomed boat or scow used in New England.—*Pickering*.

GONE GOOSE. 'It's a *gone goose* with him,' means that he is past recovery. The phrase is a vulgarism in New England. In New York it is said 'He's a *gone gander*,' i. e. a lost man; and in the West 'He's a *gone coon*.'

> If a bear comes after you, Sam, you must be up and doin', or it's a *gone goose* with you.—*Sam Slick in England*, ch. 18.

> It may be the doctor can do something for her, though she looks to me as though it was a *gone goose* with her.—*Major Downing*, p. 87.

GONE WITH, for *become of*. 'What is *gone with* it' 'or with him,' for What has become of it or him?—*Sherwood's Georgia*.

GONEY. A stupid fellow.—*New England*.

> "How the *goney* swallowed it all, didn't he?" said Mr. Slick, with great glee.—*Slick in England*, ch. 21.

> Some on 'em were fools enough to believe the *goney*; that's a fact.—*Ib.*

GOODNESS. This inoffensive word is much used in a variety of ways by people of all classes. Sometimes we hear from old ladies the exclamation, 'Oh, *my goodness!*' denoting surprise. '*Goodness me*,' '*goodness gracious*,' and '*goodness sake*,' are also common. It is not peculiar to the Americans; for we find a distinguished personage using it:

> Now don't sleep, Caudle; do listen to me for five minutes; 'tisn't often I speak, *goodness knows*.—*Punch*.

> "The devil's in the cat, I swear!
> (Cried cooky): *goodness gracious!* there!"
> Whilst Molly shrieked "Ah, wo is me!"—*Reynard the Fox*, 57.

> ——————————— *goodness me!*
> My father's beams are made of wood,
> But never, never half so good
> 　　As those that now I see.—*Wordsworth, Rejected Addresses*.

Mr. Johnson says the Railroad company charges more than he thinks himself authorized to pay; if he yields, other companies will enlarge their demands, and *goodness knows* where he will find himself landed.—*N. Y. Com. Advertiser*.

Well, *goodness me !* it's mighty strange I can't call you to mind.— *Georgia Scenes*, p. 22.

GOOSE. A tailor's smoothing-iron. It is a jocular saying that ' A tailor, be he ever so poor, is always sure to have his *goose* at the fire.'—*Grose, Dictionary.*

> Come in, tailor, here you may roast your *goose.*—*Shakspeare.*

HAVE GOT. There are several corrupt or vulgar forms of speaking which have arisen from a desire to distinguish between different uses of the same word. Thus the verb *to have* is used in the sense of to hold, to possess (Sp. *tener*), and also as an auxiliary (Sp. *haber*). In order to distinguish the former use from the latter, many persons, both in England and America, are accustomed to use the expressions ' I've *got*,' ' he's *got*,' &c., instead of simply I have, he has, &c.

> Then forcing thee, by fire he made thee bright ;
> Nay, thou *hast got* the face of man.—*Herbert.*

I *have got* a good mind to go to the play.—*Pegge's Glossary.*

GOUGE. Imposition ; cheat ; fraud.

> R—— and H—— will probably receive from Mr. Polk's administration $100,000 more than respectable printers would have done the work for. There is a clean plain *gouge* of this sum out of the people's strong box.— *N. Y. Tribune,* Dec. 10, 1845.

TO GOUGE. To chouse ; to cheat.

> Very well, gentlemen ! *gouge* Mr. Crosby out of the seat, if you think it wholesome to do it.—*N. Y. Tribune,* Nov. 26, 1845.

TO GOUGE. " *Gouging* is performed by twisting the fore-finger in a lock of hair, near the temple, and turning the eye out of the socket with the thumb-nail, which is suffered to grow long for that purpose."—*Lambert's Travels*, Vol. II. p. 300.

This practice is known only by hearsay at the North and East, and appears to have existed at no time except among the lower class of people in the interior of some of the Southern States. An instance has not been heard of for years. Grose has the word in his Dictionary of the Vulgar Tongue, and defines it as " a cruel custom practised by the Bostonians in America !"

GOVERNMENTAL. Pertaining to government; made by government.—*Webster.*

TO GRAB. To seize ; to gripe suddenly.—*Grose. Webster.*

GRADE. (French.) 1. A degree or rank in order or dignity, civil, military, or ecclesiastical. 2. A step or degree in any ascending series ; as, ' crimes of every *grade.*'—*Webster.*

This word is of comparatively modern use. It is not in the English dictionaries previous to Todd's edition of Johnson in 1818. Mr. Todd calls it " a word brought forward in some modern pamphlets," and says " it will hardly be adopted." Mr. Richardson says the word " has crept into frequent use." Mr. Knowles in the ninth edition of his dictionary introduces the word as once belonging to the language, without comment. The British Critic and other reviews have criticised the word as an unauthorized Americanism ; but, as we have seen, it has been adopted at last by the English themselves.

While questions, periods, and *grades* and privileges are never once formally discussed.—*S. Miller.*

To talents of the highest *grade* he [Hamilton] united a patient industry not always the companion of genius.—*Marshall's Life of Washington,* Vol. V. p. 213.

TO GRADE. To reduce to a certain degree of ascent or descent, as a road or way.—*Webster.*

This use of the verb is not noticed by any English lexicographer.

TO GRADUATE. To take a degree at a university. " This verb," says Mr. Pickering, " was till lately used by us as a verb neuter or intransitive. Ex. ' He graduated at the University of Cambridge ;' but many persons now say, ' he *was graduated.*' " This is merely a return to former practice, the verb being originally active transitive. Examples of both uses are found in English writers.

This freshman college lived not to be matriculated, much less *graduated,* God in his wisdom seeing the contrary fitter.—*Fuller, Worthies.*

We think dissenters, merely as such, should not be deprived of the privilege of studying and *graduating* at the English Universities.—*Eclec. Review,* April, 1811.

GRAHAM BREAD. Bread made of unbolted wheat. It is easier to digest than common wheaten bread, and is in consequence much used by invalids.

GRAHAMITES. People who rigidly follow the system of Graham in their regimen.

> A glance at his round, ruddy face would shame a *Grahamite* or tetotaller out of his abstinence principles.—*Pickings from the Picayune*, p. 130.

GRAHAM SYSTEM. A system of dietetics recommended by Sylvester Graham, a lecturer of some celebrity on temperance and dietetics, which excludes the use of all animal food and stimulating drinks, including tea, coffee, etc.

GRAIL. (Fr. *grêle*, hail.) Small particles of any kind.— *Johnson*.

> Margaret curvetted about the mounds, she leaped the hollows (in the snow), the fine *grail* glancing before her and fuzzing her face and neck.— *Margaret*, p. 175.

GRAIN. A particle; a bit. Ex. ' I don't care a *grain ;*' ' Push the candle a *grain* further from you.'

GRAIN. The universal name in the United States for what is called *corn* in England ; that is, wheat, rye, oats, barley, &c.

GRAND. Very good ; excellent ; pleasant. This is one of the words so much abused among us by its too frequent use and application in senses differing from its proper one. Ex. ' This is a *grand* day ;' ' the sleighing is *grand ;*' ' what a *grand* time we had at the ball ;' ' *grand* weather,' &c. Mr. Hamilton in his remarks on the Yorkshire dialect, in England (Nugæ Literariæ, p. 318), notices this word as common there in the same sense.

GRASS. A vulgar contraction of *sparrow-grass*, i. e. asparagus. Further than this the force of corruption can hardly go.

GRAVY. Used in New England instead of *juice*, as the *gravy* of a pie.

GREAT. This word is used variously. A *great* Christian, for a pious man ; *great* horse is applied to a small pony, meaning a horse of good qualities and bottom ; *great* plantation, a fertile one.—*Sherwood's Georgia*.

GREAT. Distinguished, excellent, admirable. As, ' he is *great* at running ;' ' she is *great* on the piano.'

GREAT BIG. Very large. Often used by children.

GREATLE. A great while. Used on Long Island.

GREAT WITH. Intimate with ; high in favor with.—*Craven Glossary.* Dr. Webster notices this word in the same sense as a vulgarism.

> Tho' he was *great with* the king, he always doubted the king's uncles.—*Froissart's Chronicles.*

> Those that would not censure or speak ill of a man immediately, will talk more boldly of those that are *great with* him, and thereby wound their honor.—*Bacon.*

GREEK. A soubriquet often applied to Irishmen, in jocular allusion to their *Milesian* (!) origin.

GREEN. Uncouth, raw, inexperienced, applied to persons, a metaphor derived from green or unripe fruit ; vegetables or fruit that are growing. It answers to the English use of the word *verdant.*

> A little sassy rascal come up before me and stood and put his thumb to the side of his nose, and looked up with an awful sassy look at me and hollered out, " Ain't ye *green !*"—*Maj. Downing, May-day,* p. 45.

GREENHORN. A raw youth, easily imposed upon, unacquainted with the world.—*Todd.*

> If by mistake, at Washington, an old-fashioned man should speak of patriotism or the welfare of his country, he would be stared at as a *greenhorn* just from the bush.—*Hon. J. Whipple on R. Island Insurrection.*

GREENS. Leaves and green vegetables used for food.—*Ash.*

GRIT. Sand ; rough, hard particles.—*Johnson.* With us it is often vulgarly used to mean courage, spirit.

> The command of a battalion was given to Mr. Jones, a pretty decided Whig in politics, and like many other men of Zacchean stature, all *grit* and spirit.—*N. Y. Com. Adv., Letter from Washington,* June 24.

> Honor and fame from no condition rise. It's the *grit* of a fellow that makes the man.—*Crockett, Tour,* p. 44.

> If he hadn't a had the clear *grit* in him, and showed his teeth and claws, they'd a nullified him so, you wouldn't see a grease spot of him no more. —*Sam Slick in England,* ch. 17.

GRITTY. Courageous ; spirited.

> My decided opinion is, that there never was a *grittyer* crowd congregated on that stream ; and such dancin' and drinkin', and eatin' bar steaks and corn dodgers, and huggin' the gals, don't happen but once in a fellow's lifetime.—*Robb, Squatter Life,* p. 106.

GROCERY. A grocer's shop.   This word is not in the English dictionaries except in the sense of *grocer's ware,* such as tea, sugar, spice, etc.; in which sense we also use it in the plural.

GROG. In the language of seamen, gin and water, or any spirit and water, usually without sugar.—*Todd.*

> We stopped serving *grog,* except on Saturday nights.—*Cook and King's Voyages.*

Grog, says Grose, was first introduced into the British navy about the year 1740, by Admiral Vernon, to prevent the sailors intoxicating themselves with their allowance of rum or spirit.

GROGGERY. A place where grog and other liquors are drunk.—*Webster.*

GRUB.   Food; victuals.—*Grose.*

> The Bengalese, in cool apparel,
> Meanwhile have reached their pic-nic barrel;
> In other words, they have tossed the *grub*
> Out of their great provision tub.—*New Tale of a Tub.*

GRUNTER. (Genus, *pogonias.* Cuvier.) One of the popular names of the fish called by naturalists the *Banded Drum.*   It is common to the Atlantic coast south of New York.   Grunts and Young Sheepskin are other names of the same fish.—*Nat. Hist. of New York.*

GRUNTER. A hog.—*Craven Dialect.*

GUBERNATORIAL. Pertaining to government or to a governor.—*Webster.*

TO GUESS. 1. To conjecture; to judge without any certain principles of judgment. 2. To conjecture rightly, or upon some just reason.—*Johnson.*

> Incapable and shallow innocents!
> You cannot *guess* who caused your father's death.—*Shakspeare.*

> One may *guess* by Plato's writings, that his meaning as to the inferior deities was, that they who would have them might, and they who would not might let them alone; but that himself had a right opinion concerning the true God.—*Stillingfleet.*

We thus see that the legitimate, English sense of this word is *to conjecture;* but with us, and especially in New England, it is constantly used in common conversation instead of *to believe, to suppose, to think, to imagine, to fancy.* From such examples as the words *to fix* and *to guess,* it will be seen that while on the one hand we have a passion for coining new and unnecessary words and often in a manner opposed to the analogies of the language, there is on the other hand a tendency to banish from common use a number of the most useful and classical English expressions, by forcing one word to do duty for a host of others of somewhat similar meaning. This latter practice is by far the more dangerous of the two ; because, if not checked and guarded against in time, it will corrode the very texture and substance of the language, and rob posterity of the power of appreciating and enjoying those master-pieces of literature bequeathed to us by our forefathers, which form the richest inheritance of all that speak the English tongue.

GUFFAW. A hearty, boisterous laugh ; a horse laugh.

"You didn't let the Judge stray away from the swamp road ?" inquired Hoss.

"Well, I predicate I didn't, for by this time he's travellin' into the diggins most amazin' innocently ;" and then the pair enjoyed a regular *guffaw !—Robb, Squatter Life,* p. 75.

GUINEA CORN. (*Holcus sorghum.*) Egyptian millet, durrah of the Arabs, a plant with a stalk of the size and appearance of maize. The grain grows in a single pendant bunch at the top.

GUINEA GRASS. A species of grass cultivated in the West Indies, used as fodder for horses.—*Carmichael's W. Indies.*

TO GULCH. To swallow voraciously.—*Todd. Webster.* In low language this word is still heard in New England.

You are all a haggling, *gulching,* good-for-nothing crew.—*Margaret.*

GULL. 1. A cheat ; a fraud ; a trick. 2. A stupid animal ; one easily cheated.—*Johnson.*

I should think this a *gull,* but that the white-bearded fellow speaks it.—*Shakspeare.*

That paltry story is untrue,
And forged to cheat such *gulls* as you.—*Hudibras.*

The author of the " Perils of Pearl Street," in describing one of the swindling auction stores in New York, says :

The auctioneer and Peter Funk were ready to burst with laughter at the prodigious *gull* they had made of the poor countryman.—P. 53.

TO GULL. To trick ; to cheat ; to deceive.—*Johnson.* Seldom employed except in familiar conversation.

> Yet love these sorc'ries did remove, and move
> Thee to *gull* thine own mother for my love.—*Dame.*

The Roman people were grossly *gulled* twice or thrice over, and as often enslaved in one century, and under the same pretence of reformation.— *Dryden.*

You colony chaps are *gulled* from year to year.—*Sam Slick.*

There is no people like unto this people [the Americans], so great yet so little, so shrewd yet so easily *gulled*, so Christian yet so easily led away from the old standards of truth.—*N. Y. Com. Adv.* Feb. 24, 1848.

GULLIBILITY. Credulity. A low expression.—*Todd.*

A silly hoax has been for some time going the rounds of the newspapers, swallowed by all with eager avidity. Verily, the *gullibility* of the age is marked and peculiar.—*New York paper.*

GULLY. A channel or hollow worn in the earth by a current of water.—*Webster.* This word is much used in the United States. It is from the French *goulet*, and in old English authors is written *gullet*.

The violent rain which had fallen in the night had suddenly brought down such torrents of water through the hollow or *gully*, where they were in the utmost danger of being swept away before it.—*Hawkesworth's Voyages.*

TO GULLY. To wear a hollow channel in the earth.—*Webster.* This conversion of the noun into a verb is an Americanism. ' The roads are much *gullied*,' is a common expression.

GUMMY ! An exclamation, used in New England.

" *Gummy !*" retorted the woman. " He has been a talkin' about me, and a runnin' of me down."—*Margaret*, p. 137.

GUMP. A foolish person ; a dolt.—*Webster.* It is provincial in England, and may be found in most of the glossaries.

GUMPTION. Understanding ; skill.—*Todd.* This vulgar word is provincial in most parts of England, and is noticed in the glossaries of Pegge, Brockett, Forby, Jennings, and Halliwell. With us it is frequently heard.

> What tho' young empty airy sparks
> May have their critical remarks ;—

'Tis sma' presumption,
To say they're but unlearned clarks,
And want the *gumption.—Hamilton, Ramsay's Poems*, II.

He's a clever man, and aint wantin' in *gumption*. He's no fool, that's
a fact.—*Sam Slick in England*, ch. 26.

GUNNING. A colloquial word from *gun*. The act of going
out with a gun in order to shoot game.—*Ash's Dictionary.*
This word is commonly used by sportsmen in the Northern
States in the sense given by Ash.   At the South they use the
word *hunting*.

The Americans were, however, mostly marksmen, having been accustomed to *gunning* from their youth.—*Hannah Adams, Hist. of N. Eng.*

SON OF A GUN. This phrase is heard in low language with
us as in England.

H.

HABITAN.   (French.)   The lower class of Canadians of
French origin.

My coachman was a *Habitan*, and I had a fine opportunity of studying
the conflicting traits of character which distinguish the race.—*Lanman's
Tour to the Saguenay.*

HACK. A hackney coach.   The term *hack* is also frequently
applied by women to any article of dress, as a bonnet, shawl,
&c., which is kept for every day use.

TO HAIL FROM. A phrase probably originating with seamen
or boatmen, and meaning to come from, to belong to ; as,
' He *hails from* Kentucky,' i. e. he is a native of Kentucky.

HAINT, for *have not*. A contraction much used in common
conversation in New England.

HALF COCK. ' To go off at *half cock*,' is a metaphorical
expression borrowed from the language of sportsmen, and is
applied to a person who attempts a thing in a hurry without
due preparation, and consequently fails.

Mr. Clayton of Georgia is a fine speaker ; he is always ready, and never
goes off *half cock.—Crockett, Tour down East.*

HALF SEAS OVER. Intoxicated ; drunk. A sailor's expression.

HALVES. An exclamation entitling the person making it to the half of anything found by his companion. In the Craven Dialect, says Mr. Carr, on such occasions, if the finder be quick he exclaims, ' No halves—finder keeper, loser seeker,' to destroy the right of the claim.

> And he who sees you stoop to th' ground,
> Cries *halves!* to ev'rything you've found.—*Savage, Hor. to Scæva.*

HAMMER AND TONGS. In a noisy, furious manner. Thus, ' They went at it *hammer and tongs*,' is said of persons quarrelling. ' To live *hammer and tongs*,' is said of married people who seldom agree.—*Holloway.*

> Jonathan and the Spaniard will be at *hammer and tongs.*—*Montreal Courier.*

HAMMOCK. (Carib *amáca.*) A swinging-bed. This word, now in such general use, especially among seamen, and the etymology of which has been so much disputed, is undoubtedly of West Indian origin.

> Cotton for the making of *hamaccas*, which are Indian beds.—*Raleigh, Disc. of Guiana*, 1596.

> The Brazilians call their beds *hamacas;* they are a sheet laced at both ends, and so they sit rocking themselves in them.—*Sir R. Hawkins, Voy. to South Sea.*

HAND AND GLOVE. Intimate, familiar; i. e. as closely united as a hand and its glove. ' They are *hand and glove* together,' meaning very intimate, is a common idiom here as in England.

TO HANDLE. To manage, to overcome an opponent; particularly in wrestling. Ex. ' You can't *handle* him.'

HANDS OFF. A vulgar phrase for keep off; forbear.—*Johnson.*

> They cut a stag into parts ; but as they were entering upon the dividend, " *Hands off!*" says the lion.—*L'Estrange.*

HANDSOME. In familiar language this word is used among us with great latitude, and, like some other words mentioned in this Glossary, is difficult to define. " In general," says Dr. Webster, " when applied to things, it imports that the form is agreeable to the eye, or to the taste ; and when applied to manner, it conveys the idea of suitableness or propriety with grace."

HAND TO MOUTH. ' To live *from hand to mouth,*' is said of a person who spends his money as fast as he gets it, who earns just enough to live on from day to day.

> In matter of learning many of us are fain to be day-laborers, and to live *from hand to mouth*, being not able to lay up anything.—*Bishop Reynolds on the Passions*, ch. 37.

> I can get bread *from hand to mouth*, and make even at the year's end.— *L'Estrange.*

HANG. ' To get the *hang* of a thing,' is to get the knack, or habitual facility of doing it well. A low expression frequently heard among us. In the Craven Dialect of England is the word *hank*, a habit ; from which this word *hang* may perhaps be derived.

> If ever you must have an indifferent teacher for your children, let it be after they have got a fair start and have acquired the *hang* of the tools for themselves.—*Prime, Hist. of Long Island*, p. 82.

> He had been in pursuit of the science of money-making all his life, but could never get the *hang* of it.—*Pickings from the Picayune.*

> Suggs lost his money and his horse, but then he hadn't got the *hang* of the game.—*Simon Suggs*, p. 44.

> Well, now, I can tell you that the sheriffs are the easiest men for you to get the *hang* of, among all the public officers.—*Greene on Gambling.*

TO HANG AROUND. To loiter about. To ' *hang around* ' a person, is to hang about him, to seek to be intimate with him.

> Every time I come up from Louisiana, I found Jess *hangin' round* that gal, lookin' awful sweet, and a fellow couldn't go near her without raisin' his dander.—*Robb, Squatter Life.*

HANGER-ON. A dependant ; one who eats and drinks without payment.—*Johnson.*

> They all excused themselves save two, which two he reckoned his friends, and all the rest *hangers-on.*—*L'Estrange.*

HANG-NAILS. Slivers, which hang from the roots of the nails, and reach to the tips of the fingers.—*Forby's Vocab.*

TO HANG UP ONE'S FIDDLE. To desist ; to give up.

> When a man loses his temper and ain't cool, he might as well *hang up his fiddle.*—*Sam Slick.*

TO HANKER. To have an incessant wish.—*Johnson.* Dr. Johnson says this word is scarcely used except in familiar language. The same observation applies to it among ourselves.

> The shepherd would be a merchant, and the merchant *hankers* after something else.—*L'Estrange.*

HANKERING. Strong desire; longing.—*Todd.*

> We shall be able to part both with the body and its delights, without any great regret or reluctancy; and to live from them for ever, without any disquieting longings or *hankerings* after them.—*Scott, Christian Life.*

> I took an awful *hankerin'* after Sofy M——, and sot in to looking anxious for matrimony, and begin to go reg'lar to meetin', to see if I could win her good opinion.—*Robb, Squatter Life.*

TO HAPPEN IN. To happen to call in; to come in accidentally.

HAPPIFYING. Making happy. This mongrel barbarism, according to Mr. Pickering, is sometimes heard in our pulpits.

HARD CASH. Silver or gold coin.

HARD DRINKER. One who drinks to excess; a drunkard.

HARDFISTED. Covetous; close-handed.—*Todd.*

> None are so gripple and *hardfisted* as the childless.—*Bishop Hall.*

HARDHACK. (*Spirea tomentosa.*) The popular name of a well known and common plant in pastures and low grounds. It is celebrated for its astringent properties.

> She made a nosegay of the mountain laurel, red cedar with blueberries, and a bunch of the white *hardhack.*—*Margaret,* p. 206.

HARDHEAD. A fish of the herring species; the menhaden; so called in the State of Maine.

HARD MONEY. A common term for silver and gold, in contradistinction from paper money.

HARD PUSHED. To be hard pressed; to be in a difficulty; and especially, as a mercantile phrase, to be hard pressed for money; to be short of cash.

> As I said, at the end of six months we began to be *hard pushed.* Our credit, however, was still fair.—*Perils of Pearl Street,* p. 123.

A HARD ROW TO HOE. A metaphor derived from hoeing corn, meaning a difficult matter or job to accomplish.

Gentlemen, I never opposed Andrew Jackson for the sake of popularity. I knew it was a *hard row to hoe*; but I stood up to the rack, considering it a duty I owed to the country that governed me.—*Crockett's Speech, Tour down East*, p. 69.

HARD RUN. To be hard pressed; and especially to be in want of money. The same as *hard pushed*.

We knew the Tammany party were *hard run*; but we did not know it was reduced to the necessity of stealing the principles of Nativism.—*N. Y. Tribune*, Nov. 1, 1845.

HARDWOOD. A term applied to woods of solid texture that soon decay, including generally, beech, birch, maple, ash, &c. Used by shipwrights and farmers in Maine, in opposition to oak and pine.

HARUM-SCARUM. A low but frequent expression applied to flighty persons; persons always in a hurry, as if they were *hared* or frightened themselves, or *haring* others by their precipitancy; as, he is a *harum-scarum* fellow.—*Johnson*.

HASTY-PUDDING. Indian meal stirred in boiling water into a thick batter cr pudding, and eaten with milk, butter, and sugar or molasses. Joel Barlow wrote a poem on the subject, in which he thus accounts for its name:

> Thy name is *Hasty-Pudding!* thus our sires
> Were wont to greet thee fuming from their fires;
> And while they argued in thy just defence
> With logic clear, they thus explain'd the sense:—
> "In *haste* the boiling cauldron o'er the blaze,
> Receives and cooks the ready-powder'd maize;
> In *haste* 'tis serv'd, and then in equal *haste*,
> With cooling milk, we make the sweet repast."
> Such is thy name, significant and clear,
> A name, a sound to every Yankee dear.—*Canto I*.

Hasty-pudding is a favorite dish in every part of the United States. In Pennsylvania and some other States it is called *mush;* in New York, *suppawn*. *Hasty-pudding* in England is made of milk and flour.

> Sure *hasty-pudding* is thy chiefest dish,
> With bullock's liver or some stinking fish.—*Dorset Poems*.

HATCHET. 'To bury the *hatchet*,' is to make peace. A phrase alluding to the Indian ceremony of burying the war-hatchet, or tomahawk, when making a peace.

TO HAVE A SAY. To express an opinion. A phrase in vulgar use.

> I picked out " Henry Clay " for my baby's name, but they all wanted *to have a say* in it, and every one had a name that they liked the best of any. —*Maj. Jones's Courtship*, p. 198.

HAW-HAW. To laugh heartily.

> I sat down in front of the General, and we *haw-haw'd*, I tell you, for more than half an hour.—*Maj. Downing's Letters*, p. 189.

> He burst out a larfin', and staggered over to the sophy, and laid down and *haw-hawed* like thunder.—*Sam Slick*, 3d ser. ch. vii.

HAY BARRACK. (Dutch, *Hooi-berg*, a hay-rick.) A straw-thatched roof, supported by four posts, capable of being raised or lowered at pleasure, under which hay is kept. A term peculiar to New York State.

TO HAZE. To haze round, is to go rioting about.

OVER HEAD AND EARS. Completely overwhelmed. ' He sank *over head and ears* in the river ;' ' He was *over head and ears* in debt.'

> In jingling rhymes well fortify'd and strong,
> He fights intrench'd *o'er head and ears* in song.—*Granville.*

HEAD-CHEESE. The ears and feet of swine cut up fine, and, after being boiled, pressed into the form of a cheese.

TO HEAD OFF. To get before ; to intercept. Ex. ' The thief ran fast, but the officer managed to *head* him *off.*'

HEAP. A crowd ; a throng ; a rabble.—*Johnson.* This very old sense of the word is now provincial both in England and in this country. The expressions, ' a *heap* of men,' ' a *heap* of horses,' are given by Holloway in his Dictionary of Provincialisms. In the Western States it is in very common use ; as, ' A *heap* of people were present at the election,' etc.

> Now is that of God a full fayre grace
> That awhiche a lewd man's wit shall pace
> The wisdom of an *heap* of lered men ?—*Chaucer, The Prologue.*

> A cruel tyranny ; a *heap* of vassals and slaves, no freeman, no inheritance, no stirp or ancient families.—*Bacon.* (*Todd's J.*)

> An universal cry resounds aloud,
> The sailors run in *heaps*, a helpless crowd.—*Dryden.*

> A *heap* of likely young fellows courted me, but I refused them all for the head coachman of Counsellor Carter.—*Davis's Travels in America in 1798*, p. 237.

HEAP. A great deal; much. So used at the South and West.

A correspondent in the Commercial Advertiser thus notices the various uses of this word at the South :

Heap is a most prolific word in the Carolinas and Georgia among the common people, and, with children at least, in the best regulated families. " How do you like Mr. Smith?" I asked. " Oh! I liked him a *heap*," will be the answer, if affirmative, in five cases out of six. It is synonymous with a majority, or a great many ; as, " We should have plenty of peaches, but a *heap* of them were killed by the frost." It is synonymous even with *very*, as, " I heard him preach a *heap* often ;" " Oh ! I'm lazy a *heap*."

I was not idle, for I had a *heap* of talk with the folks in the house.—*Crockett, Tour,* p. 87.

Baltimore used to be called Mob-town; but they are a *heap* better now, and are more orderly than some of their neighbors.—*Ibid.* p. 13.

HEARN, for *heard.*

TO HEAR TELL. To hear a report of; to hear of. This expression is frequently heard among illiterate people in familiar conversation. Examples of its use may be found in the earliest English writers.

For harde ye hau often time *heard tell.*—*Chaucer, Somp.* **P. T.**

Of which when the prince *heard tell.*—*Spenser.*

" Pray, what is the meaning of Socdolager ?" I asked. " I never heard of the term before." " Possible !" said he ; " never *heerd tell* of the Socdolager ? Why you don't say so !"—*Sam Slick in England,* ch. 15.

Now this was the very first piano that was ever *heard tell* of, in the Purchase.—*Carlton's New Purchase,* Vol. II. p. 8.

Now, Capting, I'm in distress ; and I've always *hearn tell* that you sailors was generous chaps.—*Knickerbocker Mag.* Aug. 1845.

I beg leave to suggest to you that the Tinnecum people don't care much about the elements of music, of which they've *hearn tell* these two hundred years.—*Knickerbocker Mag.* Vol. XVII. p. 37.

HEARTY AS A BUCK. A hunter's phrase, now in very common use.

Well, how d'ye do, any how ?

So, so, middlin'. I'm *hearty as a buck,* but can't jump jest so high.—*Crockett, Tour,* p. 8.

TO HEAVE IN SIGHT. To come in sight; to appear. This nautical phrase appears to have originated in the fact that an approaching vessel appears to raise or *heave* itself above the horizon.

> A Carolina waggoner had just crossed the rail-road, when the engine *hove in sight* with the cars attached.—*Crockett, Tour down East*, p. 16.

HEFT. Weight; ponderousness. A colloquial term common to England and America.

> Mr. Pickering says: " This noun is also used colloquially in America to signify the greater part or bulk of anything, in expressions of this kind: ' A part of the crop was good, but the *heft* of it was bad.' "

TO HEFT. In the United States this verb means to lift anything in order to feel or judge of its weight.

> I remember the great hog up in Danwich, that *hefted* nigh twenty score. —*Margaret*, p. 111.

HELLABALOO. Riotous noise; confusion. Provincial in England.

> And the men of one idea
> Found fault with those who had two,
> And they wrangled and jangled and got so entangled,
> That truth and plain sense were outrageously mangled
> In the terrible *hellabaloo*.—*The Devil's New Walk*, Boston.

HELP. The common name in New England for servants, and for the operatives in a cotton or woollen factory.

HELTER-SKELTER. In a hurry; without order; tumultuously.—*Todd. Johnson.*

> Sir John, I am thy Pistol, and thy friend;
> And *helter-skelter* have I rode to England,
> And tidings do I bring.—*Shakspeare.*

HEN-HAWK. (*Falco lineatus.*) The popular name of the red-shouldered hawk of naturalists.

HERN, for *hers.* A vulgarism often heard among the uneducated. It is included by Pegge in his list of cockneyisms. See *Hisn.*

HET. Pret. and part. of *to heat.*—*Pickering.* Often heard in the mouths of illiterate people.

TO HIDE. To beat.—*Carr's Craven Dialect.*

> When I was a little boy—they coaxed me to take all the jawings, and all the *hidings*, and to go first into all sorts of scrapes.—*J. C. Neal, Sketches.*

TO HIFER. To loiter. Used in North Pennsylvania.

TO HIGGLE. To chaffer; to be penurious in a bargain.—*Johnson.*

> Why all this *higgling* with thy friend about such a paltry sum? Does this become the generosity of the noble and rich John Bull?—*Arbuthnot, John Bull.*

HIGGLEDY-PIGGLEDY. In confusion. A low word.—*Webster.*

HIGHBINDER. A riotous fellow. New York slang.

HIGH ROPES. To be *on the high ropes;* to be in a passion.—*Grose.*

HIP. To have *on the hip,* is to have an advantage over another. It seems to be taken from hunting, the *hip* or *haunch* of a deer being the part commonly seized by dogs.—*Johnson.*

> If this poor brach of Venice, whom I cherish
> For his quick hunting, stand the putting on,
> I'll have our Michael Cassio *on the hip.*—*Shakspeare, Othello.*

> When you want to get a man *on the hip,* ask him a question or two, and get his answers, and then you have him in a corner.—*S. Slick in England.*

HISN, for *his,* or *his own.* A vulgarism used in the United States, and embraced by Mr. Pegge in his list of London vulgar words.

HIT OR MISS. To do a thing *hit or miss,* is to do it at all hazards; that is, with a chance of *hitting* or gaining, or of *missing* it; at all events.

HITCH. A difficulty; an impediment.

> All the *hitches* in the case of McNulty being got over, the gentlemen of the long robe set themselves at work in earnest.—*N. Y. Com. Adv.* 1845.

TO HITCH. To agree; to get along amicably.

> I've been teamin' on't some for old Pendleton, and have come to drive a spell for this old feller, but I guess we shan't *hitch* long.—*Mrs. Clavers, Forest Life,* Vol. I. p. 116.

HITHER AND YON. This expression is often used in the country towns of New England for *here and there.* It is never heard in our seaport towns.—*Pickering.* Grose has the expression in his Prov. Glossary in the same sense. He calls it a Northern phrase, though it does not appear in Brockett's Glossary.

HO. A word used by teamsters to stop their teams. It has been used as a noun, for stop; moderation; bounds.— *Webster.* See *Whoa.*

> Because, forsooth, some odd poet or some such fantastic fellows make much on him, *there's no ho with him;* the vile dandiprat will overlook the proudest of his acquaintance.—*Lingua, Old Play.*

Mr. Malone says it is yet common in Ireland; as, ' there's no *ho* in him,' that is, he knows no bounds. This expression is common in the United States.

HOBBLE. A scrape; a state of perplexity.—*Carr's Craven Glossary.*

> Now, Capt. Cleveland, will you get us out of this *hobble?*—*Pirate,* III.

HOBSON'S CHOICE. An expression often used, denoting that kind of choice in which there is no alternative. The caprice of Hobson, the Cambridge carrier, who died in 1630, is said to have given rise to it.—*Todd.* The common phrase is, ' It's *Hobson's choice*—that or none.'

> Hobson kept a stable of forty good cattle, always ready and fit for travelling; but when a man came for a horse, he was led into the stable. where there was a great choice, but he obliged him to take the horse next to the stable door; so that every customer was alike well served according to his chance, and every horse ridden with the same justice. From whence it became a proverb, when what ought to be your choice was forced upon you, to say, *Hobson's choice.*—*Spectator,* No. 509.

HOE-CAKE. A cake of Indian meal, baked before the fire. In the interior parts of the country, where kitchen utensils do not abound, they are baked on a *hoe ;* hence the name.

> Some talk of *hoe-cake,* fair Virginia's pride;
> Rich Johnny-cake this mouth has often tryed.
> Both please me well, their virtues much the same;
> Alike their fabric as allied their fame.—*J. Barlow, Hasty Pudding.*

HOG-WALLOW. On some of the Western prairies, the ground has every appearance of having been rooted or torn up by hogs, when it is very rough; hence the name.— *Kendall's Santa Fé Expedition,* Vol. I. p. 58.

HOITY-TOITY. An exclamation denoting surprise or disapprobation, with some degree of contempt.—*Webster.*

> *Hoity-toity !* what have I to do with dreams ?—*Congreve, Love for Love.*

TO HOLD FORTH. To harangue; to speak in public.—*Todd's Johnson.*

> A petty conjuror telling fortunes, *held forth* in the market-place.—*L'Estrange.*

TO HOLD ON. To wait; stop. '*Hold on* a minute;' originally a sea phrase.

TO HOLD UP. In allusion to the weather, to clear up, after a storm; to stop raining.

> Though nice and dark the point appear,
> Quoth Ralph, it may *hold up* and clear.—*Hudibras.*

TO HALLOO. }
TO HOLLOW. } To shout; to hoot; to cry out loudly.—*Todd's Johnson.* This word is generally written and pronounced *hollow*, which Dr. Johnson says is incorrect. In England as well as in the United States it is vulgarly pronounced *holler* or *hollar.*

> List, list; I hear
> Some far-off *halloo* break the silent air.—*Milton.*

> He with his hounds comes *hollowing* from the stable,
> Makes love with nods, and kneels beneath a table.—*Pope.*

> You *hollered* so, and scared Obed, he's scared now.—*Margaret,* p. 53.

HOLLOW. *All hollow* is a common expression with us, and is also given by Carr in his Craven Glossary. ' He carried it *all hollow;*' ' He beat him *all hollow ;*' that is, wholly, completely.

HOLPE, or HOLP. The old preterite and past part. of *Help.* " This antiquated inflection of the verb *to help* is still used in Virginia, where it is corrupted into *holped.*"—*Pickering.* Johnson and Webster notice the word; and Bishop Lowth observes in his Grammar, that it was used in conversation in his day.

> His great love, sharp as his spur, hath *holp* him
> To 's home before us.—*Shakspeare.*

HOLT, for *hold.* Ex. ' Death has got *holt* of him.'

HOMINY. Food made of maize or Indian corn boiled, the maize being either coarsely ground, or broken, or the kernels merely hulled.—*Flint, Mississippi Valley.* Also written *hommony.* Roger Williams, in his Key to the Indian Language, has the word *aupúminea,* parched corn—which, with the accent on the second syllable, has much the sound of hominy.

> The Indians sift the flour out of their meal, which they call *samp ;* the remainder they call *homminy.* This is mixt with flour and made into puddings.—*Josselyn's New England Rarities,* 1672, p. 53.

HONEY-FOGLE. To swindle; to cheat; to lay plans to deceive. This singular word, I am told, is used in Louisiana. *Coney-fogle,* to lay plots, a Lancashire word, noticed by Mr. Halliwell in his Dictionary of Archaic and Prov. Words, may be the origin of it.

HONOR BRIGHT! A protestation of honor among the vulgar; originating with, and still retained in commemoration of, a late well-known Newcastle worthy.—*Brockett, North Country Words.*

> Now here's another—(*honor bright !*)
> Once Reynard, as he prowled by night,
> Knew of a slaughtered pig, &c.—*Reynard the Fox.*

HOOK. (Dutch, *hoek,* a corner.) This name is given in New York to several angular points in the North and East rivers; as, *Corlear's Hook, Sandy Hook, Powles's Hook.*

BY HOOK OR BY CROOK. One way or other; by any expedient.—*Johnson.*

> It can't be done *by hook or crook,*
> Unless your Highness undertook
> To see me through the matter clean.—*Reynard the Fox.*

TO HOOK. To steal. A common vulgarism.

ON ONE'S OWN HOOK. A phrase much used in familiar language, denoting on one's own account; as, ' He is doing business *on his own hook,*' i. e. for himself.

> The South is determined that its favorite, Mr. Calhoun, shall go into the National Convention as a candidate for the Presidency; and in case he does not get the nomination, he will run *on his own hook.—Newspaper.*

> I now resolved to do business entirely alone—to go *on my own hook.* If I get rich, the money will all be mine.—*Perils of Pearl Street,* p. 195.

Are you hired to any one now, or do you go *on your own hook?—Mrs. Clavers, Forest Life*, Vol. I. p. 116.

We have every reason to believe that the time is fast approaching when we shall have our American Pope, our American Catholic Cardinals, and American Catholic everything *on our own hook.—N. Y. Herald*, Oct. 1845.

I went to the opera in London, where I kept lookin' round; and when any body laughed, I laughed too, and when they 'plauded, I 'plauded too; and sometimes, jest to make 'em think I was a reglar Frenchy, I'd laugh right out *on my own hook*, and 'plaud—then the fellers and gals would look at me, much as to say, He's got some gumption.—*N. Y. Fam. Companion.*

HOOKEY. To play *hookey*, is to play truant. A term used among schoolboys.

HOOPLE. (Dutch, *hoepel.*) The boys in the city of New York still retain the Dutch name *hoople* for a hoop.

HOOSIER. A nickname given at the West to a native of Indiana.

A correspondent of the Providence Journal, writing from Indiana, gives the following account of the origin of this term: " Throughout all the early Western settlements were men who rejoiced in their physical strength, and on numerous occasions, at log-rollings and house-raisings, demonstrated this to their entire satisfaction. They were styled by their fellow citizens, ' *hushers*,' from their primary capacity to still their opponents. It was a common term for a bully throughout the West. The boatmen of Indiana were formerly as rude and as primitive a set as could well belong to a civilized country, and they were often in the habit of displaying their pugilistic accomplishments upon the Levee at New Orleans. Upon a certain occasion there, one of these rustic professors of the ' noble art' very adroitly and successfully practised the ' fancy' upon several individuals at one time. Being himself not a native of this Western world, in the exuberance of his exultation he sprang up, exclaiming, in foreign accent, ' I'm a *hoosier*, I'm a *hoosier*.' Some of the New Orleans papers reported the case, and afterwards transferred the corruption of the epithet ' husher' (*hoosier*) to all the boatmen from Indiana, and from thence to all her citizens.

There was a long-haired *hoosier* from Indiana, a couple of smart-looking *suckers* from Illinois, a keen-eyed, leather-belted *badger* from Wisconsin;

and who could refuse to drink with such a company ?—*Hoffman, Winter in the West*, p. 210.

The *hoosier* has all the attributes peculiar to the backwoodsmen of the West. . . . One of them visited the city [New Orleans] last week. As he jumped from his flat-boat on to the Levee, he was heard to remark that he " didn't see the reason of folks livin' in a heap this way, where they grew no corn and had no *bars* to kill."—*Pickings from the Picayune.*

HOP. A dance.—*Johnson.* This word has always been used here as in England as a familiar term for *dance ;* but of late years it has been employed among us in a technical sense, to denote a dance where there is less display and ceremony than at regular balls. At Saratoga Springs, where a large majority of the people are strangers to each other, it is customary to have a dance or *hop* at the fashionable hotels three times a week, during the season when the waters are most resorted to.

HOPED. Used among the illiterate in North Carolina as the past part. of *to help.* Ex. ' It can't be *hoped.*'—See *Holp.*

HOPSCOTCH. A game well known to our boys. A figure is drawn upon the ground in the form of a parallelogram, which is subdivided in several parts. A small stone is thrown successively into each, and is knocked out by a boy hopping on one leg, without resting, until he has thrown and knocked it from every division of the figure. Mr. Hartshorn notices the word in his Shropshire Glossary.

HOREHOUND. (*Marrubium vulgare.*) One of the most common medicinal plants, celebrated for its virtues in the cure of colds.

HORN. A dram ; a glass of liquor.

The chaplain gave us a pretty stiff *horn* of liquor a-piece—and first-rate stuff it was, I swow.—*Burton, Waggeries.*

HORNS. The feelers of a snail. Hence the proverb, *To pull in the horns*, To repress one's ardor.—*Johnson.* In the United States the phrase is, *To haul in one's horns.*

I tell you what, the highfliers that's been tryin' to be 'stockracy folkes has *hauled in their horns* since Crockett cut out.—*Maj. Jones's Courtship.*

HORSE-COLT. " We frequently see in advertisements these terms, *horse-colt, mare-colt*, &c. A *horse*-colt is simply a *colt;* a *mare*-colt, merely a *filly.*"—*Portfolio*, 2d ser. Vol. II. 309.

HORSE-FOOT. (Genus, *polyphemus.* Lamarck.) The common name of a crustacea, found in our waters from Massachusetts to Virginia. In form it much resembles a horse's hoof. Also called Horse-shoe.

HOSS. (A corruption of the word *horse.*) A man remarkable for his strength, courage, etc. A vulgarism peculiar to the West.

" Well, old fellow, you're a *hoss !*" is a Western expression, which has grown into a truism as regards Judge Allen, and a finer specimen of a Western judge " aint no whar," for besides being a sound jurist, he is a great wag; etc.

Hoss Allen is powerful popular, and the " bar " hunters admire his free and easy manners, and consider him one of the people—none of your stuck-up imported chaps from the dandy States, but a genuine Westerner —in short, a *hoss !—Robb, Squatter Life,* p. 70.

HOUSEN, as the plural of *house.* This old form is still used by the illiterate in the interior of New England, as also in the State of New York. It is provincial in various parts of England.

That day at *housen* so she stopped
She was behind for dinner.—*Essex Dialect,* p. 14.

It is enacted by the court and authoritie thereof, that henceforth no person or persons shall permit any meetings of the Quakers to bee in his house or *housing.—Plymouth Colony Laws,* 1661.

HOUSEN-STUFF. Household furniture.

On the first day of May, at 12 o'clock, if the tenant isn't out, an officer goes and puts him into the street, neck and heels, with his wife and children and all his *housen-stuff.—Maj. Downing, May-day in N. Y.* p. 30.

HOUSE-WARMING. A feast, or merry-making, upon going into a new house.—*Johnson.*

Overeat himself at a *housewarming.—Addison, Guardian,* No. 136.

HOVE. (Ang. Sax. *hof,* pret. of *heafan,* to heave.) This old preterite is much used by illiterate persons in the United States.

HOW? for *what ?* Used chiefly in New England, like the French *comment ?* in asking for the repetition of something not understood.

HOW-COME? Rapidly pronounced *huc-cum,* in Virginia. Doubtless an English phrase, brought over by the original settlers, and propagated even among the negro slaves. The meaning is, How did what you tell me happen? How came it?

HOWSOMEVER, for *Howsoever*. Not peculiar to America.

HUB. The nave of a wheel; a solid piece of timber in which the spokes are inserted.—*Webster*. The word is also provincial in England.

HUBBY. Applied to rough roads, particularly when frozen; as, the road is *hubby*. In the Craven Dialect of England the word *hobbly* is applied to rough or stony roads.

HUBBUB. A shout; a tumult; a riot.—*Grose. Todd's Johnson.*

> An universal *hubbub* wild
> Of stunning sounds, and voices all confus'd,
> Borne through the hollow dark, assaults his ear
> With loudest vehemence.—*Milton, Paradise Lost.*

People pursued the business with all contempt of the government: and in the *hubbub* of the first day there appeared nobody of name or reckoning, but the actors were really of the dregs of the people.—*Clarendon.*

Agreed for all the whole inhabitants to combine to assist any man in the pursuit of any party delinquent; but if any man raise a *hubbub*, and there be no just cause for the same, then for the party that raised the *hubbub* to satisfy men for their time lost in it.—*Staples, Annals of Providence, R. I.*

The King was sorry he couldn't ask Mr. Slick to dine with him; for the Queen was very busy, as it was white-washing day, and they was all in a *hubbub.*—*Sam Slick*, 3d ser. ch. 7.

HUCKABUCK. Coarse table linen. Scottish, *hagabag*.

> Clean *hagabag* I'll spread upon this board,
> And serve him with the best we can afford.—*Ramsay's Poems.*

HUCKLEBERRY. The common *whortleberry*.

HUCKLEBERRY ABOVE THE PERSIMMON. A Southern phrase.

The way he and his companions used to destroy the beasts of the forests, was *huckleberry above the persimmon* of any native in the country.—*Thorpe, Backwoods*, p. 166.

HUFFED. Offended.

Jason insisted that the young lady was *huffed*, as he called it, and that she had thus refused to take the money merely because she was thus offended.—*Cooper, Satanstoe*, Vol. I. p. 81.

HUGE PAWS. A nickname given to the working-men of the Loco Foco party in New York.

The *huge paws* ought to have another meeting at Tammany Hall before they make their nominations.—*N. Y. Herald*, Oct. 7, 1846.

HULL. A vulgar pronunciation of the word *whole* very common in New England.

HUMBLE PIE. To make one *eat humble pie,* is to make him lower his tone, and be submissive. Forby notices this among the proverbs of Norfolk, England.

HUMBUG. An imposition; a hoax. And as a verb, to impose upon; to deceive. A low word.—*Worcester.*

"There is a word very much in vogue with the people of taste and fashion, which, though it has not even the 'penumbra' of a meaning, yet makes up the sum total of the wit, sense, and judgment of the aforesaid people of taste and fashion! 'This piece will prove a confounded *humbug* upon the nation; These theatrical managers *humbug* the town damnably!' *Humbug* is neither an English word, nor a derivative from any other language. It is indeed a blackguard sound, made use of by most people of distinction! It is a fine make-weight in conversation, and some great men deceive themselves so egregiously as to think they mean something by it!"—*Student,* Vol. II. (1751.)

> Of all trades and arts in repute or oppression,
> *Humbugging* is held the most ancient profession.
> 'Twixt nations and parties, and state politicians,
> Prim shop-keepers, jobbers, smooth lawyers, physicians;
> Of worth and of wisdom the trial and test
> Is—mark ye, my friends!—who shall *humbug* the best.—*Brookes.*

Truly as a people we are easily *humbugged,* enormously bamboozled.—*N. Y. Com. Adv.*

HUMDRUM. Dull; dronish; stupid; heavy.—*Todd's Johnson.*

I was talking with an old *humdrum* fellow, and, before I had heard his story out, was called away by business.—*Addison, Whig Examiner,* No. 3.

HUMLY or **HUMBLY,** for *homely.*

HUMPTY-DUMPTY. Short and broad; as, He's a *humpty-dumpty* fellow.—*Craven Glossary.*

HUMS AND HAHS. A familiar expression applied to one who hesitates in speaking. 'None of your *hums and hahs!*' that is, be decisive, do not hesitate. The expression is common in England.

With dimpling cheek, and snowy hand,
That shames the whiteness of his band,
Whose mincing dialect abounds
With *hums and hahs*, and half form'd sounds.—*Lloyd, Epistle.*

I know'd well enough that warn't what he sent for me for, by the way
he *humm'd and hawed* when he began.—*Sam Slick in England*, ch. 20.

HUNK. A large piece or slice; a big lump. Ex. 'A great
hunk of bread and cheese.' It is a variation of the word
hunch, which is used in England in precisely the same
manner. See Grose and Moor's glossaries.

HUNK. (Dutch, *honk*.) A goal, or place of refuge. A word
much used by New York boys in their play.

OLD HUNKER. See *Barnburners*.

HURLY-BURLY. A noise, or tumult; bustle; confusion.—
Nares's Glossary.

And to thintent the easier, to bleave his enemy's eyes with suspicion of
fearfulness, he bade that they should remove with more noise and *hurly-
burly*, than the custom of the Romans was to do.—*Udal, Luke*, ch. 21.

HURRA'S NEST. A state of confusion.

" Now just look at you, Mr. Jones! I declare! it gives me a chill to
see you go to a drawer. What do you want? Tell me! and I will get
it for you."

Mrs. Jones springs to the side of her husband, who has gone to the
bureau for something, and pushes him away.

" There now! Just look at the *hurra's nest* you have made! What *do*
you want, Mr. Jones?"—*Arthur's Ladies' Magazine.*

HURRICANE. (W. Ind. *urican*.) This word does not appear
in any English dictionary before 1720, when Phillips notices
it, as a word denoting " a violent storm of wind, which often
happens in Jamaica, and other parts of the W. Indies, making
very great havoc and overthrow of trees, houses, etc." Other
dictionaries of a later period describe it as a violent wind in
the W. Indies. It is the Carib name for a high wind, such
as is described by Phillips, and was, doubtless, carried by
seamen to Europe, whence it became introduced into various
languages.

I shall next speak of *hurricanes*. These are violent storms, raging
chiefly among the Caribee Islands; though by relation Jamaica has of late
years been much annoyed by them. They are expected in July, August,
or September.—*Dampier, Voyages*, Vol. II. ch. 6.

HURRYMENT. Hurry. Used in the Southern States.

> Somehow in my *hurryment* I drapt my pan, jest like I did when I heard Old Blaze squeel.— *Chron. of Pineville,* p. 174.

HURRY UP THE CAKES, i. e. Be quick; look alive. This phrase, which has lately got into vogue, originated in the common New York eating-houses, where it is the custom for the waiters to bawl out the name of each dish as fast as ordered, that the person who serves up may get it ready without delay, and where the order, ' *Hurry up them cakes,*' &c., is frequently heard.

HUSKING. The act of stripping off husks from Indian corn. In New England it is the custom for farmers to invite their friends to assist them in this task. The ceremonies on these occasions are well described by Joel Bárlow, in his poem on Hasty Pudding:

> For now, the cow-house fill'd, the harvest home,
> Th' invited neighbors to the *Husking* come;
> A frolic scene, where work, and mirth, and play,
> Unite their charms, to chase the hours away.
>
> *   *   *   *   *   *
>
> The laws of *husking* every wight can tell;
> And sure no laws he ever keeps so well:
> For each red ear a gen'ral kiss he gains,
> With each smut ear, she smuts the luckless swains;
> But when to some sweet maid a prize is cast,
> Red as her lips, and taper as her waist,
> She walks around, and culls one favor'd beau,
> Who leaps, the luscious tribute to bestow.
> Various the sport, as are the wits and brains
> Of well-pleas'd lasses and contending swains;
> Till the vast mound of corn is swept away,
> And he that gains the last ear, wins the day.— *Canto* 3.

> He talked of a turkey-hunt, a *husking-bee,* thanksgiving ball, racing, and a variety of things.— *Margaret,* p. 48.

HYST. (Corruption of *hoist.*) A violent fall. Ex. ' His foot slipped, and he got a *hyst.*' Mr. J. C. Neal thus discourses on this word: A *fall,* for instance, is indeterminate. It may be an easy slip down—a gentle visitation of mother earth; but a *hyst* is a rapid, forcible performance, which may be done either backward or forward, but of necessity with such violence as to knock the breath out of the body, or it is unworthy of the noble appellation of *hyst*. It is an apt, but figurative mode of expression, and it is often carried still further; for people sometimes say, "Lower him up, and *hyst* him down."—*Charcoal Sketches*.

> I can't see the ground, and every dark night am sure to get a *hyst*— either a forrerd *hyst* or a backerd *hyst*, or some sort of a *hyst*, but more backerds than forrerds.—*J. C. Neal, Sketches*.

I.

I DAD! An exclamation used in the Western States.

> "*I dad!* if I didn't snatch up Ruff and kiss him." Here the emotion of the old man made a pause.—*Carlton, The New Purchase*, Vol. I. p. 179.

IF SO BE AS HOW. A vulgar expression used by uneducated people in the interior parts of this country and in England.

ILL. The common abbreviation for *Illinois*.

ILLY. A word occasionally used by writers of an inferior class, who do not seem to perceive that *ill* is itself an adverb, without the termination *ly*.

TO IMPROVE. To occupy; to make use of, employ.— *Pickering's Vocab*. "This word," says Mr. Pickering, "in the first sense, is in constant use in all parts of New England; but in the second sense (when applied to persons, as in the following example,) it is not so common."

> In action of trespass against several defendants, the plaintiffs may, after issue is closed, strike out any of them for the purpose of *improving* them as witnesses.—*Swift's System of the Colony Laws of Connecticut*, Vol. II.

Dr. Franklin, in a letter to Dr. Webster, dated Dec. 26th, 1789, has the following remarks: "When I left New England in the year 1723, this word had never been used among us, as far as I know, but in the sense of *ameliorated* or *made better*, except once, in a very old book of Dr. Mather's, entitled *Remarkable Providences*."

> Ann Cole, a person of serious piety, living in Hartford, in 1662, was taken with very strange fits, whereon her tongue was *improved* by a demon, to express things unknown to herself.—*Cotton Mather, Magnalia*, Book VI.

IMPROVEMENT.   The part of a discourse intended to enforce and apply the doctrines, is called the *improvement.—Webster.*

> The conclusion is termed, somewhat inaccurately, *making an improvement* of the whole. The author, we presume, means, deducing from the whole what may contribute to the general *improvement.—British Critic,* Vol. I. p. 379.

IMPROVEMENTS.   Valuable additions or meliorations ; as buildings, clearings, drains, fences on a farm.—*Webster.*

IMMEDIATELY, for *as soon as.*   Ex.   ' The deer fell dead *immediately* they shot him.'

IMMIGRANT.   A person that removes into a country for the purpose of a permanent residence.—*Webster.*

IMMIGRATION.   (Lat. *immigratio.*)   The passing or removing into a country for the purpose of a permanent residence. —*Webster.*   An entering or passing into a place.—*Todd. Knowles.   Richardson.*

> The *immigrations* of the Arabians into Europe, and the Crusades, produced numberless accounts, partly true and partly fabulous, of the wonders seen in Eastern countries.— *Warton's Hist. Eng. Poetry,* Vol. I.
>
> *Immigration* has doubtless been a prolific source of multiplying words. —*Hamilton, Nugæ Literariæ,* p. 381.

Mr. Pickering, in his Vocabulary, observes that this word, as well as *immigrant,* and the verb to *immigrate,* were first used in this country by Dr. Belknap, in his History of New Hampshire, who gives his reasons for their use.   *Immigrant* is original with Dr. B. ; but the others have long been used by good English anthors, though of course less frequently than by American writers, who have more need of them.

IND.   The common abbreviation for *Indiana.*

INDIAN BED.   An *Indian bed* of clams is made by setting a number of clams together on the ground with the hinge uppermost, and then kindling over them a fire of brushwood, which is kept burning till they are thoroughly roasted.   This is the best way of roasting clams, and is often practised by picnic parties.

INDIAN FILE.   Single file ; the usual way in which the Indians traverse the woods or march to battle, one following after and treading in the footsteps of the other.

INDIAN GIVER. When an Indian gives anything, he expects an equivalent in return, or that the same thing may be given back to him. This term is applied by children in New York and the vicinity to a child who, after having given away a thing, wishes to have it back again.

INDIAN MEAL. Meal made from Indian corn.

INFLUENTIAL. Having influence.—*Pickering, Vocabulary.*

> Persons who are strangers to the *influential* motives of the day.—*Marshall, Life of Washington*, Vol. V. p. 380.

This word has been called an Americanism; but such is not the case. " I once," said Canning to Mr. Rush, " had a skirmish about language with him, (Mr. Pinckney, of Maryland, our ambassador,) but he worsted me. I said there was no such word as *influential*, except in America; but he convinced me that it was originally carried over from England." Lord Stafford has remarked, that it was so good a word, they ought to bring it back. " Yes," said Mr. Canning, " it is a very good *word*, and I know no reason why it should have remained in America, but that we lost the *thing*." —*Rush, Mem. of a Res. at London*, p. 260.

I take the following examples from Richardson:

> And now our overshadow'd souls (to whose beauties stars were foils) may be exactly emblem'd by those crusted globes, whose *influential* emissions are intercepted by the interposal of the benighting element, while the purer essence is imprisoned within the narrow compass of a centre.— *Glanville.*

> Thy *influential* vigor reinspires
> This feeble frame, dispels the shade of death,
> And bids me throw myself on God in prayer.—*Thomson, Sickness.*

IN FOR IT. Engaged in a thing from which there is no retreating.

> You may twitch at your collar and wrinkle your brow;
> But you're up on your legs, and you're *in for it* now.—*O. W. Holmes, Poems*, p. 144.

TO INHEAVEN. A word invented by the Boston transcendentalists.

> The one circumflows and *inheavens* us. The infinite Father bears us in his bosom, shepherd and flock.—*Margaret*, p. 412.

J.

TO JAB. To strike or thrust with a knife; as, 'he *jabbed* a knife into me.'

JACKASSABLE. At a call for a meeting of citizens to repair a corduroy road in Michigan, the Niles Advertiser winds up with the following stanza :

> Those who would travel it
> Should turn out and gravel it ;
> For now it's not passable,
> Nor even *jackassable*.

Compare *Boatable*.

JAG. A small load.—*Forby. Webster.*

> As there was very little money in the country, the bank bought a good *jag* on't in Europe.—*Maj. Downing's Letters*, p. 168.

JAIL BIRD. A prisoner; one who has been confined in prison.—*Webster.*

JAW. In low language, gross abuse.—*Johnson.*

TO JAW. To scold; to clamor; to abuse grossly.—*Todd.*

> He never heard freedom of speech afore, that feller, I guess, unless it was somebody a *jawin'* of him.—*Sam Slick in England*, ch. 20.

TO JEOPARDIZE. To expose to loss or injury.—*Webster.* This verb is often seen in the debates of Congress, as they are reported in the newspapers. It is, doubtless, a corruption of the ancient verb *to jeopard,* as *deputize* is of *depute.*— *Pickering.* This word is much used in the United States, and less frequently in England.

> The profound respect for the cause of truth which led Mr. Tooke not to *jeopardize* its interests by any hasty assumption of its name and pretensions for a discovery yet incomplete, constitutes one of his surest holds upon posterity.—*London Athenæum*, March 18, 1848.

JERKED MEAT. Beef and other kinds of fresh meat dried in the open air without salt. In Lower Canada and Newfoundland, fish are dried in the same manner.

> In genuine Western style they welcomed me with their dough biscuits and *jerked* venison.—*Carlton's New Purchase*, Vol. II. p. 238.

THE JIG IS UP, i. e. the game is up; it is all over with me.

> The time was when I could cut pigeon wings, and perform the double shuffle with precision and activity; but those days are over now—*the jig is up.*—*Kendall's Santa Fé Expedition*, Vol. I. p 62.

JIMINY. By *Jiminy!* An exclamation. Originally, *gemini,* or the Castor and Pollux of ancient mythology; names by which the old Romans used to swear.

JIMSON. (*Strammonium datura.*) The popular name of a poisonous weed which grows at the West and South. It bears beautiful flowers, but has a nauseous smell. In the villages on the margins of the Western rivers it is a great annoyance. Its name *Jimson* is supposed to be a corruption of *Jamestown,* the place whence it is said to have been brought. It is used in medicine in spasmodic asthma.—*Flint's Mississippi Valley.*

JOBBER. In the United States this word is applied to wholesale merchants, who operate between the importer and retailer. Importers usually sell only by the package. The *jobber* buys by the package and sells by the piece. The retailer buys of the *jobber*, and sells in smaller quantities. In England the word is used in an analogous sense, as of one who buys and sells stocks.

> There have been at times a good deal of jealousy and dissension between the *jobbers* and auctioneers. They are in some measure rivals. Both sell to the retail dealer; and the *jobbers* complain that the auctioneer injures their business by selling as low to the country and retail merchant as to them.—*Perils of Pearl Street*, p. 102.

JOLLIFICATION. A scene of festivity or merriment. Used only in familiar language.

> Mr. Tolfrey's narrative of salmon and trout fishing, and otter shooting, with private theatricals, and endless *jollifications*, come before us in a startling contrast to the received ideas of colonial service.—*Lond. Spectator.*

> I have been already twice to the top of Vesuvius: the first time we had a *jollification* near the crater—our dinner being entirely cooked in one of the *fumaroli.*—*Letter from Naples. London Athenæum*, Dec. 6, 1745.

> It was determined to commemorate our safe deliverance by a special *jollification.*—*Carlton, The New Purchase*, Vol. I. p. 224.

JOSEPH. A very old-fashioned riding coat for women, scarcely now to be seen or heard of.—*Forby's Vocabulary.*

A garment made of Scotch plaid, for an outside coat or habit, was worn in New England about the year 1830, called a *Joseph*, by some a *Josey*.

> Olivia was drawn as an Amazon, sitting upon a bank of flowers, dressed in a green *Joseph*.—*Goldsmith, Vicar of Wakefield.*

NOT BY A JUGFULL, i. e. on no consideration; on no account.

> Downingville is as sweet as a rose. But 'taint so in New York, *not by a jug full.*—*Maj. Downing, May-day in New York.*

TO JUMP AT. To embrace with eagerness; as, 'I made him an offer, and he *jumped at* it.'

JUMPER. A couple of hickory poles so bent that the runners and shafts are of the same piece, with a crate placed on four props, complete this primitive species of sledge; and when the crate is filled with hay, and the driver well wrapped in a buffalo robe, the "turn out" is about as comfortable a one as a man could wish.—*Hoffman, Winter in the West,* p. 200.

JUNK-BOTTLE. The ordinary black glass porter-bottle.

JUST NOW. Lately; now; presently; immediately. This very common phrase is, perhaps, most generally used in the western counties.—*Halliwell.* The word is used in the same senses among ourselves. Thus, many persons say, 'I was there *just now*,' i. e. a short time ago; and also, 'I will be there *just now*,' i. e. presently. This last use, however, is not regarded as correct.

K.

KATYDID. (*Platyphyllum concavum.*) The popular name of a species of grasshopper; so called from its peculiar note.

KEDGE. Brisk; in good health and spirits. Ex. 'How do you do to-day?' I am pretty *kedge.* It is used only in a few of the country towns of New England.—*Pickering.* Provincial in England.

TO KEEL OVER. A nautical term; to capsize or upset, and metaphorically applied to a sudden prostration.

> As it seems pretty evident that the sovereigns of Europe, instead of oc-

cupying or sharing thrones, are predestined to the walks of private life, it would be highly proper to cultivate in them a spirit of self-abnegation and humility. If the royal parents wish to see their offspring " let down easy " from their high estate, they will adopt this course. *Keel over* they must, and a gradual *careen* would be much better than a sudden *capsize*. Now that the people are assuming the rights and privileges of sovereignty, we trust that they will have some consideration for princes in distress.—*New York Sunday Dispatch.*

KEEP. Food; subsistence; keeping. In a letter to his brother, Bishop Heber, speaking of Bishops' College costing so much, says:

> Besides it has turned out so expensive in the monthly bills and necessary *keep* of its inmates, that my resources, &c.—Vol. II. p. 319.

> The cottager either purchased hay for the *keep* [of the cow], or paid for ·her run in the straw-yard.—*Edinburgh Review*, Vol. LXI. p. 245.

TO KEEP. The phrase *to keep shop* is often shortened into *to keep;* as, 'Where do you *keep* now?' i. e. where is your place of business. Also, in the sense of *dwelling*, which use of the word is provincial in the eastern counties of England.

TO KEEP A STIFF UPPER LIP, is to continue firm, unmoved.

> My friend, said he, don't cry for spilt milk; *keep a stiff upper lip;* all will come out right enough yet.—*Knickerbocker Magazine*, Vol. XXV.

> Tut, tut, Major; *keep a stiff upper lip*, and you'll bring him this time.— *Chron. of Pineville*, p. 150.

TO KEEP COMPANY. To court. A common term in the interior parts of New England, applied to a man whose visits to a lady are frequent, with the intention of gaining her hand. ' He *keeps company* with her,' i. e. he is courting her, or ' They are *keeping company*,' i. e. are courting.

> A young tailoress got a verdict against Mr. B——, a steady farmer who " *kept company* " with her some months, and appointed a day for the wedding. [But subsequently changed his mind.]—*N. Y. Com. Adv.*

TO KEEP IT UP. To prolong a debauch. ' He *kept it up* finely last night;' a metaphor drawn from a game of shuttle-cock.—*Grose, Slang Dictionary.*

KEEPING-ROOM. A common sitting-room; the parlor in New England. The term is chiefly used in the interior, although it may sometimes be heard in the sea-port towns. The same expression is used in Norfolk, England, for the "general sitting-room of the family, or common parlor."—*Forby's Norf. Glos.*

KEEP THE POT A BOILING, i. e. Don't let the game flag. A common expression among young people, when they are anxious to carry on their gambols with spirit.—*Brockett's North County Words.*

KETTLE OF FISH. When a person has been perplexed in his affairs in general, or in any particular business, he is said to have made a pretty *kettle of fish* of it.—*Grose, Slang Dict.* The same phrase is used in America in colloquial language.

> What a pretty *kettle of fish* we shall have to fry some of these days a looking after Uncle Sam's fortune.—*Crockett.*

KIBLINGS. Parts of small fish used by fishermen for bait on the banks of Newfoundland.

KICK. *To kick up a row.* To create a disturbance; the same as to *kick up a dust.*

> Mr. Polk admitted Santa Anna, because he knew him to be capable of fighting nothing but chickens, and *to kick up a row* in Mexico, and discon-cert government measures.—*Mr. Bedinger, Speech in House of Rep.*

TO KICK. To jilt. Ex. 'Miss A has *kicked* the Hon. Mr. B, and sent him off with a flea in his ear.' Confined to the South.

KID. A large box in fishing vessels into which fish are thrown as they are caught. In New England.

TO KILL. To do anything *to kill*, is a common vulgarism, and means to do it to the uttermost; to carry it to the fullest extent; as, 'He drives *to kill ;*' 'She dances *to kill.*'

KILLDEER. (*Charadrius vociferus.*) A small bird of the plover kind; so called from its peculiar note.

KILLHAG. (Indian.) A wooden trap, used by the hunters in Maine.

KILLING. Dangerous; heart-breaking.

> For amongst his other *killing* parts,
> He had broken a brace of female hearts.—*Hood's Miss Kilmansegg.*

> There was a pleasant, playful breeze that sported with the well curled locks of first-water dandies [on New Years Day], and gave them a certain *négligé* appearance, which must have been really *killing* 'in my lady's chamber or drawing-room.'—*N. Y. Commercial Advertiser,* Jan. 2, 1844.

The dandies forgot to oil their moustaches, or waste *killing* looks on unthinking shop girls whom they met, &c.—*Boston Times*, Nov. 13, 1845.

KILTER. (Danish *kilter*, to gird.) ' To be *not in kilter*,' or, 'to be *out of kilter*,' is to be out of order; not ready; not in good condition.

If the organs of prayer are out of *kilter*, how can we pray?—*Barrow's Sermons*, Vol. I. p. 71.

KIND OF, KIND O', KINDER. In a manner, as it were. A sort of qualifying expression; as, 'She made game on it *kind o'.'*—*Forby*.

Diogenes was asked in a *kind of* scorn, what was the matter that philosophers haunted rich men, and not rich men philosophers?—*Bacon*.

It *kinder* seemed to me that something could be done, and they let me take the colt.—*Margaret*, p. 325.

A *kinder* notion jist then began to get into my head.—*Maj. Downing*.

At that the landlord and officer looked *kinder* thunderstruck.—*Downing*.

KINDLERS. Small pieces of wood for kindling a fire; kindling-wood.

Put some *kindlers* under the pot, and then you may go.—*Margaret*, p. 6.

KINK. An accidental knot or sudden twist in a rope, thread, &c.; and, figuratively, an idea, a notion.

" It is useless to persuade him to go, for he has taken a *kink* in his head that he will not."—*Carlton, The New Purchase*.

I went down to Macon to the examination, whar I got a heap of new *kinks*.—*Maj. Jones's Courtship*, p. 20.

KINNIKINNICK. An Indian word for a composition of dried leaves and bark prepared for smoking, used in the Western States in place of tobacco. A little tobacco is sometimes mixed with it to give it a flavor.

KITE FLYING. An expression well known to mercantile men of limited means, or who are short of cash. It is a combination between two persons, neither of whom has any funds in bank, to exchange each other's checks, which may be deposited in lieu of money, taking good care to make their bank accounts good before their checks are presented for payment. *Kite flying* is also practised by mercantile houses or persons in different cities. A house in Boston draws on a house in New York at 60 days or more, and gets its bill discounted. The New York house, in return, meets its acceptance by re-drawing on the Boston house. Immense sums of money are often raised in this manner—in fact, furnishing a capital for both houses to transact their business with.

> *Flying the kite* is rather a perilous adventure, and subjects a man to a risk of detection. One who values his credit as a sound and fair dealer would by no means hazard it.—*Perils of Pearl Street*, p. 82.

KNOB. In Kentucky, round hills or knolls are called *knobs*.

> Approaching Galena, the country becomes still more broken and rocky, until at last a few short hills, here called *knobs*, indicate our approach to Fever River.—*Hoffman, Winter in the West*, p. 303.

KNOCKED INTO A COCKED HAT. Knocked out of shape; spoiled; ruined. The allusion or metaphor seems to be that of the hat of some unlucky wight, which, by a violent blow, has been knocked into a sort of flattened, three-cornered shape, resembling an old-fashioned cocked hat.

In consequence of a severe storm of rain and a freshet that followed, some time during the winter of 1842, the mails were behind several days and no news was received. In speaking of the storm, the New York Commercial Advertiser stated that they were unable to give any news, for, owing to the storm and freshet, the mails were all *knocked into a cocked hat.* A London paper, in quoting news from America, observed that a singular occurrence had taken place, which had kept back the usual supply of news from New York, as it appeared that the mails were *knocked into a cocked hat*—a most extraordinary circumstance, the meaning of which it was wholly out of their power to define.

> A tall, slatternly looking woman, wearing a dingy, old silk bonnet, which was *knocked into a cocked hat*, appeared yesterday before the Recorder.— *New Orleans Picayune.*

> At a Repeal meeting in New York, Mr. Locke was proceeding to speak of the influence this party would have, when he was interrupted by a gang of rowdies, who, with the design of disturbing the meeting, cried out, "Three cheers for O'Connell—three cheers for Repeal—and three groans for Slavery." The six cheers for O'Connell and Repeal were given, but by the time they came to the groans for Slavery, they found themselves all *knocked into a cocked hat.—New York Paper.*

> Between three and four thousand persons were assembled at the Broad-

way Tabernacle the other evening to hear a temperance lecture from the talented Mr. Gough. There were " long-robed doctors " enough to have constituted a standing army. The Rev. Dr. ——, who opened the meeting with prayer, got through in the very short space of three-quarters of an hour; but it was full long enough to *knock* the spirit of the meeting *into a* " *cocked hat.*"—*New York Tribune.*

Sometimes the dog would get hold of the coon, like he was a going to swallow him whole, and *smash him all into a cocked hat.*—*Maj. Jones's Court.*

One of the omnibuses here, run full tilt right against a cart, and *knocked* everything *into* a kind of *cocked hat.*—*Maj. Downing, May-day in N. Y.*

TO KNOCK DOWN. A word used at auctions. ' This article is *knocked down* to you, sir ;' meaning, that you are the purchaser. The phrase, ' A *knock-down* argument,' is an argument that completely overthrows one's adversary.

When I have conversed with a slaveholder—and I assure you I have done so very frequently—the only ' *knock-down* ' argument is, " They are better off than your poor whites at the North."—*Letter from N. O.—Trib.*

TO KNOCK ROUND. To go about.

I'm going to New York and Boston, and all about thar, and spend the summer until pickin' time, *knockin' round* in them big cities, 'mong them people what's so monstrous smart, and religious, and refined, and see if I can't pick up some ideas worth rememberin'.—*Maj. Jones's Sketches.*

TO KNOCK UNDER. A common expression to denote that one yields or submits.—*Johnson.*

> For ten times ten, and that's a hunder,
> I hae been made to gaze and wonder,
> When frae Parnassus thou did'st thunder,
>   Wi' wit and skill,
> Wherefore I'll soberly *knock under,*
>   And quat my quill.—*Allan Ramsay, Poems.*

Says General J——, ' Major, I reckon I can drink more Saratoga water than you.' ' I'll bet a York shillin' of that,' says I. ' Done,' says he ; and down he went to the spring with a pitcher. I got a bucket, and down I went to the spring. As soon as he saw me, he smashed his pitcher in a minit. Says he, ' Major, I *knock under.*'—*Maj. Downing's Letters*, p. 36.

TO KNOCK UP. To wear out with fatigue.—*Halliwell.*

It is the constant labour, unvaried by the least relaxation, which *knocks* me *up,* and prevents me getting back my strength.—*Lord Sydenham, Mem.*

We care not for anything but shelter and food for our horses, which are nearly *knocked up.*—*Hoffman, Winter in the West*, Let. 36.

KNOW-NOTHING. Utterly ignorant. Ex. ' A poor *know-*

nothing creature,' i. e. one exceedingly ignorant.—*Norfolk Glossary.* This word is common in New England.

KONCKS or CONKS. Wreckers are so called, familiarly, at Key West, and the place they inhabit, Koncktown.

KOOL SLAA. (Dutch.) Cabbage salad. Many persons who affect accuracy, but do not know the origin of the term, pronounce the first syllable as if it were the English word *cold.*

Ky. The abbreviation used for *Kentucky.*

L.

La. The abbreviation for *Louisiana.*

LADIES' TRACES. (*Neottia tortillis.*) The popular name in the Southern States for an herb.—*Williams's Florida.*

LAKE LAWYER. (Genus, *amia.* Linnæus.) The Western Mud-fish. It is found in Lakes Erie and Ontario, where it is known by the name of Dog-fish. Dr. Kirtland says, it is also called the *lake lawyer,* from its " ferocious looks and voracious habits."

TO LAM. (Belg. *lamen.*) To beat soundly ; to drub. Colloquial in some of the Northern States. It is provincial in Yorkshire, England.—*Willan's Glossary.*

> If Millwood were here, dash my wig,
> Quoth he, I would beat her and *lam* her weel.—*Rejected Addresses.*

LAMB'S QUARTER. (*Chenopodium authelminticum.*) The popular name of an herb at the South.—*Williams's Florida.*

LAMPER-EEL. The lamprey. A common name for lampreys in New England. It is provincial in England and Scotland.—*Forby.*

LAND-LOPER.
LAND-LUBBER. } (Dutch, *landlooper.*) A vagrant ; one who strolls about the country.—*Bailey's Dict.* Applied by sailors to landsmen by way of ridicule.

> Such travellers as these may be termed *land-lopers,* as the Dutchman saith, rather than travellers.—*Howell's Foreign Travel,* (1642.)

> He never thought how much easier it was for one of these *land-lopers* to make a city in the woods on paper, than to be at the trouble of cutting the timber all down.—*A Week in Wall Street,* p. 119.

LANDSLIDE. }
LANDSLIP. } A portion of a hill or mountain, which slips or *slides* down ; or the sliding down of a considerable tract of land from a mountain. They are common in Switzerland.— *Webster*. Johnson does not give either of these words ; which with us convey the same meaning. A remarkable *landslip* took place in the city of Troy a few years since, which swept away many houses and caused the death of some ten or fifteen persons.

> There is not an appearance in all nature, that so much astonished our ancestors, as these *landslips.*—*Goldsmith, Hist. of the Earth.*

LASSO. (Spanish.) A long rope or cord, with a noose, for the purpose of catching wild horses or buffaloes on the Western prairies.

TO LATHER. To beat.—*Wilbraham's Glossary.*

LAVE. (French, *lève*.) A term in common use among the hunters and mountaineers of the Western prairies and Rocky Mountains.

> "Lave, ho ! Lave ! Prairies on fire ! Quick—catch up ! catch up !" This startling announcement instantly brought every man to his feet.— *Scenes in the Rocky Mountains*, p. 34.

LATHY. Thin ; slender like a lath.

LATISH. Rather late.

> Last evening, in returning home at a *latish* hour, we crossed over the lot just after the pistol had been fired.—*N. Y. Commercial Advertiser.*

LAWYER. (*Himantopus. Black-necked Stilt.* Audubon, Ornith.) A small bird which lives on our shores ; known also by the names of Tilt, and Longshanks. The origin of the first-mentioned name is not known.—*Nat. Hist. of N. York.*

LAY. Terms or conditions of a bargain ; price. Ex. ' I bought the articles at a good *lay;*' ' He bought his goods on the same *lay* that I did mine.' A low word, used in New England.—*Pickering*. Probably a contraction for *outlay*, i. e. expenditure.

LAY. A word used colloquially in New York and New England in relation to labor or contracts performed upon shares ; as, when a man ships for a whaling voyage, he agrees for a certain *lay*, i. e. a share of the proceeds of the voyage.

TO LAY. To make a bet, or wager. Mr. Davis notices this word as of frequent occurrence.

> I'll *lay* you, he has got drunk again and has lost himself in the woods.— *Travels in the United States in* 1797.

TO LAY, for *to lie.* A vulgar error equally common in England and in the United States.

LAY-OVERS FOR MEDDLERS. A reply to a troublesome question on the part of a child, in answer to 'What's that?' A *turn-over* is a little pie made of one round cake of dough, doubled and joined at the edges, in which stewed apples are inclosed. Similar cakes were sold in England; and Grose suggests that they may also have been filled with *medlars*, a fruit resembling the apple; and that hence may have arisen the reply. The expression is noticed in Moor's Suffolk Glossary. I have never heard it except in New York.

TO LAZE. }
TO LAZY. } To live idly ; to be idle.—*Todd.*

> The hands and feet mutinied against the belly; they knew no reason why the one should be *lazing*, and pampering itself with the fruit of the others' labor.—*L'Estrange.*

Dr. Webster calls this a vulgar word. It is common in the familiar language of New England.

> I have work on hand that must be done. What do you do *lazying* about here like a mud turtle nine days after it is killed?—*Margaret*, p. 30.

LEAN-TO. A pent-house. An addition made to a house behind, or at the end of it, chiefly for domestic offices, of one story or more, lower than the main building, and the roof of it leaning against the wall of the house.—*Forby's Norfolk Glossary.* The word is used in New England, where it is commonly pronounced *linter.—Pickering.*

COW-LEASE. A right of pasturage for a cow, in a common pasture. Used in some towns of New England.—*Pickering's Vocabulary.* Provincial in the West of England.—*Grose's Glossary.*

TO LEGISLATE. To make laws for a community.—*Todd.* This now common and very useful word is of recent adoption by English lexicographers. It is not in the dictionaries of Johnson or Sheridan, or in Mason's supplement to Johnson.

Entick's Dictionary, of 1795, is the earliest one in which it is to be found.

LEG BAIL. To give *leg bail*, is to run away.—*Grose.*

> Sae weel's he'd fley the student's a',
> Whan they were skelpin at the ba';
> They took *leg bail* and ran awa'
> Wi' pith an' speed.—*Fergusson's Poems*, 2. 10.

LEGGINGS. (Commonly written and pronounced *leggins*.) Indian gaiters; also worn by the white hunters and trappers of the West.

> How piquantly do these trim and beaded *leggings* peep from under that simple dress of black, as its tall nut-brown wearer moves through the graceful mazes of the dance.—*Hoffman, Winter in the West*, p. 239.

LENGTHY. Having length; long; not brief; tiresomely long. Applied often to dissertations or discourses; as, ' a *lengthy* oration,' ' a *lengthy* speech.'—*Worcester.*

This word was once very common among us, both in writing and in the language of conversation; but it has been so much ridiculed by Americans as well as Englishmen, that in *writing* it is now generally avoided. Mr. *Webster* has admitted it into his dictionary; but (as need hardly be remarked) it is not in any of the *English* ones. It is applied by us, as Mr. Webster justly observes, chiefly to writings or discourses. Thus we say, a *lengthy* pamphlet, a *lengthy* sermon, &c. The English would say, a *long* or (in the more familiar style) a *longish* sermon. It may be here remarked, by the way, that they make much more use of the termination *ish* than we do; but this is only in the language of *conversation.—Pickering.*

Mr. Pickering has many other interesting remarks on this word, for which I refer the reader to his work. The word has been gradually forcing its way into general use since the time in which he wrote; and that too in England as well as in America. Thus Mr. Rush, in relating a conversation which he had in London, observes: " Lord Harrowby spoke of words that had obtained a sanction in the United States, in the condemnation of which he could not join; as, for example, *lengthy*, which imported, he said, what was tedious as well as long—an idea that no other English word

seemed to convey as well.—*Residence in London*, p. 294.
The Penny Cyclopedia remarks on it to the same effect, and
even disputes its American origin.

A writer in the Boston Daily Advertiser, under the signature of W. X., says, that he has met with the word *lengthy*
in the London Times, and the Liverpool Chronicle, in Black-
wood's Magazine, and the Saturday Magazine, in the British
Critic, Quarterly Review, Monthly Review, Eclectic Review,
Westminster and Foreign Quarterly Reviews; in the writings of Dr. Dibdin, Bishop Jebb, Lord Byron, Coleridge, &c.
&c. If the English are indebted to American genius
for the invention of this precious word, they have made
some improvements upon it, which they may boast of, for
ought that is known to the contrary, as their own. Granby,
an English author, uses the word *lengthiness*, which is a
regularly formed noun from *lengthy*. Campbell uses the
word *lengthily*. In his " Letters from the South," he says:

> I could discourse *lengthily* on the names of Jugurtha, Juba, Syphax, &c.

and again:

> The hair of the head is bound *lengthily* behind.

Here follow a few examples from English and American
writers, out of the many that present themselves:

> Murray has sent or will send a double copy of the Bride and Giaour;
> in the last one some *lengthy* additions; pray accept them according to the
> old custom.—*Lord Byron's Letter to Dr. Clarke*, Dec. 13, 1813.

> All this excitement was created by two *lengthy* paragraphs in the Times.
> —*London Athenæum*, July 12, 1844, p. 697.

> Chalmers's Political Annals, in treating of South Carolina—is by no
> means as *lengthy* as Mr. Hewitt's History.—*Drayton's South Carolina*.

> I did not mean to have been so *lengthy* when I began.—*Jefferson, Writ.*

> I forget whether Mr. Sibthorpe has mentioned, in any of his numerous
> and *lengthy* epistles, this circumstance.—*Mrs. Clavers's Forest Life*.

TO LET ON. To mention; to disclose; to betray a knowledge
or consciousness of anything. ' He never *let on*,' i. e. he never
told me. This expression is often heard among the illiterate,
and is not confined to any particular section of the United
States. It is also used in the North of England and in Scotland.

'Tis like I may,—but *let na on* what's past
'Tween you and me, else fear a kittle cast.—*Ramsay, The Gentle Shep.*

The tears were runnin' out of my eyes, but I didn't want to *let on* for fear it would make her feel bad.—*Maj. Jones's Courtship*, p. 84.

TO LET DRIVE; *to let fly ; to let slip.* To discharge; let loose a blow with the fist, a stone, a bullet from a gun, &c. Also in a metaphorical sense; as, 'He *let fly* at him a volley of abuse.'

With dreadful strokes *let drive* at him so sore.—*Spenser.*

[My gun] was already loaded, and ready *to let slip* at them.—*Sam Slick.*

TO LET OUT. To begin a story or narrative. A Western expression.

Tom squared himself for a yarn, wet his lips with a little corn juice, took a small strip of Missouri weed, and *let out.*—*Robb, Squatter Life.*

LET UP. A *let up* is a release; a relief. An expression borrowed from pugilists.

There was no *let up* in the stock market to day, and the differences paid on the maturing contracts were very large.—*N. Y. Tribune.*

DEAD LETTER. A writing or precept without any authority or force; a letter left in a post office and not called for.—*Worcester.*

LEVEE. (French.) The time of rising; the concourse of persons who visit a prince or great personage in the morning.—*Johnson.*

Such as are troubled with the disease of *levee*-hunting, and are forced to seek their bread every morning at the chamber-doors of great men.—*Addison, Spectator*, No. 547.

This word has been curiously perverted by us from its original signification, so as to mean an *evening* (!) party or assembly at the house of a great or wealthy person; as, 'the President's *levee.*'

LEVEE. (French.) An embankment on the side of a river, to confine it within its natural channel. The lower part of Louisiana, which has been formed by encroachments from the sea, is subject to be inundated by the Mississippi and its various branches, for a distance of more than 300 miles. In order to protect the rich lands on these rivers, mounds are thrown up, of clay, cypress logs, and green turf, sometimes to the height of 15 feet, with a breadth of 30 feet at the base. These, in the language of that part of the country, are called *levees*. They extend for hundreds of miles; and when the rivers are full, cultivated fields covered with rich crops, and studded with villages, are seen lying far below the river courses.— *Encyclopedia Americana.*

> The great feature of New Orleans is the *Levee*. Extending for about five miles in length, and an average of two hundred feet in width, on the west bank of this river, which here runs to the north-east, it is made the great dépôt not only for the products of the vast country bordering on the Mississippi, and its navigable tributaries, but also of every foreign port, by means of about five hundred steamboats on the one hand, and every variety of sea-craft on the other, which are at all times to be seen in great numbers along the entire length, discharging and receiving their cargoes. To the business man it is one of the most interesting scenes in the world, and for the " calculating " man here are found the " items " from which an estimate may be formed of the rapid growth and vast resources of the " Great West." Who but a " native " can see the approach of a steamer laden with forty-six hundred and odd bales of cotton, and witness casks of sugar, molasses, and tobacco by the thousand, together with the boxes and bales of merchandise from every clime which here accumulate, and not wonder whence all this is received and whither it is to go ?—*Cor. of N. Y. Tribune.*

LEVY. Elevenpence. In the State of Pennsylvania, the eighth part of a dollar, or twelve and a half cents. Sometimes called an *elevenpenny bit.*—See *Federal Currency.*

LICIT. Lawful.—*Todd, Webster.* This word was criticised in the Monthly Anthology, (1804, p. 54,) in a review of the " Miscellaneous Works of David Humphreys, Esq." The reviewers say, " There is no such word as *licit*, and we cannot allow the author, respectable as he is, to coin language."— *Pickering.* It is now found in all the later English dictionaries.

LICK. A blow. Common in vulgar language both in England and the United States.

> He turned upon me as round as a chafed boar, and gave me a *lick* across the face.—*Dryden.*

> > When he committed all these tricks
> > For which he well deserved his *licks*,
> > With red-coats he did intermix.—*Forbes's Domini Despos'd*, p. 28.

> My head was a singin' with the *licks*, when she told me how he had

done me, and if it hadn't been for her I'd gin him such a lickin', &c.—*Maj. Jones's Courtship*, p. 113.

We have had the first *lick* at him; and that, the General says, is the best part of the battle.—*Jack Downing's Letters*, p. 103.

Tom Sellers was cavortin' round Molly like a young buffalo—he was puttin' in the biggest kind a *licks* in the way of courtin'.—*Robb, Squat. Life.*

LICK, or SALT LICK. In America, a place where the beasts of the forest lick for salt at salt springs.—*Webster.* " A salt spring is called a *lick*, from the earth about them being furrowed out in a most curious manner, by the buffalo and deer, which *lick* the earth on account of the saline particles with which it is impregnated."—*Imlay's Topog. Description of the Western Territory of N. America.*

TO LICK. To beat. Common, as a colloquial expression, in many parts of England.—*Todd. To lick*, a *lick*, a *licking*, are common words in speech, though not in writing.—*Richardson.* These remarks apply with perfect accuracy to this country.

> How nimbly forward each one pricks,
> While their thin sides the rider *licks.*—*Maro*, p. 24.

What side are you on? "Well, I am for Jackson," says I. "Mister, what makes you for Jackson?" "Why," says I, "he *licked* the British at New Orleans, and paid off the national debt."—*Crockett, Tour*, p. 141.

"Don't put Spriggins in," said a ragged youth, "he's a high flyer! he *licked* Kneeland last winter, 'cause he said he warn't no gentleman."—*Mrs. Clavers's Forest Life*, Vol. II. p. 39.

Boys! behave! or if you must fight, don't let those who have offices *lick* those who haven't.—*N. Y. Tribune to Evening Post.*

LICKING. A flogging; a beating.

Come over here, you rascal, swim over the mill dam, and if I don't give you the biggest *lickin'* you ever had.—*Crockett, Tour*, p. 195.

I promised when I catched him to give him a *licking*, and I was very much afeard I'd have to break the peace.—*Neal, Charcoal Sketches.*

TO PUT THE LICKS IN, is to run very fast. A Northern phrase. Also in speaking of a ship sailing, we hear the phrase, ' She is going a pretty good *lick*,' that is, sailing at a rapid rate.

LICKSPITTLE. A mean parasite; one who will stoop to any dirty work.—*Grose.*

We saw men that had grown gray in the service of their country, hurled from their station, to make way for *lickspittles* and yelpers.—*Crockett.*

LIE.   *A lie out of whole cloth,* is an utter falsehood.

In the second place, we are authorized by these gentlemen to say that the statement is in itself utterly false—" a *lie,*" as one of the commissioners wished us to say, "*out of whole cloth.*"—*N. Y. Commercial Advertiser.*

LIEF, or LIEVE. (Sax. *leof,* past part. of *lufian,* to love.) Willingly ; gladly.—*Johnson.* This word was formerly in good repute, and was used by well-known writers. It is now a common word, but only used in familiar speech, either in England or America.

And swere that he would lodge with them yfere,
Or them dislodge, all were they *lief* or loth.—*Spenser, Fairy Queen.*

I would as *lief* the town crier spoke my lines.—*Shakspeare, Hamlet.*

She, good soul, had as *lief* see a toad, a very toad, as see him.—*Ibid. Romeo and Juliet,* II. 5.

LIFE PRESERVER.   An air-tight apparatus made of India rubber cloth for preserving the lives of persons in case of shipwreck.

LIFT.   Used by the farmers in some parts of New England to signify a sort of gate without hinges.—*Pickering's Vocabulary.* This word is also used in Norfolk, England. Mr. Forby calls it " a sort of coarse rough gate of sawn wood, not hung, but driven into the ground by pointed stakes, like a hurdle, used for the same purposes of sub-dividing lands, stopping gaps in fences, &c. and deriving its name from the necessity of lifting it up for the purpose of passing through. In Suffolk, a *lift* differs from a gate, in having the projecting ends of the back and lower bar let into mortice holes in the posts, into and out of which it must be *lifted.*"—*Norfolk Glossary.*

LIG.   A fish hook with lead cast around its upper part in order to sink it.   Maine.

LIGHT, *adj.*   *To make light of ;* to treat as of little consequence; to disregard.—*Webster.*

LIGHT, *n.*   *To stand in one's own light.*   To be the means of preventing one's own good, or frustrating one's own purposes.—*Webster.*

TO LIGHT ON. To fall on; to come to by chance; to happen to find.—*Webster*.

> As in the tides of people once up, there want not stirring winds to make them more rough; so this people did *light upon* two ringleaders.—*Bacon.*
>
> As wily reynard walked the streets at night,
> *On* a tragedian's mask he chanced to *light*.
> Turning it o'er, he muttered with disdain,
> How vast a head is here without a brain!—*Addison*.

LIKE, for *as*. As in the phrase, ' *like* I do,' for as I do. Not peculiar to America.

> Each Indian carried a great square piece of whale's blubber, with a hole in the middle, through which they put their heads, *like the Guachos do* through their cloaks.—*Darwin's Journal of a Naturalist*, ch. 10.
>
> As soon as the post office was open, I looked over the miscellany *like I* always *do*, afore I let anybody take it.—*Maj. Jones's Courtship*.

LIKELY. That may be liked; that may please; handsome. In the United States, as a colloquial term, respectable; worthy of esteem; sensible.—*Worcester*.

Mr. Webster has the following remarks on this word: " The use of *likely* (for such as may be liked; pleasing; as, a *likely* man,) is not obsolete, nor is it vulgar. But the English and their descendants differ in the application. The English apply the word to external appearance, and with them *likely* is equivalent to *handsome, well-formed;* as, a *likely* man, a *likely* horse. In America, the word is usually applied to the endowments of the mind, or to pleasing accomplishments. With us, a *likely* man, is a man of good character and talents, or of good disposition or accomplishments, that render him pleasing or respectable."

LIMITS. The extent of the liberties of a prison.—*Webster*. Called, also, *jail liberties*.

LIMSY. Weak; flexible. New England.—*Webster*.

LINER. The ships belonging to the regular lines of London, Liverpool, or Havre packets, are called *liners*, to distinguish them from transient ships sailing to the same ports.

TO LINE BEES, is to track wild bees to their homes in the woods. One who follows this occupation is called a *bee hunter*.

At killing every wild animal of the woods or prairies, at fishing, or at *lining bees*, the best hunters acknowledged his supremacy.—*Kendall.*

LINGO. (Portuguese.)   Language ; tongue ; speech.   A low cant word.—*Johnson.*

LINKS.   Sausages.   Used in the interior of New England.   It is now common in the sea-port towns to say, "*links* of sausages," meaning the *links* into which they are tied up.   In some parts of England, sausages are called links, and a number of them a "latch of *links*."—*Forby's Norf. Glossary.*

LINSEY WOOLSEY.   (A corruption of *linen* and *wool*.) Stuff made of linen and wool mixed ; light or coarse stuff.—*Todd's Johnson.*   This article is now extensively manufactured in New England ; and, among merchants, it is called *linseys*. The word appears to be a very old one.

He gave them coats of *linsey woolsey ;* for, said he, that is good and warm for winter, and good and light for summer.—*Bp. of Chichester, Ser.*

LIQUOR.   Many and very singular names have been given to the various compounds or mixtures of spirituous liquors and wines, served up in fashionable bar-rooms in the United States.   The following list is taken from one advertisement :

Plain mint julep.	I. O. U.	Milk punch.
Fancy do.	Tippe na Pecco.	Cherry do.
Mixed do.	Moral suasion.	Peach do.
Peach do.	Vox populi.	Jewett's fancy.
Pineapple do.	Ne plus ultra.	Deacon.
Claret do.	Shambro.	Exchange.
Capped do.	Virginia fancy.	Stone wall.
Strawberry do.	Knickerbocker.	Sifter.
Arrack do.	Smasher.	Soda punch.
Racehorse do.	Floater.	Slingflip.
Sherry cobbler.	Pig and whistle.	Cocktail.
Rochelle do.	Citronella Jam.	Apple-jack.
Arrack do.	Egg nog.	Chain-lightning
Peach do.	Sargent.	Phlegm-cutter.
Claret do.	Silver top.	Switchel-flip.
Tip and Ty.	Poor man's punch.	Ching-ching.
Fiscal agent.	Arrack do.	Tog.
Veto.	Iced do.	Ropee.
Slip ticket.	Spiced punch.	Porteree.
Polk and Dallas.	Epicure's do.	&c. &c.

IN LIQUOR.   Intoxicated ; drunk.

TO LIQUOR, or TO LIQUOR UP. To take a dram; or, as we more frequently say, to take a drink.

> He was the first to break silence, and jumping up, asked all *to liquor* before going to bed.—*Porter's Tales of the South-west*, p. 31.

> Arter *lickerin* and cussin a spell, we took a bee line for Skylake. Going along we *lickered* freely.—*Ibid.* p. 131.

> " The child must be named Margaret." " No ! Mary," replied the father, " in honor of my esteemed wife. Besides, that's a Bible name, and we can't *liquor up* on Margaret."—*Margaret*, p. 89.

LISTER. One who makes a list or roll.—*Webster.* This word is used in Connecticut, and is applied to those who make out lists or returns of cattle or other property. l have never heard the word used elsewhere.

LIT', past tense and part. of *to light*. Often used by the illiterate.

LOAFER. A vagabond; an idle lounger. This peculiarly American word has been gradually growing into extensive use during the last twenty years. It was applied in the first place to the vagrants of our large towns, in which sense it is equivalent to the *lazzarone* of Naples or the *lepero* of Mexico. It is now, however, frequently applied in conversation and in the newspapers to idlers in general; and seems to have lost somewhat of its original vulgarity. The Philadelphia Vade Mecum has the following remarks upon it:

" This is a new word, and, as yet, being but a colt, or a chrysalis, is regarded as a slang epithet. It is, however, a good word, one much needed in the language, and will, in time, establish itself in the most refined dictionaries. It will mount into good society, and be uttered by aristocratic lips ; for it is the only word designating the most important species of the genus idler—the most important, because the most annoying branch of that family.

" The *loafer* is not exclusively, as some suppose him, a ragged step-and-corner lounger, who sleeps in the sun, and ' hooks ' sugar on the wharf. On the contrary, the propensity to loaf is confined to no rank in life; all conditions are, more or less, troubled with it. Like squinting, the king and the beggar may be equally afflicted with the imperfection.   There be your well-dressed monied *loafer*, as well as your *loafer* who is nightly taken by the watch.

"He is that kind of a man, who, having nothing to do, or being unwilling to do anything, cannot keep his tediousness to himself, and therefore bestows it all upon others, not when they are at leisure for conversational recreation, but when business presses, and they would look black upon the intrusion of a sweetheart or a three-day wife.   He is the drag-chain upon industry, and yet so far different from the drag-chain, that he hitches to the wheel when the pull is up hill.   Loving the excitement of busy scenes, yet too lazy to be an actor in them, where men are busiest, there, too, is to be found the pure, unadulterated *loafer*, sprawling about as the hound sprawls before the fire in every body's way, and tripping up every body's heels.   In the store, he sits upon the counter, swinging his useless legs, and gaping vacantly at the movements around him.   In the office, he effectually checks necessary conversation among those who do not wish their business bruited to the world, turns over papers which he has no right to touch, and squints at contents which he has no right to know.   In the counting-house, he perches on a stool, interrupts difficult calculations with chat as idle as himself, follows the bustling clerk to the storehouse, pouches the genuine Havana, quaffs nectar from proof-glasses, and makes himself free of the good things which belong to others."

TO LOAF.   To lounge; to idle away one's time.   The verb is of still more recent origin than the noun.

> The Senate has *loafed* away the week in very gentlemanly style.—*N. Y. Com. Advertiser*, Dec. 1845.

> One night Mr. Dobbs came home from his *loafing* place—for he *loafs* of an evening like the generality of people.—*Neal's Charcoal Sketches.*

TO LOAN.   To lend.   This verb is inserted by Todd on the authority of Huloet (1552) and Langley (1664), and noted " not now in use."   It is, however, much used in this country, though rarely in England.—*Worcester.*

LOAN OFFICE.   A public office in which loans of money are negotiated for the public, or in which the accounts of loans are kept and the interest paid to the lenders.—*Webster.*

TO LOBBY. To attempt to exert an influence on the members of a legislative body, by persons not members of such body. These are confined to the lobbies of the house, where they meet the members, and by various means attempt to influence them or secure their votes for some favorite bill. So necessary has this business of *lobbying* now become, that when a petition is sent to a legislature, particularly for an act of incorporation, it is very common for one or more individuals to take it in charge for the purpose of *lobbying* it through.

There is a quarrel in Philadelphia about Mr. W——'s appointments. Some of the Loco-focos have come out to *lobby* against him.—*N. Y. Trib.*

A committee has gone to Albany to *lobby* for a new bank charter.—*N. Y. Courier and Enquirer.*

LOBBY-MEMBER. A person who frequents the lobby of a house of legislation.—*Worcester.*

TO LOCATE. To place; to set in a particular spot or position.—*Pickering. Webster.* This word is comparatively modern in England, and is not found in any of the dictionaries previous to Todd's. It is used among us much more frequently and in a greater variety of senses than in England.

Under this roof the biographer of Johnson passed many jovial, joyous hours; here he has *located* some of the liveliest scenes, and most brilliant passages, in his entertaining anecdotes of his friend Samuel Johnson.— *Cumberland, Memoirs of Himself.*

The archbishops and bishops of England can neither *locate* and limit dioceses in America, nor ordain bishops in any part of the dominions of Great Britain, out of the realm, by any law of the kingdom, or any law of the colonies, or by any canon law acknowledged by either.—*John Adams, Letter to Dr. Morse.*

A number of courts properly *located* will keep the business of any country in such condition as but few suits will be instituted.—*Debates on the Judiciary*, p. 51.

So too a town, a village, and even a piece of ground, is said to be *located*, i. e. placed, situated, in a particular position.

Baber refers to villages formerly *located*, as at the present day, on the plains, &c.—*Masson's Travels in Afghanistan*, Vol. III. p. 193.

When Port Essington was *located*, all these difficulties had to be suffered over again.—*Stokes's Australia*, Vol. I. p. 401.

A lot of earth so singularly *located,* as marks it out by Providence to be the emporium of plenty and the asylum of peace.—[London] *Observer.*

And hence arises the following American use of the word :

TO LOCATE. To select, survey, and settle the bounds of a particular tract of land, or to designate a portion of land by limits ; as, *to locate* a tract of a hundred acres in a particular township.—*Webster.*

Mistakes in *locating* land were often very serious—the purchaser finding only swamp or gravel, when he had purchased fine farming land.—*Mrs. Clavers's Western Clearings.*

It is also coming into use in the old country, as will be seen by the following example :

The banks of these rivers [the Macquarrie, &c. in New South Wales] are fast filling with settlements ; those of the Hunter, the nearest to the seat of government, being, we understand, entirely *located.*—*Edinburgh Review.*

TO LOCATE. Applied to persons, it means :

1. To place in a particular position.

The mate, having *located* himself opposite to me [at the table], began to expostulate upon the mode of sea travelling.—*Gilliam, Travels in Mexico.*

2. To place in a permanent residence ; to settle.

The Asega-bok, the book of the judge, contains the laws of the Rustringian Friesians *located* around the gulf of the Jade.—*Bosworth, Pref. to Anglo-Sax. Dic.* p. 61.

The most unhealthy points are in the vicinity of mill-dams, and of marshes, near both of which the settlers take particular pains to *locate.*—*Hoffman's Winter in the West,* Vol. I.

3. As a technical term used by the Methodists, to settle permanently as a preacher. The word is needed by them, because they have many itinerant preachers who are not *located.*

Mr. Parsons, like most *located* and permanent pastors of a wooden country, received almost nothing for his services.—*Carlton, New Purchase.*

LOCATION, *n.* That which is located ; a tract of land designated in place.—*Webster.* This application of the word is peculiar to the United States.

LOCK, STOCK, AND BARREL. The whole. A figurative expression borrowed from sportsmen, and having reference to a gun.

Look at [this carriage] all through the piece ; take it, by and large, *lock, stock, and barrel ;* and it's the dandy.—*Sam Slick in England*, ch. 19.

LOCO-FOCO. The name by which the Democratic party is extensively distinguished throughout the United States. This name originated in the year 1835, when a division arose in the party, in consequence of the nomination of Gideon Lee as the Democratic candidate for Congress, by the committee chosen for that purpose. This nomination, as was customary, had to be confirmed at a general meeting of Democrats held at Tammany Hall. His friends anticipated opposition, and assembled in large numbers to support him. " The first question which arose," says Mr. Hammond, " and which would test the strength of the parties, was the selection of Chairman. The friends of Mr. Lee, whom we will call Tammany men, supported Mr. Varian ; and the anti-monopolists, Mr. Curtis. The Tammanies entered the hall as soon as the doors were opened, by means of back stairs ; while at the same time the Equal Rights party rushed into the long room up the front stairs. Both parties were loud and boisterous ; the one declaring that Mr. Varian was chosen Chairman, and the other that Mr. Curtis was duly elected the presiding officer. A very tumultuous and confused scene ensued, during which the gas-lights, with which the hall was illuminated, were extinguished. The Equal Rights party, either having witnessed similar occurrences, or having received some intimations that such would be the course of their opponents, had provided themselves with *loco-foco* matches and candles, and the room was re-lighted in a moment. The ' Courier and Enquirer ' newspaper dubbed the anti-monopolists, who used the matches, with the name of *Loco-focos;* which was soon after given to the Democratic party, and which they have since retained."—*Hammond's Political History of New York*, Vol. II. p. 491.

LOG. A bulky piece or stick of timber unhewed. Pine *logs* are floated down rivers in America, and stopped at saw-mills. A piece of timber when hewed and squared, is not called a *log*, unless perhaps in constructing *log* huts.— *Webster.*

TO LOG.   To cut down and get out pine logs for sawing into boards, etc.

> Once more at work, he employed his leisure time in the heavy and dangerous business of *logging.*—*Mrs. Clavers's Western Clearings.*

LOGGING SWAMP.   In Maine, the place where pine timber is cut.

LOG-ROLLING.   In the lumber regions of Maine it is customary for men of different logging camps to appoint days for helping each other in rolling the logs to the river, after they are felled and trimmed—this rolling being about the hardest work incident to the business.   Thus the men of three or four camps will unite, say on Monday, to roll for camp No. 1—on Tuesday for camp No. 2—on Wednesday for camp No. 3—and so on, through the whole number of camps within convenient distance of each other.

The term has been adopted in legislation to signify a like system of mutual co-operation.   For instance, a member from St. Lawrence has a pet bill for a plank road which he wants pushed through; he accordingly makes a bargain with a member from Onondaga who is coaxing along a charter for a bank, by which St. Lawrence agrees to vote for Onondaga's bank, provided Onondaga will vote in turn for St. Lawrence's plank road.

This is legislative *log-rolling;* and there is abundance of it carried on at Albany every winter.

Generally speaking, the subject of the *log-rolling* is some merely local project, interesting only to the people of a certain district; but sometimes there is party *log-rolling*, where the Whigs, for instance, will come to an understanding with the Democrats, that the former shall not oppose a certain Democratic measure merely on party grounds, provided the Democrats will be equally tender to some Whig measure in return.   [*J. Inman.*]

> We were compelled, for electioneering objects, to attend this summer several *log-rollings.*—*Carlton, The New Purchase,* Vol. I. p. 237.

> It is to be feared that, through the pitiable system of *log-rolling* and personal favoritism that has ever cursed this city, there will be plenty of persons appointed as policemen who are utterly unfit for it.—*N. Y. Com. Adv.*

Another evil of our banking system arises from the very foolish rule, that a single director may reject any paper offered for discount, instead of making the fate of every application depend upon the decision of a majority of the board. This gives a power to individuals at variance with the interests of the community. It produces what is termed *log-rolling* in legislation, and makes good and liberal-minded men responsible for the conduct of individuals who look solely to self.—*N. Y. Cour. and Enq.*

Mr. Davis has the best prospect for speaker, without the fetters of a caucus. But with such a system of *log-rolling*, the one whose prospects are worse, or rather who has no prospects at all, has the best chance to come out successful.—*N. Y. Tribune.*

Mr. Ballou did not see the object of a postponement. If the delay was for the purpose of obtaining information for the House, he had no objections; if *log-rolling* was the motive, he opposed the postponement.— *Providence Journal.*

I doubt very much whether, with all their *log-rolling*, and caucusing, and whipping in refractory members, they will be able to carry the Annexation Bill.—*Boston Paper.*

LOGY. (Dutch, *log*, heavy, slow, unwieldy.) We have received this word from the Dutch, and apply it generally to men. He's a *logy* man, i. e. a slow-moving, heavy man. ' He is a *logy* preacher,' i. e. dull. The Dutch say, *Een log verstand*, a dull wit.

LONG AND SHORT. The end; the result; the upshot.

You see I should have bore down on Sol Gills yesterday, but she took it away and kept it. That's the *long and short* of the subject.—*Dombey and Son*, ch. 23.

The *long and short* of all this was, that the white man and Indian girl got married.—*Simon Suggs*, p. 71.

But the *long and short* of it is, that if he keeps growing stupid, I'll send him adrift.—*J. C. Neal, P. Ploddy*, p. 15.

Well, uncle, the *long and short* of the matter is, that whether you advise me or not, I am determined to be no longer a burden to mother.—*My Uncle Hobson and I*, p. 24.

BY A LONG SHOT. By a long way; by a great deal.

Mr. Divver offered a resolution summarily removing the superintendent, and was quickly told by the Recorder that he was going too fast *by a long shot*—that he was out of order.—*Proceedings in the Case of Dr. Reese.*

LONG KNIVES, or BIG KNIVES. A term applied to Europeans and their descendants, by the North American Indians. It signifies wearers of swords.

LOON. (*Eolymbus glacialis.* Wilson.)   The common name for the Northern Diver.   *As straight as a loon's leg,* is a common simile.

LOOSENESS.   Freedom.   A Western vulgarism, now becoming common at the East; as, ' He spoke with a perfect *looseness.*'

LOPE.   A leap; a long step.—*Webster.*

> A sulky ox refuses to move in the proper direction; off starts a rider, who catching the stubborn animal by the tail, it at once becomes frightened into a *lope;* advantage is taken of the unwieldy body by the hunter, as it rests on the fore feet, to jerk it to the ground.—*Thorpe's Backwoods,* p. 15.

> The mustang goes rollicking ahead, with the eternal *lope,* such as an amorous deer assumes when it moves beside its half galloping mate, a mixture of two or three gaits, as easy as the motions of a cradle.—*Ibid.* p. 13.

TO LOPE.   To leap; to move or run with a long step, as a dog.—*Webster.*

LOT.   In the United States, a piece or division of land; perhaps originally assigned by drawing lots, but now any portion, piece, or division.—*Webster.*   This application of the word is peculiar to this country, and is universally used of a parcel of land, whether in town or country.   Thus, we have city *lots,* town *lots,* house *lots,* meadow *lots,* &c.   ' I have a fine *lot* of cleared land, with a wood *lot* adjoining;' meaning a portion of the forest on which the trees are left for fuel as required.   ' In going to town, I left the road, and went across *lots,* to shorten the distance,' i. e. across the open fields or meadows.   " In the first settlement of this country," says Mr. Pickering, " a certain portion or *share* of land was allotted to each inhabitant of the town; and this was called his *lot.*   Both *lot* and *allotment* occur in our early laws."

LOT or **LOTS.**   A quantity; a large number.   A familiar expression common to England and America, but not in the dictionaries.   Thus we hear it said, ' There was a *lot* of people at the mass-meeting to-day;' ' We shall have *lots* of folks at our house to-night,' etc.

> I showed my trunk to Patrick, and then went and got into the omnibus, what took me, with a whole *lot* of other passengers, to the Charleston Hotel.—*Maj. Jones's Travels.*

My wife at home will warm us up
Some broth of well picked bones for sup;
There's *lots* of welcome in my house, &c.—*Reynard the Fox*, p. 46.

LOVIER. (A. Sax. *lufian*, to love.) A lover. A vulgarism, but no corruption, and nearer the Anglo-Saxon than the common word.—*Forby's Vocabulary*.

LUBBER. A sturdy drone; an idle, fat, bulky fellow.— *Johnson*. A name given by sailors to landsmen.—*Grose, Dic*.

LUCKS. Small portions of wool twisted on the finger of a spinner at the wheel or distaff. The same word as *lock* when applied to the hair, &c.—*Forby's Norfolk Glossary*. In New England this word is still in use.

> Miss Gisborne's flannel is promised the last of the week. There is a bunch of *lucks* down cellar, bring them up.—*Margaret*, p. 6.

LUDDY MUSSY! Lord have mercy! an exclamation of surprise, common in the interior parts of New England.

> *Luddy mussy!* can you read! Where do you live?—*Margaret*, p. 52.

LUMBER. Timber sawed or split for use; as beams, joists, boards, planks, staves, hoops, and the like.—*Webster*. The word in this sense, and the following ones derived from it, are peculiar to America.

LUMBERER.
LUMBERMAN. } A person employed in cutting timber and in getting out lumber from the forest.

LUMBERING. The business or occupation of getting out various kinds of lumber, such as timber, boards, staves, &c. ' To go a *lumbering*,' is the phrase used by those who embark in it.

LUMBERING. Strolling, lounging, walking leisurely. A vulgarism used in New York.

> As I was *lumbering* down the street, down the street,
> A yaller gal I chanc'd to meet, etc.—*Negro Melodies. The Buffalo Gal.*

LUMBER-WAGGON. A waggon with a plain box upon it, used by farmers for carrying their produce to market. It is sometimes so arranged that a spring seat may be put in it, when it is very comfortable for riding in.

TO LUMP. Used in the vulgar expression, ' If you don't

like it, you may *lump* it,' i. e. you may help yourself if you
can.

> " Hoity-toity !" exclaimed Mrs. Pipchin, plucking up all the ogress within
> her. " If she don't like it, Mr. Dombey, she must be taught *to lump* it."—
> *Dombey and Son*, Ch. XI.

LYCEUM.   A house or apartment appropriated to instruction
by lectures or disquisitions.   An association of men for literary
purposes.—*Webster.*

In New England almost every town and village of importance has its *lyceum,* where a library is formed, natural
and artificial curiosities collected, and before which public
lectures are given.   They have done a vast deal towards the
dissemination of knowledge, particularly among those classes
which have not had the advantages of a good education.

TO LYNCH.   To condemn and execute in obedience to the
decree of a multitude or mob, without a legal trial ; sometimes
practised in the new settlements in the south-west of the
United States.—*Worcester.*

LYNCH LAW.   An irregular and revengeful species of justice,
administered by the populace or a mob, without any legal
authority or trial.—*Worcester.*

M.

MAD. Inflamed with anger ; very angry ; vexed. ' I was quite
mad at him ;' ' he made me *mad.*' In these instances *mad* is only
a metaphor for angry. This is perhaps an English vulgarism,
but it is not found in any accurate writer, nor used by any
good speaker, unless when poets or orators use it as a strong
figure, and to heighten the expression, say, ' he was *mad* with
rage.'—*Witherspoon, Druid.*   No. 5.

Mad, in the sense of *angry*, is considered as a low word in
this country, and at the present day is never used except in
very familiar conversation.—*Pickering.*

This use of the word is provincial in various parts of England.   See *Halliwell, Grose*, etc.

> Indeed, my dear, you make me *mad* sometimes, you do.—*Spectator.*
> The General began to get in a passion—and says he, " Major, I'm gettin'

mad!" "Very well," says I, "General, then I'll keep cool accordin' to agreement."—*Maj. Downing's Letters*, p. 20.

Up stairs I went with them, as *mad* as thunder, I tell you, at being thought a humbug.—*Field, Western Tales.*

Jeeminy, fellows, I was so enormous *mad* that the new silk handkercher round my neck lost its color!—*Robb, Squatter Life.*

LIKE MAD. A common simile, in England and America.

A bear enrag'd at the stinging of a bee, ran *like mad* into the bee-garden and overturn'd all the hives.—*L'Estrange.*

Here's two boys a fishin,' and there a little girl a playin' with a dog, that's a racin', and a yelpin', and barkin' *like mad.*—*S. Slick in England.*

MAD AS A MARCH HARE. A common simile, used alike in England and America.

The whole's to be fourpence a quart—
　　Odswinge ! lad, there will be rare drinkin';
Billy Pitt's *mad as ony March hare,*
　　And never was reet, fwook are thinkin'.—*Westmoreland and Cumberland Poems*, p. 220.

Because I would not let Ike Tapley have the lick of the tap [after drawing some rum], he was as *mad as a March hare.*—*Margaret*, p. 39.

MADAM. In Plymouth, Massachusetts, and in some neighboring places, it has been and still is the practice, to prefix to the name of a deceased female of some consideration, as the parson's, the deacon's or the doctor's wife, the title of *Madam.*—*Kendall's Travels*, Vol. II. p. 44. "This practice," says Mr. Pickering, "like that of giving magistrates the title of 'squire, prevails in most of the country towns of New England; but is scarcely known in the sea-port towns."— *Vocabulary.*

TO MAHOGANYIZE. To paint wood in imitation of mahogany.

MAILABLE. That may be mailed or carried in the mail.—*Worcester.* In a recent suit brought by the government against Adams & Co.'s Express, for carrying letters and papers, to the injury of the post office, Judge Betts stated in his charge to the jury that "any written communication between one individual and another comes within the term *mailable matter*, and no matter in what shape it is put, it is liable to postage as if carried by mail."

All *mailable* matter intended to reach its destination without delay, must be deposited with the mail agents, on board the Stonington boats, the regular and only line for carrying the Boston, or great Eastern mail.— *Newspaper Advertisement.*

MAIZE. (W. Ind., *maiz.*) Indian corn. The name of the great staple of native American agriculture, adopted from the Carib language by the Spaniards, and thus imported into the languages of Europe. The earliest dictionary in which I find the word, is Florio's Worlde of Wordes (1598) ; the article there is " *Maiz,* a kind of grain or wheat whereof they make bread in India." Its native country is not fully determined, although it is believed to be America. Bernal Diaz speaks of it in Mexico in 1517 ; and Acosta in 1570, when treating of the plants " peculiar to the Indies," says that " the most common grain found in the new world is *mays,* which is found in all the kingdoms of the West Indies, Peru, New Spain, Guatemala, and Chili." He adds, that in Castile they call it Indian wheat; and in Italy, Turkey grain ; which seems to imply that the plant was also known in those countries.

TO MAKE FISH. To cure and prepare fish for commerce. A New England phrase.

MAKING MEAT, on the great Western prairies, consists in cutting into thin slices the boneless parts of the buffalo, or other meat, and drying them in the wind or sun. Meat thus prepared may be preserved for years without salt.—*Scenes in the Rocky Mountains,* p. 53.

TO MAKE A RAISE. A vulgar expression, meaning to raise ; procure ; obtain.

I *made a raise* of a horse and saw, after being a wood piler's prentice for awhile.—*Neal, Sketches.*

TO MAKE TRACKS. To leave ; to walk away. A figurative expression of Western origin.

He came plaguy near not seein' of me, says I; for I had just commenced *making tracks* as you came in.—*Sam Slick in England,* ch. 20.

MARM. A corruption of the word *madam* or ma'am, often used in the interior of New England for mother.

Has your *marm* got that done ?—*Margaret,* p. 39.

TO MARBLE. To move off; as, ' If you do that again, you must *marble,*' i. e. be off immediately. Used in Pennsylvania.—*Hurd's Gram. Corrector.*

MAROONING. *To go marooning.* An expression used in the Southern States. It means to make up a party and have a picnic. Such is called a *marooning* party. The difference between a *marooning* party and a picnic is, that the former is a party made up to pass several days on the shore or in the country ; the latter is a party for a day.

MARVEL. A common corrupt pronunciation of *marble.*

MASKINONGE. (Genus, *esox.* Cuvier.) An immense fish of the Pike species, caught in the St. Lawrence and the great lakes. I have seen a specimen taken at Kingston upwards of four feet in length. Dr. Richardson, in his " Fauna Borealis Am.," says that he found none in the rivers which empty into Hudson's Bay or the Polar Sea.

The *masquinonjé* is to all appearance a large species of pike, and possesses the ravenous propensities of that fish.— *Backwoods of Canada,* p. 161.

Mass. The common abbreviation for *Massachusetts.*

MASS-MEETING. A large or general meeting called for some specific purpose. The word mass is prefixed with a sort of ad captandum intent, as O'Connell called his large meetings of Irishmen, " monster meetings." Mass-meetings were first talked of in the political campaign of 1840, when Harrison was elected President. The term is now applied to any large meeting without distinction of party.

MAY-APPLE. (Genus, *podophyllum.*) A plant, the root of which is medicinal, answering as a substitute for jalup.— *Bigelow's Plants of Boston.*

Md. The common abbreviation for Maryland.

MEADOW. In New England this word means exclusively grass land, which is moist or subject to being overflowed ; and land which is not so, is called upland. In England, also, the term *meadow* is used among agriculturists in the limited sense above mentioned.—*Pickering.*

A tract of low land. In America, the word is applied

particularly to the low ground on the banks of rivers, consisting of a rich mould or alluvial soil, whether grass-land, pasture, tillage, or wood land ; as, the *meadows* on the banks of the Connecticut. The word with us does not imply necessarily wet land. This species of land is called in the Western States, *bottoms* or *bottom-land*. The word is also used for other low or flat lands, particularly lands appropriated to the culture of grass.—*Webster*.

MEAN, for *means*. Many American writers, following the Scottish models, make use of *mean* instead of *means*. But the established practice among English writers, from the time of Addison to the present day, has been to use the plural *means*.

> It was the best *mean* of bringing the negotiation to a happy issue.— *Marshall's Washington*, Vol. V. p. 546.

MEECHIN. A person with a downcast look is said to look *meechin*. Used on Long Island.

MEETING. A congregation. Among Methodists and others in the United States, it is a universal practice to say, ' we are going to *meeting*,' when going to their church or place of worship.

Me. The common abbreviation for *Maine*.

MENHADEN. (*Alosa menhaden*. Storer, Massachusetts Report.) A fish of the herring kind abounding in the waters of New England, and as far south as Chesapeake Bay. It is also known by the names of Bony-fish, White-fish, Hardhead, Mossbonker, and Panhagen. In Massachusetts and Rhode Island, they are called Menhaden ; in New York, Mossbonkers and Skippaugs. They are caught in immense quantities and used as manure, chiefly for Indian corn. Dr. DeKay, in his report on the fishes of New York, states that he has known of an instance when " 84 waggon-loads, or in other words, 168,000 of these fish were taken at a single haul " of the seine.—*Nat. Hist. of New York*.

> One day last week, Messrs. Davidson and Russel drew in at a single haul, on Mr. Hallock's shore, west side of New Haven harbor, two millions of white fish, as nearly as could be estimated, weighing on an average about three quarters of a pound each. The total weight of the haul, therefore, was about 1,500,000 lbs. or 750 tons ! It was the greatest haul of fish ever made in that harbor, and we suspect it will not

be easy to match it anywhere. The farmers from the neighboring country were engaged three or four days in carrying them off in immense cartloads. They sell at 50 to 75 cents the 1000. The fishermen are much indebted to a bevy of porpoises, who drove the white fish into the harbor, helping themselves meanwhile, no doubt, to a very large number.—*Journal of Commerce*, May 16, 1848.

MET UP WITH, for *overtook.—Sherwood's Georgia.*

MICH. The common abbreviation for *Michigan.*

MIDDLINGS. The coarser part of flour.—*Webster.*

MIDGET. The sand-fly; so called in Canada.

MIGHTILY. In a great degree; very much. A sense scarcely to be admitted but in low language.—*Todd's Johnson.*

An ass and an ape conferring grievances; the ass complained *mightily* for want of horns, and the ape for want of a tail.—*L'Estrange.*

MIGHTY. 1. Great; excellent; fine.

The old maid bridled and tossed her head, as much as to say that, in her opinion, the like of him was not so *mighty* a catch for ladies beyond their girlhood.—*Chambers's Journal (Grandmother Hook).*

2. In a great degree; very; as, ' *mighty* wise;' ' *mighty* thoughtful.'—*Webster.*

She untied her hair, then began to twirl the ringlets round her fingers and play with them in a coquettish manner, which she seemed to think *mighty* killing, for she smiled in evident self-conceit.—*London Zoist.*

The Doctor's was a *mighty* fine house, fronting the sea.—*Dickens, Dombey and Son,* ch. XI.

His face is *mighty* little for his body.—*Georgia Scenes,* p. 184.

What *mighty* hard land it is on this road. The whole face of the earth is covered with stones, as thick as Kentucky land titles.—*Crockett, Tour down East,* p. 57.

You'll be *mighty* apt to get wet, said a thorough-bred Texan, who stood watching our movements.—*Kendall's Santa Fé Expedition,* Vol. I. p. 32.

But, sir, I were *mighty* weak, and couldn't tell a stump from an old he.—*Porter's Tales of the South-west,* p. 124.

A girl belonging to the hotel was shouting to the boys, who had been dispatched to the barn for eggs, to " quit suckin' them thar eggs, or the candidates would stand a *mighty* small chance for thar dinner."—*Robb, Squatter Life,* p. 80.

MILE. Often in the singular with a numeral, instead of the plural *miles.* Mr. Hartshorne, in his Glossary, says its use is universal in England, where the vulgar never give it a plural.

" The custom," he adds, " seems to receive countenance from some of our early English poets."—*Salopia Antiqua.*

Start the horses together for a hundred and fifty *mile.*—*Georgia Scenes.*

MILEAGE is a very large and even extravagant allowance made to members of Congress, and some others of the favored, for travelling expenses—eight dollars for every twenty miles. [*J. Inman.*]

CONSTRUCTIVE MILEAGE is the same allowance for journeys supposed to be made, but not actually made, from and to the seat of Government. The allowance enures to members of the United States Senate once in every four years. When a new President comes into office, Congress adjourns, of course, on the 3d of March, the new President being inaugurated on the 4th. But the Senate is immediately called again into session, to act on the nominations of the new President; and though not a man of them leaves Washington, each is *supposed* to go home and come back again, in the course of the ten or twelve hours intervening between the adjournment and the re-assembling. For this supposed journey the Senators are allowed their mileage, just as though the journey was actually made; the sum being, in the case of Senators from distant States, from $1000 to $1500.

Many of the Senators, in 1845, when Mr. Polk was inaugurated, refused to pocket their constructive mileage, holding it to be an imposition on the public.

Constructive mileage is allowed when an extra session of Congress is called, whether the Senators and Members have actually gone to their homes or not, after the regular session. [*J. Inman.*]

The *mileage* is a still less excusable abomination. Texas sends hither two Senators and two Representatives, who receive, in addition to their pay, some $2,500 each every session for merely coming here and going away again (I would sooner pay them twice the money to stay away)—$10,000 in all for travelling expenses which are not actually $1000. Arkansas will take $6000 out of the Treasury this year merely for the travel of her Senators. When we come to have Senators and Representatives from Oregon and California, we shall have to negotiate a loan expressly to pay the *mileage* of their members.—*Letter from H. Greeley, N. Y. Tribune,* May 2, 1848.

MILK-SICKNESS.   A fatal spasmodic disease, peculiar to the Western States.   It first attacks the cattle, and then those who eat beef or drink milk.

> A few miles below Alton, on the Mississippi, I passed a deserted village, the whole population of which had been destroyed by the *milk-sickness.*— *Hoffman, Winter in the West*, Let. 2.

MILLERITES.   The name of a religious sect from its founder, William Miller.

The distinguishing doctrines of this sect are, a belief in the re-appearance of Jesus Christ on earth, " with all his saints and angels; that he will raise the dead bodies of all his saints, and change the bodies of all that are alive on the earth that are his; and that both these living and raised saints will be caught up to meet the Lord in the air.   There the saints will be judged.   While this is being done in the air, the earth will be cleansed by fire; the bodies of the wicked will be burned; the devil and evil spirits will be banished from the earth, shut up in a pit, and will not be permitted to visit the earth again until a thousand years.   This is the first resurrection and first judgment.   Then Christ and his people will come down from the heavens, and live with his saints on the new earth."   After a thousand years, a second death, resurrection, and judgment take place; when the righteous will possess the earth forever.   " The judgment-day will be a thousand years in duration.   The righteous will be raised and judged in the commencement, the wicked at the end of that day.   The millennium is between the two resurrections and the two judgments."—*Evans's Hist. Religions, American Ed.*

Believing in the literal fulfilment of the prophecies, the *Millerites* first asserted that, according to their calculations, the first judgment would take place about the year 1843.   Subsequently other periods were named; and so firm was the faith of many that the Saviour would descend from the heavens and take his followers up into the air, that they disposed of all their worldly treasures, provided themselves with ' ascension robes,' and waited with great anxiety for the sounding of the last trumpet, the signal for their aerial voyage.   Many persons became insane in consequence of the excitement and fear attending this delusion. Others have come to their senses, owing to their repeated disappointments in not being elevated according to Father Miller's promise; and at the present time the sect has happily dwindled down to an insignificant number.

MILLION. A vulgar corruption of the word *melon;* as, 'water-*millions*,' water-melons; 'mush-*millions*,' musk-melons.

TO MINCE. To diminish in speaking; to retrench, to cut off, or omit a part for the purpose of suppressing the truth; to extenuate in representation.—*Webster.*

>   And love doth *mince* this matter.—*Shakspeare, Othello.*

>   There was no *mincing* matters; it seemed as if Mr. Calhoun's presence had mesmerized the stoutest democrats into perfect agreement with himself.—*N. Y. Tribune,* Nov. 26, 1845.

TO MIND. To recollect; remember.

>   I was invited to dine out in Boston; but if I can *mind* the gentleman's name, I wish I may be shot.—*Crockett, Tour,* p. 82.

TO MIND. To take care of.

>   Yes, said Margaret, I will keep Obed. I'll *mind* the beds when the birds are about.—*Margaret,* p. 20.

MISERY. Pain; as, *misery* in my head.—*Sherwood's Georgia.*

Miss. The common abbreviation for *Mississippi.*

TO MISSIONATE. To act as a missionary. Not well authorized.—*Webster.*

Mr. Pickering notices this absurd word, which he found in the Missionary Herald.

TO MISSTATE. To state wrong; to make an erroneous representation of facts; as, ' to *misstate* a question in debate.'—*Webster.*

MISSTATEMENT. A wrong statement; an erroneous representation, verbal or written; as, a *misstatement* of facts in testimony, or of accounts in a report.—*Webster.*

Not noticed by Johnson, Todd, or Richardson. Used by the London Quarterly Review, Oct. 1837.

MITTEN. When a gentleman is jilted by a lady, or is discarded by one to whom he has been paying his addresses, he is said to have *got the mitten.*

Young gentlemen that have *got the mitten*, or young gentlemen who think they are going to *get the mitten*, always sigh. It makes them feel bad.—*Neal's Sketches.*

MITTS. A cover for the hand in which the fingers are unprotected.

TO MIZZLE. To run away; to abscond. A low word.

Mr. Buchanan was in the Senate Chamber when the Tariff was under discussion; but as soon as Mr. Bagby commenced speaking of the " odious law of 1842," the Secretary of State *mizzled.*—*Cor. of N. Y. Herald.*

A broker, named H. H. D. operated, in a financial way, day before yesterday, to the amount of $3000, and then *mizzled.*—*N. Y. Tribune.*

The Southern men will spend their last cent here; while the Northern men, if they had won, would have buttoned up their pockets and *mizzled.*—*N. Y. Herald*, May 14, 1845.

Mo. The common abbreviation for *Missouri.*

MOBEE. A fermented liquor made by the negroes in the West Indies, prepared with sugar, ginger, and snake-root. It is sold by them in the markets.—*Carmichael's West Indies.*

MOCCASON,
MOCCASIN, } Also often written and pronounced *moggason.*
(Algonkin, *makisin.*) An Indian shoe, made of soft leather without a stiff sole, and commonly ornamented round the ancle.—*Worcester.*

MONETARY. Pertaining to money, or consisting in money. —*Webster.* A word of recent origin, not in Johnson or Todd, but inserted by Richardson in his dictionary.

MONSTROUS is much used by the vulgar for very, exceedingly.

Augustus is a *monstrous* pretty city; but it ain't the place it used to was, by a great sight. It seems like it was rotting off at both ends, and ain't growing much in the middle.—*Maj. Jones's Sketches of Travel.*

It's *monstrous* inconvenient and ridiculous.—*Sam Slick in England.*

He'll cut the same capers there he does here. He's a *monstrous* mean horse.—*Georgia Scenes*, p. 27.

MOONSHINE. A trifle; nothing.—*Grose.*

The story of the Queen of Spain's secret marriage to her cousin, appears to have been all *moonshine.*—*N. Y. Com. Adv.*, Nov. 22, 1845.

MOOSE. An Indian name (Knistenaux, *mooswah*) of an animal of the genus Cervus, and the largest of the deer kind, growing sometimes to the height of seventeen hands, and weighing 1200 pounds. This animal inhabits cold northern climates, being found in the forests of Canada and New England.—*Encyclopedia.*

MORMONS.   The Mormonites, or Latter-day Saints, are a religious sect which derive their name from the ' Book of Mormon.'

This book was first published in the year 1830.   Since that period its believers and advocates have zealously propagated its doctrines through every State in the Union, and in Canada.   In England they have made some thousands of converts.

The Book of Mormon purports to be the record or history of a certain people, who inhabited America previous to its discovery by Columbus.   This history, containing prophecies and revelations, was engraven (according to it), by the command of God, on small brass plates, and deposited in the hill Comora, in Western New York.   These plates were discovered (the Mormons say) by Joseph Smith, in the year 1825 ; they contain certain hieroglyphics, in the Egyptian character, which Smith, guided by inspiration, translated.   It purported to give the history of America from its first settlement by a colony from the tower of Babel to the 5th century of our era.   It stated that the Saviour made his appearance upon this continent after his resurrection; that he planted the gospel here—had his apostles, prophets, teachers, etc. ; that the people were cut off in consequence of their transgressions ; and that the last of their prophets wrote the Book of Mormon on the brass plates above named, " which he hid in the earth, until it should come forth and be united with the Bible, for the accomplishment of the purposes of God in the last days."

Smith readily found many to believe his statements, and in 1830 organized his first church of Mormons in Manchester, Ontario county, New York.   Other preachers sprang up, who " saw visions and prophesied, cast out devils and healed the sick, by the laying on of hands," and performed other miracles.   New churches or societies were formed in other States, until in a few years their number amounted to many thousands. They removed in a body to Missouri, where a most cruel and relentless persecution sprang up against them, which forced them to quit their homes and the State. They then sought a refuge in Illinois, where they founded a city called Nauvoo, in which they erected an immense edifice or Temple, which is thus described in an Illinois paper:

" This temple stands in a prominent position, and is visible from a distance of twenty-five or thirty miles. Viewed from the bank, it is grand and imposing. It is built of white limestone, which has been worked and faced down to a perfect surface. Its length is 128 feet, width 88 feet, height to the roof 77 feet. The walls are two feet thick; and on every side are rows of pilasters, crowned with elaborately carved capitals, showing a man's face and two hands grasping trumpets. The structure is lighted with four rows of windows, two of which are quadrilateral, and two circular. All the entrances are from the West, and the immense doorways are gained by flights of steps. The interior contains a basement, in the centre of which stands the celebrated baptismal font," an immense stone reservoir, resting upon the backs of twelve oxen, also cut out of stone, and as "large as life."

Persecution followed these poor people in Illinois. They were attacked by armed bodies of men by order of the State authorities, driven out by force, and compelled to abandon or sacrifice their property. Such as survived the persecution, after traversing the boundless prairies, the deserts of the far West, and the Rocky Mountains, finally found a resting place near the Great Salt Lake in Oregon, where some 20,000 of them are now forming a settlement.

MORTAL. Used in vulgar parlance adverbially for *mortally;* i. e. excessively.

> It was a *mortal* hot day, and people actually sweated to that degree, it laid the dust.—*Sam Slick*, 3d ser. p. 102.

TO MOSEY. To be off; to leave; to sneak away. A low expression.

> After I left you, or rather after you left me, when them fellows told you to *mosey* off before the boat went to sea.—*N. Y. Family Companion.*

MOSQUITO BAR. }
MOSQUITO NET. } A net or curtain, which, in the Southern
States and in the West Indies, is placed over the bed to pro-
tect a person from mosquitoes.

MOSSBUNKER. (*Alosa menhaden*, Storer.) See *Menhaden*.

TO MOTION. To move; to make a motion; as, 'I *motion*
that the resolution pass.' An old English word rarely
used, because unnecessary.

> I want friends to *motion* such a matter.—*Burton, Anat. Melancholy.*

MOUGHT, for *might*. This old preterite is still heard among
the illiterate, especially in country places.

TO MOUSE. 'To go *mousing* about,' is to go poking about
into holes and corners.

TO MOVE, for *remove*. To change one's residence.

> These are great *moving* times. The sovereigns of Europe are being
> *moved*, much against their will—and the sovereign people of New York
> are on the eve of *moving*, according to custom, which has made the May-
> day sports of this city a very peculiar feature. Could the sovereigns of
> Europe only *move* as easily as the sovereigns of New York do, from house
> to house, palace to palace, &c., they would be well content, and not com-
> plain—as many *movers* to-morrow will.—*N. Y. Sunday Atlas*, April 30, '48.

MUD-HEN. The common name of the Virginia Rail of ornithologists. It inhabits small streams and marshes.

MUD-TURTLE. The popular name of a reptile common in
all parts of the United States. Marsh Tortoise and Mud Terrapin are other names for the same. It is the *sternothærus
odorata* of naturalists.—*Holbrook, Am. Herpetology.*

TO MULL. To soften and dispirit.—*Johnson*. The only
authority cited by Johnson is from Shakspeare :

> Peace is a very apoplexy, lethargy,
> *Mull'd*, deaf, sleepy, insensible.—*Coriolanus.*

Used in New England.

> There has been a pretty considerable *mullin* going on among the doctors
> ever sen the quack medicine came out.—*Margaret*, p. 170.

MULLEY COW. A name used for a cow chiefly among
children, or by parents when speaking to children; as, 'the
old *mulley cow*.' Provincial in England.

> In travelling homeward, buy forty good crones,
> And fat up the bodies of those seely bones :

Leave milking, and dry up old *mulley* thy *cow*;
The crooked and aged to fatting put now.—*Tusser, Husbandry.*

MUMMACHOG. (Genus, *fundulus.* Lacépède.) The popular name of the Barred Killifish of naturalists. It is a small fish from two to four inches in length, and frequents the salt water creeks and the vicinity of the wharves. This Indian name is retained in Rhode Island.

MUSH. Indian meal boiled with water, and eaten with milk or molasses. It is often called hasty pudding, and is a favorite dish throughout the United States. In Hallamshire, England, *to mush*, means to crush, or pound very small. From this our word may have originated.

E'en in thy native regions, how I blush
To hear the Pennsylvanians call thee *mush!*
On Hudson's banks, while men of Belgic spawn
Insult and eat thee by the name suppawn.—*Barlow, Hasty Pudding.*

MUSQUASH. The musk-rat among the traders in the Northern States is called the *musquash.*

TO MUSS. A corruption of *to mess.* To disarrange; disorder; put in confusion. Ex. ' I hate to ride in an omnibus, because it *musses* my clothes;' ' I'm all *mussed* up.' The word is much used in New York.

MUSS. A corruption of *mess*, a state of confusion; a squabble; a row. This vulgarism is also common in New York.

" My head aches," said he ; " they have put my mind and body both in a confounded *muss.*"—*Mrs. Child, Letters from New York*, p. 129.

I saw the British flag a flyin' from the top of the mast, and my first notion was to haul it down, and up with the stars and stripes; but I concluded I hadn't better say nothin' about it, for it might get the two nations into a *muss*, and then there would have to be a war.—*Hiram Bigelow's Letter in Fam. Companion.*

There is also an old English word *muss*, meaning a scramble; but it has evidently no connection with the above.

MUSTANG. The wild horse of the prairies, and the invariable companion of their inhabitants. Sparing in diet, a stranger to grain, easily satisfied whether on growing or dead grass, inured to all weather, capable of great labor, the *mustang* poney seems as peculiarly adapted to the prairies as the camel is to the desert.—*Thorpe's Backwoods*, p. 12.

TO MUZZLE. To loiter. In Yorkshire, England, they use
the word *muzlin*, loitering, which seems to be the same; also,
to muddle, to walk in a careless manner with the head down.—
Craven Glossary.

> The child mopes, she *muzzles* about in the grass and chips.—*Margaret.*

N.

TO NAIL. To fasten; to bind a person to a bargain. Ex.
' He offered me a dollar for this book, and I *nailed* him ;' i. e.
I accepted the offer.—*Grose.*

MISS NANCY. A name given to an effeminate man.—
Craven Glossary.

NANKEEN. (A Chinese word.) A species of light yellow or
fawn-colored cloth, made from cotton of the same color
(*gossypium religiosum*), which color is permanent. This
article was formerly imported in large quantities from China ;
but since the cultivation of the raw material in the United
States, *nankeens* have been manufactured here, in every
respect equal to, and at a less cost than those from China.

NARY-ONE, for neither. A common vulgarism.

NATION. Very; extremely; as, *nation* good, very good.
' A *nation* long way.' This word is provincial in this sense in
various parts of England.—*Junius. Brocket.*

> There were a *nation* set o' folk at kirk.—*Carr's Craven Gloss.*

> > But no sense of a place, some think,
> > Is this here hill so high ;
> > Cos there, full oft, 'tis *nation* cold,
> > But that don't argufy.—*Essex Dialect, Noakes and Styles.*

> You colony chaps are a *nation* sight too well off, so you be.—*Sam Slick.*

NATIVE AMERICANS. The name assumed by a political
party which sprang up a few years ago, to advocate the
rights and privileges of persons born in the United States, in
opposition to those of foreigners. The principal measure
advocated by them, was the extension of the time of residence required by law previous to naturalization, from seven
to twenty-one years. The extreme lengths to which this
party went, and the excesses produced in consequence of its

inflammatory appeals to vulgar prejudice, ensured its speedy defeat; and it may now be considered as, to all intents and purposes, extinct.

NEAR, for *to* or *at*; in these expressions—' The minister plenipotentiary *near* the Court of St. James's—*near* the United States,' &c. This Gallicism was first used here in translations of the diplomatic correspondence between the French and American governments; and from the language of *translations* it has been adopted in many of our original compositions.—*Pickering.*

NETOP. "This Indian word," says Mr. Pickering, "is still used, colloquially, in some towns in the interior of Massachusetts, to signify a *friend*, or (to use a cant word) a *crony*." Roger Williams, in his Key to the Indian Language, says, " What cheer, *netop?* is the general salutation of all English towards the Indians."

NIGH UNTO. Nearly; almost. A vulgarism.

> I *nigh unto* burst with madness !—I could feel every har on my head kindlin' at the eend.—*Robb, Squatter Life.*

NIGHTCAP. A glass of hot toddy or gin-sling taken before going to bed at night. When a second glass is taken, it is called ' a string to tie it with.'

> Come, now, Squire, before we turn in, let us tie the *nightcap.*—*Sam Slick in England,* ch. 3.

NIMSHI. A foolish fellow, or one who habitually acts in a foolish manner. Local in Connecticut.

NINE-KILLER. The popular name of the Northern Butcher-bird (*lanius*) of ornithologists. In Canada and the Eastern States, it is sometimes called Mocking-bird. " The name of *nine-killer*," says Dr. DeKay, " is derived from the popular belief that it catches and impales nine grasshoppers in a day."—*Nat. Hist. of New York.*

TO NIP. To pinch close in domestic management.—*Forby's Norfolk Glossary.*

> Mrs. H—— carded, spun, colored, and wove, for herself and others, *nipped* and beaked her husband, drank, and smoked.—*Margaret,* p. 14.

NIPPENT. Impudent; impertinent.—*Hurd's Gram. Corrector.*

TO NOMINATE. To name for an election, choice, or appointment ; to propose by name, or offer the name of a person as a candidate for an office or place. This is the principal use of the word in the United States ; as in a public assembly, where men are to be selected and chosen to office, any member of the assembly or meeting *nominates*, that is, proposes to the chairman the name of a person whom he desires to have elected.—*Webster.*

NOCAKE. An Indian word still used in some parts of New England.

> If their imperious occasions cause the Indians to travel, the best of their victuals for their journey is *nocake* (as they call it), which is nothing but Indian corn parched in the hot ashes ; the ashes being sifted from it, it is afterwards beaten to powder, and put into a long leathern bag, trussed at their back like a knapsack ; out of which they take thrice three spoonfuls a day.— *Wood's New England's Prospect,* 1634.

NON-COMMITTAL. That does not commit or pledge himself to any particular measure. A political term in frequent use.

> They call him [Mr. Van B——] *non-committal* too, and this is because he always looks before he leaps. They say he never gives the measure of his foot. Now how can this be, when it is shown that he speaks against the tariff at home, and votes for it in Congress ; goes for internal improvement by the General Government in New York, but against it out of it ; goes against the Bank at Philadelphia, but in favor of it at Utica ; goes for all the candidates for President in turn, Jackson last, notwithstanding which they say he is in higher favor there now than those who began before him. Went for the war, but went against Madison ; wanted to turn out Madison and put in Clinton, and then turn Clinton out from the little office he held in New York. Goes for gold and hard money, and has more rag money in his State than all the other States put together. Call you this *non-committal ?* As well may you call the fingers of a watch *non-committal,* that go regularly around to every figure on its face.— *Crockett, Tour,* p. 211.

> Extensive preparations were made [for a sketch of the Life and Times of Channing]. But experiment at length satisfied me that it was far more difficult than I supposed to shun the dishonesty of making my honored relative the exponent of my prejudices, without sinking into a tone of *non-committal,* yet more at variance with his character and with the truth.— *Preface to the Life of Dr. Channing.*

NON-COMMITTALISM. The practice or doctrine of not committing oneself.

Much of what Governor W—— says in his message is made feeble by diffuseness; and on many points he either avoids the expression of opinion, or expresses his opinion with so many qualifications as to subject himself to the charge of *non-committalism.*—*N. Y. Commercial Adv.*

He, being somewhat of a wag, handed me " Fearne on Contingent Remainders," which he remarked, with admirable *non-committalism,* was as interesting as a novel, after one got interested in it.—*My Uncle Hobson and I*, p. 20.

NON-ELECTION. Failure of election.—*Webster.*

NON-MANUFACTURING. Not carrying on manufactures; as, ' *non-manufacturing* States.'—*Webster.*

NON-PAYMENT. Neglect of payment.—*Webster.*

NO ODDS. No difference; no consequence; no matter. A common expression in low language.

There is *no* great *odds* nor difference between these two sermons.—*Bp. Latimer's Sermon before Edward VI.*

I don't ax *no odds* of nobody, shouted Boss, smacking his fists together.—*Chron. of Pineville*, p. 52.

" Now, Major," says the General, " which eend shall we begin at first ?" " It makes *no odds,*" says I.—*Maj. Downing's Letters*, p. 44.

Oh! never mind it, Mister; it aint *no odds* no how, and I guess we can soon fix it.—*Carlton, The New Purchase*, Vol. I. p. 9.

NOODLEJEES. (Dutch.) Wheat dough rolled thin and cut into strings like maccaroni. It is used for the same purpose.

NOODLE-SOUP. Soup made of the above.

NOTCH. An opening or narrow passage through a mountain or hill.—*Webster.*

NOTICEABLE. That may be observed; worthy of observation.—*Webster.* Not in any English dictionary. Mr. Pickering gives the following example of its use :

The moon's limb exhibited very little of that rough or serrated appearance, which was so *noticeable* in 1806.—*Mem. of the Amer. Acad.* Vol. III.

TO NOTIFY. 1. To make known; to declare; to publish. ' The laws of God *notify* to man his will and our duty.'

2. To give information of. 'The allied sovereigns have *notified* the Spanish court of their purpose of maintaining legitimate government.'

3. To give notice to. ' The constable has *notified* the

citizens to meet at the City Hall.' 'The bell *notifies* us of the time of meeting.'

The first of these senses, as Dr. Witherspoon long ago observed (Druid, No. 5), is the only one in which this word is employed by English writers. They use it simply in the sense of the Latin *notificare*, i. e. 'to make known,' as in the following examples from Richardson:

> His [Duke Robert's] worthie acts valientlie and fortunately atchieved against the infidels, are *notified* to the world by many and sundrie writers.—*Holinshed*.

> Such protest must also be *notified*, within fourteen days after, to the drawer.—*Blackstone, Com.*

The two significations, Nos. 2 and 3, in which the direct object of the verb is the *person* instead of the *thing*, is in accordance with the French use of the verb *notifier*. It is not improbable that they will yet be adopted in England; for the same transfer of the idea from the thing to the person took place in the Latin language itself, in which the word *notus*, known, was also used in the sense of informed of, knowing.

NOTHING TO NOBODY. Nobody's business. This singular expression is common in the language of the illiterate in some parts of the South.

> But surely no lady drank punch? Yes, three of them did, . . . and the way these women love punch is *nothing to nobody.*—*Georgia Scenes.*

NOTION. Inclination; in vulgar use; as, 'I have a *notion* to do that.'—*Webster.*

NOTIONS. Small wares or trifles.—*Worcester.* A word much used by the ingenious New Englanders.

> "Can I suit you to-day, ma'am?" said a pedlar from New England, when offering his wares for sale in Michigan. "I've all sorts of *notions.* Here's fashionable calicoes; French work collars and capes; elegant milk pans, and Harrison skimmers, and *ne plus ultry* dippers! patent pills—cure anything you like; ague bitters; Shaker yarbs; essences, wintergreen, lobely; tapes, pins, needles, hooks and eyes; broaches and bracelets; smelling bottles; castor ile; corn-plaster; mustard; garding seeds; silver spoons; pocket combs; tea-pots; green tea; saleratus; tracts; song-books; thimbles; baby's whistles; slates; playin' cards; puddin' sticks; baskets; wooden bowls; powder and shot. I shan't offer you lucifers, for ladies with such eyes never buys matches—but you can't ask me for anything I haven't got, I guess."—*Mrs. Clavers's Forest Life*, Vol. II. p. 113.

NUBBINS. Imperfectly formed ears of corn.

NURLY. A corrupt pronunciation of *gnarly*, i. e. gnarled.

Times are mopish and *nurly.—Margaret*, p. 314.

TO NULLIFY. (Lat. *nullus.*) To annul; to make void.— *Todd's Johnson.*

You will say, that this *nullifies* all exhortations to piety; since a man, in this case, cannot totally come up to the thing he is exhorted to.—*South's Sermons.*

NULLIFICATION. The act of nullifying; a rendering void and of no effect, or of no legal effect.—*Webster.* The political meaning of nullification is limited and special—at least in American politics. Some years ago, when the system of high protective duties on foreign imports was predominant in the national councils, the politicians of South Carolina— whose main article of export is cotton—were strongly desirous of free trade with England and France, the principal con- sumers of that article, believing that the consumption of it in those countries would be augmented by an augmentation of the import of their fabrics. Those politicians thought them- selves aggrieved therefore by the protection given in the United States to the manufacture of fabrics coming into compe- tition with those of England and France. But finding Congress resolute in adhering to the protective tariff, the South Carolina politicians became so exasperated that at last they proclaimed their intention to *nullify* the tariff—that is, to admit British and French goods into their ports free of duty, and not to permit the exercise of Custom House functions in their State. In other words, *nullification*, in the case of South Carolina, was simply an act, or at least a threat, of open rebellion. [*John Inman.*]

Somebody must go ahead, and look after these matters to keep down *nullification* and take care of the Gineral [Jackson] when he gits into his tantrums, and keep the great democratic party from splitting in two.— *Crockett, Tour*, p. 218.

NULLIFIER. One who believes in or maintains the right of a State to refuse compliance with a law enacted by the legislature of the whole Union. [*John Inman.*]

O.

OATS. To feel one's oats, is to feel one's importance.

> You know you *feel your oats* as well as any one. So don't be so infarnal mealy-mouthed, with your mock-modesty face.—*S. Slick in England.*

OBLIGEMENT. This antiquated word is still used by old people in New England.—*Pickering.*

OCELOT. The French popular name of a digitigrade carnivorous mammal of the cat kind.—*Webster.*

ODD FISH. A person who is eccentric or odd in his manners. The Knickerbocker Magazine, in a sketch of a learned professor of Tinnecum, says:

> He was styled unanimously an *odd fish,* by those who knew him ; nor did his appearance belie him, as he started forth on a geological excursion, making poems and tuning pianos by the way. On another occasion he won a foot race on the Union course for a hundred dollars, to enable him to pursue his studies for the ministry.—Vol. VI. p. 551.

ODD STICK. An eccentric person; as, ' John Randolph was an *odd stick.*'

OF. An action of the organs of sense may be either involuntary or voluntary. Accordingly we say *to hear, to see,* to denote an involuntary act; and *to look at, to hearken* or *to listen to,* to denote a voluntary one. With regard to the other senses we are not so well provided with words; but some people, prompted apparently by a feeling of this deficiency, endeavor to supply it by construing the verbs *to feel, to taste, to smell,* with the preposition *of,* to signify a voluntary act. Hence, to feel, taste, smell *of* a thing, is to do so intentionally. This corruption is rarely met with in writing.

> In the course of the forenoon, a few women came around our tent—*felt of* it—and peeped through the cracks, to see Mrs. Perkins.—*Perkins's Residence in Persia,* p. 103.

OFF AND ON. Vacillating, changeable, undecided ; in which sense it is much used with us. In England it is also used.—*Carr's Craven Dialect.*

> Be it so, that the Corinthians had no such contentions among them, as

Paul wrote of ; be it so, that they had not mis-ordered themselves, it was neither *off-nor-on*, to that that Paul said.—*Latimer, Sermons*, Vol. I. p. 176.

OFFISH. A word applied to a person who is distant or unapproachable in his manners.

OFFSET. In accounts, a sum, account, or value *set off* against another sum or account, as an equivalent.—*Webster.*

This word is generally used in place of the English term *set-off*. Mr. Pickering says, " it is also very common in popular language, in the sense of an *equivalent.*" None of the English dictionaries have the word in any sense except that of " shoot from a plant."

He avoided giving offence to any of the numerous *offsets* of Presbyterianism.—*Lond. Quart. Rev.*, Vol. X. p. 498.

The expense of the frigates had been strongly urged ; but the saving in insurance, in ships and cargoes, and the ransom of seamen, was more than an *offset* against this item.—*Marshall's Washington.*

Thanksgiving was an anti-Christmas festival, established as a kind of *off-set* to that.—*Margaret*, p. 61.

TO OFFSET. To set one account against another ; to make the account of one party pay the demand of another.—*Webster.*

OLD. Crafty ; cunning. Used in vulgar language.—*Webster.* When a person attempts to get the advantage of another, and is frustrated in the attempt by the sagacity or shrewdness of the other, the latter will say, ' I'm a little too *old* for you,' meaning that he is too cunning to be deceived by him.

OLD, for *stale ;* in this expression, ' *old bread.*' New England.—*Pickering's Vocab.*

Mr. P. infers from the following extract, that this is also a Scotticism :

The Scotticism *old bread*, seems no way inferior to the Anglicism *stale bread.*—*Lond. Monthly Mag.*, April, 1800.

OLD COUNTRY. A term applied to Great Britain, originally by natives from that country, but now understood and used generally in the United States.

OLD COUNTRYMAN. A native of England, Scotland, Ireland, or Wales. The term is never applied to persons from the Continent of Europe.

OLD-WIFE, or OLD-SQUAW. The popular name of a brown duck, one of the most common throughout North America, the long-tailed Duck of Pennant.—*Nat. Hist. of New York.*

OLD-MAN. (*Artemisia abrotanum.*) A popular name for the Southern-wood plant.

OLDERMOST. Oldest. Used at the West.

> Ain't that *oldermost* stranger a kinder sort a preacher ?—*Carlton, The New Purchase*, Vol. II. p. 70.

OLYCOKE. (Dutch, *olikoek*, oil-cake.) A cake fried in lard. A favorite delicacy with the Dutch, and also with their descendants, in New York. There are various kinds, as dough-nuts, crullers, etc.

ONCE IN A WHILE. Occasionally ; sometimes.

> Scarcely a day passes in which from two to half a dozen of our paragraphs are not " appropriated " by others of the city papers, without any allusion to their origin, or any complaint from us. But *once in a while*, when the " appropriation " is of a column or more, we bear the act in mind and take the first convenient occasion to retaliate.—*N. Y. Com. Adv.*

ON HAND. At hand ; present. A colloquial expression in frequent use.

> The Anti-Sabbath meeting, so long talked of, has at length taken place in Boston. About 300 females were *on hand.*—*N. Y. Express.*

> If our numerous subscribers and the public will be *on hand* about 5 o'clock this evening, we can give them the European papers by the America, containing doubtless the most critical intelligence ever transmitted to this country. So be ready.—*Burgess, Stringer & Co.*, 222 Broadway.

ONPLUSH, for *nonplus.* The expression is used in the Southern States.

> You know I tuck dinner at the Planters. Well, I was put a leetle *to the onplush* by that old nigger feller what waits on the table there. I did not know what to make of him.—*Maj. Jones's Courtship*, p. 63.

ONTO. A preposition used in some of the Northern States, but not peculiar to America.

> When the stack rises two feet high to be conveniently forked *onto* from the ground.—*Marshall, Rural Econ., Yorkshire*, Vol. II. p. 144.

Mr. Pickering quotes the following as the only example he has seen in an American book :

> Take all your cigars and tobacco, and in some calm evening carry them *onto* the common.—*Dr. B. Waterhouse, Lecture on Tobacco.*

OPINUATED. Conceited.—*Sherwood's Georgia.*

OSWEGO TEA. (Lat. *monarda didyma.*) A medicinal plant prepared by the Shakers for its aromatic and stomachic properties.

OUGHT. As this verb is defective, and has no inflection to distinguish past from present time, illiterate persons often attempt to supply the deficiency by the use of auxiliaries. Hence the expressions, *don't ought, had ought, hadn't ought.* Mr. Pegge notices the two last among the vulgarisms of London.

> Now, you *hadn't ought* to be so stingy with such charming daughters as you've got.—*Maj. Jones's Courtship*, p. 67.

> Peter Cram is an impostor and ignoramus, and you *hadn't ought* to have recommended him.—*Knickerbocker Mag.*, Vol. XVII.

> " The luggage must be brought in," said the elderly gentleman. " Yes ! I should think it *had oughter*," observed the young man in reply. " I should bring it in, if it was mine."—*Mrs. Clavers's Forest Life*, Vol. I. p. 96.

OURN, for *ours.* A vulgarism frequently heard, which is also common in the local dialect of London.

OUT AND OUT. Wholly ; completely ; without reservation. A common colloquial expression here as in England.

> Duff Green has issued proposals for a new free-trade paper in the city of New York. It will be conducted with energy, and will fail. An *out-and-out* anti-tariff free-trade paper, without commercial support, cannot obtain *that* support in any commercial city in the world.—*N. Y. Com. Adv.*

> Although an *out-and-out* democrat, by virtue of my subscription, and your well-known liberality, I claim to be heard through your columns.— *Cor. of N. Y. Tribune*, Oct. 28, 1845.

> Pliny Hopper expected to make a thousand per cent. the first year [on his morus multicaulis trees], and the second to be able to retire from business, and buy the whole State of Connecticut *out-and-out.*—*Knick. Mag.*

OUT OF FIX. Disarranged ; in a state of disorder.

> The week was the longest one ever was. It seemed to me that the axletree of the world wanted greasin', or somethin' or other was *out of fix*, for it didn't seem to turn round half so fast as it used to do.—*Maj. Jones's Conrtship*, p. 80.

OUT OF SORTS. Out of order ; disordered. Dr. Millingen, in his remarks on persons of phlegmatic temperament, says :

> They are in general good, easy persons, susceptible of kindly feelings, but, to use a common expression, easily put *out of sorts.*—*Mind and Matter*, p. 84.

OUTFIT. Money advanced to a public minister, going to a foreign country, beyond his salary.—*Webster.*

TO OUTSTORM. To overbear by storming.—*Webster.*

> Insults the tempests, and *outstorms* the skies.—*J. Barlow.*

OVER, for *under.* In these expressions, 'He wrote *over* the signature of Junius;' 'He published some papers *over* his own signature.' A few of our writers still countenance this unwarrantable innovation; but the principle, on which it is defended, would unsettle the whole language. The use of the word *under*, in phrases like those above mentioned, is as well established as any English idiom.—*Pickering.* Mr. Hoffman, in reply to a correspondent, says:

> Had our friend U., of Philadelphia, duly meditated this matter, he never would have sent us a letter with such an unpoetical expression in it as the very common blunder of " *over* the signature "—for the metaphorical phrase originally derived from the ensign of the soldier, the device of the knight, the armorial bearing of the baron, the totem, if you please, of the Indian sachem, under which he presents himself to the world. U., as a lawyer, must at least be more or less familiar with the phrase, " given under my hand and seal," as a true English idiom, albeit the hand and seal (which in this instance constitute " the signature ") are placed at the bottom of the document. We do not talk of a vessel sailing " *over* " the flag of the United States, when her ensigns are sent below at sunset !—*N. Y. Lit. World.*

OVER-CAREFUL. Careful to excess.—*Webster.*

TO OVERHAUL. To gain upon in a chase; to overtake.— *Webster.* A seaman's phrase, sometimes used in common parlance.

OVERSLAUGH. (Dutch, *overslag.*) A bar, in the marine language of the Dutch. The *overslaugh* in the Hudson river near Albany, is, I believe, the only locality to which this term is now applied among us.

TO OVERSLAUGH. (Dutch, *overslaan.*) To skip over; pass over; omit. A word used by New York politicians.

> Mr. Polk intended making Gen. Butler commander-in-chief, and to drop Gen. Scott. But it was found that public opinion would not be reconciled to *overslaughing* Taylor, and he [Gen. Taylor] was nominated.—*Washington Correspondent, N. Y. Com. Adv.,* Oct. 21, 1846.

> Van Buren is no longer feared as a candidate for the Presidency. He was *overslaughed* in May, when he was a candidate of some promise.— *Letter from Washington, N. Y. Com. Adv.,* Nov. 28, 1846.

OWDACIOUS, for *audacious*.   Southern and Western.

> He had a daughter Molly, that was the most encitin', heart-distressin' creature that ever made a feller get *owdacious.*—*Robb, Squatter Life.*

> Why, Major, you wouldn't take such a likely gall as that to New York? —the abolitionists would have her out of your hands quicker than you could say Jack Robinson.   I was never so *oudaciously* put out with the abominable abolitionists before.   It was enough to make a man what wasn't principled agin swearin', cus like a trooper.—*Maj. Jones's Travels.*

P.

PAAS.   (Dutch, *Paasch.*)   This Dutch name is still commonly applied to the festival of Easter, in the State of New York.

PACKAGE.   A general term, comprehending *bales, boxes,* &c. of merchandise.—*Pickering.*   Dr. Johnson and the early lexicographers do not notice the word.   Recent authors, however, Knowles and Reid, give it a place in their dictionaries.

PAINT.   In some of the Southern States, a horse or other animal which is spotted, is called a *paint.*

PAINTER.   In the country the popular name of the cougar or panther (*felis concolor*).   Vanderdonck, in his " History of the New Netherlands," called it a *lion;* and Mr. Emmons, in his " Massachusetts Report," speaks of it as the Puma or American Lion.

> " You don't know the way," said Obed; " snakes'll bite ye; there's *painters* in the woods, and wild cats and owls."—*Margaret,* p. 27.

PAIR OF STAIRS.   An expression often used for a *flight* of stairs.

PALMETTO.   (Genus, *chamærops.*)   A species of American dwarf palm; cabbage tree.—*Worcester.*

PALMETTO STATE or CAPITAL.   The State or capital of South Carolina; so called from the arms of the State, which contain a palmetto.

> In the delightful temperature of to-day, with the rich foliage of the trees in green luxuriance, and the perfumes of a thousand beds of flowers burdening the air, the *Palmetto Capital* is exceedingly pleasant.—*Letter from Charleston, N. Y. Tribune.*

PAPPOOS. (Algonkin.) Among the native Indians of New England, a babe or young child.—*Webster*. It is also applied to Indian infants by the whites.

PARK. A public square or enclosure is so termed in New York. The *Park*, formerly called the Commons, and in which stands the City Hall, contains nearly eleven acres of ground; *St. John's Park*, called the Hudson Square, has above four acres.

PARTLY. Mr. Pickering notices the use of this word in the sense of *nearly*, *almost*, in some towns of the Middle States. Ex. 'His house is *partly* opposite,' i. e. nearly opposite to mine. 'It is *partly* all gone;' i. e. nearly all gone.

PASSAGE. Enactment; the act of carrying through all the regular forms necessary to give validity; as the *passage* of a law, or of a bill into a law, by a legislative body.—*Webster*. Mr. Pickering says this word "is criticised by the English reviewers as an American innovation." It is not in the English dictionaries in this sense.

His agency in procuring the *passage* of the stamp act was more than suspected.—*Hosack*.

PATROON. (Dutch, *patroon*, a patron.) A grantee of land to be settled under the old Dutch governments of New York and New Jersey.

The following articles from the "Freedoms and Exemptions" granted to the Dutch West India Company, will show what were some of the privileges of the *Patroons*:

Art. 3. All such shall be acknowledged *Patroons* of New Netherland who shall, within the space of four years next after they have given notice to any of the Chambers of the Company here, or to the Commander of the Council there, undertake to plant a colonie there of fifty souls, upwards of fifteen years of age; one-fourth part within one year, and within three years of the sending of the first, the remainder, to the full number of fifty persons, to be shipped from hence, on pain, in case of wilful neglect, of being deprived of the privileges obtained, etc.

Art. 5. The *Patroons*, by virtue of their power, shall and may be permitted, at such places as they shall settle their colonies, to extend their limits four miles along the shore, that is, on one side of a navigable river, or two miles on each side of a river, and so far into the country as the situation of the occupiers will permit, etc.

Art. 8 The *Patroons* may, if they think proper, make use of all lands, rivers, and woods lying contiguous to them, for and during so long a time as this Company shall grant them to other *Patroons* or particulars.

For a further account of the privileges of the Patroons, see O'Callaghan's History of New Netherland, Vol. I. p. 112.

PAWPAW. (Lat. *annona triloba*, ficus Indicus.) A wild fruit-bearing shrub, remarkable for its beauty. The fruit is nutritious, and a great resource to the Indians. "So many whimsical and compounded tastes are contained in it," says Mr. Flint, "that a person of the most hypochondriac temperament relaxes to a smile when he tastes the *pawpaw* for the first time."—*Geog. of the Mississippi Valley.*

PAYEE. The person to whom money is to be paid; the person named in a bill or note to whom the amount is promised or directed to be paid.—*Webster.* This useful word is not in the English dictionaries.

TO PEAK.
TO PEKE. To peep; to pry into. It is quite common in the popular language of New England to hear this word, which Dr. Webster supposes to be the same as *peep.* If it is a corruption, which is doubtful, the examples will show that its use is not modern.

> Now whereof he speketh ;
> He cryeth and he creketh,
> He pryeth and he *peketh.*—*Skelton, Colin Cloute,* Vol. I. 312.

That other pries and *pekes* in everie place.—*Gascoigne,* p. 301.

He's a lazy, good-for-nothin' fellow. He's no better than a *peaking* mudsucker.—*Margaret,* p. 20.

PEAKED. Sickly looking.—*Todd.* Applied to a person who is sickly, and whose face presents sharp angles. Holloway says, that in England they say of a sickly person, " he looks pale and *peaked.*' The same expression is often heard in the Northern States.

But there was a lawyer, a standing up by the grove, lookin' as *peaked* and as forlorn as an unmated coon.—*Sam Slick in England,* ch. 11.

PEA-NUT. The common name for the fruit of the *arachis hypogea.* It is also called the *ground nut* and *earth nut.* (French, *pistache de terre.*)

PEARIFORM. Pear-shaped. A hybrid expression.

The Western mounds are usually simple cones in form; but they are sometimes truncated, and occasionally terraced, with graded or winding ascents to their summits. Some are elliptical, others *peariform*, and others square or parallelogram, with flanking terraces.—*Squier on the Aboriginal Monuments of the Mississippi Valley.*

PECCAN NUT. The *nut* of the *peccan* tree, the *carys oliviformia* of the Southern States.

PECK OF TROUBLES. Great trouble.

> Neptune at that his speed redoubles,
> To ease them of their *peck of troubles.*—*Cotton, Virgil Travestie,* B. I.

> When I wrote my last letter to you, I was in a *peck of troubles,* and it did seem to me like heaven and earth was inspired agin me.—*Maj. Jones's Courtship,* p. 106.

PECKISH. Hungry.—*Grose.*

PEEKY. A term applied to timber and trees, in which the first symptoms of decay are shown.

> The species of decay to which the cypress tree is liable, shows itself in detached spots in close proximity to each other. Timber affected in this way is denominated by raftsmen, *peeky.*—*Dickeson on Cypress Timber.*

PEEL. A broad thin board with a long handle, used by bakers to put their bread in and out of the oven.—*Johnson.* The term is by many applied to a common shovel.

PEERT. This word has the same signification as *perk*, but is much more frequently employed. It is either an altered form of the word *perk*, or a corrupt pronunciation of *pert*. The phrase, 'as *peert* as a lizard,' is sometimes heard. It is used in a good as well as a bad sense, and especially of one who is recovering, or ' looking up,' after a fit of sickness.

> I gave her the best bend I had in me, and raised my bran-new hat as *peert* and perlite as a minister.—*Robb, Squatter Life.*

Speaking of the recovery of his wife from sickness, Major Jones says:

> Mary's rite *piert,* and her child is making a monstrous good beginnin' in the world.—*Courtship,* p. 200.

> That fellow must think we were all raised in a saw mill, he looks so *peert* whenever he comes in.—*Hoffman, Winter in the West.*

> Well, I starts off pretty considerable *peert* and brisk, considering I was weak.—*Carlton, The New Purchase,* Vol. I. p. 178.

PEE-WEE. The name given by boys to a little marble.

PEET-WEET. (Genus, *totanus*.) The spotted Sandpiper or Sand-lark of ornithologists, but better known among the people by the name of *peet-weet*, in allusion to its notes; or of *teeter* and *tilt-up* from its often repeated grotesque jerking motions.—*Dr. DeKay in Nat. Hist. of New York.*

PEMICAN. A far-famed provender of man, in the wilds of North America, formed by pounding the choice parts of the meat very small, dried over a slow fire or in the frost, and put into bags made of the skin of the slain animal, into which a portion of melted fat is then poured. The whole being then strongly pressed and sewed up, constitutes the best and most portable food for the " voyageurs," and one which, with proper care, will keep a long time. Fifty pounds of meat and forty pounds of grease make a bag of *pemican*. *Sweet pemican* is another kind, made chiefly of bones.—*Dunn's Oregon*, p. 59.

PENN. The common abbreviation for *Pennsylvania*.

PERFECTIONIST. One pretending to perfection; an enthusiast in religion.—*Webster.*

> Among the highest puritan *perfectionists*, you shall find people of fifty, threescore, and fourscore years old, not able to give that account of their faith which you might have had heretofore from a boy of nine or ten.—*South's Sermons*, Vol. IV.

> There he met a *perfectionist*, ready for heaven,
> Only waiting till Heaven was willing;
> And he found him one-half a perfect fool,
> The other half a perfect villain.—*Devil's New Walk*, Boston, 1848.

PERIAUGER. (Spanish, *piragua*.) A small schooner without a bowsprit, and with a lee board, used in the waters of New York and New Jersey.

> Steamboats, lighters, *periaugers*, scows, clam-boats, and nondescript water-witches of every sort, have arrived hourly from quarantine, loaded with almost entire villages of men, women, and children [German and Irish emigrants].—*N. Y. Commercial Advertiser.*

PERIODICAL. A magazine or other publication, that is published at stated or regular periods.—*Webster.*

PERK. Lively; brisk; holding up the head.—*Webster.* This old word, still provincial in England, is used in the interior of New England, and is commonly pronounced *peark* (the *ea* as in *pear*).—*Pickering.*

> My ragged ronts
> They wont in the wind wag their wriggle tails,
> *Perk* as a peacock; but now it avails.—*Shepherd's Calendar.*

PERSIMMON. (*Diospyros Virginiana.*)   This tree is un-known in the North-eastern parts of our country ; but south of latitude 42° it is found throughout the United States.   It varies exceedingly in size, being sometimes sixty feet in height, with a trunk twenty inches in diameter, but more frequently does not attain half these dimensions.   The fruit is about an inch in diameter, and is powerfully astringent.   The wood is very hard, and is used for large screws, mallets, shoe lasts, wedges, &c.   In clearing the forests, the *persimmon* is usually preserved ; and it is probable that the quality of the fruit might be improved by cultivation.—*Encyc. Amer.*

PERTEND UP.   Better ; more cheerful.—*Sherwood's Georgia.*

PESKILY.   Very ; extremely ; confoundedly.   I know not the origin of this New England word.

> Skeered, says he, sarves him right ; he might have known how to feel for other folks, and not funkify them so *peskily.*—*Sam Slick in England.*

> I'm *peskily* sorry about that mare.—*Ibid.* ch. 28.

> The Post Office accounts were the next bother ; and they puzzled all on us *peskily.*—*Maj. Downing's Letters*, p. 139.

PESKY.   Great ; very ; exceedingly.

> I found [looking for houses] a *pesky* sight worse job than I expected.—*Downing, May-day in New York*, p. 36.

> I wonder how he's on't for face-cards; ha ! ha !   So *pesky* slow, we shan't get through to-night.—*Margaret*, p. 305.

> The thing of it is, people has got to be so *pesky* proud and perlite.—*Ibid.* p. 141.

PETER FUNK.   At the petty auctions a person is employed to bid on articles put up for sale, in order to raise their price. Such a person is called a *Peter Funk;* probably from such a name having frequently been given when articles were bought in.   At the *mock auctions*, as they are called in New York, this practice of having by-bidders is carried to a great extent ; and strangers, unacquainted with their tricks, are often cheated by them. Grose describes a person similarly employed in England, under the name of *puffer*.

PHEESE. A fit of fretfulness. A colloquial, vulgar word in the United States.—*Worcester.* The adjective *pheesy*, fretful, querulous, irritable, sore, is provincial in England.—*Forby.* Also written *feeze*, which see.

PICAYUNE. The name for the Spanish half real in Florida, Louisiana, etc. See *Federal Currency*.

PICAYUNE. Sixpenny. Sometimes used metaphorically for *small*.

> There is nothing *picayune* about the members of St. George's [Cricket] Club; for the love of sport, they will almost invariably enter upon matches that other clubs would not accept.—*N. Y. Herald.*

PICKANINNY. A negro or mulatto infant. Used in the Southern States. Mr. Boucher, in his Glossary, suggests that this word is from the Spanish *picade niño, pequeno niño.* It is more probably of African origin.

> I jest sauntered in as he was puttin' up the *pickaninny* yaller gal, about five years old.—*Robb, Squatter Life.*

PICK-BACK. On the back.—*Johnson.* We often use the word with children. To ride *pick-back*, is for a child to ride across one's back, with its arms around the neck.

> For as our modern wits behold,
> Mounted a *pick-back* on the old,
> Much farther off; much farther he,
> Rais'd on his aged beast, could see.—*Hudibras.*

TO PICK. To eat like a bird; that is, slowly and by small morsels. Ex. 'I have little appetite, but think I can *pick* a bit;' 'You will find some good *picking* on that fowl.'

PICKLE. To have *a rod in pickle*, or *in soak*, is to have a flogging prepared for one. The phrase is often used in jest, here as in England.

PICK-UP. A *pick-up*, or a *pick-up* dinner, is a dinner made up of such fragments of cold meats as remain from former meals. The word is common in the Northern States.

PIECE. A little while. 'Stay a *piece*.' Provincial in the north of England.—*Johnson.* The common expression is, 'Wait a bit.'

PIG-NUT. (Lat. *juglans porcina.*) A small species of walnut. —*Michaux, Sylva.*

PIG-YOKE. Among seamen, the name for a quadrant, from its resemblance to a pig-yoke.

PILE. (Dutch, *pyl.*) An arrow. This word is still retained by the boys of New York.

PIMPING. Little; petty; as, 'a *pimping* thing.'—*Skinner.* Used in the interior of New England.

> Was I little? asked Margaret. Yes, and *pimpin'* enough. And I fed your marm with rue and comfrey-root, or ye never'd come to this.—*Margaret*, p. 19.

ON A PINCH. On an emergency.

> At a fight in Albany, New York, on the 12th instant, one man was stabbed desperately with a dirk. *Upon a pinch*, they can stab a little at the North.—*New Orleans Paper.*
>
> They can't go ahead of us in England in racin'. We have colts that can whip chain-lightnin' *on a pinch.*—*Sam Slick in England*, ch. 19.
>
> I have the best accommodations in the city, said the landlord. I can lodge 200 persons with all the ease in the world, and 300 *upon a pinch.*— *Perils of Pearl Street*, p. 142.

PINE BARRENS. A term applied to level, sandy tracts, covered with pine-trees, in the Southern States.—*Worcester.*

> The road which I had to travel, lay through a dreary and extensive forest of pine trees, or, as it is termed by the Carolinians, a *pine-barren*, where a habitation is seldom seen, except at intervals of ten or twelve miles.—*Lambert's Travels*, Vol. II. p. 226.

PINK. Used here as in England, like the word *flower*, to denote the finest part, the essence; as, 'She is the *pink* of perfection.'

> I am the very *pink* of courtesy.—*Shakspeare, Romeo and Juliet.*
>
> Then let Crispino, who was ne'er refused
> The justice yet of being well abused,
> With patience wait; and be content to reign
> The *pink* of puppies in some future strain.—*Young.*
>
> Mr. Smoothly was the mirror of fashion, and the *pink* of politeness.— *Perils of Pearl Street*, p. 25.

PINK-STERN. (French, *pinque.*) A vessel with a narrow stern; hence all vessels so formed are called *pink-sterned.*—

Chambers. This species of craft is very common in the waters of New England.

PINION. A species of pine tree, growing on the head waters of the Arkansas; common to that region as well as to New Mexico, the Rocky Mountains, etc. Wild turkeys frequent groves of these trees for the sake of their nuts.

PINXTER. (Dutch, *pingster.*) Whitsunday. On Pinxter Monday, the Dutch negroes of New York and New Jersey consider themselves especially privileged to get as drunk as they can.

> *Pinkster* fields, and *pinkster* frolics, are no novelties to us, sir, as they occur at every season; and I am just old enough not to have missed one of them all, for the last twelve years.—*Cooper, Satanstoe,* Vol. I. p. 90.

PINXTER BLUMACHY. (Dutch.) A familiar name in the State of New York for the *Azalea nudiflora.* *May-apple* is another name for the same plant.

PIPE-LAYING. This term, in political parlance, means any arrangement by which a party makes sure of a certain addition to its legitimate strength in the hour of trial—that is, the election. In other words, to lay pipe means to bring up voters not legally qualified.

It were too long a story to tell the origin of the term at length. In brief, it arose from an accusation brought against the Whig party of this city (New York) some years ago, of a gigantic scheme to bring on voters from Philadelphia. The accusation was made by a notorious Democrat, of not very pure political character, who professed to have derived his information from the agent employed by the Whigs for the service. This agent had actually been employed by certain leaders of the Whig party, but on a service deemed legitimate and proper in the art of electioneering. He, however, turned traitor, and, as was alleged by the Whigs, concocted a plot with the notorious Democrat to throw odium upon the Whigs. A mass of correspondence was brought forward in proof, consisting mainly of letters written by the agent to various parties in New York, apparently describing the progress and success of his operations. In these letters, as if for the purpose of concealment, the form of a mere business correspondence was adopted—the number of men hired to visit New York and vote, being spoken of as so many yards of pipe—the work of laying down pipe for the Croton water being at that time in full activity.

The Whig leaders were indicted, on the strength of these pseudo revelations, and the letters were read in court; bu the jury believed neither in them nor in the writer of them, and the accused were acquitted.

The term "*pipe-laying*," however, was at once adopted as a synonym for negotiations to procure fraudulent votes. [*J. Inman.*]

PIRATE. A sea-robber; any robber; particularly a book-seller who seizes the copies of other men.—*Johnson.*

Some of our large publishing houses may not be aware that there is such good authority for applying the term *pirate* to them, as is found in the following quotation :

> This poem was written for his own diversion, without any design of publication. It was communicated but to me; but soon spread, and fell into the hands of *pirates*. It was put out, vilely mangled, and impudently said to be corrected by the author.—*Johnson, Life of J. Philips.*

PISTAREEN. The Spanish *peseta Sevillana,* or one-fifth of a dollar. A silver coin, formerly common in the United States, of the value of twenty cents. They have now become so much worn that they pass but for seventeen cents.

TO PIT. A pit is the area in which cocks fight; hence, ' to *pit* one against another,' to place them in the same *pit*, one against the other, for a contest; to put or place as a match.— *Richardson.*

> A gentleman came into our office, from Colton, and deliberately *pitted* that town against the county for tall grass.—*Ogdensburgh Sentinel.*

PIT. (Dutch, *pit*, a kernel.) The kernel or nut of fruit; as, a cherry-*pit*. Peculiar to New York.

> You put an apple-seed or a peach-*pit* into the ground, and it springs up into the form of a miniature tree.—*Prof. Bush on the Resurrection.*

ITPAN. In the West Indies, a very long, narrow, flat-bottomed, trough-like canoe, with thin and flat projecting ends.

PLAGUILY. Vexatiously; horribly. A low word.—*Johnson.*

You look'd scornful, and snift at the dean ;
But he durst not so much as once open his lips,
And the doctor was *plaguily* down in the hips.—*Swift.*

I am puzzled most *plaguily* to get words to tell you what I think.—*Maj. Downing's Letters*, p. 3.

PLAGUY. In the United States used adverbially, in the same sense as *plaguily.*

The circumstances of the case should make the committee less " avidus gloriæ," for all praise of them would look *plaguy* suspicious.—*Lord Byron to Lord Holland, Let.* 107.

The Prince de Joinville is a *plaguy* handsome man, and as full of fun as a kitten.—*Sam Slick in England,* ch. 22.

PLAGUY SIGHT. This is a very common expression in the colloquial language of New England, and means, a great deal.

Squire, said Slick, I'd a *plaguy sight* sooner see Ascot than anything else in England.—*Sam Slick in England,* ch. 19.

TO PLANK. To lay ; to put ; generally applied to money ; as, ' He *planked* down the cash.'

I've had to *plank* down handsome, and do the thing genteel, but Mr. Landlord found he had no fool to deal with, neither —*S. Slick in England.*

Why, says he, shell out, and *plank* down a pile of dollars.—*Ibid.*

During the last war he *planked* up more gold and silver to lend the government than Benton ever counted.—*Crockett, Tour,* p. 59.

PLANTER. In Newfoundland, a person engaged in the fishery.

PLANTER. A term applied to a piece of timber or the naked trunk of a tree, one end of which is firmly planted in the bed of a river, while the other rises near the surface of the water. This is the most dangerous among the " snag and sawyer " family, to which vessels, navigating the Western rivers, are exposed. See *Snag* and *Sawyer.*

PLATFORM. In some of the New England States an ecclesiastical constitution, or a plan for the government of churches ; as, the Cambridge or Saybrook *platform.*—*Webster.* The same use of this word is made by English divines.

Their minds and affections were universally bent even against all the orders and laws wherein the church is founded, conformable to the *platform* of Geneva.—*Hooker.*

A *platform* of church discipline, gathered out of the word of God, and agreed upon by the elders and messengers of the churches assembled at the synod in Cambridge in New England.—*Title of book printed, London*, 1653.

PLAY-ACTOR. A pleonastic expression for the English term *player* or *actor*. It is used only in the United States.

PLEAD or PLED, for *pleaded.* It has been correctly remarked, that there is no such word as *pled* in the English language. It is true that the preterite and past part. of the verb *to read* is pronounced *red ;* but there is no analogy between the two verbs, except their accidental similarity of sound. The former is the Anglo-Saxon verb *rædan,* and is conjugated accordingly ; whereas the latter is the old French *plaider,* and therefore cannot admit what philologists call the " strong inflexion." This vulgar mistake is often met with in our reports of legal proceedings and elsewhere. But it is not of recent origin, nor is it exclusively American, as is shown by the following example from Spenser, furnished by Richardson :

> With him . . . . . came
> Many grave persons that against her *pled.*—*Spenser, Fairy Queen.*

An old offender was caught last night in a warehouse, with a dark lantern and all the other implements of his profession, and next morning innocently *plead* " somnambulism " when brought before the magistrate—having no recollection of the doings of the night since he went to bed, early in the evening, and found himself in the watch-house in the morning.—*New York Paper.*

PLENTY. Plentiful ; in abundance.—*Webster.* Opinions differ as to this use of the word. Johnson regards it as " barbarous ;" while Webster thinks it "too well authorized to be rejected." Dr. Johnson seems clearly in the right, notwithstanding ; the word being the old French abstract noun *plenté,* which we are not entitled to turn into an adjective because it happens to end in *y.*

> To grass with thy calves
> Where water is *plenty.*—*Tusser's Husbandry.*

If reasons were as *plenty* as blackberries, I would give no man a reason on compulsion.—*Shakspeare, Henry IV.*

They were formed for those countries where shrubs are *plenty* and water scarce.—*Goldsmith.*

When laborers are *plenty,* their wages will be low.—*Franklin.*

PLUMPER. At an election, a full vote, to one candidate, not shared with another.—*Richardson.* We use the word in the same sense; for example, 'Let the Whig voters turn out in a body, and give Harry Clay a *plumper.*'

PLUNDER. Personal luggage, baggage of travellers, goods, effects. A very common word throughout the Southern and Western States. It is never heard in this sense in New England.

> When we got loaded up, I was afraid old Bosen was going to have more'n his match to pull us, they'd put in so much *plunder.* Two trunks, band-boxes, &c.—*Maj. Jones's Courtship,* p. 165.

> Help yourself, stranger, added the landlord, while I tote your *plunder* into the other room.—*Hoffman, Winter in the West, Let.* 33.

POHAGEN. A fish of the herring species. The Menhaden of Rhode Island. *Maine.*

POKE. A bag. I have heard this old word used by some persons here in the compound term *cream-poke;* that is, a small bag through which cream is strained.—*Pickering.*

POKE. A lazy person; a dawdle. 'What a slow *poke* you are!' A woman's word.

POKE, or POKE-WEED. (Lat. *phytolacca.*) A common plant, known also by the names of Garget, Cocum, Jalap, &c. It is a violent emetic.—*Bigelow's Plants of Boston.*

POKE. In New England, a machine to prevent unruly beasts from leaping fences, consisting of a yoke with a pole inserted, pointing forward.—*Webster.*

TO POKE. To put a *poke* on; as, to *poke* an ox.—*Webster.*

TO POKE FUN. To joke; to make fun. *To poke fun at,* is to ridicule, make a butt of one.

> The widow admonished Nimrod, and said, " You had better not be *pokin'* your *fun* about."—*Margaret,* p. 49.

> Jeames, if you dont be quit *poking fun at* me, I'll break your mouth, as sure as you sit there.—*Neal's Charcoal Sketches.*

POKE-BONNET. A long, straight bonnet, much worn by Quakers and Methodists.

POKE-LOKEN. An Indian word, used by hunters and lumbermen in Maine, to denote a marshy place or stagnant pool, extending into the land from a stream or lake.

POKER. A favorite game of cards among Southern gamblers.

POKER. (Dan. *pokker*, Welsh *pwca*, a hobgoblin.) Any frightful object, especially in the dark; a bugbear; a word in common use in America.—*Webster*.

POKERISH. Frightful; causing fear, especially to children. A childish or colloquial word.—*Worcester*.

> A curious old convent [in Naples] with chapels above and below—a *pokerish* looking place, fit for treasons, stratagems, and spoils.—*N. Y. Literary World*, Aug. 1847.

POLLYWOG, or POLLYWIG. A tadpole. Mr. Forby has the word *puriwiggy*, a tadpole, of which *pollywig* is a corruption. He derives it from *periwig*, from the resemblance the tadpole bears to that antiquated article of finery, the wig with a long queue, as well as to a *pot-ladle*, by which name it is also called.—*Norfolk Glossary*.

POMME BLANCHE. (Fr.) White apple. A native of the prairies and mountains, oval-shaped and about three and a half inches in circumference. It is encased in a thin fibrous tegument, which, when removed, exposes a white pulpy substance, and in taste resembles a turnip.—*Scenes in the Rocky Mountains*, p. 107.

POND. We give this name to collections of water in the interior country, which are fed by springs, and from which issues a small stream. These *ponds* are often a mile or two or even more in length, and the current issuing from them is used to drive the wheels of mills and furnaces.—*Webster*.

> There were streams meandering among hills and valleys; little lakes or *ponds*, as they were erroneously called in the language of the country, dotted the surface.—*Cooper, Satanstoe*, Vol. I. p. 144.

TO PONY UP. A vulgar phrase, meaning to pay over money. Ex. ' Come, Mr. B——, *pony up* that account;' that is, pay over the money. Grose gives a phrase similar to it : ' Post the *pony*,' i. e. lay down the money.

> It was my job to pay all the bills. " Salix, *pony up* at the bar, and lend us a levy."—*J. C. Neal, Sketches*.

POOR AS JOB'S TURKEY. A common simile.

The professor is as *poor as Job's turkey*, if it wasn't for that powerful salary the trustees give him.—*Carlton, The New Purchase*, Vol. II. p. 85.

POP. Papa. A term used in the country.

POPPED CORN. Parched Indian corn, so called from the noise it makes on bursting open. The variety usually prepared in this way is of a dark color, with a small grain.

PORGY, or PAUGIE. Pron. with the *g* hard. (Indian, *scuppaug*.) A fish of the *sparus* family, common in the waters of New England and New York. Roger Williams mentions it in his Key to the Indian Language (1643). It is singular that one half the aboriginal name, *scup*, should be retained in Rhode Island for this fish, and the other half, *paug*, changed into *paugie*, or *porgy*, in New York. The entire Indian name, however, is still common in many parts of New England.

PORTAGE. A carrying place over land between navigable waters, or along the banks of rivers, round water-falls or rapids, &c.—*Pickering*. This word has been adopted by geographers, and is universal throughout North America.

POSITION. ' *Defining one's position* ' is a political practice of modern days, generally resorted to either by gentlemen who have no other good chance or prospect of bringing themselves to the special notice of the public, as a sort of advertisement that they are in the market, or by other gentlemen who contemplate making a dodge from one side in politics to the other. It is done either orally or in writing; by a speech in Congress or at some public meeting; or by a long letter, published in some newspaper, the editor of which is always glad of something to fill his columns. The highest art in ' defining one's position ' is to leave it more indefinite than it was before, so that any future contingency may be taken advantage of. [*J. Inman.*]

The Barnburners' Mass Meeting, to *non*-respond to the nominations of Cass and Butler, will take place in the Park at 5 this afternoon, and be addressed by John Van Buren, B. F. Butler, Sedgwick, Field, Gen. Nye, &c. &c. We regret that unavoidable absence at Philadelphia will deprive us of the pleasure of hearing these gentlemen "*define their position*," especially Prince John, who has the reputation of being the most straight-forward, plain-spoken, flat-footed 'Burner in the country. It is a rare treat to hear a man speak who actually means something, and isn't afraid to say it. Let us hear what the Barnburner platform is; and when Gen. Cass comes along (probably to-morrow or next day), the Hunkers will have a chance to set forth their notions. We shall endeavor to report both.—*N. Y. Tribune*, June 6, 1848.

PORTAAL. (Dutch.) A portal, lobby. Used by people of Dutch descent, in New Jersey and New York, for a small passage or entry of a house, and pronounced *pit-áll*. The principal entrance they call the *gang;* also Dutch.

PORTMANTLE. Portmanteau; a valise.

> What do you say to a lad with a *portmantle* on his shoulders, like Ishmael Small ?—*Mathews, Puffer Hopkins*.

POST-NOTE. In commerce, a bank-note intended to be transmitted to a distant place by mail, and made payable to order. In this it differs from a common bank-note, which is payable to bearer.—*Webster*.

> *Post-notes* differ in other respects from bank-notes. The latter are payable on demand ; the former are often drawn on time, with or without interest, sometimes six or twelve months after date. This species of currency was resorted to by many banks during the great commercial revulsions in 1836–7, and thereby contributed greatly to the expansion of credits which proved so disastrous to the country.

TO GO TO POT. To be destroyed, wasted, or ruined.— *Johnson. Webster.* Though much used, it is considered a low phrase both in England and America.

> The sheep *went* first *to pot*, the goats next, and after them the oxen, and all little enough to keep life together.—*L'Estrange*.

> John's ready money went into the lawyer's pockets ; then John began to borrow money upon the bank-stock ; now and then a farm *went to pot*.— *Arbuthnot, J. Bull*.

POTTY-BAKER. (Dutch, *potte-bakker*.) A potter. This Dutch word is still common in New York. Potter's clay is here called *potty-baker's clay*.

POWER. A large quantity ; a great number. In low language ; as, ' a *power* of good things.'—*Johnson*.

> He, to work him the more mischief, sent over his brother Edward, with a

power of Scots and Redshanks, into Ireland, where they got footing.—*Spenser on Ireland.*

I think the Post Office Committees will do a *power* of good, if they can stir up the old contracts and extras.—*Crockett, Tour,* p. 118.

He made a *power* of money.—*Ibid.* p. 59.

POWERFUL. Great; very; exceedingly. A vulgar use of the word in some parts of the country.

This piano was sort o' fiddle like—only bigger,—and with a *powerful* heap of wire strings. It is called a forty piano, because it plays forty tunes.—*Carlton's New Purchase*, Vol. II. p. 8.

Yes, Mr. Speaker, I'd a *powerful* sight sooner go into retiracy among the red, wild aborigines of our wooden country, nor consent to that bill.—*Carlton, The New Purchase*, Vol. I. p. 74.

Mrs. S. Hoarhound and sugar's amazin' good.

Mrs. B. Mighty good, mighty good.

Mrs. R. *Powerful* good. I take mightily to a sweat of sugar tea in desperate bad colds.—*Georgia Scenes*, p. 193.

It may be said generally of husbands, as the old woman said of hers, who had abused her, to an old maid, who reproached her for being such a fool as to marry him : " To be sure, he's not so good a husband as he should be, but he's a *powerful* sight better than none."—*N. Y. Sunday Dispatch.*

POW-WOW. (Indian.) This is the name given by the early chroniclers to the feasts, dances, and other public doings of the red men, preliminary to a grand hunt, a council, a war expedition, or the like. It has been adopted, in political talk, to signify any uproarious meeting for a political purpose, at which there is more noise than deliberation, more clamor than counsel. [*J. Inman.*]

A murder was recently committed upon a Sioux by two Chippewas. The body of the murdered Indian was taken to the fort, where a most terrific *pow-wow* was held over it by the friends of the deceased, 300 in number.—*Western Newspaper.*

PRAIRIE. (French.) An extensive tract of land, mostly level, destitute of trees, and covered with tall, coarse grass. These prairies are numerous in the United States west of the Alleghany Mountains, especially between the Ohio, Mississippi, and the great lakes.—*Webster.*

PRAIRILLON. A small prairie.

Interspersed among the hills, are frequent openings and *prairillons* of rich soil and luxuriant vegetation.—*Scenes in the Rocky Mountains*, p. 172.

PRAIRIE-BITTERS. A beverage common among the hunters and mountaineers. It is made with a pint of water and a quarter of a gill of buffalo-gall, and is considered an excellent medicine.—*Scenes in the Rocky Mountains*, p. 133.

PRAIRIE-DOG. (*Aretomys ludovicianus.*) Called by the Indians Wistonwish. A variety of the marmot. It has received the name of Prairie-dog from a supposed similarity between its warning cry and the barking of a small dog. They live in large communities; their villages, as they are termed by the hunters, sometimes being many miles in extent. The entrance to each burrow is at the summit of the mound of earth thrown up during the progress of the excavation below. This marmot, like the rest of the species, becomes torpid during the winter, and, to protect itself against the rigor of the season, stops the mouth of its hole, and constructs a cell at the bottom of it, where it remains without injury.— *Encyclopedia Americana.* Also called Gopher.

> The good people of Porter, Wisconsin, resolved to exterminate the *gophers* in that locality, and determined to have a hunt, to see if they could not annihilate them. Twenty men were chosen on a side, and the party that was beaten was to pay for a supper for the whole party. The result was that they killed 3,196 *gophers.*— *Wisconsin Paper.*

PRAIRIE-HEN. The pinnated grouse of ornithologists. It is also called Heath-hen and Grouse in some parts of the country. —*Audubon's Ornithology.*

PRAYERFUL. Using prayer; praying; devout.—*Worcester.*

PRAYERFULLY. Devoutly. Ex. ' We may be *prayerfully* disposed.' Used by some of the clergy.—*Webster. Pickering.*

PRAYERLESS. Not praying or using prayer; indevout. This word, as also *prayerful* and *prayerfully*, though modern, are now much used.—*Worcester.*

Mr. Pickering says this word is used by Whitfield.

PRAYERFULNESS. The use of much prayer.—*Webster.*

PRAYERLESSNESS. Total or habitual neglect of prayer. —*Webster.*

PREDICATE. *To predicate on* or *upon*, is to found a proposition, argument, etc. on some basis or data.   This sense of the word, said to be purely American, is not noticed by Dr. Webster or the English lexicographers.   "Its use," as Mr. Pickering observes, "is very common with American writers, and in the debates of our legislative assemblies."

> It ought surely to be *predicated upon* a full and impartial consideration of the whole subject.—*Letter of John Quincy Adams.*

> The great state papers of American liberty were all *predicated on* the abuse of chartered, not of absolute rights.—*Gibbs, Adminis. of Washington and J. Adams*, Vol. I. p. 3.

PREHAPS, for *perhaps,* is much used at the West in familiar language when additional force is to be given to the word. It originated in a jocose mispronunciation, which appears to be becoming a fixed corruption.

> *Prehaps* Parson Hyme didn't put it into Pokerville for two mortal hours ; and *prehaps* Pokerville didn't mizzle, wince, and finally flummix right beneath him !—*Field, Drama in Pokerville.*

PRESENT.   Put on the back of letters to persons residing in the place where the letter is written.   Peculiar to the United States.   The Spanish equivalent *presente* is also used in Central America.

PRESIDENCY.   1. The office of president.   ' Washington was elected to the *presidency* of the United States by a unanimous vote of the electors.'

2. The term during which a president holds his office. 'President John Adams died during the *presidency* of his son.' —*Webster.*

PRESIDENTIAL.   Pertaining to a president.—*Webster.*   In this sense the word is an Americanism.   It is of course very common and indispensable with us, and is sometimes used by English writers in treating of American affairs.

> The friends of Washington had determined to support Mr. Adams as candidate for the *presidential* chair.—*Quarterly Rev.,* Vol. X. p. 497.

PRETTY CONSIDERABLE.   Tolerable, pretty well; tolerably, pretty.   A New England vulgarism.

> I went to the theatre in Boston, where the acting was *pretty considerable,* considering.—*Crockett, Tour,* p. 87.

> *Dear Col. Crockett*—I have heard of you a great deal lately, and read

considerable of your writings ; and I feel *pretty considerable* well acquainted with you.—*Maj Downing, Letter to Crockett, Tour*, p. 217.

There are some folks who think a good deal, and say but little, and they are wise folks ; and there are others again, who blurt out whatever comes uppermost, and I guess they are *pretty considerable* superfine fools.—*Sam Slick.*

PREVENTATIVE. A corruption sometimes met with for *preventive* both in England and America.

A cry was raised for the establishment of a *preventative* armed police ; but the madness of such a proposal could not long escape observation.—*Edinb. Annual Reg.*, Vol. V. p. 99.

PRIME. Primely ; in a first rate manner. This is one of the many English adjectives which, in our vulgar language, are transformed into adverbs.

After a little practice with my gun, she came up to the eye *prime*, and I determined to try her at the first shooting match.—*Crockett, Tour*, p. 175.

PRIMINARY. Predicament ; difficulty. Used in the Southern States.—*Sherwood's Georgia.* I am told that this word is also used by old people living on Long Island. It is provincial in the North of England.

PRINTERY. *Bakery, bindery,* have long been in use amongst us, and in New York even *paintery* and *printery.* In process of time a church may be called a *preachery.*

PROFANITY. This word is in common use here, more particularly with our clergy. It is not in the dictionaries, and I do not recollect ever meeting with it in English authors. The Scottish writers employ it ; but English writers use the word *profaneness.*—*Pickering.* It appears, however, that English authors are beginning to use it ; see Worcester on the word.

PROFESSOR. One visibly or professedly religious.—*Worcester.* A very odd use of the word to those not accustomed to it.

PROG. Victuals ; provisions of any kind. A low word.—*Johnson.* This word is often heard in New York and New England in familiar language.

O nephew ! your grief is but folly ;
In town you may find better *prog.*—*Swift, Miscellanies.*

> Spouse tuckt up doth in pattens trudge it
> With handkerchief of *prog*, like truth with budget ;
> And eat by turns plumcake, and judge it.—*Congreve.*

TO PROGRESS. To move forward ; to pass.—*Johnson.* This is not a pure Americanism, as some suppose, but an old English word which had been suffered to become obsolete. It was revived here after the Revolution (see Pickering), and has lately been taken into favor again in England.

The Penny Cyclopedia (art. *Americanism*) says, " The old verb *prógress*, which the Americans use very often and pronounce *progréss*, is now beginning to be again adopted in its native country, though we think we could do very well without it."

> Let me wipe off this honorable dew,
> That silverly doth *progress* on thy cheeks.—*Shakspeare.*

> ——Although the popular blast
> Hath reared thy name up to bestride a cloud,
> Or *progress* in the chariot of the sun.—*Ford, Broken Heart.*

Such are the inconsistencies of a flatterer, *progressing* from his butterfly state into the vermicular slime of a libeller.—*London Quarterly Review.*

" Her first teacher was but himself, at that time, a pupil ; but she *progressed* under his tuition."—*Mary Howitt, People's Journal.*

They *progress* in that style in proportion as their plans are treated with contempt.—*Washington's Writings.*

After the war had *progressed* for some time.—*Marshall's Washington.*

PROPER. Very. Colloquial in England and the United States.

> The day was gone afore I got out of the woods, and I got *proper* frightened.—*Sam Slick in England*, ch. 18.

PROPERLY. Very much. Common in New England.

> Father jest up with the flat of his hand, and gave me a wipe with it on the side of my face, that knocked me over, and hurt me *properly.*—*Sam Slick in England*, ch. 26.

PRO-SLAVERY. In favor of slavery. An expression much used by political speakers and writers, although not yet inserted in the dictionaries.

> We have devoted every inch we could spare to this debate ; and though two-thirds of what we publish was intended to favor slavery, we are confident that the whole will signally promote the cause of universal

freedom. At all events, we shall see the *pro-slavery* journals through the Free States very carefully refraining from giving it publicity.—*N. Y. Tribune*, April, 1848.

It takes a despot, a craven, and a slave, compounded together, to make a *pro-slavery* legislator in a *free State*. The last legislature of Ohio had a majority of just such creatures. Noses of wax! *stay pinched*, just as the slaveholder's thumb and finger left you. Dough-faces! wear the prints of your master's knuckles, and the traces of their spittle. They are your coats of arms, and they *fit ye*—your titles of nobility, and *they'll stick to ye*. Snow water and soap won't wash them off, nor your hot tears either—nor fire burn them out, nor paint hide them, nor plasters cover them. You have worked hard for infamy, and you have *got it*.—*Anti-Slavery Almanac.*

PROTRACTED MEETING. A name given in New England to a religious meeting, protracted or continued for several days, chiefly among the Presbyterians, Congregationalists, Methodists, and Baptists. Notice is sometimes given that a *protracted meeting* will be held at a certain time and place, where large numbers of people assemble.

PROUD. Glad; as, ' I should be *proud* to see you.'

PROX, or PROXY. The use of these words is confined to the States of Connecticut and Rhode Island. *Prox*, in Rhode Island, means the ticket or list of candidates at elections presented to the people for their votes. By a law of the colony of Providence Plantations passed in the year 1647, the General Assembly was appointed to be holden annually, " if wind and weather hinder not, at which the general officers of the colony were to be chosen." This clause made it convenient for many to remain at home, particularly as they had the right to send their votes for the officers by some other persons; hence the origin of these terms *prox* and *proxy votes*, as applied to the present mode of voting for State officers in Rhode Island.—*Staples's Annals of Providence*, p. 64.

Mr. Pickering observes that this word is also used in Connecticut, as equivalent to *election*, or *election-day*. He quotes the following instances from a Connecticut newspaper:

Republicans of Connecticut; previous to every *proxies* you have been assaulted on every side.

On the approaching *proxies* we ask you to attend universally.

Dr. Webster, with whom New England, or rather Connecticut, seems to have been a synonym for "all creation," says, the word means, "*in popular use,* an election or day of voting for officers of government."

PRY. A large lever employed to raise or move heavy substances. Used also in some parts of England.—*Worcester.*

TO PRY. To move or raise by means of a large lever.— *Worcester.*

PUBLICIST. A writer on the laws of nature and nations ; one who treats of the rights of nations.—*Webster.* It is seldom used by English writers. In this country Kent, Duponceau, Gallatin, and others have employed it.

> In this particular the two German courts seem to have as little consulted the *publicists* of Germany, as their own true interests.—*Edmund Burke.*

> There is no impartial *publicist* that will not acknowledge the indubitable truth of these positions.—*Gallatin, Peace with Mexico,* p. 8.

> At Copenhagen he rendered distinguished services, and laid the foundation of that reputation as a *publicist* which has extended to both hemispheres.—*Mem. of the Hon. Henry Wheaton, Providence Journal.*

PUBLISHMENT. A publishing of the banns of marriage, which is required by law in New England. In popular usage this is a *publishment,* as, 'Mr. Doe and Miss Roe's *publishment* took place to-day.'

> Any persons desiring to be joined in marriage, shall have such their intentions published . . . . or posted up by the clerk of each town ; and a certificate of such *publishment* . . . . shall be produced as aforesaid previous to their marriage.—*Statutes of Massachusetts,* 1786.

PUCKER. A fright ; a state of perplexity or trouble ; agitation. Provincial in England.

TO PULL FOOT. To walk fast ; to run.

> I look'd up ; it was another shower, by Gosh. I *pulls foot* for dear life.— *Sam Slick in England,* ch. 2.

> I thought I'd run round two or three streets. So I *pulled foot,* and hunted and sweat till I got so tired I couldn't but just stand.—*Maj. Downing's May-day in New York.*

TO PULL UP STAKES. To pack up one's furniture or baggage preparatory to a removal ; to remove.

> If this stranger is to receive countenance, then I'll *pull up stakes* and depart from Tinnecum for ever.—*Knickerbocker Magazine.*

PUMA. (*Felis concolor et discolor.*) This animal is also known under the names of Cougar, Panther, &c., and is the largest animal of the cat kind found in America.—*Encyc. Americana.*

PUMPKIN. The common name for the pompion throughout the United States.

PUNCHEONS. A term which, in Georgia, means split logs, with their faces a little smoothed with an axe or hatchet.

> The Squire's dwelling consisted of but one room. The house was constructed of logs, and the floor was of *puncheons.—Georgia Scenes,* p. 12.

PUNG. A rude sort of sleigh, or oblong box made of boards and placed on runners, used for drawing loads on snow by horses.—*Worcester.*

> These were sledges or *pungs*, coarsely framed of split saplings, and surmounted with a large crockery-crate.—*Margaret*, p. 174.

PUNK. Rotten wood; touchwood; spunk. A word in common use in New England, as well as in the other Northern States and Canada. Ash defines it "a kind of *fungus*, often used for tinder."—*Pickering.*

PUPELO. A name for cider-brandy, formerly manufactured in New England to a great extent.

> Han't they got any of the religion at your house? No, marm, they drink *pupelo* and rum.—*Margaret*, p. 52.

TO STAY PUT. To remain in order; not to be disturbed. A vulgar expression.

> The levees and wharves of the First Municipality won't "*stay put.*" Last evening that part of the levee opposite Custom House street, which had caved in and was since filled, sunk suddenly ten feet.—*N. O. Picayune.*

PUT OFF. An excuse, an illusory pretext for delay.—*Carr's Craven Dialect.*

> If a man tells them of the king's proceedings, then they have their shifts and their *put offs.—Latimer's Sermons.*

> The fox's *put off* is instructive towards the government of our lives, provided his fooling be made our earnest.—*L'Estrange.*

TO PUT ON AIRS. To assume airs of importance.

> You don't see no folks *putting on airs* in election time; every fellow is then as good as another, and some a darn'd sight better.—*N. O. Delta.*

TO PUT OUT. To start; to set out.

> Well, I *put out* for the Planter's as fast as I could, where you know I found you at last.—*Maj. Jones's Courtship*, p. 63.

TO PUT OUT. To offend.

> There is no affectation in passion; for that *putteth* a man *out* of his precept, and in a new case their custom leaveth him.—*Bacon.*

> The Captain's wife was at the office yesterday, and seemed a little *put out* about it.—*Dombey and Son*, ch. 23.

Q.

QUAHAUG. (Montauk Indian, *quauhaug.*) In New England, the popular name of a species of clams, having a round and very hard shell.

TO QUALIFY. To swear to discharge the duties of an office ; and hence to make oath of any fact ; as, 'I am ready to *qualify* to what I have asserted !'

QUEER FISH. An odd or eccentric person is often called a queer fish, an odd stick.

QUID, a corruption of *cud;* as, in vulgar language, a *quid* of tobacco. In Kent (England), a cow is said to chew her *quid;* so that *cud* and *quid* are the same.—*Pegge's Anonymia.*

QUILLING. A piece of reed, on which weavers wind the thread which forms the woof of cloth, is called a *quill;* an old English word. In New England a certain process of winding thread is called *quilling.*

> The child, Margaret, sits in the door of her house, on a low stool, with a small wheel, winding spools, in our vernacular *quilling.*—*Margaret*, p. 6.

R.

RACE. A strong or rapid current of water, or the channel or passage for such current ; as a *mill-race.*—*Webster.*

RADDLE. In New England, an instrument consisting of a wooden bar, with a row of upright pegs set in it, which is employed by domestic weavers to keep the warp of a proper width, and prevent it from becoming entangled, when it is wound upon the beam of a loom.—*Webster.*

RAFT. A frame or float, made by laying pieces of timber

across each other.—*Johnson*. In North America *rafts* are
constructed of immense size, and comprise timber, boards,
staves, &c.   They are floated down from the interior to the
tide waters, being propelled by the force of the current,
assisted by large oars and sails, to their place of destination.
The men employed on these rafts construct rude huts upon
them, in which they often dwell for several weeks before
arriving at the places where they are taken to pieces for ship-
ping to foreign parts.

RAFT.   This term is also given to a large collection of timber
and fallen trees, which, floating down the great rivers of the
West, are arrested in their downward course by flats or shallow places.   Here they accumulate, and sometimes block up
the river for miles.   The great raft on Red river extended
twenty miles, and required an immense outlay of money to
remove it in order to make the river navigable.

> Gigantic wrecks of the primitive forests, tossed about by the invisible
> power of the current, as if they were straws, until, finding no rest, they are
> thrown upon some projecting point of land [on the Mississippi and other
> great western rivers].   Here they lie rotting for miles, their dark forms
> frequently shooting into the air like writhing serpents, presenting one of
> the most desolate pictures the mind can conceive.—*Thorpe, Backwoods*.

RAFT.   A large quantity.   Used only in low language.

> We have killed Calhoun and Biddle ; but there is a *raft* of fellows to
> put down yet.—*Maj. Downing's Letters*, p. 93.

> We've shoals of shad, whole *rafts* of canvass-back ducks, and no end of
> terrapins.—*Burton, Waggeries*.

> Among its notices to correspondents, an exchange paper says : " A *raft*
> of original articles are on file for next week."   We hope none of them will
> prove mere lumber.—*N. Y. Tribune*.

TO RAFT.   To transport on a raft.—*Webster*.

RAFTING.   The business of [constructing and] floating rafts.—
Webster.

RAFTSMAN.   A man who follows the business of rafting.

RAIL.   A piece of timber, cleft, hewed, or sawed, inserted in
upright posts for fencing.   The common rails among farmers
are rough, being used as they are split from the chestnut or
other trees.—*Webster*.

TO RAIL IT. To travel by rail-road.

From Petersburgh I *railed it* through the North Carolina pitch, tar, turpentine, and lumber country, to the great American pitch, tar, turpentine,
and lumber depot—Wilmington. The prospect is, from the car windows,
continuously an immensity of pine, pine, nothing but pine trees, broken
here and there with openings of pine under-brush.—*Letter in N. Y. Tribune*,
May 22, 1848.

RAIL-CAR. A car for transporting passengers on rail-roads.

RAISE. *To make a raise.* A vulgar American phrase, meaning to make a haul, to raise the wind.

The chances were altogether favorable for *making a raise*, without fear
of detection.—*Simon Suggs*, p. 48.

RAISING. In New England and the Northern States, the
operation or work of setting up the frame of a building.—
Webster.

On such occasions the neighboring farmers are accustomed
to assemble and lend their assistance. In this way the frame-
work of the largest house or barn is set up in a few hours.

The spectacle of a *raising*, though so common-place an affair elsewhere,
is something worth seeing in the woods.—*Mrs. Clavers's Forest Life.*

TO RAISE. To cause to grow; to procure to be produced,
bred, or propagated; as to *raise* wheat, barley, hops, &c.; to
raise horses, oxen, or sheep.—*Webster.*

In England they use *grow* when speaking of the crops.
Raise is applied in the Southern States to the breeding
of negroes. It is sometimes heard at the North among the
illiterate; as, 'I was *raised* in Connecticut,' meaning *brought
up* there. See more in Pickering's Vocabulary.

You know I was *raised*, as they say in Virginia, among the mountains
of the North.—*Paulding, Letters from the South*, Vol. I. p. 85.

TO RAISE A BEAD. This expression is used at the West,
and means to bring to a head, to make succeed. The figure
is taken from brandy, rum, or other liquors, which will not
'raise a bead,' unless of the proper strength.

The result was, if the convention had been then held, the party wouldn't
have been able *to raise a bead.*—*Letter from Ohio, N. Y. Tribune*, 1846.

TO RAISE ONE'S BRISTLES. To excite one's anger.

I came to Congress in 1827, as honestly the friend of Gen. Jackson as any man in the world ; but when I found that his whole object was to serve party, and wreak his vengeance upon those who had voted against him, *my bristles begun to get up.—Crockett, Tour, p. 136.*

TO RAKE AND SCRAPE. To collect.

> Where under the sun, says I to myself, did he *rake and scrape* together such super-superior galls as these ?—*Sam Slick in England, ch. 23.*

RANCHO. (Span.) A rude hut of posts, covered with branches or thatch, where herdsmen or farm-laborers live or only lodge at night.

RANCHERO. (Span.) A person who lives in a rancho, and by extension to any peasant or countryman. This word and the preceding, like the word *chaporral*, have lately become familiar to us, in consequence of the present unhappy war with Mexico.

RANCHERIA. The place, site, or house in the country where a number of rancheros collect together. The collection of few or many huts or ranchos into a small village.

These three words must necessarily have a place in our vocabularies, since the acquisition of so many *ranchos* in our territory, and *rancheros* in our population.

RANTANKEROUS. Contentious ; a variation of *cantankerous*.

> She had better not come a cavortin' 'bout me, with any of her *rantanke- rous* carryings on.—*Chron. of Pineville, p. 178.*

RAPIDS. (Used in the plural.) The part of a river where the current moves with more celerity than the common current. Rapids imply a considerable descent of the earth, but not sufficient to occasion a fall of the water, or what is called a cascade or cataract.—*Webster*.

RAPPEE. An inferior quality of snuff.

RAT. A contemptuous term used by printers, to denote a man who works under price.

TO RAT. Among printers, to work under price. Among politicians, to desert one's party and go over to the opposite one. The term is used both in England and America. The London Athenæum, in a review of Campbell's Lives of the Lord Chancellors, in speaking of Wedderburn, afterwards Lord Loughborough, says :

> He panegyrized the liberty of the press ; sided with America ; clamored

for the rights of juries ; acted the part of liberal and demagogue to admiration ; all the while having his eye on the Solicitor-Generalship—for which, in the fulness of time, he *ratted* to Lord North in the most shameless manner.—*Dec.* 18, 1847.

Great was the indignation when the result was known ; and this must be confessed to be one of the most flagrant cases of *ratting* recorded in our party annals.—*Campbell, Lord Chancellors.*

RAVE. The upper side piece of the body of a cart.—*Webster.*

RAVING DISTRACTED. Stark mad.

RAW. Not worked up, manufactured, or prepared for use ; as, '*raw* materials.'—*Worcester.*

Mr. Webster presented a petition in reference to the duty proposed to be laid on *raw* copper. . . . It will be seen that nearly all the pig or *raw* copper is obtained from Chili.—*N. Y. Com. Advertiser*, July 16, 1846.

REAL. Really; truly; very; as, '*real* nice.'

TO REALIZE. To bring home to one's own case or experience ; to consider as one's own; to feel in all its force.—*Webster.*

This allusion must have enhanced strength and beauty to the eye of a nation extensively devoted to a pastoral life, and therefore *realizing* all its fine scenes, and the tender emotions to which they gave birth.—*Dwight.*

This sense of the word is not in the English dictionaries, though Mr. Pickering says it is used in Scotland.

TO RE-CHARTER. To charter again ; to grant a second or another charter to.—*Webster.*

TO RECKON. To think ; to imagine ; to believe ; to conjecture ; to conclude ; to guess. Used in some parts of the United States, as *guess* is in the Northern. It is provincial in England in the same sense, and is noticed in the glossaries of Pegge and Brockett. Mr. Hamilton, in his remarks on the Yorkshire dialect, says : "'I *reckon*' comes out on every occasion, as perhaps aliens would expect from this country of 'ready reckoners.' "—*Nugæ Literariæ*, p. 317.

General, I guess we best say nothin' more about bribin', says I. "Well," says he, " Major, I *reckon* you're right."—*Maj. Downing's Letters*, p. 208.

I say ! what do you guess about lending me your axe for a spell ? Do you *reckon* you can spare it ?—*Mrs. Clavers's Forest Life*, Vol. I. p. 84.

I *reckon* you hardly ever was at a shooting-match, stranger, from the cut of your coat.—*Georgia Scenes*, p. 198.

RED DOG MONEY. A term applied, in the State of New York, to certain bank notes which have on their back a large red stamp.

The late General Banking law of the State of New York, which was applied to all new banks, as well as to those the charters of which were renewed, obliged the parties or individuals associated to deposit securities with the Comptroller, and receive from him blank notes of various denominations, signed or bearing the certificate of the Comptroller or officer authorized by him. These notes bore a *red stamp* on their backs.

So free a system of banking induced many persons, both individually and collectively, to organize banks of issue; and, as a natural consequence, a considerable portion of the circulating medium soon consisted of the notes of the free banks, bearing the red stamp. The community, generally, did not consider these notes as safe as those issued by the old banks, and stigmatized them as *red dogs*, and the currency as *red dog money*. Since the passage of the act, however, the charters of most of the banks in the State having expired, they have been renewed under the "General Banking Law;" and, of course, the odium which existed against the first banks no longer exists. In Michigan, they apply the term *blue pup money* to bank notes having a blue stamp on their backs.

REDEMPTIONER. One who redeems himself or purchases his release from debt or obligation to the master of a ship by his services; or one whose services are sold to pay the expenses of his passage to America.—*Webster.*

RED LANE. A vulgar name for the throat, chiefly used by tipplers.

> I was ridin' in my shirt sleeves, and a thinkin' how slick a mint julep would travel down *red lane*, if I had it.—*Sam Slick in England*, ch. 22.

RED-ROOT. A shrub found upon the prairies near the Rocky Mountains, highly esteemed as a substitute for tea. It resembles the tea of commerce, and affords an excellent beverage.—*Scenes in the Rocky Mountains*, p. 26.

REGENT. In the State of New York, the member of a corporate body which is invested with the superintendence of all the colleges, academies, and schools in the State.   This board consists of twenty-one members, who are called " the *regents of the University of the State of New York.*"   They are appointed and removable by the legislature.   They have power to grant acts of incorporation for colleges; to visit and inspect all colleges, academies, and schools; and to make regulations for governing the same.—*Statutes of New York.*

TO RE-INSURE.   To insure the same property a second time by other underwriters.—*Webster.*

It is common with underwriters or insurance companies, when they find they have too large a sum insured on one ship, or in a particular district, to *re-insure* a part elsewhere.

The insurer may cause the property insured to be *re-insured* by other persons.—*Walsh, French Com. Code.*

TO RE-LOAN.   To loan again; to lend what has been lent and repaid.—*Webster.*

TO RE-INVESTIGATE.   To investigate again.—*Webster.*

TO RE-LAND.   To go on shore after having embarked.— *Webster.*

REMOVABILITY.   The capacity of being removed from an office or station ; capacity of being displaced.—*Webster.*

RENCH.   A vulgar pronunciation of the word *rinse.*

RENEWEDLY.   Again; once more.—*Webster.*

This adverb is often heard from our pulpits.—*Pickering.*

TO RE-OPEN. To open again.—*Webster.* This word is much used.   The theatre *re-opens* for the season.   The schools *re-open* after their vacations.

REORGANIZATION.   The act of organizing anew ; as, re- peated organization of the troops.—*Webster.*

REPETITIOUS.   Repeating ; containing repetition.—*Webster.*

Mr. Pickering notices this word, which he thinks is peculiar to the writer from whom the following extract is taken :

The observation which you have quoted from the Abbé Raynal, which has been written off in a succession not much less *repetitious,* or protracted, than that in which school-boys of former times wrote.—*Remarks on the Review of Inchiquin's Letters, Boston,* 1815.

TO RE-SHIP. To ship again; to ship what has been conveyed by water or imported.—*Webster*.

Much used in all our commercial cities.

RESOLVE. Legal or official determination; legislative act concerning a private person or corporation, or concerning some private business. Public acts of a legislature respect the State; and to give them validity, the bills for such acts must pass through all the legislative forms. *Resolves* are usually private acts, and are often passed with less formality.—*Webster*.

TO RESULT. To decide or decree, as an ecclesiastical council.—*Pickering*.

According to Dr. Milner, the Council of Nice *resulted*, in opposition to the views of Arius, that the Son was peculiarly of the Father, &c.—*Bible News, Rev. N. Worcester.*

RESULT. The decision or determination of a council or deliberative assembly; as, ' the *result* of an ecclesiastical council.' Peculiar to New England.—*Webster*.

RETIRACY. Sufficiency; competency. It is said, in New England, of a person who has retired from business with a fortune, that he has a *retiracy;* i. e. a sufficient fortune to retire with.

TO RETIRE. To withdraw; to take away; to make to retire.—*Johnson*. This transitive use of the verb, which had become obsolete, is now reviving in this country. Of the many examples from good old writers given by Johnson, we will quote only one from Shakspeare:

> He, our hope, might have *retired* his power,
> And driven into despair an enemy's hate.—*Richard II.*

With us it is used by military men of withdrawing troops.

General Rosas insisted on the blockade being removed before he *retired* his troops from the Banda Oriental.—*Newspaper*.

And by merchants of paying their notes.

The French houses are *retiring* their notes due next month, in advance, anticipating commercial difficulties.—*Newspaper*.

RETORTIVE. Containing retort.—*Webster*.

TO RETROSPECT. To look back; to affect what is passed.
—*Webster.*

Mr. Pickering has the following illustration:

> To give a correct idea of the circumstances which have gradually produced this conviction, it may be useful to *retrospect* to an early period.—*Letter from Alex. Hamilton to John Adams.*

This word cannot be said to be much used. The writings of Gen. Hamilton abound in peculiar expressions.

REVERENT. Strong; as, *reverent* whisky, i. e. not diluted.
—*Sherwood's Georgia.*

RICH. Luscious, i. e. entertaining; amusing in the highest degree.

> Mr. Richardson is *rich* on rabbits; and divides them into four races.—*London Athenæum*, Dec. 1847.

> Thar we was settin' on our horses, rollin' with laughin' and liquor, and thought the thing was *rich* [alluding to a dog-fight].—*Porter's South-western Tales*, p. 57.

> About as *rich* an instance of official idleness, self-conceit, and incivility, as we have seen, fell under our notice yesterday.—*N. Y. Com. Adv.*

The New York Tribune, in speaking of General Cass's book, " France; its King, Court, and Government," says:

> Mark how smoothly he glosses over the despotism of Louis Philippe—how adroitly he insinuates that all the agitation and plotting for his overthrow were impelled by atheism, thirst of blood, and an appetite for destroying and plundering. It would be *rich* indeed if the parasite should vault to the heights of power just one year after the despot he served was cast down to contempt and exile.—*N. Y. Tribune*, June 2, 1848.

TO RIDE. The use of the word *ride*, both as a verb and a noun, in the sense of *being conveyed in a carriage*, has been regarded as an Americanism. Nevertheless, it was formerly so used in England, as appears from the following example:

> He made him to *ride* in the chariot.—*Gen.* xlii. 43.

English writers of the present day, however, consider it as correct to use it only of *conveyance on horseback*, or some other motive power; but of conveyance in a carriage, they use the verb *to drive*, as in the following extract from Cowper:

> Sometimes I get into a neighbor's chaise, but generally *ride* [i. e. on horseback].

TO RIDE. To carry. In the city of New York this word is

used by carmen as well as merchants, when speaking of cart-
ing or carrying merchandise on a cart.   Thus, ' to *ride* a box
or bale of goods,' is to carry it.   I heard a witness in a court-
room testify that he had " *rode* some hogs from the wharf to
the store," by which he meant that he carried a load of dead
hogs on his cart.

RIFLE.   A whetstone for sharpening scythes.—*Todd. Worcester.*   This old English word is retained by the farmers of
New England.

> All our sports and recreations, if we use them well, must be to our body,
> or mind, as the mower's whetstone, or *rifle*, is to his scythe, to sharpen it
> when it grows dull.—*Whately, Redemption of Time* (1634), p. 11.

TO RIGHTS.   Directly ; soon.   Peculiar to America.—*Webster.*

> If folks will do what I tell 'em, things will go strait enough *to rights.*—
> *Maj. Downing's Letters,* p. 5.
>
> So *to rights* the express got back, and brought a letter.—*Ibid.* p. 129.

RIGHT AWAY, or **RIGHT OFF.**   Directly ; immediately.

RILE.   See *Roil.*

RISING, or **RISING OF.**   More than ; upwards of ; as,
' There were *rising of* a thousand men killed at the battle of
Buena Vista.'

RISKY.   Dangerous; hazardous.

RIVER.   Mr. Pickering observes that the Americans, in speaking of rivers, commonly put the name before the word *river,*
thus, Connecticut *river,* Charles *river,* Merrimack *river,*
Hudson *river,* Susquehanna *river ;*   whereas the English
would place the name after it, and say, the *river* Hudson, the
river Merrimack, &c.   There are some exceptions, however,
when speaking of the largest rivers ; for we usually say, the
river Mississippi, the *river* St. Lawrence.

RIVER DRIVER.   A term used by lumbermen in Maine, for
a man whose business it is to conduct logs down running
streams, to prevent them from lodging upon shoals or remaining in eddies.

ROARER.   One who roars ; a noisy man.—*Worcester.*

> Ben was an old Mississippi *roarer*—none of your half and half, but just

as native to the element, as if he had been born in a broad horn.—*Robb, Squatter Life*, p. 64.

ROBE. A dressed skin; only applied to that of the buffalo. *A pack of robes*, is ten skins, tied in a pack, which is the manner in which they are brought from the far West to market. For the skins of other wild animals, we always use the term *skin*, as *deer-skin, beaver-skin, muskrat-skin*, etc., but never *buffalo-skin*.

ROCK. A piece of money. A slang term peculiar to the South.

> Spare my feelings, Squire, and don't ask me to tell any more. Here I am in town without a *rock* in my pocket, without a skirt to my coat, or crown to my hat.—*Pickings from the New Orleans Picayune*.

ROCK. A stone. In the Southern and Western States, stones of any size are absurdly called *rocks*.

> Brother S—— came home in a mighty bad way, with a cold and cough; so I put a hot *rock* to his feet and gave him a bowl of catmint tea, which put him in a mighty fine sweat, &c.—*Georgia Scenes*, p. 193.

> Mr. M—— was almost dead with the consumption, and had to carry *rocks* in his pocket to keep the wind from blowin' him away.—*Maj. Jones's Travels*.

TO ROCK. To throw stones at; to stone. This supremely ridiculous expression is derived from the preceding.

> They commenced *rocking* the Clay Club House in June, on more occasions than one, and on one occasion, threw a *rock* in at the window, hitting Mr. Clem on the shoulder; and afterwards, on the Whigs leaving the Club House, the heads of Messrs. Clem and Brown were badly cut with *rocks!* A few nights before the recent election, Mr. Brown was struck with a *rock*, as the Whig procession was returning from the west end of town, the *rock* coming either from Chester's tavern, or the Office of the Sentinel.— *Jonesborough, Tennessee, Whig*.

TO ROIL. 1. To render turbid by stirring up the sediment; 2. To make angry. Provincial in England and colloquial in the United States.—*Worcester*. In both countries it is now commonly pronounced and written *rile*.

> John was a-dry, and soon cried out—
> Goon git some beer we 'ool!
> He'd so to wait, it made him *riled*,
>   The booths were all shock full.—*J. Noakes and Mary Styles*.

> I won't say your country or my country, and then it won't *rile* nobody.— *Sam Slick in England*.

> I hope you won't be *riled* at what I say.—*Maj. Jones's Courtship*, p. 63.

I tell you what, I was monstrous *riled* t'other day when I got a letter from Crockett, calling me hard names and abusin' me.—*Ibid.* p. 90.

No doubt existed in the minds of Mr. Dobbs's fellow-boarders, that the well of his good spirits had been *riled.*—*Neal's Charcoal Sketches.*

ROILY, or RILY. 1. Turbid; 2. Excited to resentment; vexed.

The boys and gals were laughin' at my scrape and the pickle I was in, that I gin to get *riley.*—*Robb, Squatter Life,* p. 64.

ROKEAGE, or YOKEAGE. Indian corn parched, pulverized, and mixed with sugar.

ROLLICKING. A peculiar gait of a horse.

Mounted by a rider that is as much a part of him as his hide, he [the mustang pony] goes *rollicking* ahead.—*Thorpe's Backwoods,* p. 13.

ROLLING. Undulating; varied by small hills and valleys, as land; so used in the Western States.—*Worcester.*

TO ROOM. To occupy a room; to lodge.—*Worcester.*

ROOSTER. The male of the domestic fowl; the cock.

As if the flourish of the quill were the crowing of a *rooster.*—*Neal's Charcoal Sketches.*

A huge turkey gobbling in the road, a *rooster* crowing on the fence, and ducks quacking in the ditches.—*Margaret,* p. 187.

TO ROPE IN. To take or sweep in collectively; an expression much used in colloquial language at the West. It originated in a common practice of drawing in hay with a rope. The hay is at first heaped in wind-rows. A rope, with a horse attached to each end, is swept like a net around the end of the row, which is thus brought together and dragged to any part of the field.

HIGH ROPES. 'Upon the *high ropes;*' i. e. elated; in high spirits.—*Grose, Prov. Dict.*

ROPING IN. Cheating. A very common expression in the South-western States.

ROSS. The rough scaly matter on the surface of the bark of certain trees. A term much used in New England.—*Webster.*

ROUND. 'To come or get *round* one,' in popular language, is to gain advantage over one by flattery or deception.—*Webster.*

ROUSING. Very great; commonly applied to a fire.—*Craven Glossary.*

> Haply, blest to my desire,
> I may find a *rousing* fire.—*Clare's Poems.*

ROUND-RIMMERS. Hats with a round rim; hence, those who wear them. In the city of New York, a name applied to a large class of dissipated young men, by others called Bowery boys and Soap-locks.

> All over the region of East Bowery is spread—holding it in close subjection—the powerful class of *round-rimmers;* a fraternity of gentlemen, who, in round crape-bound hats, metal-mounted blue coats, tallow-smoothed locks, &c., carry dismay and terror wherever they move.—*C. Mathews, Puffer Hopkins,* p. 261.

ROWDY. A riotous, turbulent fellow.

TO ROW UP. To punish with words; to rebuke. It is an essential Westernism, and derived from the practice of making refractory slaves or servants *row up* the heavy keel-boats of early navigation on the Western rivers, against the current, without being frequently relieved. It was thus regarded as a punishment.

> We should really like, of all things, to *row up* the majority of Congress as it deserves in regard to the practice.—*N. Y. Tribune,* Dec. 10, 1845.

> The most spicy part of the proceedings in the Senate was the *rowing up* which Mr. Hannegan gave Mr. Ritchie of the Union newspaper.—*N. Y. Tribune,* Jan. 30, 1846.

TO ROW UP SALT RIVER, is a common phrase, used generally to signify political defeat. The distance to which a party is *rowed up Salt river* depends entirely upon the magnitude of the majority against its candidates. If the defeat is particularly overwhelming, the unsuccessful party is *rowed up to the very head waters of Salt river.*

It is occasionally used as nearly synonymous with *to row up,* as in the following example, but this application is rare :

> Judge Clayton made a speech that fairly made the tumblers hop. He *rowed* the Tories *up and over Salt river.*—*Crockett, Tour Down East,* p. 46.

To row up Salt river has its origin in the fact that there is a small stream of that name in Kentucky, the passage of which is made difficult and laborious as well by its tortuous course as by the abundance of shallows and bars. The real application of the phrase is to the unhappy wight who has the task of propelling the boat up the stream ; but in political or slang usage it is to those who are *rowed up*—the passengers, not the oarsman. [*J. Inman.*]

ROWEN. In New England, the second growth of grass in a season. We never apply the word to a field, as in England, nor to the growth of corn after harvest.—*Webster.*

RUGGED. Hardy ; robust ; healthy. Colloquial in the United States.—*Worcester.*

RUINATIOUS. A vulgar substitute for *ruinous.*

> The war was very *ruinatious* to our profession (said the barber).—*Margaret,* p. 210.

RULLICHIES. (Dutch.) Chopped meat stuffed into small bags of tripe, which are then cut into slices and fried. An old and favorite dish among the descendants of the Dutch in New York.

RUM-BUD. A grog blossom ; the popular name of a redness occasioned by the detestable practice of excessive drinking. *Rum-buds* usually appear first on the nose, and gradually extend over the face. This term seems to have reference to the disease technically defined to be unsuppurative papule, stationary, confluent, red, mottled with purple, chiefly affecting the face, sometimes produced and always aggravated by the use of alcoholic liquors, by exposure to heat, &c.—*Rush.*

RUN. A small stream or rivulet ; a word common in the Southern and Western States, though sometimes heard at the North.

> There is no house in the main road between this and the *run* ; and the *run* is so high, from the freshes, that you will not be able to find it.—*Davis's Travels in the United States in* 1797.

TO RUN. To press with jokes, sarcasm, or ridicule.—*Webster.*

RUN. Joke ; ridicule. ' To *get the run* upon one,' is to make a butt of him ; turn him into ridicule.

> He bade him not to be discouraged at this *run* upon him ; for though they had got the laughter upon their side, yet mere wit and raillery could not hold it out long against a work of so much learning.—*Warburton on Pope.*

TO RUN ONE'S FACE. To make use of one's credit. ' To *run one's face* for a thing,' is to get it on tick.

Any one who can *run his face* for a card of pens, a quire of paper, and a pair of scissors, may set up for an editor; and by loud, incessant bragging, may secure a considerable patronage.—*N. Y. Tribune.*

RUN OF STONES. A pair of mill-stones is called a *run of stones* when in operation or placed in a mill. The Rochester flouring mills have ten or twenty *run of stones.*

RUNGS. A very common name in New England for the *rounds* or steps of a ladder. The braces or *rounds* of common chairs are also vulgarly called *rungs.* This has generally been considered as a mere corruption of *rounds;* and people of education use only this latter word.—*Pickering's Vocabulary.* It is provincial in the north of England. In New York it is applied to four upright staves fixed in a cart for supporting the load.

RUSTY DAB. (Genus, *platessa.* Cuvier.) The popular name of the Rusty Flat-fish, a fish found on the coast of Massachusetts and New York in deep water.—*Storer, Fishes of Mass.*

S.

SAFE. An iron box, frequently built into the wall, and used by merchants as a place of deposit for their books and papers. They are now generally made fire proof; and some of these are called 'salamander safes.'

TO SAG. To sink in the middle when supported at both ends; as a long pole.—*Worcester.* Provincial in England, but in common use with us.

SAGAMORE. The title of a chief or ruler among some of the American tribes of Indians; a sachem.—*Worcester.*

SADYING. A simple and unaffected mode of dancing, practised by novices in the art.

It would do you good to see our boys and girls dancing. None of your stradling, mincing, *sadying;* but a regular sifter, cut-the-buckle, chicken-flutter set-to.—*Crockett, Tour.*

S. C. The common abbreviation for *South Carolina.*

SALMAGUNDI. A Dutch dish common in New York. It is made of pickled or smoked shad, cut into thin slices or shreds, and sliced onions. The whole is then acidulated with vine-gar. This dish is generally used at tea.

SALT-LICK. A saline spring, where animals resort for drink. See *Lick*.

SALT-WATER VEGETABLES. In New York, a cant term for oysters and clams.

SAMP. (Indian, *nasaump.*) Roger Williams describes *na-saump* as "a kind of meale pottage unparched; from this the English call their *samp*, which is Indian corn, beaten and boiled, and eaten hot or cold with milke or butter, which are mercies beyond the natives' plaine water, and which is a dish exceedingly wholesome for the English bodies."—*Key to the Indian Language*, p. 33. For other dishes made of corn, see *Hominy, Mush, Suppawn, Suckatash.*

> Blue corn is light of digestion, and the English make a kind of loblolly of it, to eat with milk, which they call *sampe;* they beat it in a mortar, and sifte the flower out of it.—*Josselyn's New England Rarities*, 1672.

SANG. An abbreviation of *ginseng*. It is or was also used in Virginia as a verb ; *to go a sanging*, is to be engaged in gath-ering ginseng.

SANGAREE. (Span. *sangre*, blood.) A drink made of red wine, water, and sugar, with nutmeg grated over it. This word, now very common throughout the United States, was introduced from the West Indies.

SAND-FLEA, or BEACH-FLEA. (Genus, *orchestra*. Leach.) A small crustacea common along the shores of Long Island, and other sandy places, digging holes wherein they conceal themselves, and living upon dead animal substances.—*Nat. Hist. of New York.*

SANCTIMONIOUSLYFIED. This queer word explains itself.

> I recollect an old *sanctimoniouslyfied* fellow, who made his negroes whis-tle while they were picking cherries, for fear they should eat some.—*Crockett, Tour down East.*

SAPHEAD. A blockhead; a stupid fellow.—*Craven Dialect.*

SAPPY. Young ; not firm ; weak.—*Johnson*. Weak in intel-lect.—*Webster*. Used only in familiar language.

SAPSUCKER. A small wood-pecker (the *dentrocopus* of ornithologists), so called from a common belief that it sucks the sap of trees.—*Nat. Hist. of New York.*

SARTIN, for *certain*. A vulgar pronunciation heard in many parts of England and the United States.

SASS-TEA. A decoction of sassafras.

> In the morning, Hoss Allen became dreadful poorly. The matron of the house boiled him *sass-tea*, which the old man said revived him mightily.— *Robb, Squatter Life*, p. 72.

SATINET. A twilled cloth made of cotton and wool.

SAUCE. (Vulgarly pronounced *sass*.) Culinary vegetables and roots eaten with flesh.—*Webster*. This word is provincial in various parts of England in the same sense. Forby defines it as " any sort of vegetable eaten with flesh-meat."—*Norfolk Glossary*. *Garden-stuff*, and *garden-ware*, are the usual terms in England.

> Roots, herbs, vine-fruits, and salad-flowers—they dish up in various ways, and find them very delicious *sauce* to their meats, both roasted and boiled, fresh and salt.—*Beverly's Hist. of Virginia.*

SAVAGE AS A MEAT AXE. Exceedingly hungry. This vulgar simile is often used in the Northern and Western States.

> " Why, you don't eat nothing !" he exclaimed ; " ridin' don't agree with you, I guess ! Now, for my part, it makes me as *savage as a meat axe.*"— *Mrs. Clavers's Forest Life*, Vol. I. p. 103.

> It would be a charity to give the pious brother some such feed as chicken fixins and doins, for he looks half-starved, and as *savage as a meat axe.*— *Carlton's New Purchase.*

SAVAGEROUS. Furious. A low word.

> Well, Capting, they were mighty *savagerous* after liquor ; they'd been fightin' the whisky barrel.—*Porter's Tales of the South-west.*

SAVANNA. (W. Ind. *savana*.) An open plain, or meadow without wood.

> He that rides past through a country may tell how, in general, the parts lie : here a morass, and there a river ; woodland in one part, and *savannas* in another.—*Locke.*

> > Plains immense,
> > And vast *savannas*, where the wand'ring eye,
> > Unfix't, is in a verdant ocean lost.—*Thomson, Summer.*

SAVEY, or SABBY. (Corrupted from the Spanish *saber*, to know.) To know ; to comprehend. A word of very extensive use wherever a Lingua Franca· has been formed of the Spanish or Portuguese language in Asia, Africa, and America. It is used by the negroes in some of the Southern States.

> When I read these stories, the negroes looked delighted, and said : " We savey dat well, misses."—*Carmichael's West Indies.*

TO SAW. To hoax ; to play a joke upon one. A western term. In the State of Maine, *to saw* means to scold.

SAWYER. This may truly be called an American word ; for no country without a Mississippi and Missouri could produce a *sawyer.*

Sawyers are formed by trees, which, growing on the banks of the river, become undermined by the current, and fall into the stream. They are then swept away by the current, with the branches partly above water, rising and falling with the waves ; whence the name of *sawyer.* They are extremely dangerous to steamboats, which sometimes run foul of them, and are either disabled or sunk to the bottom.

SAW-WHET. The popular name, in some of the Northern States, for the Little Owl, or Acadian Owl of Audubon. " It has a sharp note like the filing of a saw, and another like the tinkling of a bell."—*Nat. Hist. of New York.*

SAY. A speech ; what one has to say.—*Johnson.*

> He no sooner said out his *say,* but up rises a cunning snap.—*L'Es-trange.*
>
> Gentlemen of the jury—I have as yet said nothing on the important subject engaging your attention, and I now propose to have my *say.*—*N. Y. True Sun.*
>
> Having said our *say* in the first instance, and now given place to our correspondent's replication *verbatim,* we presume we may here very fairly take leave of the matter.—*N. Y. Com. Adv.*

SCACE, for *scarce.* A vulgarism in the interior of the country.

SCALY. Mean ; stingy.—*Halliwell.*

SCALAWAG. A favorite epithet in western New York for a mean fellow ; a scape-grace.

SCAMP. A worthless fellow.

SCAPE-GALLOWS. One who has escaped, though deserving of the gallows. It seems to be synonymous with Cotgrave's *pendard,* which he defines, " a rare-hell, crack-rope, gallowclapper; one for whom the gallows longeth.'—*Carr's Craven Dialect.*

SCAPE-GRACE. A term of reproach; a graceless fellow.— *Brockett.*

> About this time of year, we notice that three young *scape-graces* infest the city, who get up their wild freaks at night, and continue them till after day.—*N. Y. Express.*

SCARLETINA. A common name for scarlet fever.—*Brande.*

SCHNAPS. Schedam gin, a kind of Hollands. A Dutch term still preserved in New York.

SCHOOL OF FISH. (Ang. Sax. *sceol.* Dutch, *school.*) Another pronunciation of the word *shoal,* and applied to a large number of fish swimming together. The expression is also provincial in England.

SCHOOL-DISTRICT. A division of a city or State for establishing schools. The State of New York is divided into more than ten thousand such partitions or school-districts.

SCHOOL-MA'AM. A school-mistress. This word is peculiar to New England.

SCHOONER. Both Webster and Todd derive this word from the German *schoner,* which means the same; but on examining the German dictionaries we find the word written *schooner, schoner,* and *schuner,* and characterized as English! The following story has a circumstantiality about it that gives it an air of truth:

"The first vessel of the kind is said to have been built at Gloucester, Mass., by Capt. Andrew Robinson, about the year 1714. The name was given to it from the following circumstance: Capt. R. had constructed a vessel, which he masted and rigged in the manner that *schooners* now are, and on her going off the stocks into the water, a bystander cried out, 'Oh how she *schoons!*' R. instantly replied, 'A *schooner* let her be;' and from that time, this class of vessels has gone by that name. Previously, vessels of this description were unknown either in this country or Europe."—*Essex, Mass. Memorial,* 1836, p. 100.

What is meant by *to schoon,* I cannot say.

SCONCE. The head ; pate.   An old English vulgarism.

> A hyst is of itself bad enough—your *sconce* gets a crack ; then you see all sorts of stars.—*J. C. Neal, Dilly Jones.*

SCOW. (Dutch, *schouw*.) A large flat-bottomed boat, generally used as a ferry boat, or as a lighter for loading and unloading vessels when they cannot approach the wharf. On Lake Ontario they are sometimes rigged like a schooner or sloop, with a lee-board or sliding keel, when they make tolerably fast sailers. The word is used in Scotland. A *mud-scow* (Dutch, *modder-schouw*) is a vessel of this description, used in New York for cleaning out the docks.

SCRANCH.   (Dutch, *schransen*.)   To crunch, crack, or break any hard thing between the teeth.—*Phillips's World of Words.* This word is in vulgar use in the United States.

> Some were coming up the hill, goreing and *scranching* the crust [of the snow] with their iron corks.—*Margaret,* p. 172.

SCRAP-BOOK. A blank book for the preservation of short pieces of poetry or other extracts from books and papers.— *Webster.*

SCRAPS. The dry, husky, and skinny residuum of melted fat.—*Forby's Vocabulary.* The common word in New England for the same.

SCRATCH. *No great scratch.* A vulgar, though common phrase, implying not worth much—*no great shakes.*

> There are a good many Joneses in Georgia, and I know some myself that ain't *no great scratches.*—*Maj. Jones's Courtship,* p. 136.

SCRATCH. *To come to the scratch.* To come to the encounter, begin a fight.

> When the landlords and tenants in New York fairly *come to the scratch* [about the first of May], they make hot work of it.—*Maj. Downing, May-day in New York,* p. 30.

SCRAWL. In New England, a ragged, broken branch of a tree, or other brushwood ; brush.—*Webster.*

SCREAMER. A bouncing fellow or girl. This, like the word *roarer,* is one of the many terms transferred from animals to men by the hunters of the West.

If he's a specimen of the Choctaws that live in these parts, they are *screamers.—Thorpe's Backwoods.*

Mary is a *screamer* of a girl ; I'd rather have her than all the rest.— *Mrs. Clavers's Western Clearings.*

What's the matter with that woman ? said the recorder. *Policeman.—* That's the way she was carryin' on last night when I arrested her—she's a *screamer*, your honor, I tell you.—*Pickings from the Picayune.*

SCREW. One who squeezes all he can out of those with whom he has any dealings ; an extortioner ; miser. Colloquial here as in England.

TO SCREW. To exact upon one in a bargain or reckoning.— *Grose.* Ex. ' He *screwed me down* to a very low price.'

SCRIMP. Short ; scanty.—*Webster.*

SCRIMP. A pinching miser ; a niggard ; a close-fisted person.—*Webster.*

TO SCRIMP. To contract ; to shorten ; to make too small or short ; to limit or straiten ; as, ' to *scrimp* the pattern of a coat.' This, as well as the previous words, are in common use in New England.—*Webster.* Used in the north of England.—*Brockett.*

TO SCROUGE. To crowd ; to squeeze. A word provincial in England and in this country. It is used in the Southern States, and among children at the North.

The ladies were obliged to stand up and be *scrouged* until chairs could be brought.—*Drama in Pokerville.*

After hard *scrouging* each way some hundred yards, we came together and held a council.—*Carlton, New Purchase*, Vol. II. p. 59.

Them boys that's a *scrouging* each other, will find plenty of room this way.—*Peter Cram, Knick. Mag.*

SCROUGER. A bouncing fellow or girl. A Western vulgarism.

Tom, the engineer, was a roaring, tearing, bar State *scrouger*—could chaw up any specimen of the human race, any quantity of tobacco, and drink steam without flinching.—*Robb, Squatter Life.*

Some of the families in them diggins had about twenty in number ; and the gals among them warn't any on your pigeon creatures, that a fellow dassent tech for fear of spilin 'em, but real *scrougers* ; any of 'em could lick a bar easy.—*Ibid.*

SCRUMPTIOUS. Nice, particular, fastidious; also, nice, excellent. Probably a corruption of *scrupulous.* A vulgarism.

> I dont want to be *scrumptious,* judge; but I do want to be a man.—
> *Margaret,* p. 304.

SCULLCAP. (Lat. *scutellaria.*) A medicinal plant; its properties tonic and sudorific.

SCUP. (Indian, *shcup-pauog.* Roger Williams.) A small
fish abounding in the waters of New York and New England.
In Rhode Island they are called *scup;* in New York, paugies,
or porgies. In speaking of this fish, which Roger Williams
calls the *breame,* he says, " there is a great abundance which
the natives drie in the sunne and smoake; and some English
begin to salt. Both wayes they keepe all the yeere; and it
is hoped it may be as well accepted as cod at a market, and
better if once knowne."—*Key to the Indian Lang.,* p. 103.
See *Porgy.*

SCUP. (Dutch, *schop.*) A swing. A New York word.

TO SCUP. (Dutch, *schoppen.*) To swing. Common in New
York.

SCUSS, for *scarce.* So pronounced by the backwoodsmen of
the West.

> The unfortunate traveller urged in vain [for food for his horse]. Hay
> was *scuss,* and potatoes were *scusser.*—*Mrs. Clavers's Western Clearings.*

SEDGE. In New England, a species of coarse grass. In England it is a small kind of flag. In New England ' a tussock
of *sedge,*' is a bunch or tuft of coarse grass, common in
swampy meadows.

> Margaret was bounding through a wet bog, springing from one tussock
> of *sedge* to another.—*Margaret,* p. 25.

SEALER. In New England, an officer appointed by the town
or other proper authority, to examine and try weights and
measures, and set a stamp on such as are according to the
standards established by the State; also an officer who in-
spects leather, and stamps such as good. These are called
sealers of weights and measures, and *sealers* of leather.—
Webster.

SEARCHING. Piercing; keen; as, ' A *searching* wind.'—
Carr's Craven Dialect.

SEAWAN. An Indian word meaning the same as *wampum*, formerly in use among the early colonists of New York.

> A quantity of Dutch commodities was purchased on this occasion by the New Plymouth people; especially *seawan* or wampum, which the English found to be afterwards very beneficial in their trade with the natives.—*O'Callaghan, Hist. New Netherland, p. 108.*

SECTION. A distinct part of a city, town, country or people; a part of a territory separated by geographical lines, or of a people considered as distinct. Thus we say, the Northern and Eastern *section* of the United States, the Middle *section*, the Southern or Western *section.*—*Webster.*

> The newly surveyed government lands at the West are laid out or divided into squares of 320 acres, which are called *sections*. These are again divided into four parts of eighty acres each, called *quarter sections*.

SECTIONAL. Pertaining to a section or distinct part of a larger body or territory.

> All *sectional* interests or party feelings, it is hoped, will hereafter yield to schemes of ambition.—*Judge Story.*

SEE, for *saw* (preterite of *to see*). I *see* him yesterday, for I *saw* him. This corruption is common among the illiterate in New England. I have heard old people use the word *seed;* as, 'I *seed* him.' Pegge says this is a common vulgarism in London, "and passes currently with the common people, both for our perfect tense *saw,* and our participle *seen.*"—*Anecdotes of the Eng. Lang.*

> He lookt, he listened, yet his thoughts deride
> To think that true which he both heard and *see.*—*Fairfax's Tasso.*

> O rare! he doth it as like one of these hartolry players as I ever *see.*—*Shakspeare, First Part Henry IV.*, II. 4.

> Mr. M—— was almost dead with the consumption, and had to carry rocks in his pocket to keep the wind from blowing him away. Well, he's a sound and well man, and looks as if he mought live to be a hundred years old. I never *seed* such an alteration in any body in my life.—*Maj. Jones's Sketches.*

TO SEE.
TO SEE ABOUT. } To attend to; to consider.

TO SEE HOW THE CAT JUMPS. A metaphorical expression meaning, to discover the secrets or designs of others.

We also say, in the same sense, *to see which way the wind blows.* Both phrases are used in England.

> I *see how the cat jumps* : here's a little tid bit of an extortion now ; but you wont find that no go.—*Sam Slick in England.*

> He has written to get up a petition in old Tammany ; and then you'll *see how the cat will jump.*—*Maj. Downing.*

> I know what I knows, I've *seen how the cat has been jumpin'.*—*Margaret*, p. 141.

TO SEE THE ELEPHANT, is a South-western phrase, and means, generally, to undergo any disappointment of high-raised expectations. It is in fact nearly or quite synonymous with the ancient " go out for wool and come back shorn." For instance, men who have volunteered for the Mexican war, expecting to reap lots of glory and enjoyment, but instead have found only sickness, fatigue, privations, and suffering, are currently said to have '*seen the elephant.*' I do not remember having ever fallen in with a good origin for the term in this employment of it. [*J. Inman.*]

A man, being brought before the Recorder in New Orleans, charged with being found drunk the previous night, after appealing to the court, closed with the following remarks :

> " Spare my feelings, Squire, and don't ask me to tell any more. Here I am in town without a rock in my pocket, without a skirt to my coat or crown to my hat ; but, Squire, I'll say no more, *I've seen the elephant.*" The Recorder let him off on condition that he would leave town, as he confessed he had *seen the elephant.*—*Pickings from the Picayune.*

> Although the merchants from the South and West may buy goods in Philadelphia, all find their way to New York to spend their pocket-money, buy brass watches at the mock auctions, and *see the elephant* generally.—*Phila. Cor. of the N. Y. Tribune.*

SEEN, for *saw.* Ex. ' I *seen* him before ;' ' I *seen* her yesterday.' This corruption is common in various parts of the country.

> Peter Cram's fits is awful, and go ahead of anything we ever *seen.*—*Knickerbocker Mag.*, Vol. XVII.

SELECTMAN. A magistrate annually elected by the freemen of a town or township in New England, to superintend and manage the affairs and government of the town. The number is commonly from three to five.—*Worcester.*

SENATE. In the United States, *senate* denotes the higher branch or house of a legislature. Such is the *Senate* of the United States, or upper house of the Congress; and in most of the States, the higher and least numerous branch of the legislature is called the *Senate.* In the United States, the *Senate* is an elective body.—*Webster.*

SERIOUS. Particularly attentive to religious concerns or one's own religious state.—*Webster.*

> *Serious* has [in New England] the cant acceptation of religious.—*Kendall's Travels.*

TO SERVE UP. To expose to ridicule; to expose.

SERVICE-BERRY. A wild fruit common to the British provinces in America, described by Sir Geo. Simpson as " a sort of cross between the cranberry and the black currant." It is a good article of food, and is sometimes mixed with pemican. The Indian name is *mis-as-quitomine.*

> Among the usual fruit-bearing shrubs and bushes, I here notice the *service-berry.*—*Scenes in the Rocky Mountains,* p. 114.

SESSIONS, in some of the States, is particularly used for a court of justice, held for granting licenses to innkeepers or taverners, for laying out new highways, or altering old ones, and the like.—*Webster.*

SET. Fixed in opinion; firm.—*Webster.* 'He is very *set* in his ways.'

A DEAD SET. A concerted scheme to defraud a person by gaming.—*Grose, Slang Dict.* This phrase seems to be taken from the lifeless attitude of a pointer in marking his game. We sometimes hear the phrase applied as in the expression, 'He made a *dead set* at the young lady,' i. e. a determined effort to win her favor.

TO SET BY.
TO SET MUCH BY. } To regard; to esteem.—*Johnson.*
Norfolk and Craven Glossaries. These are very old expressions, and were once in good use in England; they are now classed among provincialisms, and are only heard in familiar language.

> David behaved himself more wisely than all, so that his name was *much set by.*—1 *Samuel,* xviii. 30.

TO SET STORE BY. To set value upon; to appreciate. Ex. 'These things we *set* great *store by.*' Used only in familiar language. It is provincial in Yorkshire and in Norfolk.—*Forby's Glossary.*

> He [the Ohio boatman] observed very feelingly, that he *set more store to* this song than to all the rest.—*Hall, Letters from the West,* Let. 4.

SET-TO. A scientific pugilistic combat; and figuratively, an argument, debate, contest in words. Both senses are English.

SETTING-POLE. A pole pointed with iron, used for propelling vessels or boats up rivers, in shoal water.

TO SETTLE. To be ordained or installed over a parish, church, or congregation. A. B. was invited *to settle* in the first society at New Haven. N. D. *settled* in the ministry very young.—*Webster.*

TO SETTLE. To liquidate an account; to pay a debt. A sense of the word not given in the English dictionaries, but very common among our merchants and traders. On board our steamboats it is customary, soon after leaving the wharf, for one of the waiters to go about ringing a bell and crying out, 'Passengers what hain't paid their fare, will please step up to the Captain's office and *settle.*'

TO SETTLE ONE'S HASH. To properly punish one. We also say, 'to settle his business;' 'to fix his flint.'

> Brave Prudhoe triumphant shall skim the wide main,
>   The *hash* of the Yankees he'll *settle;*
> And ages hereafter shall serve to proclaim
>   A Northumberland free o' Newcastle.—*Song, Northumberlands free of Newcastle, Brockett.*

SHACK. A vagabond; a low fellow. Ex. 'He's a poor *shack* of a fellow.' It is provincial in England, and applied in the same way as here.—*Craven and Shropshire Glossaries.*

SHACKLY. Loose; rickety; as, 'What a *shackly* old carriage!'

SHAFT. A handle; as, a *whip-shaft,* the handle of a whip. —*Jamieson, Scottish Dictionary.*

SHAGBARKS. A common name in New England for a sort of Walnuts.

SHAKER. One of a religious denomination, styled the 'United Society,' which first rose in Lancashire, England, in the year 1747. In the account which the Shakers give of themselves, they mention the Quakers in the time of Oliver Cromwell, and the French prophets of a later date, as being the first who had a peculiar testimony from the Lord to deliver to the Christian world. But they complain that the former degenerated, losing that desire of love and power with which they first set out; and the latter being of short continuance, their extraordinary communications have long ago ceased. This testimony was revived in the persons of James Wardley, a tailor by trade, and Jane his wife, who wrought at the same occupation! They had belonged to the society of Shakers, but receiving the spirit of the French prophets, and a further degree of light and power, by which they were separated from that community, they continued for several years disconnected from every denomination. During this time their testimony, according to what they saw by vision and revelation from God, was, " That the second appearing of Christ was at hand, and that the church was rising in her full and transcendant glory, which would effect the final downfall of Anti-Christ."

From the shaking of their bodies in religious exercises, they were called *Shakers,* and some gave them the name of *Shaking Quakers.*

In 1757, Ann Lee joined the Society by confessing her sins to Jane Wardley. In 1772 she professed to have received a revelation from God to repair to America. Accordingly, as many as firmly believed in her testimony, and could settle their temporal concerns, and could furnish necessaries for the voyage, concluded to follow her. They arrived in New York in 1774, and in 1776 removed to Watervliet, eight miles from Albany, where a society was established, which still exists, and where they now possess 2000 acres of good land. From this society have grown several communities; one at New Lebanon, N. Y., which consists of 600 members. Others have been founded in Wayne county, N. Y., at Enfield, Connecticut, two in Ohio (one of the latter of which contains 600 members), two in Kentucky having about 500 members each, and one in Indiana.   In 1828, the number of societies was sixteen ; the number of preachers about forty-five ; members gathered into their societies, about 4500 ; those not received, 900 ; making in all about 5400.—*Evans's Hist. of Religions, Am. Ed. Rapp's Religious Denominations in the United States.*

THE SHAKES.   The fever and ague.

SHAKING QUAKER.   A member of the religious sect called *Shakers,* which see.

SHAKES.   *No great shakes.*   Of no great value ; little worth. Common in England and the United States.

> I had my hands full, and my head too, just then [when he wrote to Marino Faliero], so it can be *no great shakes.—Lord Byron to Murray.*

> Yit, if they their inquirations make,
>   In winter time some will
> Condemn that place as *no great shakes*
>   Where folks ha' the cold chill.—*Noakes and Styles, Essex Dialect.*

> Cousin Pete allowed he knowed he wasn't *no great shakes* all the time, and was makin' more noise than anybody else.—*Maj. Jones's Courtship.*

> I have forgot what little Latin I learnt to night-school ; and, in fact, I never was *any great shakes* at it.—*Sam Slick,* 3d Ser. ch. VII.

TO SHAKE A STICK AT.   A ridiculous phrase very often heard in low language.   When a man is puzzled to give one an idea of a very great number, he calls it ' more than you can *shake a stick at.*'

> New York is an everlastin' great concern, and, as you may well suppose, there's about as many people in it as you could *shake a stick at.—Maj. Downing, May-day in New York.*

> I've been licked fifty times, and got more black eyes and bloody noses than you could *shake a stick at,* for the purity of our illegal rights.—*J. C. Neal, Peter Brush.*

> We got a little dry or so, and wanted a horn ; but this was a temperance house, and there was nothing to treat a friend to that was worth *shaking a stick at.—Crockett, Tour,* p. 87.

SHAKY.   A term applied by lumbermen, dealers in timber, and carpenters, to boards which are inclined to split from defects in the log from which they have been sawed.

SHANTY. A hut, or mean dwelling.

SHARP SET. Hungry. A colloquial expression much used in the United States as well as in England.

> And so I thinke that if anie were so *sharpe set* as to eat fried flies, buttered bees, stued snailes, either on Fridaie or Sundaie, he could not therefore be indicted for haulte treason.—*Stanihurst's Ireland*, 1596, p. 19.

> I'm considerable *sharp-set* after waiting five hours and a quarter for breakfast.—*Sam Slick in England*, ch. 2.

SHARP STICK. 'He's after him with a *sharp stick;*' i. e. he's determined to have satisfaction, or revenge. Western.

SHAVER. One that is close in bargains, or a sharp dealer.—*Webster.*

To shave, is to cut off a portion of the outside; hence to strip, deprive, take away unjustly, as a robber or hard dealer; one who does this is a *shaver.* This word, in the United States, is applied to money brokers, who purchase notes at more than legal interest. Banks, when they resort to any means to obtain a large discount, are also called *shavers,* or *shaving* banks. Many such are known, but they evade the penalty of the usury laws by discounting at legal interest, and giving the proceeds of the note so discounted, in a draft on some distant place, or in uncurrent money; which are again purchased by the bank or its agents at a discount.

> They fell into the hands of the cruel mountain-people, living for the most part by theft, and waiting for wrecks, as hawks for their prey; by these *shavers* the Turks were stripp'd of all they had.—*Knolles's History of the Turks.*

> To sell our notes, at a great loss, to brokers, or, in other words, to get them unmercifully *shaved*, was what we wished to avoid.—*Perils of Pearl Street*, p. 123.

SHAVER. A *shaver* is a boy, a lad, one just beginning to shave; or else, on the *lucus a non lucendo* principle, one who does not shave, but would if he could! Comp. *Skin-flint.* The term is often humorously applied here, as in England, to boys who ape the behavior of men.

SHECOONERY. A whimsical corruption of the word *chica-nery*, used at the South.

> This town's got a monstrous bad name for meanery and *shecoonery* of all sorts.—*Chronicles of Pineville*, p. 47.

> Among other topics, he dwelt upon the verdancy of his neighbors, and the *shecoonery* which had been practised upon them.—*Ibid.* p. 48.

TO SHELL OUT, means to hand over money.

> Witness the testimony of Major Noah and others in New York, who prove that the office-holders had to *shell out* a part of their salary, to support Jacksonism.—*Crockett, Tour*, p. 163.

> The rich folks have pretty much all the money; but as we can out-vote them, they ought to *shell out.*—*Maj. Downing's Letters*, p. 98.

> If I could *shell out* ideas as easy as you do words, I could soon write another book.—*Crockett, Tour down East*, p. 5.

SHERRYVALLIES. (Fr. *chevalier.*) Pantaloons made of thick velvet or leather, buttoned on the outside of each leg, and generally worn over other pantaloons. They are now chiefly worn by teamsters. Mány years ago, when the facilities for travelling were not as great as now, and when journeys were made on horseback, *sherryvallies* were indispensable to the traveller.

SHET. A vulgar pronunciation of *shut;* also used in England.

> Here slouthe brouyte it so aboute,
> Fro him that they ben *schet* withoute.—*Gower, MS. quoted by Halliwell.*

> Hey, mister! said a shop-boy at last, I want to get shut of you, cause we're goin' to *shet* up.—*Neal's Sketches.*

SHEEPSKIN. The parchment diploma received by students for taking their degree at college. In the back settlements are many clergymen who have not had the advantages of a liberal education, and who consequently have no diplomas. Some of these look upon their more favored brethren with a little envy. A clergyman is said to have a *sheepskin,* or to be a *sheepskin,* when educated at college.

> This apostle of ourn never rubbed his back agin a college, nor toted about no *sheepskins*—no, never! . . . . . How you'd a perished in your sins, if the first preachers had stayed till they got *sheepskins.*—*Carlton's New Purchase.*

> I can say as well as the best ou them *sheepskins,* if you don't get religion

and be saved, you'll be lost, tetotally and for ever. [Sermon of an itinerant preacher at a camp-meeting].—*Ibid.* Vol. I. p. 203.

SHEER. Applied in the United States to fabrics of cotton or silk ; as, *sheer muslin;* meaning very thin, clear, or transparent.

SHEW, (pron. like *shoe*,) for *showed*. Ex. ' I *shew* him the difference between black and white.' This corruption is so common among all classes in the " American Athens," as to form a sort of shibboleth for distinguishing a Bostonian.

Several years ago this corrupt preterite was very common in New England ; but it is now much less used than formerly. Mr. Pegge, in his ironical defence of *know'd* for *knew*, mentions the following singular instances of irregular preterite verbs ending in *ew* or *ow:* " The modern past tense, *I knew*, seems to have been imported from the north of England, where the expressions are, ' I *sew* (instead of I *sow'd*), my corn ;' ' I *mew* (that is, I *mow'd*) my hay ;' and, ' it *snew*,' for it *snowed*."—*Pickering*.

TO SHIN. To borrow money. A word well understood in New York in times when money is scarce. The author of the amusing work, entitled " Perils of Pearl Street," page 123, thus describes it :

" By *shinning*, in mercantile phrase, is meant running about to one's acquaintance, to borrow money to meet the emergency of a note at bank. It is doubtless so called, because in the great hurry of picking up cash to meet the hour of three, which perchance is just at hand, the borrower, not having the fear of wheelbarrows, boxes, barrels, piles of brick, &c. before his eyes, is very apt to run furiously against them with his *shins*, the bark whereof is apt to be grievously battered off by the contact. . . . . So fares it with the poor merchant, while he is looking out for an acquaintance of whom he may ask, *Anything over?* This is an expression used by *shinners*, on applying to their acquaintances for the needful ; and means, Have you any money over and above the sum requisite for discharging your own notes ? If so, it is of course expected, that, in the way of mercantile courtesy, or of a friendly reciprocity, you will oblige the *shinner* so far as to hand it over to him.   It is a common way, amongst those who have business in banks, of obliging one another.   If they have anything over, they do not withhold it from their neighbor, lest in turn he should do the same towards them.

"*Shinners* may be divided into two classes : those who *shin* from necessity, and those who *shin* from profit.   The latter may be called professional *shinners;* and they consist of merchants of some standing, who make it their business to find out, and get into the good graces of those who are just starting in trade.   Correctly judging that these last will have no notes to pay under six months, and that they will take in considerable money in that time, they borrow their surplus cash, promising in their turn to lend whenever the other shall stand in need.   But when the time comes, these cunning old *shinners* take especial care to have nothing over ; then coldly turn their back upon the young merchant, and commence a new *shinning* account with some fresh dupe, who, in like manner, is to be abandoned whenever he requires an interchange of the favor."

The Senator was *shinning* around, to get gold for the rascally bankrags, which he was obliged to take.—*N. Y. Com. Adv.*, Dec. 13, 1845.

SHINDY.   `A row ; a spree.

If this 'ere isn't that 'are singing chap agin.   He's on a *shindy* somewhere or other every night.—*J. C. Neal, P. Ploddy*, p. 18.

TO SHINE.   In the Southern States the deer is often hunted by torch-light.   The custom is thus described in the ' cracker' dialect of Georgia : " You see the way we does *to shine* the deer's eyes is this—we holds the pan of fire so, on the left shoulder, and carries the gun at a trail in the right hand. Well, when I wants to look for eyes, I turns round slow, and looks right at the edge of my shadder, what's made by the light behind me in the pan, and if there's a deer in gun-shot of me, his eyes'll *shine* 'zactly like two balls of fire."—*Chronicles of Pineville*, p. 169.

He often urged me to accompany him to see how slick he could *shine* a buck's eyes.—*Ibid.* p. 162.

SHINE.   *To take the shine off*, is to surpass in beauty or excellence.

Cousin P——, with his dandy cut trousers, and big whiskers, tried *to take the shine off* everybody else.—*Maj. Jones's Courtship,* p. 111.

I'm sorry he didn't bring his pitch-pipe with him, jest *to take the shine off* them 'are singers.—*Maj. Downing's Letters,* p. 37.

SHINE. *To take a shine to* a person, is to take a fancy to him or her.

SHINE. *To cut* or *make a shine,* is to make a great display.

All the boys and gals were going to camp-meetin'; so, to *make a shine* with Sally, I took her a new parasol.—*Robb, Squatter Life.*

SHINER. (Genus, *Leuciscus.*) The popular name of the fish known to naturalists as the Dace. In different parts of the country, however, other small fish are called *shiners,* from their glittering or shining appearance. In New York a small fish of the genus *stilbe,* is known to naturalists as the New York Shiner. It is also found in the adjoining States.—*Nat. Hist. of New York.*

SHINGLE. A jocose term for a sign-board, placed over a shop-door or office.

Doctors and dentists from the United States have stuck up their *shingles* in Mexico.—*N. Y. Com. Adv.,* Dec. 24, 1848.

Several made bold to peep inside, in spite of the " No Admittance !" which frowned from a *shingle* over the door.—*Drama at Pokerville.*

SHINPLASTER. A cant term for a bank-note, or any paper money. It probably came into use in 1837, when the banks suspended specie payment, and when paper money became depreciated in value.

The people may whistle for protection, and put up with what *shinplaster* rags they can get.—*N. Y. Tribune,* Dec. 3, 1845.

TO SHIRK. To procure by mean tricks; to steal.—*Todd.* To live by one's wits; also to *shirk off,* to sneak away.

Tell me, you that never heard the call of any vocation, that are free of no other company but your idle companions, that *shirke* living from others, but time from yourselves.—*Bp. Rainbow, Sermons* (1635), p. 40.

SHIRTING. A fabric of cotton or linen of a suitable width for making shirts. Goods which are a yard or more wide are called sheeting; when less than a yard, *shirting.*

TO SHOAL. To lounge about lazily.

You shuffled up to the counter as if you were *shoaling* through the market, according to your well known habits, stealing pig's feet to make broth of, &c.—*Mathews, Puffer Hopkins*, ch. 14.

SHOEMAKE. A common name for the *sumach*-tree.

SHOO! A word commonly used to drive away fowls.—*Brockett*.

SHOOT, or SHUTE. A passage-way on the side of a steep hill or mountain down which wood and timber are thrown or slid. There are many such on the Hudson and Mohawk rivers. In the West the term is applied to places where a river is artificially contracted in order to increase the depth of water. In Lower Canada a *shoot* is a place where the stream, being confined by rocks which appear above water, is shot through the aperture with great force.—*Cartwright's Labrador*, p. 14. In the West, ' to take a *shoot* after,' is to take a fancy to.

> That gal was the prettyest creatur I ever *took a shute after;* her eyes jest floated about in her head like a star's shadow on a Mississippi wave.—*Robb, Squatter Life.*

TO SHOOT ONE'S GRANDMOTHER, is a common though vulgar phrase in New England, and means to be mistaken, or to be disappointed; to imagine oneself the discoverer of something in which he is deceived. The common phrase is, ' You've shot your granny.' It is, in fact, synonymous with ' You've found a mare's nest.'

SHOOTING IRON. A common Western term for a rifle, or fowling piece.

SHOPPING. The act of frequenting shops.—*Jodrell's Philology.* This very useful word is not noticed by Dr. Johnson; and Mr. Todd calls it a cant word of modern origin.

> For those the hour of retirement is three, which gives, till noon the next day, nine hours for rest; and after that sufficient time for a ride, auctions, or *shopping*, before the dinner-hour.—*Hawkins, Life of Johnson*, p. 262.

> What between *shopping*, and morning visits with mamma, &c., I contrive to amuse myself tolerably.— *Cœlebs*, Vol. I. p. 356.

> Mr. Smoothly was the very prince of retailers. His store was the great *shopping* mart—or perhaps the great *shopping* theatre; for the goods were rather exhibited than sold. The ladies, too, while examining the merchandise, had a chance of exhibiting themselves to the lounging beaux, and thus under pretence of *shopping*, might possibly make a market for themselves.—*Perils of Pearl Street*, p. 26.

SHOPPER. One who frequents shops.

> It is a most provoking thing to have anything to do with professed *shoppers*. They require more attention, without offering an equivalent, than any other class of people in the world.—*Ibid.* p. 27.

SHORT-COMINGS. Defective performance ; deficiency as to duty.—*Worcester.*

> Here is proof that very little was known of the life of St. Clair by the author ; and the question instantly arises, Has he any excuse for such *short-comings ?*—*Review of Headley's Washington, Literary World.*

> We are willing to receive the rebukes, and suffer the exhortations of our brethren in view of our *short-comings.*—*Princeton Rev.*, July, 1847.

SHORTS. The bran and coarse part of meal, in mixture.

SHORTS. Small-clothes ; breeches.—*Webster.*

SHOT. Another pronunciation of the word *scot*, a reckoning.

> As the fund of our pleasure, let each pay his *shot* ;
> Far hence be the sad, the lewd fop, and the sot.—*B. Jonson.*

> I called for oysters and whisky, and waited for him to come back and *pay* his share of the *shot.*—*Sam Slick*, 3d *Series*, ch. 9.

SHOT IN THE NECK. Drunk. A Southern phrase.

SHOTE. A young hog ; a pig partially grown. This old English word is written in different forms in several of the counties of England. Cotgrave (1611) spells it *shote, shoat,* and *shoot,* and defines it, " a hog that is a year or under a year old." Bailey, Martin, and Johnson, spell it *shoot ;* Ainsworth, *shote ;* Lemon, *shot ;* Moor and Forby, *shot* and *shoat ;* Holloway, *shoot* and *sheet ;* Ray, *sheat, shote,* and *shoot ;* and Ray remarks, that " In Essex they call it a *shote.*" In this country the common form is *shote,* used for a young hog.—*Worcester.*

SHOTE. An idle, worthless man. ' A poor *shote.*' It is also provincial in England in this sense.

SHRINKAGE. A shrinking or contraction into a less compass. ' Make an allowance for the *shrinkage* of grain in drying.'— *Webster.*

> A new carriage-wheel has been invented, the spokes of which, should they become loose through wear or *shrinkage,* are made tight by a few turns with a wrench.—*N. Y. Tribune.*

SHUCK. The outer husk or shell of the walnut, chestnut, &c. ; or the husk of Indian corn. In England, the word is applied to pods as well as husks ; as, *pea-shucks*. *Not worth shucks*, is a Southern expression meaning good for nothing.

> If them thar is all he's got to offer, he aint worth *shucks*; and if you don't lick him, you aint worth *shucks*, neither.—*Robb, Squatter Life.*

> They had three or four hounds, and one great big yellow cow, what wasn't worth *schuks* to trail.—*Maj. Jones's Courtship*, p. 48.

SHUT. Quit; rid. *To be shut of*, or *to get shut of*, signifies to be or to get rid of. We also say, to be or get *shot* of. The expression is common in England.

> " Do you call those houzen—those things that have stoops to them ?" as he saw here and there a log cabin or unpainted hut, such as abound in the sparsely settled regions of the South. " They pass for houses hereabouts," replied Mr. S——, " though the original owners have generally contrived to get *shut* of them and gone coon-hunting to the Mississippi."—*Letter in N. Y. Journal of Commerce.*

TO SHUT UP. To hold one's tongue. A vulgar expression.

> Jones was singing, " 'Tis the Star Spangled Banner ;" but was soon made *to shut up*, and Leviller's name was called.—*Pickings from the Picayune.*

> Did you ever see a marmaid ? Well, then, I reckon you'd best *shut up* ; 'cause I have—and marmen too, and marmisses.—*Burton, Waggeries.*

> I order you again *to shut up*, said the watchman. There aint no two ways about it—you must either *shut up* yourself, or I'll *shut you up* in a winking.—*N. O. Picayune*, p. 119.

SHY. A fling.

> Lord Brougham could not lay the first stone to University College Hospital without having a fling at Oxford and Cambridge. If his Lordship gets a stone in his hand, he must, it seems, have a *shy* at somebody.—*London Punch.*

TO SHY. To throw a light substance, as a flat stone, or a shell, with a careless jerk.

> Just to make matters lively, I headed up alongside of Molly, and *shyed* a few soft things at her, such as asking how she liked bar steaks cooked, and if Jim warn't equal in the elbow to a mad panter's tail, and such amusin' conversation.—*Robb, Squatter Life.*

TO SHY. To turn aside, or start, as a horse; to *sheer*.— *Forby.*

> This horse don't *shy*, does he ? inquired Mr. Pickwick. *Shy*, sir ? He wouldn't *shy*, if he was to meet a vaggin load of monkeys with their tails burnt off.—*Pickwick Papers*, Ch. V.

They drove to his assistance, but the horses *shyed* off at the terrific conduct of the bull.—*Knickerbocker Mag.*, Vol. VI. p. 550.

TO SHY. To hang about.

I was kind of *shying* round and looking at the everlastin' sight of books, when he came in.—*Maj. Downing, May-day in New York*, p. 1.

SICK AS A HORSE. 'I'm *as sick as a horse,*' is a vulgar phrase which is used when a person is exceedingly sick. As a horse is larger than a man, it is customary to use it by way of comparison to denote largeness or excess either in a serious or ludicrous way, as horse-chestnut, horse-leech, horse-laugh, &c. We also say, *as sick as a dog.*

SIDE-SADDLE FLOWER. (Lat. *Sarracenia.*) A plant, as well as its whole genus, of very singular structure. It grows in swamps and meadows.—*Bigelow's Plants of Boston.*

SIGHT. A great many.—*Brockett, Glossary. A sight of people,* is a great multitude. *A sight of things,* a great many. The same expressions are used in Yorkshire, England, where they also say, a ' vast of folks,' which is hardly more elegant than our Western phrase, ' a heap of folks.' *Sight* is used in most of the Northern and Eastern, and *heap* in the Southern and Western States.

SIGHT. In North Carolina the distance that can be seen on a road is called a *sight.*

TO SIGNALIZE. To communicate information by means of signals or telegraph. A new and absurd use of the word.

The ship was *signalized* about eight o'clock this morning, and came up the harbor in fine style.—*N. Y. Com. Adv.*, Jan. 17, 1848.

SILVER FOX. A black fox, with white king-hairs interspersed on the back of it.—*Cartwright's Labrador.* Like the *cross-fox*, this variety is rare. They are found in the United States and Canada. Their skins are used for ladies' muffs, and bring a high price.

SIMON PURE. ' The real *Simon Pure,*' is a phrase meaning the genuine article; the real thing; as, ' This whisky is the real *Simon Pure.*'

SIRS. This plural is adopted by many persons in commercial correspondence in beginning their letters. Instead of the word *gentlemen,* addressed to a firm, they write, *Dear Sirs.*

SCARY, or SKEARY. Frightened.

> I got a little *scary*, and a good deal mad; there I was perched up on a sawyer, bobbin' up and down in the water.—*Robb.*

SIXES AND SEVENS. ' To be at *sixes and sevens*,' is to be in a state of disorder and confusion. A ludicrous expression that has been long in use.—*Johnson.*

> John once turned his mother out of doors, to her great sorrow ; for his affairs went on at *sixes and sevens.*—*Arbuthnot.*

> California is less than ever attached to the central authority of Mexico Everything is at *sixes and sevens.*—*N. O. Paper*, Sept. 7, 1845.

> In Mr. Johnson's arrangement of the mails, he throws everything into *pi*, and all are at *sixes and sevens* under his vigilant administration.—*N. Y. Com. Adv.*, Jan. 10, 1848.

TO SIZZLE. To hiss from the action of fire.—*Forby.*

> From the ends of the wood the sap fries and drips on the *sizzling* coals below, and flies off in angry steam.—*Margaret*, p. 159.

SKEERSOME. Frightful.

> It's cruel *skeersome* about there.—*Margaret*, p. 275.

SKETCHILY. In a sketchy manner.

> The short papers in Mr. W. A. Jones's Essays are generally analytical, political, or *sketchily* descriptive.—*Southern Quart. Rev.*, March, 1837.

TO SKEW. To walk obliquely.—*Todd.*

> Child, you must walk strait, without *skiewing* and shailing to every step you set.—*L'Estrange.*

> Thus linked, sideling, *skewing*, filing as they could through the trees and brush, they soon emerged in the road.—*Margaret*, p. 27.

> The sleds *skewed*, brushed, and bumped along.—*Ibid.*

SKID. A piece of light timber from ten to twenty feet in length, upon which heavier timber is rolled or slid from place to place.

SKILTS. A sort of brown tow trowsers formerly worn in New England, very large, and reaching just below the knees.

> The lad's *skilts*, through which were thrust his lean dry shanks, gave him a semblance to a peasant of Gascony on *stilts.*—*Margaret*, p. 22.

SKIN-FLINT. A niggardly, close-fisted person—one so parsimoniously mean, that he would perform that operation were it possible.—*Brockett's North County Words.*

TO SKINK. (Ang. Sax. *scencan*.) To serve drink. Dr. Johnson says this word is wholly obsolete in England.

Come, crush a glass with your dear papa, and all this nice company. You have *skinked* long enough.—*Margaret*, p. 300.

SKIPPER. The cheese maggot.—*Webster*.

SKRIMMAGE. A corruption of *skirmish*, used in the Western States; probably of Irish origin.

We felt confident that we should meet with large bands of Indians, with whom we should have an occasional "*skrimmage*."—*Kendall's Sante Fé Expedition*, Vol. I. p. 66.

SKUNK. (*Mephitis putorius*.) A small, carnivorous American quadruped, allied to the weasel and badger, and very fetid. An aboriginal or Indian term.—*Worcester*.

SKUNK CABBAGE. (Lat. *Ictodes fœtidus*.) A strong-scented, repulsive plant, exceedingly meritorious of the name it bears. The odor depends on a volatile principle not separable by distillation. This plant has been found useful in asthma and some other diseases.—*Bigelow's Plants of Boston*.

SKUNKHEAD. The popular name, on the sea-coast, of the Pied Duck of ornithologists.—*Nat. Hist. of New York*.

TO SKY A COPPER. To toss up a cent.

Didge said he was like *skying a copper*—head or tail.—*Crockett, Tour*.

SKY-RACKET. The vulgar pronunciation of *sky-rocket*.

SLANG-WHANGER. This curious word is defined by Mr. Pickering, as signifying "a writer or noisy talker, who makes use of that sort of political or other cant, which amuses the rabble, and is called by the vulgar name of *slang*." The word frequently occurs in Paulding's Salmagundi; but it is now seldom or never heard.

SLANG-WHANGING. Political cant.

Part of the customary *slang-whanging* against all other nations is habitual to the English press.—*N. Y. Com. Adv.*, Oct. 10, 1845.

TO SLAB OFF. I do not know the exact meaning of this expression.

You must take notice that I am *slabb'd* off from the election, and am nothing but a "voter;" and this gives me a right to dictate to the rest.—*Crockett, Tour*, p. 212.

SLAB. The outside of a piece of timber or log sawn off at a mill. As the bark is on one side, it is useless as merchandise.

The same term is employed in England, and is noticed by Ray and Grose.

SLANTENDICULAR. Aslant; oblique. Used in low language.

> Pony got mad and sent the Elder right slap over his head *slantendicularly*, on the broad of his back into the river.—*Sam Slick in England*, ch. 28.

SLAP-JACKS. Pancakes made of the whole size of the frying-pan or spider. A country girl formerly was not considered eligible for marriage until she could make a shirt, and toss a slap-jack fairly right into the middle of the pan. In Norfolk, England, they are called *flap-jacks*.

SLAT. A narrow piece of board or timber, used to fasten together large pieces; as, the *slats* of a cart or chair.—*Webster.* Mr. Worcester calls it "an American corruption of the word *sloat.*"

ΓO SLAT. A word of uncertain derivation, signifying to throw down with violence.—*Toone's Glossary.*

> *Slatted* his brains out, then soused him in the briny sea.—*Old Play, The Malcontents.*

> With that, I handed him my axe, and he *slatted* about the chamber a spell.—*Maj. Downing's Letters*, p. 200.

> Suz alive! but warn't my dander up to hear myself called a flat? down I *slat* the basket and upsot all the berries.—*Lafayette Chronicle.*

> Aunt Nancy would retire to the kitchen, and, taking up the dipper, would *slat* round the hot water from a kettle.—*N. Y. Com. Adv.*, May 15, 1846.

SLAZY. A corrupt pronunciation of *sleazy* or *sleezy;* i. e. weak, wanting substance; thin; flimsy. It is also pronounced so in some parts of England.

SLED. A carriage or vehicle moved on runners; much used in America for conveying heavy weights in winter, as timber, wood, stone, and the like.—*Webster.*

SLEDDING. The means of conveying on sleds; snow sufficient for the running of sleds.—*Webster.*

TO SLEEP. Sometimes used as an active verb; as, 'This steamboat can *sleep* three hundred passengers,' i. e. can furnish sleeping accommodations for them. We have heard of a landlady who said 'she could *eat* fifty people in her house, but could not *sleep* half the number.'

SLEIGH. A vehicle moved on runners, and greatly used in America for transporting persons or goods on snow or ice.— *Webster*. In England it is called a *sledge*. During the winter of 1844, after a fall of snow in London, an English newspaper observed that " the Queen was making preparations for *sledge-driving*," which in America few would understand to mean, that Her Majesty was about taking a *sleigh-ride*.

SLEIGHING. The state of the snow which admits of running sleighs.—*Webster*. As, ' good sleighing,' ' bad sleighing;' and in the winter when there is no snow, we say there is ' no sleighing.'

2. The act of riding in a sleigh.—*Webster*.

SLEIGH-BELL. A small hollow ball, made of bell-metal, having a hole in it that passes half round its circumference, and containing a small solid ball, of a size not to escape. These bells are fastened to leathern straps, which commonly pass round the necks of horses. They were formerly, by the Dutch, attached to small plates, which were buckled to various parts of the harness ; but this caused a motion annoying to horses.—*Cooper, Satanstoe*, Vol. I. p. 216.

SLEIGH-RIDE. Used both as a noun and as a verb.

> In winter we *sleigh-ride*, coast, skate, and snow-ball.—*Margaret*.

TO SLEW, or SLUE. In seaman's language, to turn anything, as a barrel, &c., about its perpendicular axis ; to turn around.

SLEWED. Moderately drunk. A common expression in the United States, and also used in Yorkshire, England.

SLICE. A common name in parts of New York and Canada for a large fire-shovel formed of a bar of iron flattened at one end.

SLICK. The popular pronunciation of *sleek*, and so written by some authors.—*Webster*. It is also used adverbially in vulgar language, like many other adjectives.

" This word," says Todd, " was formerly written *slick;* and *slick* or *slicken* is still our northern word." It is also provincial in Kent, while, in other parts of England, the verb *to slick,* to comb or make sleek the hair, is provincial.—*Hollo-way's Prov. Dict.*

Dr. Jamieson also notices it as used in Scotland, *slik,* smooth, slippery, for *sleek.*

> Her flesh tender as is a chicke,
> With bent browes, smooth and *slike.*—*Chaucer, Rom. of the Rose.*

> When silver bow'd Apollo bred, in the Pierian mead,
> Both *slicke* and daintie, yet were both in war of wound'rous dread.—
> *Chapman, Homer.*

> Glass attracts but weakly; some *slick* stones, and thick glasses indiffer-ently.—*Brown, Vulgar Errors.*

> That the bodie thereof is not all over smoothe and *slicke* (as we see in birds' eggs), is shewed by good arguments.—*Holland, Trans. of Pliny.*

> The rail-road company, out of sheer parsimony, have neglected to fence in their line, which goes *slick* through the centre of your garden.—*Black-wood's Mag.,* July, 1847 [*Letter from a Rail-way Witness*].

> Well! one comfort is, that there ain't many folks to see how bad you look here in the woods! We ain't used to seein' folks look so dreadful *slick,*—so it don't matter.—*Mrs. Clavers's Forest Life,* Vol. I. p. 114.

> Singin' is a science which comes pretty tough at first; but it goes *slick* afterwards.—*Peter Cram of Tinnecum, Knick. Mag.,* 1841.

> Then here's to women, then to liquor;
> There's nothing swimmin' can be *slicker.*—*Boatman's Song.*

> The Senate could not pass Mr. Stevenson through for England. The reason was, he was a-going through right *slick,* till he came to his coat-pockets, and they were so full of papers written by Ritchie, that he stuck fast, and hung by the flaps.—*Crockett, Tour,* p. 120.

TO SLICK UP. To dress up; to make fine.

> Mrs. Flyer was *slicked up* for the occasion, in the snuff-colored silk she was married in.—*Mrs. Clavers, A New Home,* p. 211.

> The house was all *slicked up* as neat as a pin, and the things in every room all sot to rights.—*Maj. Downing, May-day,* p. 43.

> The caps most in vogue then were made of dark, coarse, knotted twine, like a cabbage-net, worn, as the wives said, to save *slicking up,* and to hide dirt.—*Carlton, The New Purchase,* Vol. I. p. 72.

SLICK AS A WHISTLE. A proverbial simile, in common use throughout the United States. To do anything as *slick as a whistle,* is to do it very smoothly, perfectly, adroitly.

> You know I told you in my last letter, I was going to bring Miss Mary up to the chalk at Christmas. Well, I done it as *slick as a whistle.*—*Maj. Jones's Courtship,* p. 94.

SLICK AS GREASE. Another *classical* expression, conveying the same idea as the foregoing.

TO LET SLIDE. To let go; as, ' that fish you have hooked
is not fit to eat; *let him slide.*'

SLIM. Weak; slight; slender; feeble; worthless.—*Worcester.*

> The church of Rome indeed was allowed to be the principal church.
> But why? Was it in regard to the succession to St. Peter? No, that
> was a *slim* excuse.—*Barrow on the Pope's Supremacy.*

> Now how vain and *slim* are all these [arguments of fatalists], if com-
> pared with the solid and manly encouragement which our religion offers.—
> *Killingbeck, Sermons,* p. 376.

> From this central spot, the condition of things is more apparent, and
> could Mr. Calhoun's friends see the truth, they might readily discover how
> *slim* was his chance for election.—*Newspaper.*

> *Gen.* What! not homesick, are you?
> *Doolittle.* I guess I be; for I feel pretty *slim.* But how to get hum is
> the devil on't, as Jack the sailor says.—*D. Humphreys, The Yankee in
> England.*

SLIMSEY. Flimsey; frail. Most frequently applied to cotton or other cloth.

> The building is old and *slimsy.*—*Margaret,* p. 329.

SLING. A drink composed of equal parts of rum and water
sweetened.—*Rush.*

SLINK. A sneaking fellow.

> I despise a *slink.*—*Chron. of Pineville,* p. 139.

SLINKY. Thin; lank.

SLIP. 1. The opening between wharves or in a dock.—*Webster.*

This word is peculiar to New York, where we have Peck
Slip, Burling Slip, Old Slip, Coenties Slip, etc.

2. In New England, a long seat or narrow pew in a church.
—*Webster.* When there is a door, they are called pews;
when without doors and free to all, *slips.* This, I believe, is
the difference between them.

SLIP. An escape; a desertion.—*Johnson.* ' To give one the
slip,' means to escape, or run away.

> The more shame for her goody-ship,
> To give so near a friend the *slip.*—*Hudibras.*

The daw did not like his companion, and gave him the *slip*, and away into the woods.—*L'Estrange.*

SLIPE. A distance.

Well, I've got a long *slipe* off from my steamboat, the Hunter; and I had better look up the Captain.—*Crockett, Tour,* p. 145.

SLIPPER-DOWN. A vulgar name in some parts of Connecticut for hasty pudding. The etymology is obvious.

SLIPPERY. Uncertain; changeable.—*Johnson.* That man's a *slippery* fellow; i. e. no dependence can be placed in him. One who is disposed to cheat or obtain undue advantage, is called a *slippery* fellow. It is used alike in England and America.—See *Grose, Prov. Dict.*

Merchants who resort to drumming as a means for selling their goods are apt to be considered as very *slippery* fellows.—*Perils of Pearl Street.*

SLIVER. A piece of any substance; as wood torn or split off. This word is, in this country, commonly pronounced slĭver; but the English orthoëpists all pronounce it slīver.—*Worcester.*

When frost will not suffer to dike and to hedge,
Then get thee a heat, with thy beetle and wedge;
Once Hallowmas come, and a fire in the hall,
Such *slivers* do well for to lie by the wall.—*Tusser, Husbandry.*

Alas! that he all hole or of him some *slivers*
Should have his refute in so digne a place,
That Jove, him sone out of your herte race.—*Chaucer, Troil. and Cress.* B. 3.

In New England this word is used as a verb as well as a noun.

As there was nothin' else to get hold of, I just *slivered* a great big bit off the leg of the chair, and made a tooth-pick of it.—*Sam Slick in England.*

TO LET SLIVER. To let slip, let fly, i. e. to fire.

Old Yelp smelled the bar; and as soon as I clapped peeper on him, I let *sliver*, when the varmint dropped.—*Robb, Squatter Life.*

SLOMMACK. A slattern.

TO SLOPE. To run away. A new but very common vulgarism.

As the officers approached, some hid themselves in their ovens, some under their beds; but a majority *sloped* without hats, shoes, or coats.—*N. Y. Com. Adv.,* Nov. 3, 1845.

The instant an English mob sees two dragoons coming, they jist run like a flock of sheep afore a couple of bull-dogs, and *slope* off, properly skeered. —*Sam Slick in England*, ch. 27.

The editor of the Eagle cannot pay his board bill, and fears are entertained that he will *slope* without liquidating the debt.—*Robb, Squatter Life.*

The constables appeared with attachments ; each person interested seized his own goods, while the master and clerk *sloped* to parts unknown.—*Baltimore Patriot*, July 10, 1846.

SLOPS. Large and loose trowsers, from which loose clothing is called slops. The word, says Todd, was formerly used in the singular ; as in Chaucer :

His overest *slop* is not worth a mite.

Slop-clothing is the term now universally applied to ready made clothing for seamen. It was so used in 1691.

The *slop-seller* is a person crept into the navy, I mean to monopolize the vending of clothing only, but since the restoration of King Charles the Second.—*Maydman, Naval Speculat.* (1691).

SLOP-SHOP. A place where slop-clothing is sold.

SLUMP. A favorite dish in New England, called an *apple slump,* is made by placing raised bread or dough around the sides of an iron pot, which is then filled with apples and sweetened with molasses. Called in other parts of the country an *apple pot-pie.*

TO SLUMP. To slip or fall into a wet or dirty place.— *Brockett's North County Words.* Provincial in various parts of England, and also used in New England. Mr. O. Wendell Holmes, in describing the school-boy, in a short poem read at the late festival in Berkshire, Massachusetts, says :

By the side of yon river, he weeps and he *slumps,*
His boots filled with water, as if they were pumps,
Till, sated with rapture, he steals to his bed
With a glow in his heart and a cold in his head.

SLUMPY. Marshy ; easily broken through.—*Jamieson. Worcester.*

We came back by another path that's *slumpier* than t'other [in consequence of the rain.]—*Sam Slick in England*, ch. 23.

SLUNG (the pret. of *sling*), is often heard instead of *swung.*

We swung round the wharf; and when the captain told the people who I was, they *slung* their hats, and gave three cheers.—*Crockett, Tour down East*, p. 37.

SLUNG-SHOT. An offensive weapon formed of two leaden or iron bullets fastened together by a piece of rope five or six inches long. One bullet is held in the hand, while the other hangs outside by the rope which passes between the second and third fingers. A blow from it on the head will fell the strongest man.

SLUSH. Grease or fat from salt meat.—*Worcester.* The refuse grease from cooking on board ship, which is one of the perquisites of the cook.

SLUSH, or SLOSH. This term is often used by the people of New England, in speaking of the state of the roads, when they are covered with snow, and a thaw takes place. It is very common to hear people say, ' the roads are *sloshy ;* it is very *sloshy going,*' &c. None of the English dictionaries have this word; but all of them, I believe, except Bailey's, have the term *sludge,* and define it as Dr. Johnson does— ' Mire, dirt mixed with water.' Grose has *sludge* in the same sense, as a provincial term, peculiar to the North of England. Marshall also has *sludge* among his provincialisms of the Midland counties, *sluss* among those of Norfolk, and *slush* among those of Yorkshire ; and he defines them all nearly in the same words.—*Pickering.*

> It sometimes happens that a fall of snow in the night time will cover the deep water where the feiths are, with snow and *slush.*—*State, Leslie of Powis,* 1803.

SLUSHY. Consisting of soft mud, or of snow and water.— *Webster.*

SMALL FRY. Young children ; persons of little importance.

> Let there be any question to be decided, which Gen. Jackson has set his heart on, and you will see all the *small fry* as busy as pismires, and the big bugs drumming up the drones, &c.—*Crockett, Tour down East,* p. 20.

SMALL POTATOES. An epithet applied to persons, and signifying mean, contemptible ; as, ' He is very *small pota- toes.*' *Small potatoes* are not fit for eating, and except for the feeding of hogs and cattle, are worthless; hence the expression as applied to men. It is sometimes put into the more emphatic form of *small potatoes and few in a hill ;* see Sam Slick in England for an explanation of the latter, ch. 6.

Give me an honest old soldier for the Presidency—whether a Whig or Democrat—and I will leave your *small potato* politicians and petty-fogging lawyers to those who are willing to submit the destiny of this great nation to such hands.—*N. Y. Herald*, Dec. 13, 1846.

The very incidents of the meeting, and the names of the speakers [noticed by the Washington Union], induce a strong suspicion that it was rather *small potatoes.*—*N. Y. Com. Adv.*, April 15, 1848.

SMART. Quick; active; intelligent. 'He is a *smart* business man.' The word appears to be not now used in this sense in England, although Johnson gives several meanings very nearly allied to it. The corresponding English term is *clever.*

SMART CHANCE. A good opportunity; a fair chance. A vulgar expression.

He has a *smart chance* of getting a better character.—*S. Slick in England*, ch. 9.

Says I, "Friend Wolfe," for I seed there was a *smart chance* of a row, "play I won't."—*S. Slick*, 3d Ser. p. 117.

SMART CHANCE. A good deal; a large quantity; large company; a great number. A singular expression used in the Southern and Western States, but never heard in the Eastern.—*Sherwood's Georgia.*

I don't pretend to say, stranger, what sort of cattle you have in your country, but I reckon there's a right *smart chance* of self-conceit among you Yankees.—*Letter from the South, N. Y. Journ. of Com.*

There's a *smart chance* of cigars there in the bar, stranger, if you'll try some of them, said one of the hooshiers.—*Hoffman, Winter in the West.*

We had a "*smart chance*" of snow on Thursday; it fell during the day to the depth of two inches, which makes a considerable snow-storm in this part of the world.—*Wilmington, N. C. Commercial*, Dec. 10.

SMART SPRINKLE. A good deal; a good many. Used in the interior of the Western States.

In answer to some query about snakes, our landlord said there was a *smart sprinkle* of rattlesnake on Red Run; and a powerful nice day to sun themselves.—*Carlton, The New Purchase*, Vol. I. p. 85.

SMASHER. A low word denoting anything very large, or larger than another of the same kind. It is used in the same sense in the North of England.—*Brockett's Glossary.*

Put up your benefit for that night; and if you don't have a *smasher*, with at least six wreaths, say I don't understand managing the theatres.—*Field, Drama at Pokerville.*

SMEAR-CASE. (Dutch, *Smeer-kaas.*) A preparation of milk made to be spread on bread, whence its name; otherwise called Cottage-cheese.

TO SMOKE. To find any one out; to discover anything meant to be kept secret.—*Halliwell.*

> The two free-booters, seeing themselves *smoaked*, told their third brother he seemed to be a gentleman and a boone companion; they prayed him, therefore, to sit down with silence, and sethence dinner was not yet ready, he should heare all.—*Dekker's Lanthorne,* 1629.

> The fellow takes me for a country dealer. Good! I'll *smoke* him. Ahem! sir, how do you sell iron feather beds by the gross?—*Perils of Pearl Street,* p. 77.

SMOOTH. A meadow, or grass field.

> Get some plantain and dandelion on the *smooth* for greens.—*Margaret.*

TO SMOUTCH. To gouge; to take unfair advantage. Colloquial in New York.

TO SMOUZE. To demolish, as with a blow. Used in Ohio.

SMUDGE. A heap of damp combustibles placed on the windward side of the house and partially ignited, that the inky steam may smother or drive away mosquitoes.—*Mrs. Clavers.*

> I have had a *smudge* made in a chafing dish at my bedside, after a serious deliberation between choking and being devoured at small mouthfuls; and I conscientiously recommend choking.—*Mrs. Clavers's Forest Life.*

TO SMUTCH. To blacken with smoke, soot, or coal.—*Webster.* 'I have *smutched* my fingers.' The word is provincial in England, and is found in the old writers. In the United States, as in Scotland, it is pronounced *smootch,* and is never heard except colloquially.

> Thou hast *smutched* thy nose.—*Shakspeare, Winter Evening Tale,* I. 2.

> Have you mark'd but the fall of snow,
> Before the soil hath *smutched* it.—*Ben Jonson, Wanderer.*

SNAG. A tree having its roots fastened in the bottom of a river; or a branch of a tree thus fastened. These are common in the Mississippi and Missouri rivers, and frequently destroy steamboats which come in contact with them by piercing their bows, or sides. This word is not a new one, and is defined by Johnson as " a jag or sharp protuberance."

SNAGGED. Run against a snag, or projecting branch of a sunken tree.

SNAKE-HEAD. An object of dread to travellers on railways. The end of an iron rail, which sometimes is thrown up in front of the car wheels, and passes through the cars. Serious accidents have been caused by them. They occur, however, only with flat rails.

> The road to Petersburg consists of an iron strap laid upon pine timber, and is beautifully diversified with that peculiar half horizontal, vibrating rail, known as " *snake's head*." Frequently, during our short ride, an iron *snake* would strike his heavy *head* against the iron fenders of our car ; and then, as we rolled on unharmed, he would shake himself as if in wrath awaiting another opportunity for vengeance.—*N. Y. Tribune.*

TO SNAKE. To crawl like a snake. A common expression at the West. A fine example of the use of this term is given in the N. Y. Tribune, from one of the Western newspapers :

> In Iowa, as in other new countries, the duties of a judge often begin before a court-house or place of shelter has been provided. Not long since, Judge Williams was obliged to hold his first court beneath the shade of a large tree, where logs were rolled up for seats, a larger one being provided for the Judge. The clerk used a shingle on his knee for a desk ; and the jury, after being charged by the judge, were sent in care of a sheriff to a hollow, or ravine, where they could sit in conclave beyond the view of the court or spectators.
>
> The grass grew very tall in the neighborhood, and the jurymen lay down in a ring in the grass, where they could more perfectly exclude themselves from observation. The jury had not been long in their quarters, when a tall, raw-boned fellow, rose up and addressed the judge as follows :
>
> " May it please your honor, I wish to speak to you." " Order, sir ; what is it ?" " Judge," continued he, with the utmost gravity, " is it right for fellows to *snake* in the grass ?" " How ? what is that, sir ?" " Why, you see," said the Yankee, " there's some fellows who's tarnal fraid the Grand Jury will find something agin 'em, which they desarve, and they are *snaking* up to the Grand Jury, on their bellies in the grass, kind of trying to hear what the Jury are talking about." " No," responded the Judge, with as much gravity as he could command, " I do not allow of *snaking*. Here, Mr. Sheriff, go station a guard around each *Jury's hollow*, and if a man is found ' *snaking* ' have him brought before me, and I will cause him to be punished. Indeed, if this *snaking* is persisted in, I shall recommend a special act to be passed, making it a misdemeanor."
>
> The fact was, as the Judge said, there were present at the time some

barefooted, vagrant rascals, who were, probably, justly suspected of horse-stealing, and had " *snaked it* " on the Grand Jury, in order to find out whether the Jury intended to present them ; and, if so, to gain time by this clandestine warning, and flee the jurisdiction of the Court by escaping into Missouri.

TO SNAKE OUT. To drag out ; to haul out, as a snake from its hole. A farmer in clearing land, attaches a chain to a stump or log, whereby to draw it out ; this he calls, *snaking it out.* Maj. Downing says, in speaking of a person who fell into the river :

> We *snaked* him *out* of that scrape as slick as a whistle.—*Letters*, p. 14.

> I went down again and found the cow as dead as a herrin'. We skinned her and *snaked* her *out* of the barn upon the snow.—*Evidence before a Court in Boston, Daily Adv.*, March, 1848.

SNAP. Applied to the weather ; as, ' a cold *snap*,' i. e. a period of sudden cold weather. A common expression.

SNAPS. Young kidney-beans in the pod.

SNAPPED. Drunk. Used at the South.

> I like to forgot to tell you 'bout cousin Pete. He got *snapt* on egg-nog when he heard of my engagement.—*Maj. Jones's Courtship*, p, 102.

SNAPPING-TURTLE. (Genus, *chelonura*.) A reptile common to all parts of the United States, so named from its propensity to snap at everything within its reach.

SNARL. An entanglement, as a twisted thread ; a quarrel ; an angry contest. Provincial in England, and colloquial in the United States.—*Worcester.*

> Her mother gets her to pick a *snarl* out of the yarn she is winding.—*Margaret*, p. 160.

> This gallant officer and estimable man [Sir John Harvey] has been transferred from Nova Scotia to Newfoundland, where Lord Falkland had got into a *snarl*.—*Com. Adv.*, April 1, 1846.

> The members of the House of Representatives got themselves into a most admirable *snarl* on Saturday afternoon, by their proceedings in reference to the recent case of resistance to the serving of a habeas corpus writ. —*Boston Traveller*, Feb. 12.

> Men, you have all got into a sort of *snarl*, as the militia Captain said to his men, when he could not keep them in line.—*Georgia Scenes*, p. 149.

SNATCH. A hasty repast ; a snack. Scottish.—*Jamieson.*

> Our kind host and hostess would not go before taking a *snatch*, as they called it ; which was in truth a very good dinner.—*Boswell's Journal.*

The most relishing *snatch* of slumber out of bed, is the one which a tired person takes, before he retires for the night, while lingering in his sitting-room.—*Leigh Hunt, Indicator*, ch. 21.

SNATHE. } SNEAD. } The crooked handle of a mowing scythe. An agricultural term common with the farmers both of England and of this country.

This is fixed on a long *sneed*, or strait handle.—*Evelyn*, B. II. ch. 6.

When stormy days constrain to quit the field,
The house or barn may useful business yield ;
There crooked *snathe* of flexile sallow make,
Or of tough ash, the fork-stall and the rake.—*Scott, Amœbæan Ecl.*

SNEAKING NOTION. To have a *sneaking notion* for a lady, is to have a timid or concealed affection for her.

Well, I always used to have a sort of a *sneakin' notion* of Mary Stallins. —*Maj. Jones's Courtship*, p. 11.

An army such as me would fright the devil—
What are ye giggling at ? Can't ye be civil ?
There—that's well done ; now I've a *sneaking notion*—
When I git hum—I'll git some grand promotion.—*D. Humphreys, The Yankee in England*, p. 102.

TO SNICKER, or SNIGGER. To laugh slily, wantonly, or contemptuously ; to laugh in one's sleeve.—*Johnson*.

Then I heard the gals *snickering* and laughing in the next room, and I began to see how it was.—*Maj. Jones's Courtship*, p. 18.

Ha, ha, ha ! *snickered* out the woman, more afraid of paper money than the doctor's knife.—*Margaret*, p. 273.

Never mind, says the General, if you can't get them 'are pantaloons mended, the State'll give you a new pair. And then we all snorted and *snickered*.—*Maj. Downing's Letters*, p. 15.

A hyst is bad enough, without being *snickered* at.—*Neal's Sketches*.

TO SNIGGLE. A method of fishing for eels in small streams and ponds.

Sniggling is thus performed. In a warm day, take a small strong hook, tied to a string about a yard long ; and then into one of the holes, where an eel may hide herself, with the help of a short stick, put in your bait leisurely, and as far as you may, conveniently ; if within the sight of it, the eel will bite instantly, and as certainly gorge it ; pull him out by degrees.—*Izaak Walton, Angler*.

In the darkest nights we rowed across the pond and *sniggled* for eels.— *Margaret*, p. 234.

SNIPPER-SNAPPER.   An effeminate young man ; a trifler.

SNIPPY.   Finical ; and substantively, a finical person.   A woman's word.   In the South they use the word *sniptious*.

SNIPSNAP.   Tart dialogue ; with quick replies.—*Todd's Johnson*.

> Dennis and dissonance, and captious art,
> And *snipsnap* short, and interruption smart.—*Pope, Dunciad*.

> Plucks *snipsnaps* with his wife, cracks on Hash, shows his white teeth to Margaret.—*Margaret*, p. 161.

TO SNOOP.   (Dutch, *snoepen*.)   Applied to children, servants, and others, who clandestinely eat dainties or other victuals which have been put aside, not for their use.   A servant who goes slyly into a dairy-room and drinks milk from a pan, would be said to be *snooping*.   The term is peculiar to New York.

SNOOZE.   Sleep ; as ' he lay in a drunken *snooze*.'

SNOOZER.   A thief who follows the business of robbing the boarders at hotels.   He takes board and lodgings, and endeavors to share a room and become familiar with some country merchant; after which, by various tricks, he succeeds in robbing him.   The police reports of New York exhibit frequent cases of this system of depredation.

SNORE.   *I snore!*   An exclamation used in New England.

> I hain't lived in the woods to be skeered at owls, *I snore*.—*Margaret*.

SNORE.   (Dutch, *snoer*.)   A string with a button on one end to spin a top with.   This term is retained by the boys of New York.

TO SNORT.   To laugh outright.—*Brockett's Glossary*.   Used in low language in New England.

> We all *snorted* and snickered.—*Maj. Downing's Letters*, p. 15.

SNORTER.   A dashing, riotous fellow.   A vulgar Western term.

> " I'm a roaring earthquake in a fight," sung out one of the half-horse, half-alligator sort of fellows, " a real *snorter* of the universe. I can strike as hard as fourth proof lightning, and keep it up, rough and tumble, as long as a wild cat."—*Thorpe's Backwoods*, p. 183.

SNOWBALL.   A jeering appellation for a negro.

TO SNUGGLE. To lie close for convenience or warmth.— *Johnson.* Seldom used except in familiar language.

SO is often improperly used for *such*, as in the phrase :

> Prof. W——, who has acquired *so* high distinction in teaching the elements of music and singing.—*N. Y. Tribune.*

TO SOAK. To bake thoroughly. It is particularly applied to bread, which, to be good, must be macerated, as it were, in the caloric of the oven. If it be dough-baked, the complaint is, that it has not been sufficiently *soaked.*—*Holloway, Forby's Vocabulary.* This word is used in the same sense in New England.

TO SOAK. To drink intemperately.—*Johnson.*

> Let a drunkard see that his health decays, his estate wastes, yet the habitual thirst after his cups drives him to the tavern, though he has in his view the loss of health and plenty ; the least of which he confesses is far greater than the tickling of his palate with a glass of wine, or the idle chat of a *soaking*-club.—*Locke.*

SOAKER. A great drinker. In low language.—*Johnson.* 'An old *soaker*,' is a common name for a drunkard. *Groses's* definition is, " one that moistens his clay to make it stick together."

SOAP-LOCK. A lock of hair made to lie smooth by soaping it. Hence also a name given to a low set of fellows who lounge about the markets, engine-houses, and wharves of New York, and are always ready to engage in midnight rows or broils. It is, in fact, but another name for a Rowdy or Loafer. The name comes from their wearing long side locks, which they are said to smear with soap, in order to give them a sleek appearance ; whence the name.

> The way my last letter has cradled off the *soaplocks*, and imperials, and goat-knots, and musty shows, is truly alarming.—*Maj. Jones's Courtship.*

SOCIETY. In Connecticut, a number of families united and incorporated for the purpose of supporting public worship, is called an *ecclesiastical society.* This is a parish, except that it has not territorial limits. In Massachusetts such an incorporated society is usually called a parish, though consisting of persons only, without regard to society.—*Webster.*

SOCDOLAGER. A patent fish-hook, having two hooks which

close upon each other by means of a spring as soon as the fish bites.

TO SOCK.　To press by a hard blow a man's hat over his head and face.　Used in Rhode Island.　I have never heard it elsewhere.　The New York term is, *to crown.*

SOFT SOAP.　Flattery; blarney.　A vulgar phrase, though much used.

TO SOFT SOAP.　To flatter; to blarney.

> I am tired of this system of placemen *soft-soaping* the people,—telling them just before an election what fine, honest, noble, generous fellows they are, and then, just after election, turning their backs on them.—*Mike Walsh, Speech*, Sept. 1843.

SOFT SAWDER.　Flattery; blarney.

> Then he did a leadin' article on slavery and non-intervention, and spoke a little *soft-sawder* about America.—*Sam Slick in England*, ch. 20.

> The Washington Union cracks the whip gently about the ears of the Democracy, and winds up with a counter-application of *soft-sawder*, in the shape of appeals to patriotism.—*N. Y. Com. Adv.*, Jan. 6, 1847.

TO SOFT SAWDER.　To flatter.

> I don't like to be left alone with a gall; it's plaguy apt to set me a *soft-sawderin'* and a courtin'.—*Sam Slick in England*, p. 19.

SOME.　Somewhat; something.　**Ex.** ' He is *some* better than he was ;' ' it rains *some*,' &c.　Used chiefly by the illiterate.—*Pickering's Vocabulary.*

SOPHOMORE.　This word has generally been considered an American barbarism, but was probably introduced into our country at a very early period from the University of Cambridge, England.　Among the cant terms at that University, as given in the Gradus ad Cantabrigiam, we find Soph-Mor as the next distinctive appellation to Freshman.　It is added, that a writer in the Gentleman's Magazine thinks Mor an abbreviation of the Greek μωρία, introduced at a time when the Encomium Moreæ, the Praise of Foll y by Erasmus, was so generally used.　The ordinary derivation of the word, from σοφὸς and μωρὸς would seem, therefore, to be incorrect.　The young Sops at Cambridge appear, formerly, to have received the adjunct mor, μωρὸς, to their names, either as one they courted for the reason mentioned above, or as one given them in sport for the supposed exhibition of inflated feeling in entering upon their new honors. The term thus applied, seems to have passed at a very early period from Cambridge in England to Cambridge in America, as the next distinctive appellation to Freshmen, and thus to have been attached to the second of the four classes in our American Colleges, while it has now almost ceased to be known, even as a cant word, at the parent institution in England, from whence it came. This derivation of the word is rendered more probable by the fact that the early spelling was, to a great extent at least, Sophimore, as appears from the manuscripts of President Stiles of Yale College, and the records of the Harvard College, down to the period of the American Revolution. This word would be perfectly natural if Soph or Sophistu was considered as the basis of the word, but can hardly be explained if the ordinary derivation had then been regarded as the true one.—*Prof. Goodrich, new ed. Webster's Dic.*

SOSSLE, or SOZZLE. A lazy or sluttish woman. Provincial in Connecticut.

Mr. Todd gives this word, which he defines as a lazy fellow, on the authority of Cotgrave and Sherwood. In the south of England, a *soss-brangle* is a slatternly, lazy wench. This is precisely the sense in which *sossle* is used with us.

TO SOZZLE. To loll; to lounge; to go lazily or sluttishly about the house. A term used by housekeepers in certain parts of Connecticut. ' This woman *sozzles* up her work.' *To sozzle* is provincial in England, and means the same as *to soss;* i. e. to lounge, to loll.

> A sandpiper glided along the shore; she ran after it, but could not catch it; she sat down and *sozzled* her feet in the foam.—*Margaret,* p. 8.

SPACK AND APPLEJEES. (Dutch.) Pork and apples, cooked together. An ancient Dutch dish made in New York.

SPAKE. (Preterite of *speak*.) This antiquated word is still heard occasionally from the pulpit, as well as in conversation. —*Pickering's Vocab.*

SPAN. A span of horses consists of two of nearly the same color, and otherwise nearly alike, which are usually harnessed side by side. The word signifies properly the same as yoke, when applied to horned cattle, for buckling or fastening together. But in America, *span* always implies resemblance in color at least; it being an object of ambition with gentlemen, and with teamsters, to unite two horses abreast that are alike. —*Webster.* This use of the word is not mentioned in any of the English dictionaries or glossaries.

TO SPAN. To agree in color, or in color and size; as, 'The horses *span* well.' New England.—*Webster.*

SPAN-CLEAN.
SPANDY-CLEAN. } Very clean; perfectly clean.

TO SPARK IT. To court. Used chiefly in New England.

> You were a nation sight wiser than brother Jonathan, sister Keziah, poor little Aminadab, and all the rest; and above all, my owny, towny Lydia, the Deacon's darlin darter; with whom I've *sparked it*, pretty oftentimes, so late.—*D. Humphreys, The Yankee in England.*

SPARKING. 'To go a *sparking*,' is to go a courting; a common expression in the Northern States.

> Mr. Justice Crow was soon overtaken; Lieut. Col. Simcoe accosted him roughly, called him " Tory," nor seemed to believe his excuses; when, in the American idiom for courtship, he said, " he had only been *sparking*."—*Simcoe, Military Journal,* p. 73.

> He rolled his eyes horribly, and said that that was the way the young men cast sheep's eyes when they went a *sparking.*—*Mrs. Clavers's Western Clearings,* p. 16.

SPARROW GRASS. A vulgar pronunciation of *asparagus* both in England and America. Hence the celebrated charade by a certain alderman :

> " My first is a little thing vot hops,—(*sparrow*)
> My second brings us good hay crops,—(*grass*)
> My whole I eats with mutton chops,"—(*sparrow grass.*)—*Pegge, Anecdotes of the Eng. Lang.,* p. 54.

SPAT. A petty combat; a little quarrel or dissension. A vulgar use of the word in New England—*Webster.*

> The National Bank and the Mechanic's Banking Association have had a standing *spat* for some time.—*N. Y. Com. Adv.*

> We do not believe that Messrs. Buchanan and Walker have resigned their seats in the cabinet. There has been a *spat* of course; but there may be many more before either of the Secretaries will resign $6000 a year.— *N. Y. Tribune.*

TO SPAT. To dispute; to quarrel. A low word. New England.

TO SPAT THE HANDS. To slap the hands.

> The little Isabel leaped up and down *spatting her hands.*—*Margaret.*

SPEC. A bit; in the least.

> I doubled up my fist, for I did not like the treatment a *spec.*—*S. Slick in England,* ch. 2.

SPEC, for *speculation*; as, 'He made a good *spec* in flour.'

TO SPEECHIFY. To make a speech; to harangue.—*Webster.* A rather low word, and seldom heard except among bar-room politicians. It is not peculiar to America, though not in any English dictionary.

> The treaties continually going on in the bazaar for buying and selling, are carried on by *speechifying,* rather than by mere colloquies.—*Eöthen.*
> We'll forth in *posse comitatus,*
> And take the Fox, ere he escape us;
> Without a moment's pause he dies;—
> We'll hang him ere he *speechifies!*—*Reynard the Fox,* p. 143.

> The Dyaks of Borneo are very fond of *speechifying.*—*Keppel's Borneo.*

SPELL. (From Ang. Sax. *spelian,* to supply another's room; to act or be proxy for.—*Bosworth.*) A turn of work; a vicissitude of labor.—*Todd's Johnson.* It is often used in a secondary sense, to denote a short turn; a little time; a bout; a fit; and is applied particularly to work, to sickness, or to the weather. Provincial in England and colloquial in the United States.

> Their toil is so extreme as they cannot endure it above four hours in a day, but are succeeded by *spells;* the residue of their time they wear out at coytes and kayles.—*Carew.*
> Come, thou's had thy *spell,* it's now my time to put in a word.—*Carr's Craven Glossary.*
> Josiah Norton said he had come home from the South, where he had been pedling a *spell.*—*Crockett, Tour,* p. 90.
> Spain has obtained a breathing *spell* of some duration from the internal convulsions which have, through so many years, marred her prosperity.—*President Tyler's Message to Congress,* 1844.
> I and the General have got things now pretty considerable snug; public affairs go on easier than they did a *spell* ago, when Mr. Adams was President.—*Maj. Downing's Letters,* p. 35.
> During the same *spell* of weather, two waggoners and some oxen were frozen on the prairie.—*Hoffman, Winter in the West,* Let. 26.

SPIDER. A cast iron frying-pan with three legs.

SPIKE TEAM.   A waggon drawn by three horses, or by two oxen and a horse, the latter leading the oxen or span of horses.

SPILL.   A strip of paper rolled up to light a lamp or acigar. Provincial in England.

SPITTOON.   A spitbox; a box or vessel to spit in.—*Worcester.*

> Now, Caudle, I won't have my dear child lost by any of your *spittoon* acquaintance, I can tell you.—*Mrs. Caudle's Curtain Lectures.*

SPLENDIFEROUS.   Splendid; fine.   A make-believe word used only in jest.

> A *splendiferous* white horse, with long tail and flowing mane.—*S. Slick in England*, ch. 13.

An itinerant gospeller was holding forth to a Kentuckian audience, on the kingdom of Heaven :

> " Heaven, my beloved hearers," said he, " is a glorious, a beautiful, a *splendiferous*, an angeliferous place. Eye hath not seen, ear hath not heard, it has not entered into the imagination of any cracker in these here diggings what carryings on the just made perfect have up thar."

SPLIT.   A division.

> The fiery spirit which has occasioned a *split* among the British Archæologists, would appear not yet to have burnt itself out, &c.—*London Athenæum*, p. 840.

> There was a *split* in the Democratic Convention in Baltimore, caused by the Old Hunkers and Barnburners of New York.—*Newspaper.*

> The *split* in the Whig organization, if it come to anything serious, will extend beyond the Presidential election.—*Letter from Boston, New York Herald*, June 21, 1848.

SPLIT.   A rapid pace or rate of going.   ' He went full *split*,' i. e. as hard as he could drive.   ' To go like *split*,' is a common expression in New England.

> There was no ox-teams [in New York] such as we have in Downingville; but there was no end to the one-hoss teams, goin' like *split* all over the city.—*Maj. Downing, May-day in New York*, p. 64.

TO SPLIT.   To go at a rapid pace; to drive along.   Used in the phrase, ' As hard as he could *split*.'

> The thing tuk first rate, and I set the niggers a drummin' and fifin' as hard as they could *split* right afore the cabin door.—*Maj. Jones's Courtship.*

TO SPLURGE.   To make a blustering demonstration in order to produce an effect.   A term in common use at the South and West.

Cousin Pete was thar *splurgin* about in the biggest, with his dandy-cut trowsers and big whiskers.—*Maj. Jones's Courtship*, p. 101.

Well, them was great times, but now the settlements is got too thick for them to *splurge.*—*Porter's Tales of the South-west*, p. 54.

SPLURGE. A great effort; a demonstration.

Members of Congress should not forget when Senator Benton was shinning around, making what they call in Missouri a great *splurge* to get gold.—*N. Y. Com. Adv.*, Dec. 13, 1845.

SPOOK. (Dutch.) A ghost; hobgoblin.

SPOONEY. A man who has been drinking till he becomes disgusting. A stupid or silly fellow.—*Grose.* We use the word only in the latter sense. The Hon. Mr. Preston, in his remarks on the Mexican war, thus quotes from Tom Crib's remonstrance against the meanness of a transaction, similar to our cries for more vigorous blows on Mexico when she is prostrate:

> Look down upon Ben—see him, *dunghill* all o'er,
> Insult the fallen foe that can harm him no more.
> Out, cowardly *spooney!* Again and again,
> By the fist of my father, I blush for thee, Ben.

Ay, you will see all the *spooneys*, that ran, like so many *dunghill* champions, from 54 40, stand by the President for the vigorous prosecution of the war upon the body of a prostrate foe.—*N. Y. Tribune*, 1847.

I shall escape from this beautiful critter, for I'm gettin' *spooney*, and shall talk silly presently.—*Sam Slick.*

TO SPORT. To exhibit; to make a show of; as, 'Mr. A *sported* a new carriage yesterday;' 'I shall *sport* a new coat to-day.' "The word *sport* in this sense," says Grose, "was in great vogue in the years 1783 and 1784."

SPORTSMAN. A term often applied to a gambler.

SPOSH. A mixture of mud and water. See *Slush.* The New York Tribune, in speaking of the falling of rain and snow, at the same time, adds:

The morning was blue and streaked, and the streets were one shining level of black *sposh.*—Nov. 25, 1845.

SPOTTED TREES. Equivalent to *blazed trees*, which see. Maine.

TO SPOUT. To make a speech, especially in debating-clubs, etc.

SPREE.   A merry frolic.—*Halliwell.*

> A *spree* is to come off to-night.—*Neal's Sketches.*

SPRINKLING.   A small quantity scattered.—*Todd.*

> [Infidels] by giving a *sprinkling* of irreligion to all their literary productions, aim to engross the formation of the public mind.—*Robert Hall, Modern Infidelity.*
>
> There is a good *sprinkling* of distinguished personages at Saratoga Springs.—*N. Y. Com. Adv.*, July 10, 1845.

TO SPRUCE UP.   To dress oneself sprucely.   In Sussex (England) they say, *to sprug up*, in the same sense.

> To-night we're goin' to a quiltin' at Uncle Josh's.   The Deacon's eldest daughter is *sprucin'* up for it.—*Maj. Downing, Letters*, p. 27.
>
> " What ! would you not have the child exhilarate and *spruce up* a little ?' cried the father.—*Margaret*, p. 28.

SPRY.   Having great power of leaping or running ; nimble ; active ; vigorous.—*Webster.*

> This word is much used in familiar language in New England.   It is not in the English dictionaries, but Jennings notices it among the provincialisms of Somersetshire.
>
> In a Fable by R. W. Emerson, " The Mountain and the Squirrel," Squirrel says :
>
>> If I'm not so large as you,
>> You are not so small as I,
>> And not half so *spry*.
>
> She is as *spry* as a cricket.—*Margaret*, p. 58.
>
> " How are you, Jeremiah ?" " Why, I'm kinder sorter midlin', Mr. Slick, what you call considerable nimble and *spry*."—*Sam Slick.*

SPUNK.   Mettle ; spirit ; vivacity.—*Brockett's Glossary.*   A colloquial word, considered in England extremely vulgar.

> I admire your independent spirit, Doolittle.   I like to have people think well of themselves.   You have convinced me of your *spunk*.   I am your friend.—*D. Humphreys, The Yankee in England.*

SPUNKY.   Sparkling ; fresh ; spirited.—*Brockett's Glossary.* Forby also mentions the word as provincial in Norfolk.

SPUR.   A mountain that shoots from any other mountain or range of mountains, and extends to some distance in a lateral direction, or at right angles.—*Webster.*

SQUADDY.   Short and fat.   A vulgar word formed from *squat.*

I had hardly got seated, when in come a great, stout, fat, *squaddy* woman. —*Maj. Downing, May-day.*

SQUALLY. Windy; gusty. A sailor's word.—*Johnson.* It is often used by us in a figurative sense; so that *to look squally,* means to bode a quarrel; and especially as applied to political meetings and debates.

TO SQUALE. To throw a stick or other thing with violence, and in such a manner that it skims along near the ground. New England.—*Pickering's Vocabulary.*

According to Grose, it is provincial in the west of England, and means, " to throw a stick, as at a cock."

TO SQUARE UP. To put oneself in an attitude fit for boxing. Provincial in various parts of England.—*Halliwell.*

> You will remember that Mr. Polk asserted that our title to Oregon was " clear and unquestionable." Well, how was that settled? There were Polk and Cass fidgeting and *squaring up* to Queen Victoria, one declaring that unless England or the United States backed out, war was " inevitable."—*Speech at a Whig Meeting in Baltimore,* June, 1848.

TO SQUAT. To squeeze; to press. Ex. The boy has *squat* his finger. Used by the vulgar in New England.—*Pickering's Vocabulary.*

Mr. Todd has this word in his dictionary from Barret (1580): " To bruise or make flat by letting fall." Provincial in the south of England.

TO SQUAT. In the United States, to settle on another's lands, or on public lands, without having a title.—*Worcester.*

> On either side of the bank the colonists had been allowed *to squat* on allotted portions until the survey of the town should be completed.—*Wakefield's Adventures in New Zealand in* 1844.

SQUATTER. In the United States, one that settles on new land without a title.—*Webster.*

> When I was at Prairie du Chien, there were several of the officers who had been cited to appear in court, for having, pursuant to order, removed *squatters* from the Indian lands on the Mississippi.—*Hoffman, Winter in the West,* Let. 29.

> The Western *squatter* is a free and jovial character, inclined to mirth rather than evil; and when he encounters his fellow-man at a barbecue, election, log-rolling, or frolic, he is more disposed to join in a feeling of hilarity, than to participate in wrong or outrage.—*Robb, Squatter Life.*

The London Spectator has the following remarks on this word, occasioned by the removal of a number of the occupants of Glenculvie, in Scotland, who had *squatted* there as under-tenants :

The term "*squatter*" is very ambiguous. In America it denotes a ragged rascal without a cent in his pockets, and with a rifle or woodman's axe in his hand. In Australia, it designates a young Oxonian or retired officer of the army or navy, possessed of stock to the value of some thousands. In Scotland it seems to designate a person very differently circumstanced from either of the preceding. . . . . The Scotchmen who "squat under tenants," are men who have followed their fathers and grandfathers for unknown generations in the occupancy of their huts and kail-yards. Their families are of older standing in the district than those of the tacksmen or the lairds. The Scotch *squatter* is no clandestine intruder upon the soil ; he stands in the place of his forefathers, and the act which ejects him is a violent innovation on the customs of the country—a forcible change in a mode of tenancy, sanctioned by the " use and wont " of all ages.— June 7, 1845.

SQUAW. (Narragansett Indian.) An Indian woman. Mr. Duponceau, after giving a list of the languages and forms in which this word occurs, observes : " On voit que la famille de ce mot s'étend depuis les Knisténaux en Canada, et les Skoffies et Montagnards d'Acadie, jusqu'aux Nanticokes sur les confins de la Virginie."—*Mém. sur les Langues d'Amérique du Nord*, p. 333.

SQUAW-ROOT. (Lat. *macrotys racemosa.*) A medicinal plant put up by the Shakers. It is recommended for correcting the secretions, and possesses narcotic properties.

SQUAW-WEED. (Lat. *senecio obovatus.*) A medicinal plant used for diseases of the skin.

SQUETEAGUE, or SQUETEE. (*Labrus Squeteague.*) A very common fish in the waters of Long Island Sound and adjacent bays. It never visits rivers, and is similar in habits to the tautog. In New York it is called *Weak-fish,* owing to the feeble resistance it makes when caught with a hook.

TO SQUIB. To throw squibs ; to utter sarcastic or severe reflections ; to contend in petty dispute ; as, 'two members of a society *squib* a little in debate.' Colloquial.—*Webster.* This word is not in the English dictionaries.

TO SQUIGGLE. To move about like an eel. New England. Often figuratively used in speaking of a man who evades a bargain as an eel eludes the grasp.—*Pickering*.

Forby's Glossary of Norfolk contains the word in the sense of " to shake a fluid about the mouth."

TO SQUIRM. To wriggle or twist about, as an eel. Provincial in England, and colloquial in the United States.—*Bailey. Worcester*.

TO SQUIRM. To climb by embracing and clinging with the hands and feet, as to a tree without branches. Johnson writes this word *swarm;* and this is probably the original word. Bailey writes it *squirm.—Webster*.

SQUIRT. A foppish young fellow; a whipper-snapper. A vulgar word.

> If they won't keep company with *squirts* and dandies, who's going to make a monkey of himself?—*Maj. Jones's Courtship*, p. 160.

SQUIRTISH. Dandified.

> It's my opinion that these slicked up *squirtish* kind a fellars ain't particular hard baked, and they always goes in for aristocracy notions.—*Robb, Squatter Life*, p. 73.

SQUSH. To crush. A vulgarism.

> The next time I meet the critter, I'll take my stick and kill it—I'll *sqush* it with my foot.—*Neal's Charcoal Sketches*.

STADDLE. A young tree; a tree left to grow when others are cut; standard.—*Worcester*.

> Leave growing for *staddles* the likeliest and best,
> Though seller and buyer despatched the rest.
> In bushes, in hedge-row, in grove, and in wood,
> This lesson observed, is needful and good.—*Tusser, Husbandry*.

> At the edge of the woods a rude structure had been thrown up, of *staddles* interlaced with boughs.—*Margaret*, p. 274.

STAFF. 'To have the *staff* in one's own hand,' is to keep possession of one's own property, and, consequently, to retain authority and obedience. A very common expression used in good language. Mr. Carr has it in his Craven Glossary.

STAG. In the New York courts, a *stag* is the technical name for a man who is always ready to aid in proving an alibi, of course " for a consideration."

STAG-DANCE. A dance performed by males only, in bar-rooms, &c. Also called a *bull-dance*.

STAGE. A carriage for conveying passengers; a stage-coach. —*Worcester.* We sometimes use *mail-stage* for mail-coach, which is hardly allowable.

> To pay my duty to sweet Mrs. Page,
> A place was taken in the Stamford *stage.*
> Our coachman, Dick, the shades of night to shun,
> Had yok'd his horses long before the sun.—*Hawkes, The Stage Coach.*

STAGE DRIVER. A stage-coachman.

STAGING. Scaffolding. Used in New England, and I believe in other parts of the United States.—*Pickering.*

STAMPEDE, or **STAMPADO.** (Span. *estampado*, foot-steps, noise of stamping feet.) A general scamper of animals on the Western prairies, generally caused by a fright. Mr. Kendall gives the following interesting account of them :

> ' A *stampede!*' shouted some of the old campaigners, jumping from the ground and running towards their frightened animals ; ' a *stampede!* look out for your horses, or you'll never see them again!' was heard on every side.
>
> It is singular, the effect that sudden fright has, not only upon horses, but oxen, on the prairies. The latter will, perhaps, run longer and farther than the former ; and although not as difficult to ' head,' because they cannot run so fast, their onward course it is impossible to stay. Oxen have been known to run forty miles without once stopping to look back. Not one in fifty of them has seen the least cause of fear, but each simply ran because his neighbor did. Frequent instances have occurred where some worthless but skittish horse has caused the loss of hundreds of valuable animals.
>
> Nothing can exceed the grandeur of the scene when a large *cavallada*, or drove of horses, take a ' scare.' Old, weather-beaten, time-worn, and broken-down steeds—horses that have nearly given out from hard work, or old age—will at once be transformed into wild and prancing colts. When first seized with that indescribable terror which induces them to fly, they seem to have been suddenly endowed with all the attributes of their original wild nature. With heads erect, tails and manes streaming in the air, eyes lit up, and darting beams of fright, old and jaded hacks will be seen prancing and careering about with all the buoyancy of action which character-

izes the antics of young colts. The throng will sweep along the plain with a noise which may be likened to something between a tornado and an earthquake, and as well might feeble man attempt to arrest either of the latter.

Were the earth rending and cleaving beneath their feet, horses, when under the terrifying influence of a *stampede*, could not bound away with greater velocity, or more majestic beauty of movement.—*Santa Fé Expedition*, Vol. I. p. 96.

The boys leaped and whooped, flung their hats in the air, chased one another in a sort of *stampede*, &c.—*Margaret*, p. 120.

After him I went, and after me they came, and perhaps there wasn't the awfullest *stampede* down three pair of stairs that ever occurred in Michigan!—*Field, Western Tales*.

TO STAMPEDE. To cause to scamper off in a fright.

> Col. Snively was on the point of marching in pursuit of the Mexicans, when an incident occurred which frustrated the purposes of the expedition. This was effected by a war party of Indians, who succeeded in *stampeding* a large band of the army horses.—*Scenes in the Rocky Mountains*, p. 268.

STANCHEOUS. Strong; durable. Western.

> I tell you what, it's a mighty *stancheous* looking building, and looks far off at a distance when you're going up to it.—*Maj. Jones's Courtship*, p. 33.

TO STAND IN. To cost. 'This horse *stands* me *in* two hundred dollars.'

TO STAND IN HAND. To concern; to behoove.—*Holloway, Prov. Dict.* This phrase is a colloquial one in New England. Ex. 'It *stands* you *in hand* to attend to your business.'

STAND-POINT. (Germ. *stand-punkt*.) Place of standing; point of view. An expression lately introduced from the German.

TO STAND UP TO THE RACK. A metaphorical expression of the same meaning as the like choice phrases, ' to come to the scratch;' ' to toe the mark.'

> I begun a new campaign at Washington. I had hard work, but I *stood up to the rack*, fodder or no fodder.—*Crockett, Tour*, p. 137.

> By making a great rush upon these free-thinkers, we can whip them back into the party, and make them *stand up to the rack*, fodder or no fodder.—*Ibid.*, p. 212.

> It was the hottest night's work ever old Wolf undertook; and it tuck a mighty chance of hollerin' to make him *stand up to his rack* as well as he did.—*Maj. Jones's Courtship*, p. 64.

STARS. A Southern pronunciation of the word *stairs*, like *bar* for *bear*; also heard in New England.

STATE-ROOM. A small room in a ship or steam-vessel for one or two passengers.—*Worcester*.

TO STAVE. To break a hole in; to break; to burst; as, 'to *stave* a cask.'—*Webster*. This is the legitimate use of the verb; but sometimes we make it govern the instrument directly, as in the following example:

> I'll *stave* my fist right through you, and carry you on my elbow, as easily as if you were an empty market-basket.—*Neal's Charcoal Sketches*.

TO STAVE. To hurry; to press forward.

> A president of one of our colleges once said to a graduate at parting, "My son, I want to advise you. Never oppose public opinion. The great world will *stave* right on!"—*Am. Review*, June, 1848.

> Hilloa! Steve! where are you a *staving* to? If you're for Wellington, scale up here and I'll give you a ride.—*Mrs. Clavers's Forest Life*.

TO STAVE OFF. To push away as with a staff; to delay; as, 'to *stave off* the execution of the project.—*Webster*.

> Humane, divine laws, precepts, fear of God and men, fame, honor, cannot oppose, *stave off*, or withstand the fury of illicit passion.—*Burton, Anat. of Melancholy*.

> We hope that Congress will sink all party jealousies, and go for such measures as will show an undivided front. It is the way *to stave off* a war; because the enemy is calculating upon a division among the people upon the Oregon question.—*N. Y. Herald*, March, 1848.

> In the mean time, this new episode [Mr. Webster's speech on the Ashburton treaty] will *stave off* the Oregon question.—*N. Y. Com. Adv.*

STEAL (pronounced *stail*). The handle of various implements; as a *rake-steal*, a *fork-steal*. Used by the farmers in some parts of New England. Provincial in various parts of England.—*Pickering*.

STEBOY. ⎫
SEBOY. ⎬ A word used to set dogs upon pigs or other animals.

> "There it is—that black and white thing—on that log," says Tom. "*Steboy*; catch him!" say he [to the dog]. Ben run up with his light, and the first thing I heard him says was, "Peugh! oh, my Lord! look out, fellers, it's a pole-cat."—*Maj. Jones's Courtship*, p. 55.

STEVEDORE. A man employed in loading and unloading vessels.—*Worcester*.

STEW. *To be in a stew*, is to be in a heat, a confusion of mind. According to Grose, however, who is followed by Todd and Webster, a *stew* is " confusion, as when the air is full of dust, smoke, or steam."

> Incensed were Isengrim and Bruin,
> To see the couple such a *stew* in.—*Reynard the Fox*, p. 189.

> It aint such an easy thing to feel mad at a rite pretty gall; and the more he feels mad, the more he's apt to feel sorry too. I tell you what, *I was in a stew*. I didn't know what to do.—*Maj. Jones's Courtship*, p. 77.

> Clay, Calhoun, Van Buren, Benton, Cass, Webster, and all the intriguing politicians, who have kept the country in a *stew* for years past, may be considered as effectually laid on the shelf.—*Newspaper*.

TO STICH. To form land into ridges. Common in New England.—*Webster*. The word is not new, though it does not seem to be used now in England.

> Many men at plough he made, and drave earth here and there
> And turn'd up *stitches* orderly.—*Chapman, Iliad*.

TO STICK. To take in; to impose upon; to cheat in trade. 'I'm *stuck* with a counterfeit note;' 'He went to a horse sale, and got *stuck* with a spavined horse.'

> As soon as the whole class of small speculators perceived they had been *stuck*, they all shut their mouths; no one confessing the ownership of a share.—*A Week in Wall Street*, p. 47.

> Very often is a client *stuck* for a heavy bill of costs, which he would have saved but for the ignorance of his attorney.—*Newspaper*.

STICK-CHIMNEY. In newly settled parts of the country, where log-houses form the first habitations of the settlers, the chimneys are made with sticks from one to two inches square, and about two feet in length, which are laid crosswise and cemented with clay or mud. The fire-places are built of rough stone, and the *stick-chimneys* are merely the conductors of the smoke.

> The *stick-chimney* [of this house] was like its owner's hat, open at the top, and jammed in at the *sides*.—*Mrs. Claver's Western Clearings*, p. 7.

STICKER. An article of merchandise which sticks by the dealer and does not meet with a ready sale, is technically called a *sticker*.

STICKLING. Hesitating; delaying.—*Dr. Humphreys*.

STILL-HOUSE. A common term in the United States for a distillery.

> Despise it not, ye Bards to terror steel'd,
> Who hurl'd your thunders round the epic field;
> Nor ye who strain your midnight throats to sing
> Joys that the vineyard and the *still-house* bring.—*Joel Barlow,
> Poem on Hasty Pudding.*

STIMULUS. This very common word is not mentioned by any English lexicographer, though it is used by good English writers. Our American lexicographers, Pickering, Webster, and Worcester, have noticed it.

1. Literally, a goad; hence something that rouses the mind or spirits; as, 'the hope of gain is a powerful *stimulus* to labor and action.'

2. In medicine that which produces a quickly diffused or transient increase of vital energy and strength of action in the circulating system.—*Webster.*

3. In vulgar use, intoxicating drink.

> Those young academicians will receive, from the perusal of his book, a powerful *stimulus* to their ambition.—*British Critic*, Vol. III. p. 518.

> We should expect even the voluntary productions of the pen, without this violent *stimulus*, to be sufficient to satisfy the expectations of the public.—*Ibid.*, Vol. I. p. 362.

TO STIVE UP. To stuff up close.—*Johnson.*

> Things are a good deal *stived up*. People's minds are sour, and I don't know what we can do.—*Margaret*, p. 329.

> You would admire, if you saw them *stive* it into their ships.—*Sandy's Travels.*

> "Oh, marcy on us," said a fat lady who was looking for a house, "this'll never do for my family at all. There's no convenience about it, only one little *stived up* closet. . . . . And the bed-rooms,—she would as soon sleep in a pig-pen and done with it, as to get into such little mean *stived up* places as them."—*Downing, May-day in New York.*

TO STIVER. To run; to move off. A low word used in the Northern States.

STIVER. A Dutch coin about the value of a cent. A common expression in New York is, 'He's not worth a *stiver*,' i. e. he's very poor.

STOCK. Cattle in general; the cattle belonging to a farm. Provincial in the North of England.—*Pegge's Glossary.*

STOCKHOLDER. One who is proprietor of stock in the public funds, or in the funds of a bank or other company.— *Webster.* This is not in the English dictionaries. In England when speaking of the same, they say *shareholders, members,* or *proprietors,* generally the former. Mr. Pickering, however, cites the Edinburgh Review for the use of the word :

> The *stockholders* who allow inferior capitalists to derive a profit from commission, will diminish that allowance.—Vol. III. p. 475.

STOOL-PIGEONING. One of the old standing and oft-repeated charges urged with great pertinacity against the police of this city in olden times, was that of " stool-pigeoning." As this term may not be familiar to our readers, we will briefly explain it. " Stool-pigeoning " is for an officer to arrest a party of doubtful or perhaps decidedly bad reputation on suspicion, and making him or her give up money or valuables to obtain liberty, when the officer would set the party free, and nothing would be heard by the public or any one else of the arrest, or anything else connected with it.—*N. Y. Courier and Enquirer.*

STONE-ROOT. (Lat. *Collinconia Canadensis.*) A plant used in medicine. Its properties are diuretic and stomachic.

STOOP. (Dutch, *stoep.*) The steps at the entrance of a house ; door-steps. It is also applied to a porch with seats, a piazza, or balustrade. This, unlike most of the words received from the Dutch, has extended, in consequence of the uniform style of building that prevails throughout the country, beyond the bounds of New York State, as far as the backwoods of Canada.

> About nine o'clock all three of us passed up Wall street, on the *stoops* of which no small portion of its tenants were already seated.—*Cooper, Satanstoe,* Vol. I. p. 69.

> Nearly all the houses [in Albany] were built with their gables to the streets, and each had heavy wooden Dutch *stoops,* with seats at the door.— *Ibid.* p. 161.

> There was a large two story house, having a long *stoop* in front.—*Margaret,* p. 63.

> I shall step back to my party within the *stoup.*—*Backwoods of Canada.*

> The *stoup* is up, and I have just planted hops at the base of the pillars. —*Ibid.* p. 309.

TO STOP. To visit; to stay; as, 'When you come to New York, *stop* with me instead of going to a hotel.'

> Those who remain at home know little of the newer portions of our country, and of the primeval style of living. I recently *stopped* with a friend on court-day. The court-house was of logs, without a floor, etc.— *Corresp. of Newark Daily Adv.*

STORE. In the United States and Canada, shops of every kind for the sale of goods whether at wholesale or retail, are commonly called *stores*. Thus we have dry goods *stores*, shoe *stores*, book *stores*, hardware *stores*, etc. etc. This use of the word, whose proper meaning is a magazine or storehouse, where merchandise or movable property is kept, seems to arise from that tendency to the magniloquent with which Americans have been charged.

TO SET STORE BY. To value; esteem; regard. This sense of the word *store* is not noticed by the English or American lexicographers, though it comes to us from a good source. It is much used in New England in familiar conversation, and is also provincial in England, according to Halliwell.

STOREKEEPER. In America, a man who has the care of a store or warehouse; a shopkeeper. The officer who has charge of the government warehouse, where property to the value of millions is deposited for inspection, or for safe keeping, is a *storekeeper;* so too is the man who stands behind the counter of a shop, and sells his yard of tape, or paper of pins.

STORM. A violent wind; a tempest. Thus, 'a *storm* of wind' is correct language, as the proper sense of the word is rushing, violence. It has primarily no reference to a fall of rain or snow; but, as a violent wind is often attended with rain or snow, the word *storm* has come to be used, most improperly, for a fall of rain or snow without wind.—*Webster.*

TO STORM. To blow with violence; impersonally, as, *it storms.*—*Webster.* We use it improperly in the sense of to rain or to snow.

STORY. A floor; a flight of rooms.—*Johnson.* In the United

States, the floor next the ground is the first story. In France and England, the first floor or *story* is the second from the ground.—*Webster.*

STRAIGHT AS A LOON'S LEG, is a common simile in New England.

> They were puzzled with the accounts; but I saw through it in a minit, and made it all as *straight as a loon's leg.*—*Maj. Downing's Letters*, p. 42.

STRANGER. It is the common practice in the Western States to accost a person whose name is not known by this title. In England, for example, a person would say, 'Can you tell me, sir, if this is the road to B?' At the West he would say, '*Stranger*, is this the road?' &c.

STRAPPER. A woman of a bulky form. A large, tall person.—*Carr's Craven Dialect. Jodrell's Philology.* This vulgar word is used in the same sense with us.

> Your mother! by St. Anthony, she's a *strapper;* why, you are a dwarf to her.—*Mrs. Centlivre, The Wonder*, Act IV.

STRAPPING. Huge, lusty, bouncing; as, 'a *strapping* lass.' —*Philips, New World of Words.*

> Then that t'other great *strapping* lady.—*Congreve, The Double Dealer.*
> Wi' kindly welcome Jenny brings him ben,
> A *strappin* youth; he takes the mother's eye.—*Burns.*

STREAKED, or **STREAKY.** 'To feel *streaked*,' is to feel confused, alarmed.

> I begun to feel *streaked* enough for our folks, when I see what was done on Boston Common.—*Maj. Downing's Letters*, p. 18.

> Polly begun to look a little *streaked.*—*May-day in New York*, p. 49.

> People felt considerable *streaked* [about the executions in Canada], in consequence of the rebellion in 1837.—*Sam Slick*, 3d Series.

> Oh what a beautiful sight the ocean is when there aint no land in sight! There we was in a little shell at the mercy of them big waves, higher than father's barn. I never did feel so *streaky* and mean afore—talk of a grain of sand; why I felt like a starved speck of dust cut up into homœopathic doses for a child two minits old.—*Hiram Bigelow, Letter in Family Companion.*

> *Gen.* Tell the truth—keep back nothing—I promised no harm shall happen you.

> *Doolittle.* Oh, I'll tell all now—I won't stay to be hanged first. Oh.—

the good, gracious suzz ! how *streaked* I feel all over !—*D. Humphreys, The Yankee in England.*

TO STREAK, or TO STREAK IT, is to run as fast as possible.

> O'er hill and dale with fury she did dreel,
> A' roads to her were good and bad alike ;
> Nane o't she wyl'd, but forward on did *streak.*—*Ross's Helenore.*

I was certain it wasn't no fox or wolf, but a dog ; and if I didn't *streak* off like greased lightnin'.—*Carlton, The New Purchase,* Vol. I. p. 78.

I *streaked* it for Washington, and it was well nigh upon midnight when I reached the White House.—*Maj. Downing's Letters,* p. 91.

When I did get near, he'd stop and look, cock his ears, and give a snuff, as if he'd never seen a man afore, and then *streak it* off as if I had been an Indian.—*Porter's Tales of the South-west,* p. 165.

STRETCHER.   A notorious lie.—*Carr's Craven. Brockett.*

> Whenever Mrs. Oscar Dust told a *stretcher,* old Waters was expected to swear to it.—*Field, Drama at Pokerville.*

STRICKEN.   " This ancient participle," says Mr. Pickering, " is much used in Congress and our other legislative assemblies. A member moves that certain parts of a bill should be *stricken* out," &c.—*Vocabulary.*

The use of the word referred to by Mr. Pickering is peculiar to us, though there are examples of its occasional use in England applied in other ways.

> Many of the foreigners were much *stricken* with the splendor of the scene.—*London Statesman,* June 10, 1814.

TO STRIKE, among workmen in manufactories, in England and America, is to quit work in a body or by combination, in order to compel their employers to give them higher wages. —*Webster.*

STRIKE.   A combination among workmen to obtain an advance in wages.   This, as well as the verb *to strike,* is new, and has not yet found its way into the English dictionaries. Its use is now common both in England and America.

STRING.   A common name among teamsters for a whip.

> With some judicious touches of the *string,* the horses are induced to struggle as for their lives.—*Mrs. Clavers, A New Home,* p. 9.

STRING-BEANS.   The common name for French beans ; so

called from the string-like substance stripped from the side of the pod in preparing it for the table.

STRIPPINGS. The last and consequently the richest milk drawn from a cow in milking. It is provincial in England.

> When they were about breaking up the meeting, Deacon Ramsdell said, "Shan't we have a collection? We have had nice times, but *strippins* arter all is the best milk."—*Margaret*, p. 159.

GOOD STROKE. Used in the sense of considerable; as, 'a *good stroke* of business.'—*Brockett's North County Words*.

STRONG. *To go it strong*, means to do a thing with energy or perseverance.

> The pilot on duty above; another was calling out the Captain, who *went it strong* at cards.—*Porter's Tales of the South-west*, p. 107.

> You should *go it*, remarked Spifflekins, *go it strong*—that's the way to scatter the blue devils, *go it strong*; and as the poet judiciously remarks, *go it* while you're young.—*Neal's Peter Ploddy*, p. 46.

TO STUB, or STUMP. 'To *stub* one's toe,' is to strike it against anything in walking or running; an expression often used by boys and others who go barefoot.

STUBBY. ⎫
STUBBED. ⎬ Short and thick; truncated.—*Todd. Webster*.

This word is now provincial in England. In the United States it is colloquial and not much used. It is found in well known authors.

> A pain he in his head-piece feels,
> Against a *stubbed* tree he reels,
> And up went poor Hobgoblin's heels.—*Drayton*.

It is also used to signify hardy; not delicate.—*Todd's Johnson*. In this sense it is heard with us. Ex. That is a '*stubbed* child;' meaning hardy, plump, or strong.

> The hardness of *stubbed* vulgar constitutions renders them insensible of a thousand things.—*Bishop Berkeley*.

> If he thinks I'll put that treatment to my wife, he's mistaken. He may be *stubbeder* than I be, Uncle, that's a fact; but if he was twice as *stubbed* I'd walk into him like a thousand of brick.—*Sam Slick in England*, ch. 29.

> However, I can always help a gentleman, if he asks me like a gentleman; and, upon the whole, I guess I'm rather *stubbeder* than you be.— *Mrs. Clavers, Forest Life*, Vol I. p. 97.

STUD. A collection of breeding horses and mares.—*Johnson*.

In the United States we use the term *stud-horse*, or simply *stud*, to signify a breeding horse ; a stallion.

STUFFY. In Scotland, stout, mettlesome, resolute.—*Jamieson.* In the United States, angry or sulky ; obstinate. Colloquial. —*Worcester.*

STUFFENING. Stuffing ; seasoning for meat or poultry, usually made of bread and herbs to give it a higher relish. Western.

> By way of amends [for the dried up turkey] quarts of gravy were judiciously emptied on our plates from the wash-basin bowls. That also moistened the *stuffinin*, composed of Indian meal and sausages.—*Carlton, The New Purchase*, Vol. I. p. 182.

TO STUMP. To challenge ; to defy.—*Webster. Worcester.* The more usual meaning, however, is to puzzle ; to confound.

> Dabbs turns up his nose at betting. Instead of *stumping* his antagonist by launching out his cash, he shakes a portentous fist under his nose, and the affair is settled.—*Neal's Charcoal Sketches.*
>
> When you see Lord Sydenham, *stump* him ; and ask him, when a log is hewed and squared, if he can tell the tenth side of it.—*Sam Slick.*
>
> Heavens and earth ! thinks. I, what does all this mean ? I knowed I hadn't done anything to be put in prison for, and I never was so *stumped*. —*Maj. Jones's Courtship*, p. 135.
>
> At this the parson appeared as if he was *stump't.*—*Crockett, Tour*, p. 16.
>
> I put a conundrum to them. They were all *stump't* and gave it up.— *Ibid.*

TO STUMP. ' *To stump it*,' or ' *take the stump*.' A cant phrase signifying to make electioneering speeches.—*Worcester.* This is a term borrowed from the backwoods, where the stump of a tree often supplies the place of the English hustings.

STUMPER. A puzzler.

> My note was a *stumper* to Sally ; so she got Jess to explain it, and the way he did it was enormous.—*Robb, Squatter Life.*

STUMP ORATOR. A man who harangues the people from the stump of a tree, or other elevation.

STUMP ORATORY. The sort of popular speaking used by stump orators.

STUMP SPEECH. A speech made from a stump or other

elevation; i. e. an electioneering speech in favor of one's self, or some other political candidate.

> We had of course a passion for stump speaking. But recollect, we often mount the stump only figuratively; and very good *stump speeches* are delivered from a table, a chair, a whiskey-barrel, and the like. Sometimes we make the best *stump speeches* on horseback.—*Carlton, The New Purchase*, Vol. I. p. 211.

STUMP SPEAKER. A popular political speaker.

> The Hon. W. R. Thompson, of Indiana, one of the most popular *stump speakers* of the day, addressed a large meeting of Whigs from the stoop of Barnum's Hotel, Baltimore, in support of the nominations of the late Whig Convention.—*Letter from Washington, N. Y. Herald*, June 21, 1848.

The New York Commercial Advertiser, in giving the requisites of a good *stump speaker*, says:

> A less objectionable pre-requisite is self-reliance. A man may be pardoned for faltering in delivering a lecture; or for showing sweet confusion and charming hesitation in addressing a fashionable audience on manners and taste; a man may even be agitated by the conflict of natural bashfulness and a desire to advocate a good cause; but woe, confusion and utter rejection as an instrument of power await him who breaks down in a political *stump speech*. Right or wrong, well-informed or ignorant, he must be bold in speech and dogmatical in his assertions, and the weaker he feels his cause to be, the more vehemently and confidently he must advocate it. His self-reliance had better rise into impudence than sink into modesty, if he desires to make an impression; at least we have heard speakers who seemed to act on this principle. Seriously, however, nerve, and energy, and self-reliance of a high order, *are* pre-requisites for those who enter upon the work of itinerant speech-makers among either party.

> But we cannot longer dwell on this view of the matter. Other pre-requisites there are, as experience has shown, but they must be summarily dismissed: a good, meaning thereby a convenient, memory, that will retain the slightest incident or the most apocryphal anecdote that will tell in favor of the speaker's candidate and against his opponent, but will prove a very open sieve in the matter of a favorite's follies or an opponent's virtues. Then the campaigner should have the last edition of the political jest book; a vocabulary of hard names; a dictionary of offensive epithets; a text book of political phrases and clap-trap expressions; with a general assortment of "principles," "issues," "consequences," and a package of "patriotism," "devotion," "free republics," "enlightened people," &c. &c., and thus armed he may go forth to political war.—June 23, 1848.

STUMPAGE. The sum paid to owners of land for the privilege of cutting the timber growing thereon. State of Maine.

STUN, for *stone*, so pronounced in the back parts of New England.

> Captain Stone, I've been clean away amongst the Yankees, where they call your name *Stunn.*—*Crockett, Tour*, p. 145.

STURTION. A common pronunciation for *nasturtion*.

TO STUTTER. To saunter lazily, with a slip-shod movement. This is not a common word. I have never met with it except in the example quoted.

> I *stuttered* up to No. 4 yesterday arter the funeral; but they are so grown over with rum there, you can hardly tell what is nater and what is not.—*Margaret*, p. 327.

SUABILITY. Liability to be sued; the state of being subject by law to a civil process.—*Webster*.

SUABLE. That may be sued; subject by law to be called to answer in court.—*Webster*.

SUANT. Even; uniform; spread equally over the surface. Provincial in England.—*Holloway's Prov. Dict.* Used by farmers in some parts of New England, and applied thus: ' The grain is sowed *suant*,' i. e. evenly; regularly.—*Pickering*.

TO SUBSIST. To feed; to maintain.—*Todd*. This and the following verb are sometimes, though rarely, used transitively.

> Instructions have been given by the Department, to cause the officers and men of the California regiment, left on shore, to be quartered on Governor's Island, where they will be *subsisted* and provided for until a transport can take them to their place of destination.—*Washington Union*.

TO SUCCEED. To prosper; to make successful.

> Sincerely praying and desiring for your Excellency's highest personal happiness, and the smiles of Heaven *to succeed* your present and very important embassy, I have the honor to remain, &c., &c.—*J. Perkins, Residence in Persia*, p. 219.

SUCKATASH, or **SUCCOTASH.** (Narragansett Ind., *msickquatash*, corn boiled whole.) Green Indian corn and beans boiled together. It is a favorite dish wherever these plants are cultivated.

Joel Barlow, in his admirable poem on Hasty-pudding, thus compares *succotash* with it:

Let the green *succotash* with thee contend,
Let beans and corn their sweetest juices lend ;
Not all the plate, how fam'd soe'er it be,
Can please my palate like a bowl of thee.—*Canto I.* p. 6.

SUCKER.   A nickname applied throughout the West to a native of Illinois.   The origin of this term is as follows :

The Western prairies are, in many places, full of the holes made by the " crawfish," (a fresh water shell-fish similar in form to the lobster,) which descends to the water beneath. In early times, when travellers wended their way over these immense plains, they very prudently provided themselves with a long hollow weed, and when thirsty, thrust it into these natural artesians, and thus easily supplied their longings.   The crawfish-well generally contains pure water, and the manner in which the traveller drew forth the refreshing element gave him the name of " *Sucker.*"—*Let. from Illinois, in Providence Journal.*

A correspondent of the New York Tribune, writing from Illinois, says :

> We say to all friends of association, come West ; to the land of *suckers* and liberal opinions.

SUCKER.   A greenhorn ; an awkward country fellow.   Western.

SUCKER.   A hard drinker ; a drunkard.

SUCKER.   A tube used for sucking sherry-cobblers.   They are made of silver, glass, straw, or sticks of maccaroni.

SUCKER.   A very common fish of the genus *labeo*, and of which there are many varieties, including the Chub, Mullet, Barbel, Horned Dace, etc.   They are found in most of the lakes and rivers of North America.

TO SUCK IN.   To take in ; to cheat ; to deceive.   A figurative expression, probably drawn from a sponge, which sucks up water.   *To be sucked in*, is to be ' sponged ' out of one's money, or to be cheated in a bargain.   It is a low expression, though often heard, and is understood by all.

> " I ain't bound to drive nobody in the middle of the night," said the driver ; " so you don't try *to suck me in* there."—*Mrs. Clavers's Forest Life*, Vol. I. p. 109.

Who was the first unfortunate speculator ? Jonah. Ah ! why ? Because he got *sucked in !—Newspaper.*

SUGAR MAPLE. (*Acer saccharinum.*) A handsome forest tree from 50 to 80 feet high, from the sap of which is made the well known *maple sugar.* The wood is valuable for fuel ; and accidental varieties of it are the *birds-eye maple* and *curled maple* of cabinet makers.—*Dr. Torrey, in Nat. Hist. of New York.*

SUGAR ORCHARD. A collection of maple trees selected and preserved in the forest for the purpose of making sugar therefrom.

SULKY. A carriage for a single person ; generally in the form of a chaise.

He bought him a *sulky* and a fast trotter.—*J. C. Neal*, p. 40.

SU MARKEE. (French, *sou marqué.*) Used in the sea-port towns of New England and in New York. Ex. ' I would not give a *soo markée* for it,' i. e. a single cent.

SUNDOWN. Sunset. Peculiar to the United States.

SUPAWN. An Indian name, in universal use in New England, New York, and other Northern States, for boiled Indian meal.

The common food of the Indians is pap, or mush, which in the New Netherlands is named *supaen.* This is so common among them, that they seldom pass a day without it, unless they are on a journey or hunting. We seldom visit an Indian lodge at any time of day, without seeing their *supaen* preparing, or seeing them eating the same. It is the common food of all ; and so fond of it are they, that when they visit our people, or each other, they consider themselves neglected unless they are treated with *supaen.—Van der Donck's New Netherlands*, (1656,) *N. Y. Hist. Soc. Collections.*

The flour [of maize] makes a substantial sort of porridge, called by the Americans *supporne ;* this is made with water, and eaten with milk.—*Backwoods of Canada*, p. 189.

SUPPLE JACK. (Lat. *rhamnus volubilis.*) The popular name of a vine common to some of the Southern States. Twisted walking canes made of it are much admired.—*Williams's Florida.*

SUSPENDERS. Braces ; straps worn over the shoulders for

holding up pantaloons ; also called *gallowses* in many parts of the country.

SURE AS A GUN. Absolutely certain. A common colloquial expression.—*Brockett.*

> There's luck, says auld Lizzy, in facin' the sun ;
> Thou's young, lish, and clever, may wed a feyne leady,
> And come home a nabob—aye, *as sure as a gun.*—*Westm. and Cumb. Dialect*, p. 256.

SUZZ ! A common pronunciation of *sirs !* An exclamation much used in New England, as *sirs* is in Scotland.

SWACKING. Huge ; robust.—*Forby's Vocabulary.*

SWAD. In New England, a lump, mass, or bunch; also, a crowd.—*Webster.* This is a vulgar word. In the North of England it is the common name for the pod or shell of peas. May not our word be derived from this ? A pod is a quantity, a bunch of peas. A quantity or large pile of potatoes, would be called ' a *swad* of potatoes '—so, ' a *swad* of people.' (See *Dreadful.*)

> There was a *swad* of fine folks, and the house was well nigh upon chuck full.—*Maj. Downing's Letters*, p. 35.
> How is a colonist able to pay for this almighty *swad* of everlasting plunder, seein' he has no gold or silver.—*Sam Slick*, 3d Ser. ch. 6.

SWAG. A term used in speaking of booty lately obtained. I have never seen the word used except by Mr. Greeley, who has good authority for its use in Grose's Slang Dictionary.

> Between Gen. Storms and the late Comptroller, there have been at least $20,000 lost to the State ; and though Mr. Flagg seems to have been exceedingly remiss and blameworthy in the premises, it will not be easy to make the people of New York believe that any of the *swag* has found its way into *his* pocket.—*N. Y. Tribune*, April 21, 1848.

SWALE. A local word in New England, signifying an interval or vale ; a tract of low land.—*Webster.* This word is provincial in Norfolk, England, and means a low place ; and shade, in opposition to sunshine.—*Forby's Vocabulary.*

TO SWALE. ⎫
TO SWEALE. ⎭ To melt and run down, as the tallow of a candle ; to waste away without feeding the flame ; to blaze away.—*Pickering. Webster.* This word is provincial in England, and is mentioned by Ray, Grose, and other writers. —*Craven Glossary.*

TO SWAMP. To plunge into inextricable difficulties.—*Webster*. To whelm or sink as in a *swamp.—Todd*. The former use of the word is not in Todd's Johnson, or other English dictionaries. Dr. Webster quotes the Quarterly Review as authority. It is common in the United States, though not elegant. Ex. ' He invested a large sum of money in land speculations, which *swamped* him ;' i. e. ruined him.

I SWAMP IT ! An interjection of the same meaning as *I swan !* which see.

> Had that darn'd old vessel—that frigate there—bin a stone's throw farder off from land, I should never have swimmed to shore, dead or alive, to all eternity, I *swamp it.—D. Humphreys, The Yankee in England.*

SWAMP-PINK. (Lat. *Azalea Viscosa.*) A popular name for the Wild Honeysuckle.—*Bigelow's Plants of Boston.*

SWAN ! A euphemistic pronunciation of the word *swear ;* as, *I swan !* Used chiefly in New England.

> " Well ! *I swan !*" exclaimed the mamma, giving a round box on the ear to a dirty little urchin, " what made you let the little huzzy have your specs ?"—*Mrs. Clavers's Forest Life*, Vol. I. p. 29.
>
> I took a turn round Halifax, and *I swan* if it aint the thunderinest, drearyest place I ever seen, and the people they call blue-noses.—*Hiram Bigelow's Lett. in Family Companion.*

SWANGA. A word used among the negroes in some parts of the South in connection with *buckra*, as *swanga buckra ;* meaning a dandy white man, or literally, a dandy devil. *Swanga* is an African word, and belongs to the language spoken near the Gaboon river, where anything gay or elegant is *swanga*. The Rev. J. L. Wilson, long a resident in Africa, and acquainted with the language, recognises this word among the Southern negroes.

TO SWAP. To exchange ; to barter.—*Johnson*.

This word has often been noticed by English travellers in this country, and may, perhaps, be more common here than in England ; but it is also used by the vulgar in that country. —*Pickering*.

> When I drove a thrust home, he put it by,
> And cried as in derision, " Spare the stripling."
> Oh, that insulting word ! I would have *swopp'd*

Youth for old age, and all my life behind,
To have been then a momentary man.—*Dryden, Cleom.*

He makes me an offer to *swap* his mare.—*Edgeworth's Castle Rack Rent.*

I'm for a short talk in a horse-*swap*, and always tell a gentlemen what I wish to do.—*Georgia Scenes,* p. 28.

SWEEP. The pole or piece of timber moved on a fulcrum or post, used to lower and raise a bucket in a well for drawing water.—*Webster.*

The same is used in England. In Yorkshire it is called a *swape;* in Norfolk a *swipe.* It is written *swipe* in Bailey's Dictionary.

SWEET TOOTH. A person who is fond of sweet things is said to have a *sweet tooth* in his head. And so in England. —*Carr's Craven Glossary.*

SWEET OIL. The common name for olive oil.

TO SWINGE. 1. To whip; to bastinade; to punish.—*Johnson.*

And that baggage, Beatrix, how I would *swinge* her if I had her here.— *Dryden, An Evening's Love,* Act V.

Go it, old fellow; give the goats a *swinging* every time you come across them.—*Maj. Jones's Courtship,* p. 180.

2. To singe. Provincial in various parts of England.— *Halliwell.*

The weather has been monstrous hot here, and I don't think I ever did see things jest sprawled out and *swinged* up so with the sun before.—*Maj. Jones's Courtship,* p. 185.

SWINGLE-TAIL. (Genus, *carcharias.* Cuvier.) The popular name for the Thresher Shark, from the use it makes of its long flexible tail, " with which," says Dr. De Kay, " it literally threshes its enemies."—*Nat. Hist. of New York.*

SWITCHEL. Molasses and water; a common beverage in New England.

TO SWATE, pron. *swot.* (Dutch, perf. of *suizen,* to make the ears tingle.) To give a violent slap or blow in the face with the open hand. A low word.

Tell me that again, and I'll *swot* you over the mug.—*Report of the Hunker Meeting in Albany,* June, 1848.

SWOT. A violent slap or blow with the open hand.

I SWOW! An exclamation.

TO SYSTEMIZE. To systematize. A word rarely used by good writers.—*Worcester.* Dr. Webster, however, gives it the preference over *systematize*, which he denounces as "ill formed." What would he have thought of *dogmize* and *stigmize*, by way of ' improving ' the language?

T.

TO SUIT TO A T. To suit or fit exactly. This old English phrase is often used by ourselves in colloquial language.

TO TACKLE. To attack. Provincial in England.—*Halliwell.*

> Well, I tell you what, it tuck a feller mighty wide between the eyes to *tackle* that tree, for it was a whopper.—*Maj. Jones's Courtship,* p. 53.

> I shook the two fellows off my trunks monstrous quick, and was going to *tackle* the chaps what had my carpet-bag.—*Maj. Jones's Travels.*

TACKLE. A horse's harness. Provincial in various parts of England.

TO TACKLE. To tackle a horse, is to harness him.

TAFFY. A kind of candy made of molasses, flour, and butter, baked in a pan. New York.

TO TAG AFTER. To follow closely after.—*Forby.*

TAIL-RACE. The water course leading from a mill after it has passed the water-wheel.

'TAINT. A corrupt abbreviation for *it is not.*

> " Wonder what time it is?" said Miss Mary. " Oh, *taint* late," says he. " Is there going to be any preaching here to-morrow ?"—*Maj. Jones's Courtship,* p. 69.

TAKING. Distress of mind.—*Johnson.*

> What a *taking* was he in, when your husband asked who was in the basket ?—*Shakspeare.*

> > What! alack!
> > Yours is the last year's almanack!
> > And so the day you made mistake in ?
> > The king is in a dreadful *taking !*—*Reynard the Fox,* p. 60.

> I told you I was goin' to get things to rights; and when I got here, I found them in a terrible *takin.*—*Maj. Downing's Letters,* p. 18.

TO TAKE ON.   To grieve ; to fret at a misfortune or disappointment.

> " Why, Polly, what's the matter, gal," inquired he ; " what in thunder makes you *take on* so ?   Come, out with the cause, or I shall get a blubberin' too."—*Robb, Squatter Life.*"

TO TAKE TO DO.   To take to task ; to reprove.

TO TAKE THE SHINE OFF.   To surpass ; excel.

> Dublin is worth seein' ; it *takes the shine off* of most cities.—*Sam Slick,* 3d Series.

TALENTED.   Furnished with talents ; possessing skill or talents.—*Webster.*   This word is not noticed by any English lexicographer except *Knowles.*

The London Monthly Magazine (Sept. 1831) blames Mr. Stanley for using this word.   " Sir Robert Peel referred it to his American associations, and prayed him never to employ it again, with all the strenuousness of Oxonian adjuration." The Philadelphia Nat. Gaz., in speaking of the above, adds, " Sir Robert was right in protesting against the word, but wrong in his reference.   It is of London cockney derivation, and still more employed in Great Britain than in America."

> Mr. Bulwer is not yet ' *talented,*' a pseudo-participle, which no one will use who is not ripe for any atrocity ; but he ' progresses ' at a fearful rate.— *Edinburgh Rev.*, Vol. LXV. p. 240.

TALKING-IRON.   A comical name for a gun or rifle ; called also a *shooting-iron.*

> I hops out of bed, feels for my trunk, and outs with my *talkin'-iron*, that was all ready loaded.—*Sam Slick in England*, ch. 2.

TALL.   Sturdy ; lusty ; bold ; spirited ; courageous.—*Johnson.*

> Spoke like a *tall* fellow, that respects his reputation.—*Richard III.*
> They, leaping overboard amidst the billows,
> We pluck'd her up, unsunke, like stout *tall* fellows.—*Taylor's Works*, 1630.

In the United States, and especially at the South, the word is often used in the analogous sense of great ; excellent ; fine.

> Stump straightened up and started at a pace that would have staggered Capt. Barclay, Ellsworth, or the greatest pedestrian mentioned in the annals of ' *tall* walking.'—*Kendall's Santa Fé Expedition*, Vol. I. p. 398.

> A pretty *tall* excitement came off at Coney Island on Saturday.—*N. Y. Tribune.*

TALL, as an *adv.*   Finely ; exceedingly ; highly ; very much. Western.

> I will walk *tall* into varmint and Indian ; it's a way I've got, and it comes as natural as grinning to a hyena.   I'm a regular tornado, tough as hickory, and long-winded as a nor'-wester.—*Thorpe's Backwoods*, p. 131.

> I seed Jess warn't pleased, but I didn't estimate him very *tall*, so I kept on dancin' with Sally, and ended by kissin' her good bye, and making him jealous as a pet pinter.—*Robb, Squatter Life.*

TANTRUM.   Affected airs ; insolences ; whims.—*Halliwell.*

> I thought where your *tantrums* would end.—*Jamieson's Popular Ballads.*

> A scolding woman, in one of her *tantrums*, told an old parson, that she could preach as well as he could, and he might select the text.—*Crockett, Tour down East*, p. 83.

TO TAP.   To add a new sole or heel to a shoe.   Hertford-shire, England.—*Worcester.*

TAPIOCA.   A substance much used in the United States for puddings and other culinary purposes.   It is extracted from the *manioc* (*gatropha manihot*), a shrub indigenous to tropical America, and now cultivated from Florida to Magellan. It is said that an acre of manioc will nourish more persons than six acres of wheat.   Its roots attain the size of the thigh.   Every part of the plant is filled with a milky juice, which is a very violent and dangerous poison, producing death in a few minutes, when swallowed ; yet human ingenuity has converted its roots into an article of food.   This is done by grinding them in wooden mills, after which the paste is put into sacks, and exposed to the action of a powerful press.   The poisonous juice is thereby extracted, and the residue is the substance known as *cassava*, or *mandioca*, a nutritious flour, preferred by the natives to that from wheat. When kept from moisture, this flour will keep good for fifteen or twenty years.   The *tapioca* is made by separating from the fibrous part of the roots a small quantity of the pulp, after the juice is extracted, and working it by hand till a thick white cream appears on the surface.   This, being scraped off and washed in water, gradually subsides to the bottom.   After the water is poured off, the remaining moisture is dissipated by a slow fire, and the substance being constantly stirred, gradually forms into grains about as large as those of sago. This is the purest and most wholesome part of the manioc.—*Encyc. Americana.*

TO BE ON ONE'S TAPS, is to be always ready on one's feet, literally on one's shoes; a metaphor borrowed from the shoemaker, *taps* being a cant word for shoes among the fraternity.

> Your editor, when times are dull, must be ' on his *taps*,' as the saying is. When the mail comes through and brings news enough to make things look lively, why then he must work, and cut, and paste, as though the world depended on him.—*N. Y. Tribune.*

TARBOGGIN. In Canada, a light sleigh.

TARNATION. A common oath.—*Halliwell*. In vulgar use in New England.

> Poor honest John! 'tis plain he know'd
> But liddle of live's range,
> Or he'd a know'd, gals oft, at fust,
> Have ways *tarnation* strange.—*Essex Dialect*, p. 11.

TARRING AND FEATHERING. A punishment sometimes inflicted by indignantly virtuous mobs in Southern and Western States, on persons who have committed an offence of which they fear the law will not take cognizance, by daubing them all over with tar, and afterwards covering them with feathers. " A practice," says Grose, " lately inflicted by the good people of Boston, in America, on any person convicted or suspected of loyalty."

TAUTAUG. The name of the Blackfish caught in the waters of Rhode Island. It is an Indian word, and may be found in Roger Williams's Key to the Indian Language, where, however, he calls it the Sheepshead, an entirely different fish. In New York it is called Black Fish. Dr. Mitchell gave the generic name of *Tautoga* to it, which name it retains among naturalists; see Storer, Cuvier, and De Kay.

TO TAX. To charge; as, ' What will you *tax* me a yard for this cloth?' i. e. what will you charge for it, or what is the price of it?

TEETER. To see-saw on a balanced plank, as children for amusement.—*Worcester*. The English pronunciation is *titter*.

TEETER-TAWTER. The act of see-sawing. In England pronounced *titter-totter.*—*Halliwell.*

TEE-TOTAL. Entire; total. A modern cant word, formed by reduplication, the syllable *tee* being used for the letter *t.*— *Worcester.*

> Reading books is enough to ruin anybody. There ought to be *tee-total* societies against it.—*J. C. Neal, Peter Ploddy,* p. 15.

> He lodged at a strictly *teetotal* house,
> That he might not be shocked with hilarity,
> And found among other *teetotalisms,*
> A total exclusion of charity.—*The Devil's New Walk.*

The Preston (Eng.) Chronicle gives an account of the funeral of Richard Turner, who, it says, was the originator of the term *tee-totaller,* as applied to those who abstain from intoxicating drinks.

The deceased had been upwards of fourteen years a member of the Temperance Society, having signed the pledge in October, 1832, while in a state of intoxication. It may not be generally known (says the Chronicle) how the term "*tee-totallers*" became first adopted by the members of the Total Abstinence Society, but we may inform our readers that Dickey, (that being the name by which Mr. Turner was familiarly called,) in one of his speeches, which were generally characterized by an equal mixture of wit and blunders, being at a loss for a word which would convey to the audience that he was an out-and-out total abstinence man, said, " I have signed the *tee, tee-total* pledge."

This speech was delivered in the Cockpit, at the latter end of the year 1833. The word, being short and expressive, was immediately adopted by the abstainers of Lancashire, and ultimately throughout England—nay, we may say throughout the world, for both in America and India the term is adopted by those who are pledged to abstain from all intoxicating liquors.

TEE-TOTALLER. A thorough temperance man, who avoids every kind of ardent spirits, wine, and beer.

A stump orator in Michigan, in his appeal to the electors, uses the following language:

> I'm a man that will never refuse to take a glass of grog with a fellow-

citizen because he wears a ragged coat. Liberty and equality, I say. Three cheers for liberty and equality, and down with the *tee-totallers!*— *Mrs. Clavers's Forest Life*, Vol. II. p. 39.

Candidates for office ain't never near-sighted; they sees every body; there ain't no *tee-totallers* among them neither, for they treat every body.— *N. O. Delta.*

TEE-TOTALLY. Entirely; totally.

The meetin' houses on one side of the water, how *tee-totally* different they be!—*Sam Slick in England*, ch. 12.

Stranger, I'm powerful sorry, but we're *tee-totally* out; he took every bit of food with him.—*Carlton's New Purchase*, Vol. II. p. 245.

Things weren't going on right; so I pretty nearly gave myself up *tee-totally* to the good of the republic.—*J. C. Neal, Peter Brush.*

TELL. A saying; generally, however, a good one, or a complimentary one. A young lady will say to another, " I've a *tell* for you," i. e. I've a compliment for you, or I have heard some one speak highly of you. Not elegant.

In his dealings with the other sex, he is a little twistical according to their *tell.*—*Humphreys, The Yankee in England.*

TO TELL ON. To tell of; to tell about.

" Well," says the Gineral, " I am glad I didn't understand him, for now it stumps me considerable. Major, who was that?" " Why," says I, " Gineral, he is the son of a man I've heard you *tell on* a thousand times."— *Maj. Downing's Letters*, 29.

TO TELL. To have effect.—*Worcester.*

President Everett's letter read at the Tabernacle, at the meeting in favor of Pope Pius IX., contained good counsels of a *telling* character.—*N. Y. Express*, Dec. 1, 1847.

The admirable pamphlet of Mr. Gallatin on the Mexican War, has *told* in every part of the country.—*Newspaper.*

In this vicinity we are all perfectly satisfied with the nominations of Taylor and Fillmore. I think that we can beat the free trade party with ease, having old Rough and Ready as a leader. With the Germans he is a great favorite, and their votes *tell* in Pennsylvania.—*N. Y. Com. Adv.*

TO TELL APART. To distinguish; as, ' Their resemblance was so striking, that I could not *tell* them *apart.*' We also use the phrase, ' To know apart,' in the same sense.—*Hurd's Corrector.*

TELL'D, for *told.* Provincial in England.—*Halliwell.*

Now I guess you'd better stayed at hum with mother, next time. She *tell'd* you about the perils of the salt sea.—*Humphreys, The Yankee in England.*

DO TELL. See page 119.

TENDSOME. Requiring much attendance; as, ' a *tendsome* child.'—*Webster.* This word is used in Connecticut.

TENN. The abbreviation for *Tennessee.*

TEND, for *attend.*

Most of the passengers in the cars were preachers what had been up to Augusta to *tend* the convention.—*Maj. Jones's Travels.*

TERRAPIN. A name given to a species of tide-water tortoise. —*Webster.*

TERAWCHY. This word is evidently of Dutch origin, though I cannot discover its derivation. It is a very common word in the nursery, and is always accompanied by a peculiar motion of the fingers, with the palm of the hand presented to the child. It is as well known among the old English families of New York as among those of Dutch descent.

THICK. Intimate; familiar. ' They are very *thick* just now.' Provincial in the North of England, and in Yorkshire.— *Craven Glossary and Brockett.*

It was lucky I leet of a man that went to school wi' me when I was a lile lad; we were devlish *thick.*—*Westm. and Cumb. Dialect,* p. 127.

THICK. The midst, i. e. of a crowd.

I met a large concourse of people at Louisville. I had no idea of attracting so much attention; but there I was in the *thick* of them.—*Crockett, Tour,* p. 159.

THIMBLE BERRY. The Black Raspberry, so called by many.

THIMBLE WEED. (Lat. *Rudbeckia.*) A tall plant six or eight feet high, resembling the sunflower. It is one of the herbs prepared by the Shakers, and is used in medicine for its diuretic and tonic properties.

THIS HERE, and **THAT THERE.** These vulgar pleonasms are often heard in this country as well as in England.

THOROUGHWORT. (Lat. *eupatorium perfoliatum.*) A plant used in medicine for its tonic properties.—*Bigelow, Medical Botany.*

LIKE A THOUSAND OF BRICK. A queer simile very often heard. It means, of course, very heavily; and then, vigorously; vehemently.

A huge negro woman threw herself convulsively from her feet, and fell *like a thousand of brick* across a diminutive old man.—*Simon Suggs.*

The new " Yankee Doodle," by George P. Morris, created an immense noise. Nobody could sit still; hands and feet came into the chorus of their own accord, and the house was down " *like a thousand of brick.*"— *New York Paper.*

I see he was gettin riled some, and I thought he'd bile over. You see that's the way with us Western folks. If folks is sassy, we walk right into 'em *like a thousand of brick.*—*Mrs. Clavers, Forest Life,* Vol. I. p. 109.

THUNDERING. Very; exceedingly. A vulgar word used with pretty much the same latitude as the English *devilish.*

I was told that Faneuil Hall was called the " cradle of liberty." I reckon old King George thought they were *thundering* fine children that were rocked in it, and a good many of them.—*Crockett, Tour down East,* p. 61.

If a chap only comes from the North, and has got a crop of hair and whiskers, and a coat different from everybody else, and a *thunderin'* great big gold chain about his neck, he's the poplerest man among the ladies.— *Maj. Jones's Courtship,* p. 82.

TICK. A ticket; score; debt; trust; credit.—*Worcester.* This word, says Dr. Johnson, seems contracted from *ticket,* a tally on which debts are scored. Mr. Halliwell says it signifies a tradesman's bill, formerly written on a card or *ticket.*

You may swim in twentie of their boates over the water upon *ticket.*— *Decker's Gull's Horn Book.*

Taking up arms and ammunition from the States united, with whom they went on *ticket,* and long days of payment, for want of ready money for their satisfaction.—*Heylin, Hist. of the Presbyterians* (1670), p. 437.

To buy on tick, to go on tick, are the common phrases wherein this now vulgar word is heard. Like many other words once used in good society and by learned men, ' *tick* ' has almost had its day, and is fast sinking into obscurity.

When the money is got into hands that have bought all that they have need of, whoever needs anything else must *go on tick* or barter for it.— *Locke.*

Wild. Play *on tick* and lose the Indies, I'll discharge it all to-morrow.— *Dryden, An Evening's Love,* Act 3.

They call this the age of inventions; but why does not some fellow take out a patent for providing drinks *on tick*—he would be a benefactor to his species.—*N. O. Delta.*

TICKLER. A common name among merchants and bankers for a book in which a register of notes or debts is kept, for reference.

TIE. The state produced by an equal number of votes on two opposite sides.—*Worcester.* I have not found this very common use of the word in any other dictionary or glossary, English or American.

TIGHT. Close; parsimonious; saving; as, 'a man *tight* in his dealings.' Close; hard; as, 'a *tight* bargain.'—*Webster.* To these American uses of the word is to be added another similar to the last. When money is difficult to be procured by discounting, &c., business men say, 'the money-market is *tight*,' or 'money is *tight*.' In this sense it is the opposite of *easy*, which see.

> The money market, except on the best stocks, is getting *tight*, and there is a general calling in of loans upon the "fancies."—*N. Y. Tribune.*

TIGHT MATCH. A close or even match, as of two persons wrestling or running together; and hence a difficulty. 'The Loco-focos may succeed in electing Cass, but they will have a *tight match* to do it.'

TIGHT SCROUGING, i. e. hard squeezing. Said of anything difficult to accomplish.—*Sherwood's Georgia.*

TILT-UP, or **TIP-UP.** The popular name of the Sand-piper. See *Peet-weet.*

TIME, for *hour*, in the phrase, 'What *time* are you?' meaning, What o'clock is it?

TIMOTHY GRASS. (*Phleum pratense.*) The common name for the Herd's Grass; said to be derived from Timothy Hanson, one of its early propagators.—*Bigelow's Flora Bostoniensis.*

TIN. A slang word for money. 'Kelter,' 'dimes,' 'dough,' 'rocks,' and many other words are used in the same manner.

TINKER. Small mackerel. New England.

TO TIP OVER. To turn over; to capsize.—*Worcester.*

TO TIP UP. To raise up one end, as of a cart, so that the

contents may pass out.—*Worcester*. Both this and the preceding expressions are used in England, although not in the
dictionaries.

TIP-TOP. An expression often used in common conversation,
denoting the utmost degree, excellence or perfection.—*Todd's
Johnson*.

> If you love operas, these will be the most splendid in Italy; four *tip-top*
> voices; a new theatre.—*Gray to West*, Let. (1741).

> Had I come a few minutes sooner, I might have heard Geeho Dobbin
> sung in a *tip-top* manner by the pimple-nosed spirit at the President's right
> elbow.—*Goldsmith, Essays*, p. 114.

> Knowing as I'm a man of *tip-top* breeding,
> That great folks drink no healths whilst they are feeding.—*Peter
> Pindar, Bozzy and Piozzi*.

At the Democratic meeting, held in New York, June 12th,
1848, to ratify the nomination of Gen. Cass for the Presidency, Gen. Houston, who addressed the meeting, closed as
follows:

> I am, fellow citizens, exceedingly obliged to you for the notice you have
> extended to me, and am happy on turning round, to touch upon my friend
> Senator Bright, who is proud of being from Kentucky, proud of Virginia,
> and proud of New York. He is a *tip-top* half-horse, half-alligator, from
> Kentucky, and I recommend him to your keeping.—*Report in N. Y. Her-
> ald*, June 13, 1848.

> To crown his accomplishments, Simon was *tip-top* at the game of 'old
> sledge,' which was the fashionable game of that era.—*Simon Suggs*, p. 14.

> He allowed the gentleman to be right good company, and he did not
> mistrust but what we'd have a *tip-top* time of it.—*Hoffman, Winter in the
> West*, Let. 33.

> This day is a *tip-topper*, and it's the last we'll see of the kind 'till we get
> back to America again.—*Sam Slick in England*, ch. 3.

TO TITIVATE. To dress up. 'To *titivate* oneself,' is to
make one's toilet. Provincial in various parts of England.

> Well, I'll arrive in time for dinner; I'll *titivate* myself up, and down to
> drawin'-room.—*Sam Slick in England*, ch. 23.

TIT FOR TAT. The phrase "*tit for tat*, if you kill my dog
I'll kill your cat," is among the provincialisms of Hants, and
means, that I shall treat you as you treat me.—*Holloway*.
In the United States this phrase is very common.

> " Ah, me ! your reverence's sister,
> Ten times I carnally have——kissed her."
> " All's fair," returns the reverend brother ;
> " I've done the samer with your mother
> Three times as aft ; and sae for that
> We're on a level, *tit for tat.*"—*Allan Ramsay, Poems.*

TITHING-MAN. In New England, a parish officer appointed to preserve order at public worship, and enforce the proper observance of the Sabbath.—*Worcester.*

TITTER. An eruption on the skin. This is merely another pronunciation of *tetter*, used in New England, and, according to Forby, provincial in England.

TO, for *at* or *in,* is an exceedingly common vulgarism in the Northern States. We often hear such vile expressions as, ' He was not *to* home,' ' He lives *to* York ;' and the opposite mistake of *in* for *into* (see Appendix) is hardly less frequent.

> I have forgot what little I learnt *to* night school ; and, in fact, I never was any great shakes at it.—*Sam Slick.*

TOBACCO. (Span. *tabaco.*) An American plant ; the dried leaves of the plant used for smoking, chewing, and for making snuff. The name is supposed to be derived from *Tabaco*, a province of Yucatan, where it was first found by the Spaniards.—*Worcester.* According to Gilii, it is the name of an instrument which the Indians used for smoking.—*Storia Americana.*

Among the host of names given to the weed according to the various modes in which it is prepared for *chewing* are, Pig-tail, Ladies' twist, Cavendish, Honey-dew, Negro-head (pron. Nigger-head), Long cut, Short cut, Bull's eye, Plug, Oronoko leaf, Nail-rod or 32's, Roll, Fine spun, Pound, &c. &c. There is besides *smoking* tobacco put up in papers of various kinds, as Canaster, Kite-foot, Cut-stems, &c. In the form of *snuff*, there are also many terms for it, as Maccoboy, Rappee (American and foreign, named after the places it is manufactured in), American gentleman, Demigros, Pure Virginia, Copenhagen, Nachitoches, Bourbon, St. Domingo, Scotch of various qualities in bladders, High toast, Irish blackguard, Irish High toast, &c. &c.

TODDY. Originally a tree in the East Indies ; afterwards, a liquor extracted from it; and latterly a kind of punch made of rum, water, sugar, and nutmeg.—*Todd.*

> The *toddy* tree is not unlike the date or palm.—*Sir T. Herbert, Travels.*

> The wine, or *toddy,* is got by piercing the tree, and putting a jar or pitcher under, so as the liquor may distil into it.—*Ibid.* p. 29.

TO TOLL. To entice; to lead on. Western.

TOMAHAWK. Common to several Indian languages of the Atlantic coast of the United States. Micmac, *tomehagen;* Abenakis, *temahigan;* Mohegan, *tumnahegan;* Delaware, *tamoihecan.* An Indian hatchet, or axe.—*Gallatin's Synopsis.*

It was and is the custom of the Indians to go through the ceremony of burying the *tomahawk* when they made peace; when they went to war, they dug it up again. Hence the phrases 'to bury the *tomahawk,*' and 'to dig up the *tomahawk,*' are sometimes used by political speakers and writers with reference to the healing up of past disputes or the breaking out of new ones. See *Hatchet.*

TOMCOD. (Genus, *Morrhua.* Cuvier.) A small fish common to our coast, but which become very abundant after the first frost; hence the name of Frost Fish by which it is also known. —*Storer, Fishes of Massachusetts.*

Dr. J. V. C. Smith believes the *tomcod* to be the same as a fish known in Europe as the *tacaud* of Cuvier, and that *tomcod* is a corruption of the Indian name, *tacaud,* i. e. plenty fish, as this little fish was well known to our aborigines.

TONGS. A name for pantaloons and roundabouts formerly in use in New England.

> Children were playing on the green, the boys dressed in *tongs;* some in skirt-coats, &c.—*Margaret,* p. 34.

TOO BIG FOR HIS BREECHES, is said of a man who is above his business; arrogant; haughty.

> Gentlemen, I was one of the first to fire a gun under Andrew Jackson. I helped to give him all his glory. I liked him well once; but when a man gets *too big for his breeches,* I say good bye.—*Crockett, Tour,* p. 152.

TOOTHACHE GRASS. (Lat. *monocera aromatica.*) A singular kind of grass which grows in Florida, with a naked stalk four feet high. It affects the breath and milk of cows, which eat it when young and tender. The root affects the salivary glands.—*Williams's Florida.*

TOOTIES. A common term in nursery language for the feet. A corruption of *footies*, i. e. feet. Used in England as well as with us.

> One luckless day last week the poet met
>> A maid of such perfection, such a face,
>> Such form, such limbs, such more than mortal grace,
> Such dark expressive eyes, such curls of jet,
> Arched brows, straight nose, round chin, and lips a prince
>> Might sue to kiss—in brief, so many beauties,
>> Such hands, such waist, such ankles—O such *tooties!*
> He really has not been his own man since :
> Rum-punch will not restore his appetite,
> Nor rarebits even make him sleep at night !—*Am. Rev.*, July, 1848.

TOPPER. Anything superior; a clever or extraordinary person; but generally in an ironical sense.—*Brockett's North County Words.*

> The king's meade a bit of a speech,
>> And gentlefolk says it's a *topper.*—*Poems in Westm. and Cumb. Dialect,* p. 220.

TOPPING. Fine; gallant; proud; assuming superiority.—*Johnson. Webster.* In New England much used among the common people.

> *Doolittle.* Why ! what's a ladyship more than any other woman ? and wherein lies the odds ?
> *Newman.* Odds ! It lies in everything. They are often very odd.
> *Doolittle.* As how, in this particular case ?
> *Newman.* She's lofty—*topping*—has her highs sometimes.—*D. Humphreys, The Yankee in England.*

TORE. The dead kind of grass that remains on the ground in winter. This word, says Webster, is used in New England.—*Ash.*

TORE. The place where one stands to shoot marbles from. Used by the boys of New York.

TORY. The name of a political party. It originated in Ireland, and is derived from *toraigham*—to pursue for plunder. (Lingard, Hist. England, XI. 135.) It imported a leaning towards popery and despotism, and was first applied to the natives of Ireland, who having been deprived of their estates, supported themselves by depredations on the English settlers.—*Wade's British History,* p. 237.

TO TOTE. To carry. A queer word of unknown origin, much used in the Southern States. It has been—absurdly enough—derived from the Latin *tollit*.

> The militia had everlastin' great long swords as much as they could tote.—*Maj. Jones's Courtship*, p. 39.

> Here a boy was ferociously cutting wood—there one *toting* wood.— *Carlton, The New Purchase*, Vol. I. p. 167.

> My gun here *totes* fifteen buckshot and a ball, and slings 'em to kill.— *Chron. of Pineville*, p. 169.

> "Goodness gracious!" said old Miss Stallins; " white servants! Well. the Lord knows I wouldn't have none on 'em about me; I could never bear to see a white gall *toatin* my child about, and waitin' on me like a nigger; it would hurt my conscience."—*Maj. Jones's Travels.*

> And its oh! she was so neat a maid,
> That her stockings and her shoes
> She *toted* in her lily white hands,
> For to keep them from the dews.—*Ohio Boatman's Song.*

> Tom was liberal [with his honey], and supplied us all with more than we wanted, and *toted* his share to his own home.—*Thorpe's Backwoods.*

> The watchman arrested Mr. Wimple for disturbing the peace, and *toted* him off to the calaboose.—*Pickings from the N. O. Picayune*, p. 120.

STONE TOTER. The most singular fish in this part of the world [the Southern States] is called the *stone-toter*, whose brow is surmounted with several little sharp horns, by the aid of which he *totes* small flat stones from one part of the brook to another more quiet, in order to make a snug little inclosure, for his lady to lie in in safety.—*Paulding, Lett. from the South.*

TOUCH. *No touch to it*, i. e. not to compare with it. A common expression in vulgar language.

> The children of Israel, going out of Egypt, with their flocks and their little ones, is *no touch to it* [i. e. the first day of May in New York].— *Maj. Downing*, p. 30.

TOUCH-ME-NOT. (Lat. *impatiens noli tangere*.) A plant found about brooks, and in moist places.—*Michaux, Sylva.* A popular name for the common balsam, so named from the bursting of the capsules when touched with the fingers.

TOUSE. A noise, or disturbance.—*Halliwell.*

> The Loch Katrin, they [the Scotch] make such a *touss* about, is jest about equal to a good sizeable duck-pond in our country.—*Sam Slick in England*, ch. 30.

TRACK-SPRINKLER. A contrivance recently invented in Providence, R. I., and now in use on the railroads in that State, for sprinkling railroad tracks. A tank of 2000 gallons has been found sufficient to sprinkle a track or railway of 47 miles, the train going at the rate of 20 miles an hour.

TRAIL. Scent left by a track; track followed by the hunter; an Indian footpath.—*Worcester.*

> It was the policy of the President of Texas to open a direct road to Santa Fé by a route much nearer than the great Missouri *trail.*—*Kendall's Santa Fé Expedition,* Vol. I. p. 14.

> It is suggested that the respective locations for the Indians might be made, apart from the great Northern and Southern *trails*, thoroughfares of migration, and the settlements limited within certain prescribed boundaries, where the government might protect them from the encroachments of white men.—*Report of the Philadelphia Committee at a meeting in behalf of the Indians,* March 31, 1848.

TO TRAIL. 'Not worth shucks *to trail*,' is a Southern phrase, meaning that anything is of little value, not fit to draw home *shucks;* and probably equivalent to the classical expression, ' not fit to carry guts to a bear.'

> They have three or four hounds, and one great big yellow one, what wasn't *worth shucks to trail.*—*Maj. Jones's Courtship.*

TRAIN. (Fr. *traineau.*) A peculiar kind of sleigh used for the transportation of merchandise, wood, &c., in Canada.

TRAINERS. The militia when assembled for exercise.

> The gentler sex partake, by sympathy at least, in the excitement, by running after the *trainers.*—*Mrs. Clavers's Western Clearings,* p. 28.

TRAINING-DAY. The day when the militia are called out to be reviewed.

TO TRAIPSE. To walk in a careless or sluttish manner.—*Johnson.* It is almost exclusively a woman's word.

> Two slip-shod nurses *traipse* along,
> In lofty madness meditating song,
> With tresses staring from poetic dreams,
> And never wash'd, but in Castalia's streams.—*Pope, Dunciad.*

TO TRAMPOUS. To walk; to lounge or wander about; to tramp. The origin of this word is doubtful; there is nothing analogous to it in the English provincial glossaries.

I felt as lonely as a catamount, and as dull as a bachelor beaver, so I *trampousses* off to the stable.—*Sam Slick in England*, ch. 2.

So we *trampoused* along down the edge of the swamp, till we came to a track.—*Porter's Tales of the South-west*, p. 44.

> When I get hum, I guess that my narration
> Will make some little stir among the nation.
> Some years ago, I landed near to Dover,
> And seed strange sights, *trampoosing* England over.—*D. Humphreys, The Yankee in England.*

So away goes lunch, and off goes you and the " Sir " a *trampousin'* and a *trapsein'* over the wet grass agin.'—*Sam Slick in England*, ch. 23.

TRANSCENDENTALISM. The state or quality of being transcendental ; a transcendental notion or system ; transcendental philosophy.—*Worcester.* This word and most of the following are used by English writers, but having been but lately introduced into the language, they have not yet found a place in the dictionaries.

TRANSCENDENTALIST. One who adheres to transcendentalism.—*Worcester.*

TRANSCENDENTALITY. The quality of being transcendental.—*Worcester.*

TRANSCENDENTALLY. In a transcendent manner.—*Webster.*

TO TRANSMOGRIFY. To change; to alter; to metamorphose. A low word. It is provincial in the North of England, and in Craven Districts.—*Glossaries of Carr and Brockett.*

> Some friends of John's, who at him now
>   Had tuk a squint, they cried,
> " Sen' John's kep comp'ny with that gal,
>   He's quite *transmogrified.*"—*Essex Dialect, Noakes and Styles.*

> See social life and glee sit down
>   All joyous and unthinking,
> Till quite *transmogrified* they're grown,
>   Debauchery and drinking.—*Burns.*

I went to the calaboose to see my friend, Joe Head, and found him *transmogrified* into Mounsheer Tate.—*Crockett, Tour*, p. 146.

TRAPS. Goods; household stuff; baggage. English and American.

Well, when we alighted, and got the baggage off, away starts the guide with the Judge's *traps* to a settler's.—*Sam Slick in England*, ch. 9.

TRASH. The leaves of the sugar cane, in the West Indies, stript from the cane to permit it to ripen. These leaves are laid upon the ground, to prevent the sun's influence on the earth, that every moisture possible may be retained for the nourishment of the plant. *Trash* is also used for foddering cattle and thatching houses.—*Carmichael's West Indies.*

TO TRASH. *To trash the cane*, is to strip off the dry leaves.

TRAVELLER'S JOY. (Lat. *clematis*.) The popular name of a hardy climbing vine, common in low grounds. When in fruit, the long feathery tails of the seeds appear like tufts of wool.—*Bigelow's Plants of Boston.*

TO TREE. To take refuge in a tree, said of a wild animal; to force to take refuge in a tree, drive to a tree, said of the hunter. *To tree oneself*, is to conceal oneself behind a tree, as in hunting or fighting. This hunter's word is purely American.

> Besides *treeing*, the wild cat will take advantage of some hole in the ground, and disappear as suddenly as ghosts at cock-crowing.—*Thorpe's Backwoods*, p. 180.

TRICKY. Trickish ; practising tricks.—*Forby. Halliwell.* Provincial in England and colloquial in the United States.

TO TRIG A WHEEL. To stop a wheel so as to prevent its going backwards or forwards.—*Bailey.* Still used in New England in the same sense.

> I remember when Hash was driving a cart up a hill, I used *to trig the wheels*, that is, put under a stone.—*Margaret*, p. 455.

TRIMMINGS. Bread and butter and other necessary eatables for the tea-table.

> A cup of tea with *trimmings*, is always in season ; and is considered as the orthodox mode of welcoming any guest.—*Mrs. Clavers, A New Home.*

> The party luxuriated at Florence's [eating house] on lobster and *trimmings.*—*Knickerbocker Mag.*, Aug. 1845.

TO TROLL. A method of fishing, by a long line attached to the stern of a boat, which is set in motion by sails or muffled oars. A piece of tin, or a strip of red and white cloth, is attached to the hook, which, passing rapidly along the surface of the water, is seized by the fish. Bass are generally caught in this way.

TO TROUNCE. To beat.—*Halliwell.* Colloquial in England and the United States.

> The Lord *trounced* Sisera, and all his chariots.—*Mathews' Trans. of the Bible,* 1537. Judges, v. 15.

> Sit down and eat your supper, or I'll *trounce* you in two minutes.—*Maj. Downing,* p. 165.

TRUCK. Medicine.—*Sherwood's Georgia.*

TRUCK. Produce; cloth, or almost anything.—*Ibid.*

> They purchased homespun, calico, salt, rum, tobacco, and such other *truck* as their necessaries called for.—*Chronicles of Pineville,* p. 40.

> The fact is, if the people of Georgia don't take to makin' homespun and sich *truck* for themselves, and quit their everlastin' fuss about the tariff and free trade, the first they'll know, the best part of their population will be gone to the new States.—*Maj. Jones's Travels.*

> Now they passed down into Punkatees Neck; and in their march they found a large wigwam full of Indian *truck,* which the soldiers were for loading themselves with.—*Church's Indian War,* 1716.

> " What do the doctors give for the fever and ague ?"
> " Oh, they give abundance o' *truck.*"—*Georgia Scenes,* p. 192.

TRUCK. A two-wheeled vehicle drawn by a horse, and used for carrying merchandise; a cart.

TRUCKMAN. The driver of a truck.

TRUCKAGE. The charges for carrying on a truck; the cartage. These words are commonly used in New England instead of cart, carman, and cartage, elsewhere employed.

TO TRY. To purify; to refine.—*Johnson. Webster.* A common use of this word in the United States, and the only one connected with purifying, is in connection with tallow: ' *To try out* tallow or lard,' is to melt it down, for the purpose of purifying. It is provincial in England in the same sense.—*Forby. Halliwell.*

TUK, for *took.* A vulgar pronunciation, common to the North and South.

TO TUCK. To gather into a narrow compass; to crush together; to hinder from spreading.—*Johnson.*

In the United States we use the phrase, *to tuck on*, in two different senses or applications. It means in the first place to lay on; as, 'having caught the thief, he *tucked* it *on* to him without mercy.' 'How you *tuck* the price *on* these goods,' i. e. how dear they are. It also means, to force a bad article on a person in buying or exchanging; as, 'We swapped horses, and I got this miserable old animal *tucked on* to me.'

TUCKAHOE. (*Lucoperdon solidu.* Clayton, *Flora Virginica*.) The Virginia truffle. A curious vegetable, sometimes called by the name of Indian Bread, or Indian Loaf, found in the Southern States, bordering on the Atlantic. It is a natural production, the origin of which has greatly perplexed naturalists, as it is commonly found several feet under the surface, and, like the truffle of Europe, has apparently no stem or leafy appendage connecting it with the external atmosphere. They are generally found through the instrumentality of hogs, whose acute sense of smelling enables them to fix upon the spot where they lie buried. They are usually of a globular or flattened oval shape, and rather regular surface, the large ones resembling somewhat a brown loaf of coarse bread. The size varies from an acorn to the bigness of a man's head. Its name *tuckahoe* is Indian, and is said to designate bread. When examined with a microscope, it exhibits no fibres or pores, or any other indications of organization, so easily detected in roots and other vegetable productions of ordinary growth. The Southern botanists regard the *tuckahoe* as a fungus.—*Farmer's Encyclopedia.*

The term *tuckahoe* is often applied to an inhabitant of Lower Virginia, and to the poor land in that section of the State.

TUCKERED OUT. Tired out; fatigued. Used in New York and New England.

I guess the Queen don't do her eating very airly; for we sot and sot, and waited for her, till we got eenamost *tuckered out.*—*N. Y. Family Comp.*

TO TUMP. Probably an Indian word. It means to draw a deer or other animal home through the woods, after he has been killed.   Ex. 'We *tumped* the deer to our cabin.'   Used in Maine.

TUMPLINE.   A strap placed across the forehead to assist a man in carrying a pack on his back.   Used in Maine, where the custom was borrowed from the Indians.

TUM-TUM.   A favorite dish in the West Indies, made by beating the boiled plantain quite soft in a wooden mortar. It is eaten like a potato pudding, or made into round cakes and fried.—*Carmichael's West Indies*, Vol. I. p. 183.

TO TURN IN.   To go to bed.   Originally a seaman's phrase, but now common on land.

TUSSLE.   The verb *to touse* is given by both Johnson and Webster, to pull; to tear; to haul.   Both have also the word *tussle*, a struggle; a conflict, which they call a vulgar word.

> Thus Envy, the vile hag, attacks my rhymes,
> Swearing they shall not peep on distant times;
> But violent indeed shall be the *tussel.*—*P. Pindar, Royal Tour, Proem.*

> In New York the *tussle* is all about the price of rents; the landlords want to get them up higher, and the tenants want to get them down lower —*Maj. Downing, May-day in New York*, p. 30.

> I'll give the old dog a *tussel* when it comes to my turn.—*Simon Suggs.*

'TWA'N'T, for *it was not.*   New England.

TO TWIG.   To observe.   A flash word common to England and the United States.

> Your responsibility men want no endorsers, do you *twig?*—*Sam Slick.*

> I'm a regular patriot—look at my coat.   I'm all for the public good—*twig* the holes in my trowsers.—*Neal's Sketches.*

TWISTICAL.   Tortuous; unfair; not quite moral.   Used in New England.

> He may be straight going, farzino, manwards; but in his dealings with t'other sex, he is a leetle *twistical*, according to their tell.   I wouldn't make a town talk of it.—*D. Humphreys, The Yankee in England.*

TO TWITCH.   To draw timber along the ground by a chain. Used by lumbermen in Maine.

TYKE.   In Scotland and the North of England, a dog; and hence a contemptible person.

Base *tyke*, call'st me host? now
By this hand, I swear I scorn the term.—*Shakspeare.*

I never had but six months' schooling in all my life, and I confess, I consider myself but a poor *tyke* to be here addressing the most intelligent people in the world.—*Crockett's Speech, Tour,* p. 82.

U.

UGLY. Ill-tempered; bad. New England. Ex. 'He is an *ugly* fellow,' i. e. of a bad disposition; wicked. The compound *ugly-tempered* is also used. They are both heard only among the illiterate.—*Pickering.*

UGLY CUSTOMER. A disagreeable or troublesome companion.

Capt. H——, whom we met at St. Francisco, carried a number of horses, rather *ugly customers,* for the occasion, in an undecked vessel, from California to Woahoo.—*Simpson's Overland Journey,* Vol. I. p. 224.

UMBRELLA TREE. (Lat. *magnolia tripetala.*) The popular name of this tree in the Southern States.

UNBEKNOWN. Unknown. Various dialects of England.— *Halliwell.* This is a very common word in familiar language in New England. It is regularly formed from the Ang. Sax. *be-knowen,* to know; to recognise; to acknowledge; pret. *bi-knewe ;* past part. *bi-known ;* all of which are used by Piers Ploughman.

And though it hadde costned me catel
Bi-knowen it I nolde.—*Piers Ploughman, Vision,* l. 407.

For I am *bi-knowen,*
Ther konnynge clerkes
Shul clokke bi-hynde.—*Ibid.* l. 1422.

The sooty wretches [chimney sweeps] stole four good flitches of bacon, as was up the kitchen chimbly, quite *unbeknown* to me.—*T. Hood, The Pagsley Paper.*

UNCLE SAM. The cant or vulgar name of the United States Government; sometimes called Brother Jonathan. It is used as John Bull is in England. Mr. Frost, in his Naval History of the United States, gives the following account of the origin of the name:

" Immediately after the last declaration of war with England, Elbert Anderson of New York, then a contractor,
visited Troy, on the Hudson; where was concentrated, and
where he purchased, a large quantity of provisions, beef,
pork, &c. The inspectors of these articles at that place were
Messrs. Ebenezer and Samuel Wilson. The latter gentleman (invariably known as ' *Uncle Sam* ') generally super-
intended in person a large number of workmen, who, on this
occasion, were employed in overhauling the provisions purchased by the contractor for the army. The casks were
marked 'E. A.—U. S.' This work fell to the lot of a facetious
fellow in the employ of the Messrs. Wilson, who, on being
asked by some of his fellow-workmen the meaning of the
mark (for the letters U. S. for United States, were then almost
entirely new to them), said, ' he did not know, unless it meant
Elbert Anderson and *Uncle Sam* '—alluding exclusively, then,
to the said ' *Uncle Sam* ' Wilson. The joke took among the
workmen, and passed currently; and ' *Uncle Sam* ' himself,
being present, was occasionally rallied by them on the in-
creasing extent of his possessions." P. 297.

"Many of these workmen, being of a character denominated ' food for powder,' were found, shortly after, following the recruiting drum, and pushing toward the frontier
lines, for the double purpose of meeting the enemy, and of
eating the provisions they had lately labored to put in good
order. Their old jokes accompanied them, and before the
first campaign ended, this identical one first appeared in
print; it gained favor rapidly, till it penetrated and was
recognised in every part of the country, and will, no doubt,
continue so while the United States remain a nation." Ibid.

UNCOMMON. Exceedingly; very.

> It struck me with astonishment to hear people huzzaing for me; and
> took me so *uncommon* unexpected, as I had no idea of attracting atten-
> tion.—*Crockett, Tour down East*, p. 17.

UNCONSCIONABLE. Enormous; vast. A low word.—
Johnson. Used adverbially at the West, as in the following
example:

> " That's an *unconscionable* slick gal of your'n," says I; and it did tickle

his fancy to have her cracked up, 'cause he thought her creation's finish-in' touch—so did I!—*Robb's Squatter Life.*

UNDERDONE. Cooked rare. A very common word with us. Used in the London Quarterly Review, but not noticed by Johnson or Todd.

TO UNDERPIN. To place something for support or foundation; to prop; to support.—*Worcester.*

UNDERPINNING. Act of supporting something placed under; stone-work or masonry on which a building rests.—*Worcester.*

TO UNIFY. To form into one; to reduce to unity.

> Supposing, which requires some confidence, the reader to be able to collect and *unify* these discursive remarks, we will refer to the previous question.—*Am. Review*, Vol. I. N. S. p. 583.

UP-A-DAY. A fondling expression of a nurse to a child, when she takes it up in her arms, or lifts it over some obstacle. The author is informed by a friend, that he heard it used on the same occasions, by nurse-maids in Normandy. It may come from the Anglo-Saxon *up-adon*, to lift up; but is more probably a mere contraction for the equally common phrase *up-a-daisy.*

UPPISH. Proud; insolent.—*Halliwell.* Colloquial in England and the United States.

> You pretend to think everybody alike; but when it comes to the pint, you're a sight more *uppish* than the ra'al quality at home.—*Mrs. Clavers's Western Clearings.*

UPPER CRUST. The aristocracy; the higher circles.

> I want you to see Peel, Stanley, Graham, Shiel, Russell, Macauley, old Joe, and so on. They are all *upper crust* here.—*Sam Slick in England.*

THE UPPER TEN THOUSAND, and contracted, THE UPPER TEN. The aristocracy; the upper circles of our large cities. A phrase invented by N. P. Willis.

> The Biscaccianti troupe commence their season of Italian Opera at the Chestnut to-morrow night. The seats for the first night are already many of them engaged; and engaged, too, by the very cream of our " *upper ten ;*" while the moderate democratic prices of admission which have been wisely adopted, will invite large slices of the honest and hearty masses.—*Letter from Philad. N. Y. Herald.*

UPPER STORY. The brain; as, 'He's not right in his

upper story.'—Carr's Craven Dialect. This same expression is sometimes heard in the United States, to denote a person who is deranged. I have never heard it applied in any other way.

UP TO. 'To be *up to* a thing,' is to understand it. A common English and American vulgarism.

> Have you ever tried faro? whispered Spifflekins; there's considerable fun at faro, when you are *up to it.—J. C. Neal, P. Ploddy,* p. 50.

UP TO THE HUB. To the extreme point. The figure is that of a vehicle sunk in the mud *up to the hub* of the wheels, which is as far as it can go.

> *Newman.* I am sorry not to have your good opinion. I don't doubt your courage.
>
> *Doolittle.* No, you ought not. I've been *up to the hub,* and didn't flinch. No, nor won't back out now. I'll tell you what, Mister! if we Yankees come to loggerheads, we'll show whose heads are hardest.—*D. Humphreys, The Yankee in England,* p. 33.
>
> " You've hearn tell of the bank and tarriff questions?"
>
> " Yes," replied the new editor of the Eagle newspaper.
>
> " Well, hoss, we expect you to be right co-chuck *up to the hub* on them thar questions, and pour it into the enemy in slashergaff style."—*Robb, Squatter Life,* p. 31.

UP TO SNUFF. To be flash; to be shrewd. *Up to snuff and a pinch above it,* is a common cant phrase.—*Grose.* Both these expressions are familiar in the United States.

> "Oh, you remember me, I suppose?" said Mr. Pickwick. " I should think so," replied Sam. " Queer start that 'ere, but he was one too many for you, wasn't he? *Up to snuff and a pinch or two over*—eh?"—*Pickwick Papers.*
>
> A Blue Nose or a John Bull, are a primitive, unsuspectin' sort of folks not exactly *up to snuff.—Sam Slick,* 3d Ser., p. 121.
>
> Then putting his fingers to his nose, says he, " Mr. Slick, I see you are *up to snuff.*"—*Ibid.,* ch. 7.
>
> I'm *up to snuff,* I can tell ye. The master 'll have to kiss the cook this time; he han't enough left for the cat to lick.—*Margaret,* p. 305.
>
> The editor of the Herald has commenced several libel suits against Major Noah. We learn that the Major is *up to snuff,* and announces his intention of bringing thirty or forty suits against Bennett.—*N. Y. Tribune.*

UP TO TRAP. Knowing; shrewd. English and American.

> Phrenology is a little bit dangerous. It is only fit for an old hand like me, that's *up to trap.—Sam Slick.*

Mr. Richardson is evidently a man who has lived among foxes and rabbits—who has seen warrens, knows weazles, associates with terriers, and is perfectly "*up to trap.*"—*London Athenæum*, Dec. 4, 1848.

TO UPSET. To overturn; to overthrow; to overset.—*Todd. Webster.* This word is now so universal both in England and America, that it may appear unnecessary to give it a place. Its use, however, is quite modern, as it is not in any of the English dictionaries before Todd, who calls it a low word.

UPSET PRICE. At public auctions an article is sometimes 'set up,' or 'started,' by the auctioneer at the lowest price at which it can be sold. This is called the *upset price.*

TO USE. To frequent a place. This word is employed in the following sense among the hunters of the West: 'I can see where the deer *used,*' i. e. where the deer have been, or where they have fed. The sense intended to be conveyed, is that the deer has left tracks and other marks on the ground *used* by him. This term is also noticed by Mr. Sherwood as provincial in Georgia; as, 'The sheep *used* in that field.'

TO USE UP. To discomfit; destroy. Grose has this word, which he calls a military one, meaning killed.

> I have promised to write the life of the magician of the North [Mr. Van Buren], and I'll do it; and if, when you read it, you don't say I've *used him up*, I'm mistaken, that's all.—*Crockett, Tour*, p. 234.

> Moving on the first day of May in New York, has *used* me *up* worse than building forty acres of stone wall.—*Maj. Downing, May-day in New York.*

> In 1836, New York went Loco-foco by 26,000 majority, and the Whig party was thought, by its adversaries, to be *used up* for some years.—*N. Y. Tribune*, Nov. 1, 1845.

USED TO COULD. A vulgarism used in the Southern States for *could formerly;* as, 'I cannot do it now, but I *used to could.*'—*Sherwood's Georgia.* We had set this down as a native vulgarism, until we discovered it in the poem called John Noakes and Mary Styles, illustrating the Essex dialect of England.

> I don't think I cud clime it now,
> Altho' I *uster could* ;
> I should't warsley loike to try,
> For guelch cum down I should.

V.

VACHER. (French.) The stock or cattle keeper on the prairies of the South-west. His duty is also to break wild horses, to run cattle, and to brand calves.

TO VAMOS. A Spanish word signifying *let us go*. Fr. *allons!* This and other Spanish expressions have lately become familiar to us through the letters of soldiers and officers from Mexico in the public prints.

> I couldn't stand more than this stanza, coming from a street voice compared with which the notes of a hand-saw are positively dulcet, and I accordingly *vamosed*.—*N. Y. Mirror*, May, 1848.

> Yankee Sullivan's house, corner of Frankfort and Chatham streets, is in a dangerous condition; its foundation walls having been partially undermined for the purpose of excavating a cellar. Its occupants received some very ominous premonitions of a downfall, early yesterday morning, and forthwith *vamosed* with their baggage.—*Journ. of Com.*, June, 1848.

> Madame Anna Bishop gave, on Monday evening last, a spirited exhibition, and not exactly of the vocal powers, for which she is celebrated, but of the woman's temper of which she has undoubtedly her due portion. The saloon was duly lighted up, and very soon after the doors were opened a respectable number of ladies and gentlemen took their seats. But the Madame appears to have been dissatisfied at the number, and before waiting to see if others would assemble, the audience was unceremoniously dismissed, the lights blown out in a huff, and Madame and Monsieur, fiddles, harps, rosin, catgut and all, *vamosed*.—*Vicksburgh Sentinel*, May, 1848.

> On Sunday our city was thrown into a state of intense excitement. Between seventy and eighty slaves had disappeared. Several negroes who had made arrangements to *vamose*, were left behind, and, to be revenged, they gave the alarm.—*Washington Paper*.

> And flinging down a dollar on the table, he seized his white bell-top from the hand of the trembling waiter, and *vamosed*. Down Washington and State streets, he streaked it like a comet, and never slackened his pace till he pulled up on board the Kennebec.

> "Cap'n," said he to the commander, " cast off your lines jest as quick as you're a mind to—and ef you catch me wanting to see Boston again, jest take me by the slack and throw me right into that ere biler, boots and all, by gravy !"—*Sunday Atlas*.

VARMINT. A corrupt pronunciation of the word *vermin*. Applied to noxious wild beasts of any kind.

I shot tolerably well, and was satisfied the fault would be mine if the *varmints* did not suffer.—*Crockett, Tour*, p. 125.

The idea of a man's keeping two *varmints* in a grass, when he might shoot a dozen by going a little way into the woods. These *varmints* were two beautiful deer.—*Thorpe's Backwoods*, p. 156.

VENDUE. (French *vendre*, to sell, *vendu*, sold.) Auction ; a public sale of anything by outcry to the highest bidder.— *Webster.* This word is in use in the United States and the West Indies ; but it is not common in England, though it is found in the recent English dictionaries of Knowles, Oswald, and Smart.

VEST. A waistcoat, or garment worn under a coat. We almost always use this word instead of *waistcoat,* which we rarely apply to anything but an under garment, as ' a flannel waistcoat.'

VETO. A prohibition; negative. A word frequently trans- ferred from political to ordinary life.

The cold, miserable, rainy, unseasonable weather yesterday, put a *veto* on all out-door operations.—*N. Y. Paper.*

VINE-FRETTER. (Lat. *aphis puceron.*) An insect very de- structive to vines, rose bushes, cabbages, &c. in the Southern States. There are said to be 150 species. On every plant they vary in form and color. They have many enemies, among them the caterpillar which will destroy about a hun- dred in an hour.—*Williams's Florida.*

VOYAGEUR. (French.) A Canadian boatman.—*Worcester.*

Vt. The common abbreviation for *Vermont.*

I VUM! An exclamation often heard in New England.

"*I vum,*" said he, " I'm sorry ; what's the matter ?"—*Margaret,* p. 86.

W.

TO WABBLE. In the Western States, to make free use of one's tongue; to be a ready speaker.

TO WABBLE. To move from side to side ; to vacillate. A low and barbarous word, says Dr. Johnson. It is provincial in England.—*Forby's Glossary.*

The sleighs *wabbled* and warped from side to side, the riders screamed and hooted at each other.—*Margaret*, p. 174.

WABBLING.   Moving from side to side ; vacillation; oscillation.

Leverrier's calculations gave the mass of the unknown planet, by which the "*wabblings*" of Herschell were to be set right, at so much ; but the mass of the known planet proves to be less than a quarter of what Leverrier figured out ; and the result is, in short, that yet another and much larger planet must be found to make Leverrier's theory good.   Here's a pretty kettle of fish !—*N. Y. Com. Adv.*

WAFFLE.   (Dutch *wafel.*)   A wafer; a soft indented cake baked in an iron utensil on coals.

WAFFLE-IRON.   (Dutch *wafelyzen.*)   A wafer-iron ; a utensil for baking waffles.

TO WALK THE CHALK.   To walk straight.

"The Tallapoosa volunteers," said Capt. Suggs; "so let every body look out and *walk the chalk.*"—*Simon Suggs*, p. 89.

TO WALK INTO.   To get the upper hand of; to take advantage of; to punish.   A common vulgarism.

To walk into a down-east land-jobber, requires great skill, and a very considerable knowledge of human nature.—*Sam Slick*, 3d series, p. 122.

Senator Benton's speech at St. Louis will amply reward a perusal.   The way it *walks into* Tyler and Calhoun for the Texas iniquity fully atones for all its nonsense about the surrender of Texas in 1819.—*New York Tribune*, May 24, 1847.

I went into the dining room, and sot down afore a plate that had my name writ on a card onto it, and I did *walk into* the beef, and taters, and things, about east.—*Hiram Bigelow's Lett. in Family Comp.*

WALKING TICKET. }
WALKING PAPERS. } Orders to leave ; a dismissal.   When a person is appointed to a public office, or receives a commission, he receives papers or documents investing him with authority ; so when he is discharged it is said in familiar language that ' he has received his *walking papers,* or his *walking ticket.*'

It is probable, that "*walking papers*" will be forwarded to a large proportion of the *corps diplomatique* during the session of Congress.   B—— and B—— are already admonished to return, and the invitation will be pretty general.—*N. Y. Herald, Letter from Washington.*

We can announce with certainty that the Hon. Mr. D—— has received his *walking ticket*, accompanied with some correspondence with his Excellency that has given him offence.—*Kingston, Canada, Whig*, Dec. 1843.

Mr. Duane was ordered to remove the deposits. He answered that his duty did not require it. In a few hours he got his *walking ticket* that his services were no longer wanted.—*Crockett, Tour down East*, p. 30.

TO WALK THE PLANK. This is an expression borrowed from the horrible practice of pirates, who, when they determine to destroy those on board a captured vessel, place a plank projecting over the side, and force the unfortunate wretches to walk out on it till they slip off into the water.

WALL, for *well*, is a common vulgarism in the Northern States.

TO WALLOP. To beat. Provincial in England and colloquial in the United States.

> For sic an infair I've been at
>   As he's but seldom been,
> Whar was sec *wallopin'* and wark
>   As verra few hev seen.—*Poems, Cumberland Dialect*, p. 133.

I grabs right hold of the cow's tail, and yelled and screamed like **mad**, and *wallopped* away at her like anything.—*Sam Slick in England*, ch. 18.

There's nothing like *walloping* for taking the conceit out of fellows who think they know more than their betters.—*J. C. Neal, Orson Dabbs*.

All I know was *walloped* into me. I took larnin' through the skin.—*Neal's Charcoal Sketches*.

WALT. Crank. A ship is said to be *walt*, when she has not her due ballast, that is, not enough to enable her to bear her sails, and keep her stiff. Hubbard in his History of New England, speaking of Lamberton's ill-fated ship, says, that "she was ill-built, very *walt*-sided."—*Rev. Alex. Young, note, Chron. of Massachusetts.*

The next year brought a Flemish fly-boat of about 140 tons, which being unfit for a fishing voyage, and wanting lodging for the men, they added unto her another deck, by which means she was carried so high that she proved *walt* and unable to bear sail.—*White, The Planter's Plea*, 1630, p. 1.

In the North of England *walt* means to totter; to overthrow.—*Halliwell.*

WAMBLE-CROPPED. Sick at the stomach; and figuratively, wretched; humiliated. New England.

There stood Capt. Jumper, shaking General Taylor's hand when he came on board the " Two Pollys," trying to get a start in the address, but could not; and then I tried it. I never saw Capt. Jumper so melted down before—and that made me feel so *wamblecrapt* I could not say a word.— *Maj. Downing, Letter from Baton Rouge*, June 15, 1848.

WAMPUM. (A term in the Massachusetts Indian language signifying *white*, the color of the shells most frequent in *wampum* belts.) Shells, or strings of shells, used by the American Indians as money. These when united form a broad belt, which is worn as an ornament or girdle. It is sometimes called *wampumpeage*, or *wampeage*, of which *wampum* seems to be a contraction.—*Encyc. Americana*.

> A Sagamore with a humberd in his eare for a pendant, a black hawk on his occipit for a plume, good store of *wampompeage* begirting his loynes, his bow in hand, his quiver at his back, with six naked Indian spatterlashes at his heels for his guard, thinks he is all one with King Charles.—*Wood's New England*, 1634, p. 66.

WANGAN. (Indian.) In Maine, a boat for carrying provisions.

WASHY. Weak, not firm or hardy.—*Webster*. Used in New England in various senses. A *washy* horse is one that sweats easily and profusely with labor. An insipid discourse, &c. is often termed by us, as in England, *wishy-washy*.

> " Let the dog alone," he replied, speaking in a blubbering *washy* manner. "You'll spoil him; would you make a goslin of him ?"—*Margaret*, p. 275.

TO WAP. To throw quickly ; to flap.—*Jamieson*. See *Whap*.

> Day is dawen, and cocks hae crawen,
> And *wappit* their wings sae wide.—*Jamieson, Pop. Ballads*, I. 95.

WAY-BILL. A list of the passengers in a stage-coach, railroad car, steamboat, or other public conveyance.

WAYS AND MEANS. The committee of ' *ways and means*,' in legislation, is a committee to whom is intrusted the consideration of the affairs relating to the revenue or finances of a country.—*Worcester*.

WAYS, for way, distance, space. A very common vulgarism.

> It's only a little *ways* down to the village.—*Margaret*, p. 123.

THERE'S NO TWO WAYS ABOUT IT, i. e. the fact is just so, and not otherwise. A vulgarism of recent origin, equivalent to the common phrase, ' *there's no mistake about it*,' or ' the fact is so and so, *and no mistake*.'

Jist so, jist so, stranger; you are just about half right and *there's no two ways about it.*—*Sam Slick*, 3d ser. ch. 7.

There's no two ways about that, sir; but arn't you surprised to see such a fine population ?—*Hoffman, Winter in the West.*

WEATHER-BREEDER. A cloudless sky, after a succession of rainy weather, denotes rain, and is said to be a *weather-breeder.*—*Carr's Craven Dialect.* This expression is frequently applied by seafaring men to certain appearances in the heavens which denote an approaching storm.

WEED. A common term for tobacco; as, 'Do you use the *weed?*' meaning, 'Do you chew tobacco?'

Those who were not dancing, were seated around the room, some smoking, others chewing the *weed*, still others drinking.—*Mysteries of New York*, p. 89.

WEEDY-WEEDY. A plant resembling spinach, much used in the West Indies.—*Carmichael's West Indies.*

WELL-TO-DO. In a state of ease as to pecuniary circumstances; well off.—*Holloway.*

In speaking of the emigration from Stockholm to the United States, the Liverpool Times (June 19, 1846) says :

The greater part of the emigrants are artisans and agriculturists, and many of them are tolerably *well-to-do* in the world.

Each sectary, *well-to-do*, in Persia or India, leaves a portion of his wealth to the mosques of Kerbela, that his body may be received there.—*London Athenæum*, 1845, p. 1246.

By all accounts you are considerable *well-to-do*, and have made an everlastin' sight of money among the Blue Noses of Nova Scotia.—*Sam Slick.*

The old lady being now *well-to-do*, in a spiritual sense.—*Boston Times.*

WELL TO LIVE. To be in easy circumstances; to live comfortably.

I wanted to see how these Northerners could buy our cotton, carry it home, manufacture it, bring it back, and sell it for half nothing; and, in the mean time, be *well to live*, and make money besides.—*Crockett, Tour.*

WENCH. In the United States, this word is only applied to black females.

WHANG. Sinews of the buffalo or other animal, or small strips of thin deer-skin, used by the dwellers and hunters of the prairies for sewing.

WHALING. A lashing; a beating.

But it is possible that we may, at some future time, go to war with England—her writers and speakers having spoken disparagingly of us, while her actors, half-pay officers and other travelling gentry carry their heads rather high in passing through our country—for which "arrogant" demeanor we are bound to give her a *whaling!*—*N. Y. Tribune*, Aug. 1847.

WHALER. A big, strapping fellow.

He's a *whaler!* said Rory; but his face is mighty little for his body and legs.—*Georgia Scenes*, p. 184.

WHAP. A quick and smart stroke.—*Jamieson.*

He hit him on the wame ane *wap,*
It buft lyke ony bledder.—*Chr. Kirk, st.* 12.

WHAP! An interjection expressive of a sudden blow, like whack! slap! bang! &c.

But a day of payment is coming; and if the money ain't forthcoming, out comes a Randolph writ, and *whap* goes your money and liberty.—*Crockett's Speech, Tour,* p. 109.

I began to think smokin' warn't so bad after all, when *whap* went my cigar right out of my mouth into my bosom.—*Sam Slick in England,* ch. 2.

TO WHAP OVER. To turn over. (New England.)

WHAPPER. ⎱
WHOPPER. ⎰ Anything uncommonly large; as, 'That's a *whopper,*' meaning a monstrous lie. 'In angling to-day, I caught a *whopper,*' i. e. a very large fish. This word is provincial in various parts of England, and is a common one here. In his paper on the ancient words in Yorkshire, Dr. Willan observes that, "in many other instances, our forefathers seem to have estimated weights and magnitudes by the force of their blows. Thus, they employed in gradation, the terms *slapper, smacker, banger, thumper, twacker, swinger,* and *rattler.* The word *bumper,* concerning which much has been said and surmised, is not of a more exalted origin than that which is here stated."—*Archæologia,* Vol. XVII. p. 162.

WHAPPING. Very large.

We've got only one crib, and that's a *whappin'* one too.—*Maj. Downing's Letters,* p. 67.

A *whappin'* big pan of mush stood in the centre of the table, and a large pan of milk beside it, with lots of corn-bread and butter.—*Robb, Squatter Life,* p. 61.

WHARVES, plur. of *wharf.* Mr. Pickering notices this form of the plural of *wharf,* as peculiar to Americans. The

English say *wharfs*. In the Colony and Province Laws of Massachusetts, Mr. Pickering says he has observed the plural *wharfs* (or *wharfes*) as late as the year 1735; but after that period the form *wharves* is used.

WHAT NOT. In New York a piece of furniture usually placed in a parlor, consisting of several shelves, upon which are placed articles of vertu, porcelain, small bronzes, etc.

WHAT'S WHAT. ' To know *what's what*,' is to know the nature of things, or as we classically express it, ' to be up to a thing or two.'

> I know *what's what*. I know on which side my bread is buttered.— *Ford, The Lady's Trial,* II. 1.

> I knew the time would come when they would say I knew *what was what.*—*Maj. Downing's Letters,* p. 190.

> A tame, vacant, doll-faced, idle gall. What a fate for a man who knows *what's what.*—*Sam Slick,* 2d series.

> Why, Mr. Bott, if I wasn't a married man, I'd soon know who's who and *what's what.*—*C. Mathews, The Motley Book,* p. 13.

TO WHEAL. To swell.

> The father discovered a gainsome expression of face. . . . His cheeks *whealed* and puffed, and through his lips his laughter exposed his white teeth.—*Margaret,* p. 10.

WHEEL-HORSE. An intimate friend; one's right hand man. Western.

WHELK. An old name for a pustule, a pimple. The word is not much used in America.

> White cohush will bring out the *whelk* in less than no time; and brook lime will break any fever.—*Margaret,* p. 375.

We have authority for this word from Shakspeare, Henry V.:

His face is all bubukles and *whelks*, and knobs, and flames of fire.

WHELKY. Protuberant; rounded.—*Todd.* Still heard sometimes in New England.

> Ne ought the *whelky* pearls esteemeth he,
> Which are from Indian seas brought far away.—*Spenser, Virg. Gnat.*

> Pluck, unchilled by the coolness of the drench, stood, sunk to his chin in the snow, his shining bald pate and *whelky* red face streaming with moisture.—*Margaret,* p. 167.

WHIG AND TORY. Names of political parties. The history

of the origin of these names is thus given by Cooke : " According to Roger North, the country party were the first to brand their opponents with the name by which they were afterwards to be designated. The Duke of York naturally affected the society of those whose religion was the same as his own, and the Catholic Irish were, therefore, in great favor with him. This circumstance occasioned the popular party to call all the opponents of the Exclusion Bill, Irishmen. The hatred the majority of the English bore to popery, rendered this an opprobrious term ; but it required to be strengthened before it could express the animosity of a hostile party. The epithet became successively " Wild Irish," and " Bogtrotter ;" but it was yet imperfect until some zealous member of the opposition found invective and euphony united in the word *Tory*, a name applied to a set of ruffians in the disturbed districts of Ireland—according to North, to the most despicable savages among the wild Irish. The word *Whig* is of Scotch origin. It was, say some writers, used in that country for the curd into which milk was reduced previous to being converted into cheese ; it was thence deemed applicable to the sour and curdled tempers of the persecuted Covenanters. The rebellion of that ill-used sect, of course, rendered them an object of the greatest abhorrence to the high church and high monarchical *Tories*, and they bestowed this name upon their opponents in England as the most reproachful they could discover.

"Bishop Burnet, however, gives another derivation of this word. He dates it from the year 1648, when the Scotch people, excited by their ministers, rose and marched to Edinburgh to oppose the prosecution of Duke Hamilton's attempt in favor of the captive king. The south-west counties of. Scotland, producing little corn, were obliged to send to Leith for stores of that article, which were supplied by the superior facilities of the northern counties. The carriers who repaired to Leith for this purpose were then called *Whiggamors*, from the word *wiggam*, which they used in driving their cattle. The inhabitants of Leith and Edinburgh very naturally extended this epithet to the whole of the inhabitants of the counties whence these men came; and as the insurgents who occupied Edinburgh sprang chiefly from the West, that circumstance was called the *Whiggamors'* inroad. The name was afterwards applied to the whole body of Covenanters, gradually shortened into *Whig*, and thence, as already mentioned, the word was introduced into England." —*Cooke's Hist. of Parties*, Vol. I. p. 138.

> Let such men quit all pretences to civility and breeding,—they are ruder than *Tories*, and wild Americans; and were they treated according to their deserts from mankind, they would meet everywhere with chains and strappadoes.—*Glanville, Sermons*, 4.

During the war of the American Revolution, the terms *Whig* and *Tory* were applied—the former to those who supported the revolutionary movement; the latter to the royalists, or those who adhered to the Britsh government. *Tory* was then a stigma of the most reproachful kind.

WHIGS AND DEMOCRATS. It is very difficult to give a precise, accurate, and satisfactory definition of the principles distinctively held by the two great political parties into which the population of the American Union is divided—one popularly styling itself the *Democratic*, the other the *Whig* party. In point of fact, the satirical definition of the *outs* and the *ins* would not be *very* far out of the way; for the doctrines of government and legislation theoretically advanced by the *Democratic* party, when out of power, are not so radically diverse from those of the *Whigs*, in the same condition, as are the practices of either, when in power, from their professions. As times change and circumstances, the demands or wishes of these parties change also; so that what was *Whig* doctrine in 1830, may be *Democratic* doctrine in 1850, and *vice versa*.

The nominal distinctions, some years ago, were, on the *Whig* side, a Protective Tariff, a National Bank, Division of the Proceeds of the Public Lands among all the States, and the duty of the General Government to carry on works of Public Improvement, such as Canals, Roads, &c. &c.

The *Democrats* were for Free Trade, no connection of the Government with Banking, Distribution of the Proceeds of the Public Lands among the States in which the lands lie, and Non-interference by the Government with Internal Improvements.

But all these questions have rarely been brought to the practical test. Absolute free trade has ever been impracticable, because it would deprive the Government of the revenue derived from imposts. The Government has always been obliged to carry on some kind of financial operations, differing more in name than in reality from a system of banking considered as a means of supplying a currency. The public lands have rarely yielded any proceeds beyond the wants of the Government. And the only real question, fairly at issue, has been that of improvement in public works.

The Democrats popularly charge upon the *Whigs* a desire to strengthen and centralize the National Government—declaring themselves to be in favor rather of strengthening the local Governments of the several States, and of limiting, as far as constitutionally possible, the agency of the National Government, or Government of the Union; but in practice the Democratic party is ready enough to assume power for the General Government, when anything is to be gained by so doing; and in this, as in most other instances, the difference between the two parties lies rather in words than in deeds.

The Whigs, on the other hand, popularly charge upon the *Democrats* an undue degree of subserviency to the Executive, especially since the elevation of General Jackson to the Presidency, in 1829; and this charge seems to have more foundation in truth. It is certain, at all events, that the three Democratic Presidents, Jackson, Van Buren, and Polk, have found a more zealous and unscrupulous support in questionable measures than was ever given to a Whig President, or indeed to any of their predecessors.

Perhaps, on the whole, it may be truly said, that the main practical difference between the *Whigs* and *Democrats* lies in the fact that the latter give a more unhesitating and thorough-going support to all measures which involve the question of party-measures, which become, by any means, party tests, whether emanating from the Executive or adopted by him under impulse from his adherents.   [*J. Inman.*]

WHIGGISM.
WHIGGERY.   Whig principles; the doctrines of the Whig party.   These words have, in the United States, lost their original opprobious meaning, and are now frequently used by the Whigs themselves in speaking of their doctrines.

> The Whigs in Boston see by the movement in New York, and by accounts from Ohio, that there is a chance, at least, of General Taylor being vigorously opposed by some men of undoubted *Whiggery* in influential States.—*Let. from Boston, in N. Y. Herald,* June 21, 1848.

> Professor Amasa Walker here came forward, and said they all stood together upon the same platform, and he had heard too much of *Whiggery* about their proceedings already ; and as they stood upon a broad platform, he as a Democrat protested against their throwing in so much *Whiggery,* and entertaining them about Gen. Taylor's white horse.—*Rep. of a Free-soil Convention at Worcester, Mass.,* June 28, 1848.

WHILE, for *till.*   'Stay *while* I come,' instead of stay *till* I come.   Used in the Southern States.—*Sherwood's Georgia.*

WHIM-WHAM.   A toy; a freak; a strange fancy.—*Jodrell's Philology.*

> Another gentleman declares that if we make them and their *whim-whams* the subject of any more essays, he shall be under the necessity of applying for satisfaction.—*Paulding, Salmagundi,* Vol. I. p. 283.

WHIFFLE-TREE.
WHIPPLE-TREE.   The bar to which the traces of a carriage are fastened for draught.—*Webster.   Whipple-tree* is the form used in England.—*Halliwell.*

WHISTLE.   The throat.   It is never used in this sense except in the phrase to ' wet one's *whistle,*' to take a draught of liquor.   It is a corruption of *weesle ;* an old term for the weasand, or windpipe.—*Carr's Craven Dialect.*

> So was hire joly *whistle wel ywette.*—*Chaucer, Reeve's Tale.*

> Let's turn to the fire, drink the other cup to *wet our whistles.*—*Izaak Walton.*

> > Youn' John seem'd nut at all to be
> > A chip ov the old block ;
> > To see some *wet their whistles* so,
> > It oft gave him a shock.—*John Noakes, Essex Dialect,* p. 7.

I can talk all day, and most of the night, only stopping to *wet my whistle.—J. C. Neal, Peter Brush.*

TO WHISTLE. *To whistle before you are out of the woods,* is to exult before you are out of danger.

But let not the Pennsylvanians rejoice—let them not *whistle before they are out of the woods.* The duties on iron will have to come down too.— *N. Y. Tribune.*

WHOLE. *Made out of whole cloth,* i. e. altogether an invention.

Isn't this entire story about your Jersey grandmother *made out of whole cloth*—spun on your own wheel, with your tongue for the spindle ?—*C. Mathews, The Motley Book,* p. 68.

WHOLE HEAP. Many ; several ; much ; a large congregation. An expression peculiar to certain parts of the South and West.—*Sherwood's Georgia.*

WICKET. A place of shelter, or camp made of the boughs of trees, used by lumbermen in Maine.

WIDE AWAKE. On the alert ; ready ; prepared.

The Captain was *wide awake,* but said nothing.—*Simon Suggs,* p. 37.

WIGWAM. An Indian cabin or hut, usually made of skins. The word is Algonkin, and occurs in variously modified forms in the languages of that family. See Gallatin's Synopsis, p. 322.

WILD CAT BANK. One of the various terms applied at the West to some of the irresponsible banks of the country. A bank in Michigan had a large vignette on its notes representing a panther, which animal is familiarly called there a *Wild cat.* This bank failed, having a large amount of its notes in circulation, which notes were afterwards denominated *Wild cat money,* and the banks issuing them, *Wild cat Banks.* Other banks were compelled to stop payment soon after, in consequence of the want of confidence in them ; and the term became general in Michigan, to denote banking institutions of an unsound character. The term *Blue-pup money* had a similar origin, as distinguished from *Red Dog,* which see.

We had to sell some of our land to pay taxes on the rest—and then took our pay in *Wild-cat money,* that turned to waste paper before we could get it off our hands.—*Mrs. Clavers's Forest Life,* Vol. I. p. 91.

TO WILT. To droop; to wither, as plants or flowers cut or plucked off.—*Holloway.* A word common in the United States, and provincial in England, where *welk* and *welt* are used in the same sense.—*Worcester.*

> Miss Amy pinned a flower to her breast; and when she died, she held the *wilted* fragments close in her hand.—*Margaret*, p. 213.

> Some cotton fellar here bid sixty dollars [for the slave], and she *wilted* right down.—*Robb, Squatter Life.*

TO WIND UP. To close up; to give the quietus to an antagonist in a debate; to effectually demolish.

> John Bell, of Tennessee, that unmistakable Whig, has rung out a clear and far-sounding note of alarm concerning this Mexican war. He is as serious as a preacher, and as downright as a sailor in the delivery of his sentiments. A lively dialogue, constituting a kind of interlude to his speech, sprang up between him and Mr. Cass, in which he pretty effectually ' *wound up* ' the Senator from Michigan.—*N. Y. Com. Adv.*

WINKLE-HAWK. (Dutch *winkel-haak.*) A rent in the shape of the letter L, frequently made in cloth. It is also called a *winkel-hole.* A New York term.

WINSOME. (Ang. Sax. *winsum.*) Lively; cheerful; gay. Provincial in the North of England.—*Brockett.*

> The curls that overhang her face
> In clusters rich and *winsome* grace.—*American Anthology.*

WIRE-PULLERS. A term denoting those who, by their secret plots and intrigues, control the movements of the puppets on the political stage.

> Baltimore is now the great Babel of Loco-Focoism. All the office-holders, office-seekers, hangers-on, and *wire-pullers* of that craft are here. What a happy country this would be if Baltimore should sink, or swim off somewhere! I have no doubt that some righteous would perish, but there would be so much demagogueism swamped with them, that the political atmosphere would be renovated for half a century!—*N. Y. Tribune.*

> The coming contest is to decide whether the people have the privilege of electing a chief magistrate of their own selection, or only the privilege of electing one of two candidates whom self-elected cliques of nominators choose to designate. The Philadelphia Convention will assemble on Wednesday; already that city is filled with *wire-pullers*, public opinion manufacturers, embryo cabinet officers, future ambassadors, and the whole brood of political make-shifts, who contrive to live out of the public purse, by abusing public credulity.—*N. Y. Mirror*, June 5, 1848.

WITCH-HAZEL. The popular name of the *Hamamelis*, so called from its reputed power of bending towards water, when a forked branch is held in the hands.

WITNESS-TREES. In newly settled countries at the West, every mile square is marked by "blazed" trees, and the corners especially distinguished by stakes whose place is pointed out by trees called *witness-trees.—Mrs. Clavers's Western Clearings*, p. 3.

WOLFISH. Savage; savagely hungry. A Western word.

> You must fight or play; so take your choice, for I feel most *wolfish* and savagerous.—*Sam Slick*, 3d ser. p. 117.

> They'd been fightin' the barrel of whiskey mightily comin' up, and were perfectly *wolfish* arter some har of the dog.—*Porter's Tales of the Southwest*, p. 121.

WONDERMENT. Astonishment; amazement. Wonderful appearance. Not in use except in low or sarcastic language.—*Johnson*. Examples of the use of this word may be found in many of the old authors.

> When my pen would write her titles true,
> It ravish'd is with fancy's *wonderment.—Spenser*.

> Those things which I here set down, do naturally take the sense, and not respect petty *wonderments.—Bacon*.

> The neighbors made a *wonderment* of it, and asked him what he meant·—*L'Estrange*.

> All was *wonderment* and curiosity, and Jim for once experienced the inadequacy of the human capacity for such extraordinary occasions.—*Chronicles of Pinevelle*, p. 12.

WONT. A common contraction for *will not*. In New England, generally pronounced *wunt*.

TO WOOD. To supply or get supplies of wood.—*Webster*. The boats on the Ohio and Mississippi rivers, in their long voyages, are obliged to make frequent stops for supplies of wood. The common phrase is *to wood up*.

> The process of *wooding-up* is one of the first the passenger is made acquainted with. The steamer approaches a dreary shore, without any thing to indicate that civilized man has ever set his foot upon it for many miles above or below, save the wood-pile and a small cabin of the rudest description. The terms are usually agreed upon before the boat touches the bank; and when it does, fifteen or twenty hands throw on board from

twenty to fifty cords, at a price varying from $2 to $3, for which the woodman pockets his money and seems a happy man, although cut off from the world.—*N. Y. Tribune*, 1848.

WOODING-PLACE. A station on the banks of a river where the steamboats stop to take in supplies of wood.

WOODCHUCK. In New England, the popular name of a rodent mammal, a species of the marmot tribe of animals, the *Arctomys monax*. The ground hog. It burrows and is dormant in winter.—*Webster.*

> Yea, verily, this is like a *woodchuck* in clover.—*Margaret*, p. 48.

WORM-FENCE. A rail fence laid up in a zig-zag manner.

> Mr. Haskell, one of the delegates from Tennessee, told a story about a man in his " diggins," who was once struck by " Joe Larkins," by which he was knocked at least forty rods. He fell against a *worm-fence*, and carried away about forty panels, rail-riders and all.—*N. Y. Mirror.*

WORRY. Perplexity; trouble. In familiar language, this word is often used with us; and, although it does not appear in any of the English glossaries, it is also employed colloquially in England. We say, ' the *worry* of business ;' ' the *worry* of politics,' &c.

> I am in the midst of the bustle attending the opening of the session [of Parliament]. . . . . But the excitement and *worry* are more than I can stand in the present state of my health.—*Lord Sydenham, Memoirs.*

WORSER, instead of *worse*, is often heard among the vulgar. It is common in the dialect of London, and like other words enlarged from the comparative degree, is supported by eminent writers.—*Pegge, Anecdotes of the English Lang.*

> Let the *worser* spirit tempt me again.—*Shakspeare, King Lear.*

> Changed to a *worser* shape thou canst not be.—*Ibid. King Henry VI.*

WRATH. *Like all wrath*, i. e. violently; vehemently; angrily. A Southern simile.

> There ain't much to interest the traveller on the railroad from Hamburg to Charleston. Most of the passengers in the car were preachers what had been up to Augusta to attend the convention. They was the dryest set of old codgers I ever met with, till the jolting of the cars shook up their ideas a little, and then they fell to disputin' *like all wrath.*—*Maj. Jones's Travels.*

WRATHY. Very angry. A colloquial word.—*Webster.*

> Oh! you're *wrathy*, ain't ye ? Why, I didn't mean nothin' but what was civil !—*Mrs. Clavers's Forest Life*, Vol. I. p. 103.

The General was as *wrathy* as thunder; and when he gets his dander up, it's no joke.—*Maj. Downing's Letters*, p. 34.

WRINKLE. An idea; notion; fancy. Colloquial in England and America.

Such was, after a little experience, the *wrinkle* adopted by Mr. Lear. —*Quarterly Rev.*, Vol. LXXXI. p. 462.

WRAPPER. A loose dress or gown.

Her dress was a blue-striped linen short-gown, *wrapper*, or long-short, a coarse petticoat, checked apron, &c.—*Margaret*, p. 14.

Y.

TO YANK. To twitch or jerk powerfully; a term used in New England.

YARN. A story. A word chiefly used by seamen. *To spin a long yarn*, is to tell a long or tedious story.

YEATH, for *earth*. A vulgar pronunciation among the illiterate at the South.

" Why you don't look like the same man. I never should have know'd you. What upon *yeath* has brung you out so ?"—*Maj. Jones's Sketches*.

YEATHQUAKE, for *earthquake*. A Southern vulgarism like the previous word.

The Girard College is all solid brick and marble. Fire can't get hold of wood enough to raise a blaze, and the walls are so thick and strong that nothin' short of Florida lightnin' or a South American *yeathquake* couldn't knock it down.—*Maj. Jones's Sketches*.

YELLOW-HAMMER. (*Picus auratus.* Wilson, Ornith.) The popular name of the Golden-winged Woodpecker, the most beautiful of the genus. It is known by other names in different parts of the country, as High-hole, Yacker, Clape, &c.

YELLOWS, often pronounced *yallers*. A disease of horses and cattle, which is indicated by a yellow appearance of the eyes, inside of the lips, &c.—*Farrier's Dict.* This word is old and is used by Shakspeare :

His horse sped with spavins and raied with the *yellows.*—*Taming of the Shrew*.

Ask the widder if she can cure the *yallers* in Bright [the ox].—*Margaret*, p. 17.

YOU DON'T ! for *you don't say so ;* really ! indeed ! as, 'Mr. A threw a back somerset out of a three-story window. *Ans.* Now, *you don't !'*

YOUNG DEMOCRACY. See *Barnburners.*

YOURN.   This is a contraction of *your own,* or a change in the termination of the pronoun *yours,* in conformity with *mine,* and which is much used by the illiterate and vulgar.   It is also used in London, and in the West of England.   " The cockney," says Mr. Pegge, " considers such words as *our own* and *your own* as pronouns possessive, a little too much expanded ; and, therefore, thinks it proper to curtail them, and to compress them into the words *ourn* and *yourn,* for common daily use."—*Anecdotes of the English Lang.*, p. 193.

He might have added *hisn,* as in the famous distich:

> Him as prigs vot isn't *hisn,*
> Ven he's cotch'd 'll go to pris'n.

APPENDIX.

A.

AMBIA. Used in Virginia and the Carolinas for tobacco juice. It is a euphemism for the spittle produced by this voluntary ptyalism.

AVAILABILITY. Quality of being available.—*Worcester*. That qualification in a candidate which implies or supposes a strong probability of his success, apart from substantial merit—a probability resulting from mere personal or accidental popularity. The thing has long existed in the Papal Government, where the advanced age of a candidate for the triple crown has often been the motive of his election; the idea being that he would soon die out of the way and leave the chair vacant for a new trial of strength under more favorable auspices, perhaps, for some of the electing cardinals.

Inoffensiveness—exemption from strong hostility in any quarter—is a frequent element of availability. [*J. Inman.*]

As this word is not noticed by any lexicographer except Dr. Worcester, and is now much used, it is thought advisable to give several examples of its use.

> For some months past, a regular system of crying down Mr. Clay as *unavailable*, has been prosecuted with indefatigable energy and adroitness throughout the Union. . . . . . Mr. Clay is a great man—able statesman —all of us prefer him to anybody else *if* he could be elected, *but* I'm afraid he isn't *available.—Letter in N. Y. Tribune*, May, 1848.

> The only possible motive for the choice of Mr. Cass that we can imagine, is his presumed "*availability*," the elements of this being his known predilection, real or assumed, for territorial acquisition'in all quarters, by

warlike means as well as others, and his avowed devotion to the Southern or slave-holding interest.—*N. Y. Com. Adv.*, May 26, 1848.

These political Conventions are certainly becoming more odious and objectionable from year to year, and *availability*, not merit or qualifications, is the only requisite to secure a nomination.—*Baltimore Cor. of the N. Y. Herald*, May, 1848.

At a Democratic meeting held in New York to ratify the nomination of Gen. Cass, Mr. McAllister, of Georgia, said that—

Henry Clay, about whom the Whig party had professed such ardent attachment, had been carried upon the altar of *availability*, and there sacrificed by the hands of his pretended friends, and inquired what kind of a spectacle it presented to the young men of our country with ardent spirits —young men who have attached themselves for a time to the car of Whigism.—*N. Y. Herald*, June, 1848.

At the same meeting the Hon. James Bowlin, of Missouri, thus expressed himself, in relation to General Taylor :

The Whigs within the last few days have presented candidates for the highest office in the gift of the people, who are without any principles. . . . What do they mean by this in thus presenting candidates who have no principles ? They proceed on the principle of mere *availability*, and nothing else. They are again going to insult your judgments, and tarnish the character of the nation by their exhibitions of coon-skins and hard cider, and their midnight debaucheries, as they did in 1840.—*Report in N. Y. Herald*, June 12, 1848.

B.

BAY STATE. The State of Massachusetts. The original name of the Colony was *Massachusetts Bay*. Hence, among the New England people it was usually called the *Bay State*.

BEAR STATE. A name by which the State of *Arkansas* is known at the West. I once asked a Western man if Arkansas abounded in bears, that it should be designated as the ' *Bear State?*' " Yes," said he, " it does ; for I never knew a man from that State but he was a *bar*, and in fact the people are all *barish* to a degree."

BELIKED. Liked ; beloved. A Western term.

I do believe me and Nancy was *beliked* by the Indians, and many's the venison and turkey they fotch'd us as a sort of present, and may be a kind of pay for bread-stuffs and salt Nancy used to give them.—*Carlton, The New Purchase.*

BOLIVAR HAT.   A Leghorn bonnet, with a broad brim, worn a few years since.

BUCK.   A frame or stand of peculiar construction on which wood is sawn for fuel.   In New England it is called a *saw-horse.*

BULLION STATE.   The State of Missouri ; so called in consequence of the exertions made by its Senator, Mr. Benton, in favor of a gold and silver currency, in opposition to banks and a paper currency.   The honorable Senator was often nicknamed *old Bullion,* and the State he represented, the *Bullion State.*

At the Democratic meeting in New York, June 12, 1848, to ratify the nomination of Gen. Cass, the Hon. James Bowlin, of Missouri, in denouncing the Whig party, said :

> I deny that the election of 1840 was carried by the people.   It was carried by duplicity.   It was carried by the unfortunate state of the times, which was not the result of Democratic rule, and by false charges against the American Democracy ; and, thank God, in my own State, in the *Bullion State,* they did not succeed in depreciating our majority.—*N. Y. Herald,* June 13, 1848.

BUNGO.   A kind of boat used at the South.

> The most urgent steps were being taken to press every *bungo* and canoe to the immediate relief of the people along the coast, in order to embark them without delay.—*N. O. Picayune.*

BURGALL.   (*Ctenolabrus ceruleus.*)   A small fish very common in New York ; also found on the coast of New England, and as far South as Delaware Bay.   The usual length is about six inches, though they are sometimes found twelve inches.   Other names for the same fish are Nibbler, from its nibbling off the bait when thrown for other fishes, Chogset, the Indian name, and in New England, those of Blue Perch and Conner.

C.

CABOODLE.   *The whole caboodle* is a common expression, meaning the whole.   I know not the origin of the word.   It is used in all the Northern States and New England. The word *boodle* is used in the same manner.

> They may recommend, to the electors of Hamilton county, to disregard so much of the law as constitutes two election districts of Hamilton county. Having done this, Medary will be looking out for a job—Olds will be often in Fairfield, cozening for a nomination to Congress—and the *whole caboodle* will act upon the recommendation of the Ohio Sun, and endeavor to secure a triumph in the old-fashion way.—*Ohio State Journal.*

CARLACUE. A caper; a boyish trick. '*To cut up carla-cues,*' is a common expression, equivalent to '*cutting up di-does.*' Used in New York.

CASTOR. (Latin.) A beaver; hence, a hat.

> " I trembled, I own, where the bravest would shrink,
>   Each moment expecting some horrid disaster ;
>   Then my head gave a spin, and I lost—what d'ye think ?"
>   Said St. Peter, " Most likely your *castor.*"—*New York Sunday Courier.*

CATCH. A term used among fishermen to denote a quantity of fish taken at one time.

> It is said that the *catch* of blue fish in the inlet and river is greater than ever known so early in the season, and that they are served up *secundem artem* at Mr. Williston's.—*N. Y. Courier and Enquirer,* June 24.

CHAISE. A light two-wheeled pleasure carriage drawn by one horse. In New England it is called a *chaise,* in New York, a *gig.*

CHOGSET. The Indian name of a small fish known in New York as the *Burgall,* which see.

CHUNK or CHUNKEE YARD. A name given by the white traders to the oblong four-square yards adjoining the high mounts and rotundas of the modern Indians of Florida. In the centre of these stands the obelisk, and at each corner of the farther end stands a slave post, or strong stake, where the captives that are burnt alive are bound.—*Bartram.*

> The pyramidal hills or artificial mounts, and highways or avenues, lead-ing from them to artificial lakes or ponds, vast tetragon terraces, *chunk-yards,* and obelisks or pillars of wood, are the only monuments of labor, ingenuity, and magnificence, that I have seen worthy of notice.—*Bartram, Travels in Florida* (1773), p. 518.

This is doubtless an Indian term, and the enclosure a place

where the natives played a game called *chunkee,* as will appear by the following extract from Du Pratz :

" The warriors practise a diversion which they call the *game of the pole,* at which only two play at a time. Each pole is about eight feet long, resembling a Roman f, and the game consists in rolling a flat round stone, about three inches in diameter and one inch thick, and throwing the pole in such a manner, that when the stone rests the pole may be at or near it. Both the antagonists throw their poles at the same time, and he whose pole is nearest the stone counts one, and has the right of rolling the stone."—*Hist. of Louisiana,* 1720.

Adair speaks of the same game, which is by the Indians called *chungke.*—*History American Indians,* p. 402. Catlin notices the same among the Mandans and Creeks, called by them *Tchungkee.*—*Catlin's Indians,* Vol. I. p. 132.

TO CIRCULATE. To travel. Used in this sense many times in a pamphlet on the " Frauds, Extortions, and Oppressions of the Railroad Monopoly in New Jersey." In comparing the rates of travel in various States, by which it is shown that the rates in New Jersey are the highest in the world, the author says :

Arriving in Maryland, a slave State, he *circulates* at a cost of from three to five cents per mile.

COME-OUTERS. This name has been applied to a considerable number of persons in various parts of the Northern States, principally in New England, who have recently *come out* of the various religious denominations with which they have been connected ; hence the name. They have not themselves assumed any distinctive organization. They have no creed, believing that every one should be left free to hold such opinions on religious subjects as he pleases, without being held accountable for the same to any human authority.

They hold a diversity of opinions on many points—some believing in the divine inspiration of the Scriptures, and others that they are but human compositions. They believe Jesus Christ to have been a divinely inspired teacher, and his religion, a revelation of eternal truth ; that according to his teachings, true religion consists in purity of heart, holiness of life, and not in opinions ; that Christianity, as it existed in Christ, is a life rather than a belief.—*Evans's History of Religions, with Additions by an American Editor.*

CONIACKER. A counterfeiter of coin.

CONNIPTION FIT. This term is exclusively used by the fair sex, who can best explain its meaning. As near as I can judge, *conniption fits* are tantrums.

TO COUNT. To reckon ; suppose ; think.

> *Newman.* You'll pass muster ! a proper fine fellow.
> *Doolittle.* I calculate I be.
> *Newman.* Ready to enter on duty ?
> *Doolittle.* I should be glad to know what kind of way you *count* to improve me.—*D. Humphreys, The Yankee in England.*
> *Count St. Luc.* Read the superscription. You can read ?
> *Doolittle.* I *count* I can—and spell, too.—*Ibid.*

D.

DARN. An expletive in very general use among the vulgar, instead of *damn.*

> Now let me see, that isn't all ; I used 'fore leaving Jaalam,
> To count things on my finger-ends, but something seems to ail 'em.
> Where's my left hand ? O, *darn it,* yes, I recollect what's come on 't,
> I haint no left arm but my right, and that's got jest a thumb on 't.—*Poetical Epistle from a Volunteer.*

DASSENT, for *dares not.* It is vulgarly used in all persons and numbers.

DEAD HEADS. Persons who drink at a bar, ride in an omnibus, or railroad car, travel in steamboats, or visit the theatre without charge, are called *dead heads.* These consist of the engineers, conductors, and laborers on railroads ; the keepers of hotels ; the editors of newspapers, &c.

DEAD HORSE. Work for which one has been paid before it is performed. When a workman, on Saturday night, includes in his bill work not yet finished, he is said the following week to ' work off a *dead horse.*'

DIPSY. A term applied in some parts of Pennsylvania to the float of a fishing-line.

DOBBER. A float to a fishing-line. So called in New York.

DOUGH-FACES. This term may be regarded as nearly or quite synonymous with another not very much unlike it in form—the English " nose of wax." Generally it means a pliable politician—one who is accessible to personal influences and considerations. It was first applied, however, by John Randolph, of Roanoke, to such Northern members of Congress as manifested especial willingness to fall in with the views and demands of the South on questions involving the " peculiar institution," alias slavery. " These Northern *dough-faces,*" he said, with an intensity of contempt, which may be imagined only by those who have seen and heard him in his sarcastic mood. [*J. Inman.*]

> Thanks to a kind Providence, and the manly straight-forwardness of John C. Calhoun, the great question of extension or non-extension of human slavery under the flag of this Republic is to be pressed to a decision now. Desperate, idolatrous, and blind as is his devotion to slavery, we would sooner see him President to-morrow than any *dough-face* in the Union. He is no smooth-tongued parasite—no oily wriggler between resorts which he pronounces more and most detestable. He always strikes directly for what he wants, and boldly for *all* he wants, and in this boldness finds the elements of success.—*N. Y. Tribune,* June 29, 1848.

This term has very recently been taken up by the Southerners themselves, to denote men who are false to the principles of slavery, as Northern *dough-faces* are to the principles of freedom.

> There was a disposition in the Senate to evade the question—to slip a bill for the establishment of the Oregon territory through the Senate, without calling attention to the Slavery question, and under the immediate pressure of the demand made for the military defence of the territory from the Indians. The Whigs of the North and of the South were silent. The Democratic Cass men of the North and of the South were *mum.* Two-thirds of the Senate were *dough-faced.* There are Southern as well as Northern *dough-faces;* men looking to the spoils care not for principles,—whether they be of the North or of the South.—*Washington Cor. N. Y Com. Adv.,* June 4, 1848.

> I say to our Southern friends, deliver to us the *dough-faces;* deliver them to our tender mercies. We Democrats of the West and of the North-west will take care of our interests and of yours also. We keep our eyes on the old land-marks—on the letter of the Constitution. You have rights guaranteed to you in the South, and we in the West. You have one species of property, and we another. We have been charged with being *dough-faces;* and gentlemen who make this charge not only go

the *dough-face*, but the *dough-head*. What is the meaning of *dough-face*? I believe it is, that the *dough*, being soft, can be pinched and made to exhibit any aspect you please. I believe that animal magnetism has been almost reduced to a science. The principle is, that, by touching a certain part of the cranium, certain effects are produced. If you touch one of the bumps of the *dough-head*, benevolence turns out for the negro; there is no sympathy for any other kind of person. Touch another bump of the *dough-head*, and the *dough-face* will go against every slaveholder for President; but when you touch another, the *dough-face* will hurrah for old Zack Taylor, although he is a large slaveholder.—*Mr. Foote of Mississippi, Debate in Senate,* June 22, 1848.

E.

EAST. *About east,* is about right; in the proper manner. A common slang expression in New England. See *walk into,* for an example.

EMPIRE STATE. The State of New York; so called from the enterprise of its people, its wealth, population, extent of canals, railroads, etc. In fact everything done by New York is on a grand scale. Hence the name.

F.

FARZINO. As far as I know. See *Farziner.*

Gen. And what kind of characters are the Count and Countess?

Doolittle. Why, I ha'nt been here such a despud while, as to have larnt myself much about the matter. But by hearsay, they are a topping sort of people, and pretty much like the Boston folks, full of notions. At times, he is obstropulous. He may be a straight-going critter, *farzino,* manwards; but in his dealings with t'other sex, he is a little twistical.— *D. Humphreys, Yankee in England.*

FENCE-RIDING. Sitting on the fence, i. e. keeping neutral in politics.

The South, will not vote for a Northern candidate, who is nominated as such, nor the North for a Southern man, who is nominated on exclusive Southern principles. In this matter there can be no neutral ground. The dividing line is narrow, but distinct; it admits of no *fence-riding;* the candidate must be on one side or the other; and when the time shall come, that either the North or the South adopts a candidate on sectional grounds, it will not be difficult to foretell the issue.—*N. Y. Mirror.*

FRESH. Forward ; as, ' don't make yourself too *fresh* here ;' that is to say, not quite so much at home.

> Considering that this man is so new a recruit in the party, it is not exactly modest for him to make himself quite so *fresh* in its counsels.—*Newspaper.*

G.

GAL. A vulgar pronunciation of *girl,* common alike in England and America.

GALLS. A kind of low lands in Florida. They consist of a matted soil of vegetable fibres, spongy and treacherous to the foot, unpleasant as well as dangerous to cross.—*Vignoles, Florida*, p. 91.

TO GOOSE BOOTS. To repair them by putting on a new front half way up, and a new bottom.

GOPHER. In Georgia a species of land turtle, burrowing in the ground in the low country. It is able to walk with a heavy man on its back.—*Sherwood's Georgia.*

GOPHER. A little animal found in the valleys of the Mississippi and Missouri rivers. See *Prairie Dog.*

GRANITE STATE. The State of New Hampshire, so called from the abundance of this material found in it.

GREEN MOUNTAIN STATE. The State of Vermont.

H.

HAMMOCK. In Florida, a term given to a particular kind of land. The *low hammocks* are the richest in the country, and are capable of producing, for many successive years, rich crops of sugar, corn, hemp, or other equally exhausting productions. In their primitive state they are clothed with so heavy a growth of timber and underwood, that the task of clearing them is appalling. The *low hammocks* are, if possible, more dense in their growth than the others, but the coat of vegetable matter is thin, and the white sand lies within a foot or eighteen inches of the surface. They are also very productive.—*Vignoles, Florida,* p. 87.

> "HEAD QUARTERS, ARMY OF THE SOUTH,
> "FORT BROOKE, July 29th, 1838.
>
> "SIR :—I have the honor to inclose you a communication this moment received, on the subject of procuring bloodhounds from the Island of Cuba, to aid the army in its operations against the hostiles in Florida.
>
> "I am decidedly in favor of the measure, and beg leave to urge it as the only means of ridding the country of the Indians who are now broken up into small parties, and take shelter in swamps and *hammocks* as the army approaches, making it impossible for us to follow or overtake them without the aid of such auxiliaries.
>
> "I wish it distinctly understood that my object in employing dogs, is only to ascertain where the Indians can be found, not to worry them.
>
> "I have the honor to be, Sir, &c.,
> "Z. TAYLOR, Brevet Brig. Gen.
> "U. S. A. Commanding."

HAT. Our American women have almost discarded the word *bonnet*, except in "*sun-bonnet,*" and use the term *hat* instead. A like fate has befallen the word *gown*, for which they commonly use *frock* or *dress*.

HAW-BUCK. A term used by the farmers in driving their oxen; and hence often applied to a rough and unpolished man from the country.

> "Mr. Jones," says a sleek, cunning, demure expectant of something nice in case of a Whig triumph, to a bluff, *haw-buck* sort of a fellow whom he drops in upon on one of his circuits, "who do you think we ought to run for President this time?" "Run who?' retorts Mr. Jones, "Harry Clay, to be sure—I haven't heard anybody else talked of up our way."—*N. Y. Mirror.*

HELP. The common term in New England for a domestic servant—also for the operatives in a cotton or woolen factory.

> *Newman.* I speak; I command; all budge; all jump. I don't often stand to hear *servants* argue.
>
> *Doolittle.* *Servants* argue !! Do you mean me, Mister?
>
> *Newman.* I say, all that wear the Countess's livery, serve her. You are a footman; you have not the honor of being her *body servant.*
>
> *Doolittle.* *Body servant !* Hah! no; I hope, I ben't her *body servant,* nor anybody's *servant,* nor your *servant.* I don't choose to be a *servant* of *servants,* and a slave to the devil.
>
> (High words follow, Doolittle gets into a passion—Newman becomes alarmed, and thus explains himself :)

Newman. You are our principal *help.* That is all. I told you at first I wanted you to *help* the Countess. You know that is a descriptive term in New England. *Help* is not a discreditable name—not at all derogatory. There is nothing degrading in *helping,* is there?

Doolittle. Why—no—I believe there an't. You now begin to seem rational, and I'll make up with you.—*D. Humphreys, The Yankee in England,* Act I.

HOUSE-HUNTING. In the city of New York all houses are let from the 1st day of May, and the landlords have assumed to themselves the right of requiring from their tenants a decision, as to whether they will keep their houses or not, three months before the period for which they hired them expires. On those houses which are not hired for another term (usually a year) " bills " are put up by the landlords, signifying that they are to let. Persons who intend to " move," traverse that section of the city in which they desire to establish themselves, in search of a suitable house, in which search they are guided by the landlord's " bills." This is called *house-hunting,* and is practised by thousands every year in the city of New York.

Polly began to grow uneasy now, because we hadn't got no house, and said I ought to go a *house-hunting* as everybody else did, or else we should be turn'd out of doors.—*Maj. Downing, May-day in New York.*

HOW FARE YOU? This is a common expression in those parts of New England for 'How do you do?' It is pronounced short, as, ' *How fa' ye ?* '

Newman. What, come back so soon? *How fare you,* Doolittle?
Doolittle. Cleverly. Steady, pretty steady, and quite chirk again; I thank you.—*D. Humphreys, The Yankee in England.*

HUM, for *home,* common in New England.

Well, well, I know it now—' *hum* is *hum,* be it ever so humbly.' I am desperd sick of being in strange parts. I wish I was at *hum* agin, under mother's own ruff, I guess—I know I do.—*D. Humphreys, The Yankee in England.*

HURRYMENT. Hurry; confusion.

I always hate to kiss old women what hain't got no teeth, and I was monstrous glad old Miss Stallins had her handkerchief to her face, for in the *hurryment* I kissed it.—*Maj. Jones's Travels.*

I.

IN, for *into.* Mr. Coleman, in remarking upon the prevalence of this inaccuracy in New York, says: "We get *in* the stage, and have the rheumatism *into* our knees."—*N. Y. Evening Post*, Jan. 6, 1814. An observing English friend at Philadelphia also speaks of its frequent use there in the following terms: "The preposition *into* is almost unknown here. They say, 'When did you come *in* town?' 'I met him riding *in* town.' "—*Pickering.*

INDIAN SUMMER. A period of warm weather late in autumn, when, it is said, the Indians go hunting to supply themselves with the flesh of wild animals for provisions in the winter.—*Webster.*

J.

JOHNNY-CAKE. A cake made of Indian meal mixed with milk or water. A New England *Johnny-cake* is invariably spread upon the stave of a barrel-top, and baked before the fire. Sometimes stewed pumpkin is mixed with it.

> Some talk of *hoe-cake*, fair Virginia's pride,
> Rich *Johnny-cake* this mouth has often tried.
> Both please me well, their virtues much the same;
> Alike their fabric, as allied their fame,
> Except in dear New England, where the last
> Receives a dash of pumpkin in the paste.—*Joel Barlow, Poem on Hasty Pudding.*

K.

KEYSTONE STATE. The State of Pennsylvania. So called from its being the central State of the Union at the time of the formation of the Constitution.

KILL. (Dutch *kil.*) A channel, or arm of the sea; a stream; river. This Dutch appellation is still preserved in several instances; thus the channel that separates Staten Island from

Bergen Neck, is called the *Kills;* to which we may add the names *Schuylkill* and *Catskill,* applied to streams.

KILLIFISH. (Genus *fundulus*.) A small fish found in the salt water creeks and bays, from one to five inches in length. It is only used for bait for larger fish. The name is Dutch from *kill*, a channel or creek (which see), where the fish is only found. They are often called *killies.*

KISS-ME-QUICK. A homemade quilted bonnet which does not extend beyond the face. They are chiefly used to cover the head by ladies when going to parties, or the theatre.

KIT. *The whole kit.* An expression common in various parts of the country.

> The clymit seems to me jest like a teapot made o' pewter
> Our Prudence had, that wouldn't pour (all she could do) to suit her;
> Fust place the leaves would choke the spout, so's not a drop would
>   dreen out,
> Then Prude would tip, and tip, and tip till the whole *kit* bust clean out,
> The kiver-hinge-pin bein lost, tea leaves, and tea, and kiver
> Would all come down *kerswosh!* as though the dam broke in a river.—
> *Poetical Epistle from a Volunteer.*

L.

TO LINE. To fish with a line. So, *to seine,* i. e. to fish with a seine. I have never seen these words used except by Dr. J. V. C. Smith, in his History of the Fishes of Massachusetts; and for so interesting a book the Doctor is well entitled to the privilege of coining a phrase or two.

> The squeteague is taken both by *lining* and *seining,* and because it makes such feeble exertion and resistance, in being drawn in by a hook, it has received the appellation of *weak fish.—Fishes of Massachusetts.*

LINES. The reins, or that part of the bridle which extends from the horse's head to the hands of the driver or coachman.

LITTLE END OF THE HORN. 'To come out at the *little end of the horn,*' is said when a ridiculously small effect has been produced after great effort and much boasting.

LOAFER. The origin of this word is altogether uncertain. Two etymologies have been suggested for it, viz. the German *laufer,* a runner; and the Spanish *gallofo* (whence the Ital. *gagloffo,*) a wandering mendicant; a vagabond.

TO LOGICIZE.   To reason.

> And I give the preliminary view of the reason; because, since this is the faculty which reasons or *logicizes,* &c.—*Tappan's Elements of Logic,* Preface, p. 5.

M.

TO MAKE ONESELF SCARCE, is to leave; to go away.

ME, for *I.*   The objective case of pronouns is often used for the nominative by the illiterate.   In New York it is very common to hear such choice expressions as ' *Me* and *him* went to the play last night.'

METAPHENOMENA.   The primordial facts of our being, which, although known by necessity of reason to exist, are not the immediate objects of consciousness.—*Tappan.*

METAPHENOMENAL.   Relating to *metaphenomena.*

> The immediate objects of our consciousness are *phenomena,* and these only are *phenomenal;* while those objects which, by supposition, lie beyond immediate consciousness, are *metaphenominal.*—*Tappan's Elements of Logic,* p. 12.

MOOSE-YARD.   In the State of Maine, an area in which *moose* tread down the deep snow in winter.

N.

NIGH UPON.   Nearly; almost.

> I got your letter and razor-strap.   It's a complete strap as you ever see; and as soon as it was known about here that I had received it, *nigh upon* all our folks have been sendin' to borrow it.—*Maj. Downing, Letter* 27.

NOMOLOGY.   That branch of philosophy which treats of law in general.

> This at once introduces us to the Doctrine of Law or *Nomology,* which is the second grand division of philosophy.—*Tappan's Elements of Logic.*

NOMOLOGICAL.   Relating to *nomology.*

> The observations of the senses yield us only limited successions and recurrences of phenomena.   These have antecedence in the order of time. But Law, eternal, absolute, and universal, has antecedence in the order of necessary existence, and is an idea of the Reason.   It is the Idea of Ideas under the *nomological* conception.—*Ibid.*

O.

OLD DOMINION. The State of Virginia.

OUTSIDER. A term of recent origin among politicians, applied to persons belonging to parties unconnected with the two great leading political divisions of the country, Locofocos and Whigs. The term was first used in the Baltimore Convention in May, 1848, when a leading politician stigmatized that portion of the Democratic party known as the Barnburners, as *outsiders*, classing them among the Abolitionists, Agrarians, Native Americans, etc.

> With the *outsiders* of all descriptions, Barnburners, and everybody else with a spark of independent patriotism, the nomination of General Taylor is equally a cause of delight. All the Whig papers give in readily, manfully, and sincerely.—*N. Y. Mirror*, June 10, 1848.

> Why do we find the *outsiders* of all creation—Tylerites, nullifiers, Locofocos, and no-party men—going in with such a rush for General Taylor? It looks odd that the Journal of Commerce, Herald, Sun, etc., should become so enamored all at once of a straight-forward Whig, as to urge his election to the Presidency!—*N. Y. Tribune.*

OUT AND OUT. Thorough.

> Henry Clay is such a statesman as the country wanted. We want a long tried, well known, universally understood, undeniable, straight-forward, *out and out* Whig.—*Mr. Fowler's Speech at the Clay meeting in New York*, June 2, 1848.

P.

TO PARMATEER. To electioneer; evidently a corruption of *parliamenteer*, to electioneer for a seat in parliament. This term is very common in the State of Rhode Island, beyond which I think it does not extend.

TO PETTIFOG. To play the pettifogger.—*Johnson.* This old verb has just been revived by political writers.

> On Saturday evening Gen. Cass reached this city from New York. Persons were sent about to drum up a crowd; but free white men could not be found or hired, to welcome the embodiment of slavery-propagandism. The thing was a dead failure. When Mr. Peckham, who has *pettifogged*

many a desperate case with unwavering assurance, undertook to welcome the conservative leader in the name of the Democracy of Albany, he broke down.—*Albany Atlas*, June 13, 1848.

Senators Allen, Houston, and Bright *pettifog* for Cass to-night in Albany, this being the tenth or twelfth day since they did anything for the eight dollars per day that they are steadily drawing from the Nation's consumptive Treasury—or rather adding to its plethoric debt.—*N. Y. Tribune*.

PICK. In mercantile usage, and among manufacturers, a *pick* is a thread. The relative quality of cotton cloth is denoted by the number of *picks* it has to the inch.

PINKY. (Dutch, *pink*.) The little finger. A very common term in New York, especially among small children, who, when making a bargain with each other, are accustomed to confirm it by interlocking the little finger of each other's right hands and repeating the following doggerel:

> *Pinky, pinky*, bow-bell,
> Whoever tells a lie,
> Will sink down to the bad place,
> And never rise up again.

TO PLAY POSSUM. ' He's *playing possum* with you,' is a common expression at the South and West, and means that he is deceiving you. The *opossum*, it is said, when attacked by a dog, will pretend to be dead, and often deceives his pursuers; hence the expression.—*Sherwood's Georgia*.

POLT. A blow. ' He gave him a *polt* on the head.' Used in New England and New York.

PLAY-ACTOR. A theatrical performer. The expression is objectionable, because the term *actor* is itself a technical word, which expresses the full meaning conveyed by the compound. In England they always say simply *actor* or *player*.

POT-PIE. A pie made by spreading the crust over the bottom and sides of a pot, and filling up the inside with meat, i. e. beef, veal, mutton, or fowls.

An enormous *pot-pie*, and piping hot, graced our centre, overpowering, with its fragrance and steam, the odors and vapors of all other meats; and *pot-pie* was the wedding dish of the country, par excellence! The pie to-day was the doughy sepulchre of at least six hens, two chanticleers, and four pullets! What pot could have contained the pie is inconceivable. Why, among other unknown contributions, it must have received one half peck of onions! And yet it is to be feared that many would be *pot-pieless*. —*Carlton, The New Purchase*, Vol. I. p. 181.

PROSPECTING. Hunting or searching for lead. The process is thus described in a sketch of Life on the Upper Mississippi :

"The chief mart of the lead trade is in the town of Galena, built upon a small, sluggish stream. In travelling through the upland prairie of this neighborhood, you will see many hillocks of earth, as far as the eye can reach, as if some huge animal had been burrowing beneath, and had thrown up the dirt in that manner ; but you may, by chance, meet two or three men with a bucket, a rope, a pick-axe, and a portable windlass, and the difficulty is explained. This, in the language of the country, is a *prospecting* party ; which, being interpreted, means that they are on the look-out for ore, if it is to be found within ten or fifteen feet of the ground ; having come to the end of the rope at about that depth, and found nothing, they remove elsewhere, the *prospect* not being good. When ore is found, they either sell out their discovery, or mine the vein on a small scale themselves."—*N. Y. Literary World*, June 3, 1848.

TO PUT OUT. To remove ; to be off. A Western expression. *To put* is used in the same sense.

As my wife's father had considerable land on Blue Fox river, and as we wanted a little more elbow-room, I says one day to Nancy, "Nancy," says I, "Idad, 'spose we *put out* and live there."—*Carlton, The New Purchase*, Vol. I. p. 172.

ROLLING PRAIRIE. The following excellent definition of this term is from the pen of Judge Hall :

"The vast plains or prairies of the West, although preserving a general level in respect to the whole country, are yet in themselves not flat, but exhibit a gracefully waving surface, swelling and sinking with an easy slope, and a full rounded outline, equally avoiding the unmeaning horizontal surface, and the interruption of abrupt or angular elevations. It is that surface which, in the expressive language of the country, is called *rolling*, and which has been said to resemble the long, heavy swell of the ocean, when its waves are subsiding to rest after the agitation of a storm. Such are *rolling prairies.*"—*Judge Hall, Notes on the Western States.*

S.

SABBADAY. Sabbath day, Sunday ; so called in the interior of New England.

> *Newman.* You look better ; I hope you feel better, and are better ?
> *Doolittle.* Why, I expect I do, and I guess I be, all three. I know I be, as to the first particular, changing my old shabby duds, for these new *Sabbaday* clothes, for a go-to-meeting day, anywheres.—*D. Humphreys, The Yankee in England,* p. 29.

SARVES, for *preserves.* So pronounced in some parts of the West.

> We had also [for dinner] custard pies, and maple molasses, (usually called 'them 'are molasses,') and preserved apples, preserved water-melon-rinds, and preserved red peppers and tomatoes—all termed, for brevity's sake, (like words in Webster's Dictionary,) *sarves.*—*Carlton, The New Purchase,* Vol. I. p. 183.

SALAD. In the Northern States often used specifically for *lettuce,* of which salad is frequently made.

SAULT. (French.) The rapids of the St. Lawrence, and those connecting the Upper Lakes, retain the French name ; as, *Sault* St. Mary, etc. Pronounced *soo.*

TO SEE HOME. '*To see* a lady *home,*' is to wait upon or attend her home from a party or elsewhere.

> The eventful day was closing, and some had already taken French leave. But at the request of some young fellows, who offered *to see the galls home,* we left our helps to have some fun after the graver people should be gone away.—*Carlton, The New Purchase.*

SHANTY. A mean cabin or shed.—*Worcester.*

> The best residences in the slave States are made disagreeable by the proximity of huts and *shanties* for negroes, which, in Charleston, offend the eye everywhere except in the streets devoted to trade.—*Letter from Charleston, N. Y. Tribune,* April, 1848.

SHINGLES. The name of an eruptive disease which takes the form of a belt (cingulum) around the body.

SHORT GOWN. A short gown with hardly any skirt, worn by women when doing household work, as washing, &c.

TO SIMILATE. To put on the appearance of that which does not really belong to the subject.

And this holds true both of actions which *similate* the intellect, and those which *similate* the moral sense, such as gratitude and shame in a dog.—*Tappan's Psychology* (*not published*).

SIMON PURE. Genuine; real.

A merchant in Boston paid $500 for a portrait of Washington by Winstanley, believing it to be by Stuart, which he presented to the town. It was put up in Faneuil Hall. . . . . The connoisseur was laughed at. He had been deceived; he thought it a real *Simon Pure.*—*Dunlap, Arts of Design.*

SISTERN, for *sisters.* A vulgar pronunciation sometimes heard from uneducated preachers at the West.

"Brethurn and *sisturn*, it's a powerful great work, this here preaching of the gospel, as the great apostle hisself allows in them words of hissin **what's** jest come into my mind; for I never knowed what to preach till I ris up." —*Carlton, The New Purchase*, Vol. I. p. 203.

TO SKUNK. To utterly defeat. In games of chance, if one of the players fails to make a point, he is said to be *skunked.* A presidential candidate who fails to secure one electoral vote is also *skunked.*

SMACK SMOOTH. At the West, a term applied to land which is thoroughly cleared; i. e. smoothly cleared; level. It is also used in England in the sense of level.—*Craven Glossary.*

SOCIALISM. A social state in which there is a community of property among all the citizens—a new term for Agrarianism.—*Webster.*

SOCIALIST. An advocate of socialism.—*Worcester.*

SOCIALISTIC. Appertaining to the principles of socialism.

And now let us briefly assure the Courier that it is greatly, grievously wrong in supposing that we shrink, or falter, or despond with regard to the future of France, in view of the prominence and imminence given to social theories and ideas by the new Revolution. On the contrary, our columns will bear witness that we have, from the hour that the fall of Louis Philippe was known here, to this moment, profoundly rejoiced in the Revolution itself, and more especially in its *socialistic* aspects and tendencies.—*N. Y. Tribune*, April 25, 1848.

SOME PUMPKINS. A term in use at the South and West in opposition to " small potatoes." The former is applied to anything large or noble ; the latter to anything small or mean.

> Although the Mexican women are not distinguished for beauty, I never remember once to have seen an ugly woman. Their brilliant eyes make up for any deficiency of feature, and their figures are full and voluptuous. Now and then, moreover, one does meet with a perfectly beautiful creature ; and when a Mexican woman does combine such perfection, she is "*some pumpkins*," as the Missourians say when they wish to express something superlative in the female line.—*Ruxton's Adventures in Mexico*, p. 57.

> Cass is *some pumpkins*, and will do the needful in the office line if he is elected, which I hope and trust will be his fate. I am no Democrat, as embraced on their whole platform, but I am, what I conceive to be, a least evil man.—*Letter from New Orleans, N. Y. Herald*, June 21, 1848.

SOUTHRON. A term borrowed from Scotland, and often applied to natives of the South ; a Southerner.

> Walker is a dexterous, busy intriguer, and may shuffle the cards so as finally to turn himself up for President ; but we think he sees that the skies are squally, and will insist on running a Northern man now, so that he may cut in for himself in 1852. If so, he will prevent the nomination of Gen. Butler, or any other Southron.—*N. Y. Tribune*, May 22, 1848.

SPLIT TICKET. When two or more important offices are to be filled at the same time, the wire-pullers of each party select the men they wish their party to support, and print their names on a ticket to be deposited in the ballot-box. It sometimes happens, however, that individuals choose to think for themselves, and consequently erase one or more of the names and substitute others more to their liking. This is called a *split ticket.*

> Well, Jonathan, you intend voting for Gen. Cass and the regular Democratic nomination, don't you ?
> *Jonathan.* Not by a jug full, I can tell you. I am an out-and-out Democrat—dyed in the wool, and have stood up to the party through thick and thin. But I'll vote for no Northern men with Southern principles—no dough-faces for me. Vote for Cass ?—why, he's the very boss of dough-faces. No, I'll vote a *split ticket.* I'll scratch out the dough-face and put in a Free Soil name. I'll go the regular nomination, only substituting the name of Van Buren for Cass.—*Newspaper*, June, 1848.

SPOILS, i. e. *the spoils of office.* The pay and emoluments of official station—specifically referred to as the leading inducements to partisan activity, and as distinct from political zeal generally. [*J. Inman.*]

> It has been asserted that to the victors belong the *spoils*. Let us determine that we will be the victors, and that if we must have the *spoils* they shall be appropriated to the good of the country.—*Speech of the Hon. Mr. Morehead to the Whig National Convention in Philadelphia*, June, 1848.

> There is a slight misgiving in the minds of the Loco-focos, that Gen. Cass will not have it in his power to reward many partisans; and by filling the important offices just on the eve of departure from office, they hope to perpetuate their possession of the *spoils* for four years after they shall have sunk to that profound depth to which Senator Hannegan consigned them, in spite of the impotency of the arm of political resurrection!—*Cor. of N. Y. Tribune.*

> Men looking to the *spoils* care not for principles,—whether they be of the North or of the South.—*Washington Cor. of N. Y. Com. Adv.*

> It is estimated that there are at least sixty thousand office-holders under the general administration, and that the amount of plunder annually distributed by government, is equal to forty millions of dollars, which is expended in a thousand and one ways. The party which has the command of these office-holders, and the scattering of this vast amount of *spoils*, is possessed of a potent weapon.—*N. Y. Herald*, June, 1848.

SQUASH. A culinary vegetable. (Genus, *cucurbita.*) It is not necessary to resort to the Greek σιχυος, as certain lexicographers do, for the etymology of this word. It is Indian, and is often mentioned by the early writers.

> In summer, when their [the Indians'] corn is spent, *squonter squashes* is their best bread, a fruit like a young pumpion.—*Wood's New England*, 1634, p. 67.

STORE PAY. Payment made for produce or other articles purchased, by goods from a store, instead of cash. This is a common way of buying produce in the country. Sometimes a merchant agrees to pay half in cash and half out of his store, i. e. *store pay.*

SWASH. To shake water about from side to side, as in a tub or barrel.

T.

TAG. A slight touch. A boy touched by one who is in the first instance fixed upon to commence the game, is in his turn obliged to overtake and touch another of the party, when he cries *tag*, and so the game proceeds.   According to Mr. Halliwell the same game is played in Warwickshire, where it is called *tick*.

W.

WHAT, for *that* or *who*.   A vulgarism often heard amongst us, but probably still more common in England.